Offended Freedom

Offended Freedom

The Rise of Libertarian Authoritarianism

Carolin Amlinger and
Oliver Nachtwey

Translated by Jan-Peter Herrmann
with David Broder

polity

First published in German as *Gekränkte Freiheit. Aspekte des libertären Autoritarismus*
© Suhrkamp Verlag AG Berlin, 2022. All rights reserved by and controlled through Suhrkamp Verlag AG Berlin.

This English edition © Polity Press, 2025.

The translation of this book was supported by a grant from the Goethe-Institut.

Polity Press
65 Bridge Street
Cambridge CB2 1UR, UK

Polity Press
111 River Street
Hoboken, NJ 07030, USA

ISBN-13: 978-1-5095-6084-4
ISBN-13: 978-1-5095-6085-1 (paperback)

A catalogue record for this book is available from the British Library.

Library of Congress Control Number: 2024934472

Typeset in 10.5 on 12.5 pt Sabon
by Fakenham Prepress Solutions, Fakenham, Norfolk NR21 8NL
Printed and bound by CPI Group (UK) Ltd, Croydon, CR0 4YY

The publisher has used its best endeavours to ensure that the URLs for external websites referred to in this book are correct and active at the time of going to press. However, the publisher has no responsibility for the websites and can make no guarantee that a site will remain live or that the content is or will remain appropriate.

Every effort has been made to trace all copyright holders, but if any have been overlooked the publisher will be pleased to include any necessary credits in any subsequent reprint or edition.

For further information on Polity, visit our website:
politybooks.com

CONTENTS

ACKNOWLEDGEMENTS

This book is the outcome of a collaboration between a literary scholar and a sociologist. The research on which it is based is likewise the result of collaborative study. Without the support of our fellow researchers and assistants, it would have been impossible to gather and analyse our empirical material. We therefore owe our greatest thanks to all of them. We are especially grateful to Nadine Frei, Maurits Heumann, Johannes Truffer, Daria Wild, Matthias Zaugg, Clara Balzer-Nelson, Max Kaufmann, Verena Hartleitner and Robert Schäfer for their collaboration in the empirical research projects and their assistance in preparing the manuscript for this volume.

We would also like to thank the participants in the research colloquium on socio-structural analysis at the Department of Sociology, University of Basel, for their thoughts and suggestions. Besides the aforementioned names, they include Helene Thaa, Mirela Ivanova, Linus Petermann, Jacqueline Kalbermatter and Simon Schaupp. Furthermore, we are infinitely grateful to Nicola Gess and the Swiss National Science Foundation (SNF) project on 'Halbwahrheiten' ('Half–Truths') at the University of Basel – specifically, to Silvan Bolliger, Hevin Karakurt, Lea Liese and Cornelius Puschmann – for creating such a productive intellectual atmosphere.

We would like to thank Sidonia Blättler, Ulrich Bröckling, Adrian Daub, Alex Demirovic, Wolfgang Eßbach, Philipp Felsch, Johannes Franzen, Gunnar Hindrichs, Agnes Hoffmann, Vera King, Piotr Kocyba, Albrecht Koschorke, Nils C. Kumkar, Andrea Maihofer, Julian Müller, Johannes Paßmann, Dieter Rucht, Astrid Séville, Markus Steinmayr, Ferdinand Sutterlüty, Simon Teune, Hubert Thüring, Niels Werber and Eberhard Wolff for many inspiring conversations and discussions at conferences, workshops, in the context of research networks, or even just on faculty corridors.

We are grateful to our agent Aenne Glienke for her committed effort on our behalf. We would also like to thank our son for his stoic patience in those moments in which we had to once again hammer at the keyboard. He has our undying appreciation! Finally, we are forever indebted to our copyeditor for the German edition, Heinrich Geiselberger, for a particularly outstanding and reliable collaboration.

INTRODUCTION

My freedom needn't be your freedom, too.
My freedom: yes! Your freedom: no!
My freedom is guaranteed by the constitution,
Yours has never mattered so far.

[Meine Freiheit muss noch lang' nicht deine Freiheit sein.
Meine Freiheit: ja! Deine Freiheit: nein!
Meine Freiheit wird von der Verfassung garantiert,
Deine hat bis jetzt nicht interessiert]
Barbara Peters and Georg Kreisler, 'Meine Freiheit, deine Freiheit'
(1985)

It might be an old friend from school, a colleague or a family member
– and they have begun moaning that their freedom has come under
attack. Probably, most of us have had this kind of encounter. Our
conversations with them have changed. We avoid certain topics
because we know that the argument may escalate all too easily.
Sometimes, it is only the thread of a conversation, but in more serious
cases even a longstanding relationship may be broken off. Children
become estranged from their parents. Some even end all contact with
them, as they can no longer bear to witness the process of mounting
radicalization.

Often, the individuals concerned would describe themselves as
open-minded and liberal and often they have a broad education. It
is not so much the emergence of authoritarian populists like Donald
Trump or Vladimir Putin that concerns them, nor that of right-wing
populist parties. Rather, they feel suffocated by encroaching rules,

1

regulations and prohibitions. They believe these latter have been devised by the 'mainstream' or, more recently, by the 'woke' crowd. They often perceive themselves as victims of a sinister establishment in which liberals, the political Left, the world of science and global corporations have joined forces to prepare a totalitarianism of unprecedented scale.

Many of the current conflicts in society eventually reach a point at which someone invokes the right to individual freedom. However, these struggles defend a concept of freedom that differs considerably from that once pursued by the emerging bourgeoisie and the workers' movement. In these historical cases, the call for freedom was directed against an absolutist monarchy, feudal dependencies, the rule of the church and the guilds as well as state censorship. The concept of freedom was associated with the demand for equal civil rights, including free speech and universal suffrage. Today, civil liberties implying protection from a despotic state have largely been codified.

Freedom conflicts

The fact that we are generally protected from a despotic state does not mean that we are free to do whatever we want. Given the continuing highly unequal distribution of economic power (which is why some people – including ourselves – speak of a class society), 'social advancement' passes many people by. We have to stop at a red light, pay taxes and, when we are young, go to school. In other words, every society has rules that restrict its members' freedom; including ones with an official, formal character, enforced by the state, for instance road traffic rules. At the same time, there are norms and conventions of a more informal nature: if an older person asks you to help them cross the road, you are not legally obliged to do so – you are free to ignore the request and continue on your way. Similarly, of course, you are allowed to eat a kebab on a crowded train – that is, should you be indifferent to the many appalled faces of your fellow passengers.

What we can frequently observe today is a libertarian notion of freedom. The rise of libertarianism is arguably the most astonishing phenomenon of these strange times.[1] They traditionally privilege individual freedom over, and at the expense of, collective freedom. But another emerging characteristic, shared by its most prominent adherents – Peter Thiel, Elon Musk, and the anarcho-capitalist Javier Milei – is that their libertarianism is infused with authoritarian tendencies. Like neoliberals, libertarians are sceptical of the democratic state, not as a threat to smoothly functioning markets, but as a machine that restricts individual freedoms. Neoliberals use the state to strengthen the market, whereas libertarians consider the state itself, the authorities and their regulations, to be invasive and harmful.[2] Current libertarian prophets also mobilize against multiculturalism and what they perceive to be enforced solidarity with vulnerable groups, such as asylum seekers or minority groups, and were vehemently opposed to lockdowns associated with the COVID-19 pandemic. Libertarian prophets are not new – the twentieth-century writer Ayn Rand is the best-known representative. But also, economists like Milton Friedman and philosophers like Robert Nozick are intellectual exponents of libertarianism. With his support for the Chilean dictator Pinochet, Friedman is also a drastic representative of libertarian authoritarianism.

What is new, and worrying, is that in Germany, and across Europe, the libertarian social base has expanded significantly in recent decades. A new social character is emerging in modern Western societies: the libertarian-authoritarian personality. Together with our various research teams, we surveyed individuals who have started *drifting* in some way or another. Our research draws on more than sixty interviews with people from what is widely referred to in Germany as the *Querdenker*[3] scene (forty-five) and followers of the AfD who are active in civil society (sixteen). Many of the encounters preyed on our minds for quite some time. Usually, our conversation partners did not initially strike us as the aggressive characters some of them ultimately turned out to be. We got to know them as friendly, even warm-hearted people. Yet, at the same time, they did give us the impression of being oddly disgruntled and disappointed with the world – we might say, offended. Over the course of the interviews, ever-new aspects of their personalities emerged, in particular their radical and authoritarian traits. They freely indulged in their rage – presumably also because our role as sociological observers compelled us to remain silent and refrain from objecting. Instead, we were there to listen, and only from time to time ask questions.

One of our interview partners was Mr Rudolph, the impoverished son of the owner of a manufacturing company. He had bought an assortment of cakes especially for the interview and, to go with it, he had prepared coffee: one pot regular, one pot decaf. A member of the Green Party from day one, a cosmopolitan who had travelled the world extensively, he related the turbulent story of his life and his never-ending commitment to the good cause. Rudolph sacrificed himself for his family, but no one appreciated it. Pouring coffee into our mugs politely and attentively, he told us that 'half the world' has already sat here at his kitchen table. And yet, there he was, flying into a fury when speaking about 'foreigners swamping' his homeland (*Überfremdung*). There was no stopping him, and the situation became particularly uncomfortable as he began fantasizing about taking revenge on those he deems responsible for this whole malaise.

Ms Weber, by contrast, yearns for a world of harmony. She meditates for world peace and teaches classes on this technique. What matters to her is human closeness, contact, touching – all of which children were entirely deprived of during the COVID-19 pandemic. She claims that this issue has been ignored by everyone, particularly by the media who have been 'forced into line' (*'gleichgeschaltet'*).[4] She strongly believes that 'something is rotten' in the state of Germany, that something is fundamentally wrong. The detail that far-right groups participate in the marches she attends does not bother her.

Whereas Ms Weber repeatedly apologizes for her inconsistent use of gender-neutral language, for others the 'gender asterisk' (*Gendersternchen*)[5] used to this end has become the embodiment of the mounting *un*freedom. Various intellectuals believe that it is increasingly impossible to defend positions that deviate from the 'mainstream', and issue warnings of a 'dictatorship of opinion'. Many of them are erstwhile adherents of subversive theories and were once committed to an emancipatory transformation of the existing order. Today, they fight for a nostalgic 'retrotopia' (Zygmunt Bauman) in which everything will be restored to how it allegedly used to be. They traipse from one TV talk show to the next, spreading their sour breath of resentment and claiming in front of an audience of millions that they are being silenced.

As for the topic of this book: it is not a study of the libertarian prophets, but rather an investigation of the changes in individualism, the transformation of the political and intellectual public sphere, and, finally, the protest movement that can be subsumed under the term libertarian authoritarianism. Here, individual freedom is not social, but absolute.

The adherents of such an understanding of freedom perceive wearing a mask to cover their mouth and nose, or indeed gender-sensitive language conventions as obstacles that are holding them back. They regard any new or altered social conventions as externally imposed restrictions that illegitimately limit their scope for self-realization. Some go even further and turn against the very preconditions for freedom: they do not want to pay taxes (or only very low tax rates) but do not hesitate to use the roads that are paid for with tax money. They ignore the fact that cutting-edge medical research would be inconceivable without public funding and that a publicly provided school education is the very basis of individual self-development.

Today's freedom conflicts represent the culmination of a process that has already been building over the past decades. It is manifested in the return of an interventionist state that decisively interferes with individual behaviour. In contrast to the traditional far right, those taking to the streets today are not in favour of a strong state but rather a weak, essentially absent state. Their almost frivolous subversion and furious rejection of other opinions, however, simultaneously indicate authoritarian attitudes. They deny solidarity to vulnerable groups, use a markedly martial tone of speech and are highly aggressive towards those they consider responsible for the restriction of their freedom. They spread far-right conspiracy theories but categorically reject the accusation of being in any way right-wing. This authoritarianism, which so vehemently insists on the individual's autonomy, is an indicator that the established political coordinates are in disarray. What is the reason for this change? Have these people always been sympathetic to authoritarianism – and were we simply unaware? Or have they performed an abrupt biographical U-turn?

Although we are unable to deliver any final answers to these questions here, in this book we nevertheless present indicators that the root causes are to be found in the historical development of capitalist societies. In this sense, we regard libertarian authoritarianism not as an irrational movement in opposition to, but as a dark side-effect of, late modern societies. Their promise of individual self-fulfilment harbours a potential for disappointment that can flare up as frustration and resentment. The people we met were defending their freedom – albeit in a peculiarly apodictic, almost authoritarian manner. We understand this libertarian authoritarianism as a symptom of an individualist concept of freedom which defies social

5

interdependence. From this perspective, freedom is not a collective and shared condition of society but a personal possession. Although the libertarian-authoritarian protest is directed against late modern society, it is a rebellion in favour of the latter's core values: self-determination and sovereignty.

This is true for the man demonstrating against a patronizing government; the pensioner who feels harassed as a 'staff member' of the so-called *Deutschland GmbH* ('Germany Ltd')[6]; or those intellectuals whose scepticism turns into new ultimate justifications. Even when facing opposition, they stand by their views and are willing to accept significant detrimental consequences like losing their job or being shunned by their social circles. Furthermore, they want to understand the problems around them: either as part of their work or in their free time, they pore over heaps of books or scour alternative online news outlets. They are sceptical of authorities and generally recognized knowledge. But these claims to autonomy and self-fulfilment often remain unattainable, and so the promises of late modern societies seem hollow to them. As a result, they develop a grudge towards those people and institutions they hold responsible for their own failure. They are unwilling to accept the slight that they have suffered and fight back, either by joining the self-proclaimed resistance or incessantly posting comments against their enemy stereotypes on social media. Frequently, a logic of escalation sets in that compels them to adopt increasingly more radical positions.

The libertarian authoritarians we engage with in this volume at times feel helpless in the face of social change. This is not to say that the reverse also applies, namely that frustrating experiences must necessarily prompt anomic or even authoritarian reactions. Besides, the extent of 'freedom' in the pursuit of one's own interests varies strongly between different classes, strata and occupational groups. There is no question that people are leading successful lives, they are in fact in the majority. People are able to adjust their claims and standards to the available options. However, some are fiercely determined to defend their individual scope of action against any potential restrictions. What drives them is a late modern sense of powerlessness, which we refer to as offended freedom. Regardless of whether these individuals participate in protest marches against an imagined dictatorship, indulge their proclivity for conspiracy fables or in their resentment against minorities – they all consider

6

themselves to be among the few who see through the overbearing injustices of late modernity. They virtually never run out of energy and consider themselves freedom fighters or the vanguard in a new and fundamental social conflict.

Libertarian authoritarianism

In parallel with social change itself, authoritarianism has also undergone modifications.[7] We consider libertarian authoritarianism to be a metamorphosis of the 'authoritarian personality' as described by Critical Theory in the twentieth century. In the studies on the *Authoritarian Personality* from 1950, co-authored by sociologist and philosopher Theodor W. Adorno, the authoritarian syndrome is characterized by a combination of distinct features, including, among other things, the rigorous adherence to conventional values, the subordination to an idealized authority, a binary concept of power, fantasies of superiority or general hostility.[8] As we illustrate throughout this book, the first two of these characteristics were observable only to a very limited extent among the groups we surveyed. As libertarian authoritarians, conventionalism and, particularly, subordination are alien to them. In this sense, they display similarities with a type that the representatives of Critical Theory had identified early on but considered to be a marginal figure at the time. According to the social psychologist Erich Fromm, the authoritarian 'rebels', as he called them in 1936, 'automatically react defiantly and rebelliously [...] whenever such people encounter authority'.[9] Yet, the one thing they most certainly were not was libertarian. They were 'indifferent' to a value such as 'freedom'.[10]

The individuals we surveyed stubbornly defy social conventions, and are animated by the anarchic impulse to assert their objectives against all and any outside opposition. In the process, they frequently develop an untiring destructive activity that is framed as a heroic courage to stand by one's principles. Their form of authoritarianism is libertarian, then, because it constitutes a resistance against any form of restriction of individual behaviour. It revives a negative concept of freedom in which the individual is situated in contradistinction to the social order. Libertarian authoritarians identify not with a leader figure but with themselves and their own autonomy.

7

An authoritarian rebellion may occur in social situations in which political authorities are losing legitimacy. In other words, when the promises coming from the self-proclaimed custodians of unsatisfied aspirations are no longer credible. At this point, popular admiration turns into hatred. During the second half of her time in office, former German chancellor Angela Merkel was commonly perceived as too weak by her critics from the right: during the euro crisis she was seen as being too yielding and soft towards the southern European countries. During the migration crisis of 2015, she was chided for having 'opened the borders'. Following her famous statement, '*Wir schaffen das*' ('We can do this'), the accusation of weakness grew into a rancour that went far beyond right-wing circles.

Defiance of authority arises from the frustrated insight that this authority is flawed and fallible. And yet, even though this leads to a rebellion against authorities, the character structure remains essentially authoritarian. Libertarian authoritarianism fights against false authority and in the name of the legitimate authority of freedom. However, its attainment is no longer entrusted to some powerful leader figure but to the self-empowered individual. In the process, libertarian authoritarians also latch on to a binary 'power complex' which dwells on one's own superiority and the opponent's weakness.[11] While one's own group is glorified, there is a kind of 'craving for punishment' ('*Strafsucht*') of the outsider group.[12] In contrast to more traditional authoritarians, who seek to point out their opponent's alleged moral weakness, libertarian authoritarians indulge in exposing their opponent's bigotry.

Critical Theory referred to the authoritarian personality of the twentieth century, which was submissive towards authority figures and hostile towards dissenters and minorities. Today's libertarian authoritarians do not primarily yearn for the reinstatement of traditionalist values, nor do they submit uncritically to leaders. They consider themselves altogether modern and progressive, even though they are animated by their own power and superiority. They are authoritarian in the sense that they recognize no plausible values nor reasonable interests whatsoever – which might render compromise at least conceivable – among their democratic opponents. For these libertarian authoritarians, there can be no balanced, sober negotiation, seeing as their opponents unvaryingly pursue sinister objectives and secret plans.

The structure of this book

Before we engage with the character and social location of libertarian authoritarianism in greater depth, in the first chapter we turn to the 'Aporias of enlightenment', i.e., the critical potential inherent in the concept of freedom, indeed in a double sense. On the one hand, it constitutes the starting point for social movements that mobilize people in the name of freedom. On the other hand, the norm of freedom always implies a call to reflect on its contradictions and self-endangerment and critically inquire as to what extent it has been established in social reality. The central finding of Critical Theory with regard to fascism and capitalist mass democracies is that bourgeois freedom entails the possibility of regression. According to this understanding, although modern society creates material prosperity, it also restricts the scope of individual emancipation. It was assumed that the aporias of modern freedom harbour an authoritarian potential.

The second chapter, 'Freedom in dependence', traces these aporias and starts off by revisiting the historical origins of the modern individual. The emancipation from feudal dependencies failed to create truly autonomous individuals: instead, bourgeois society's individualism fused with inequalities and difference. While the (propertied) bourgeois and merchants were free, the workers were 'free in the double sense': the latter were additionally free of private property and thus dependent on wage labour. Today, the basic constitution of late modern individuals is ambivalent. They are able to independently determine their own lives, but they are simultaneously subjected to social constraints. Proceeding from the sociologist Ulrich Beck, we analyse forms of negative individualization that limit the continued expansion of the individual's scope for action.

In contemporary societies, the individual is performance-oriented and adapts to the law of competition in the capitalist market. At the same time, ever since the emergence of counter-cultural alternative movements post-1968, the concept of the 'authentic self' has become ever more influential. Particularly among the middle classes, the yearning for self-fulfilment merges with the urge for success and recognition. It is a blend that systematically causes disappointment. As a result, a reified notion of freedom develops, understood as an individual trait, not a social relation. Any dependencies experienced are ignored, even denied. The affirmation of such a purely negative freedom is a key source of libertarian authoritarianism.

In the third chapter, 'The order of disorder', we situate the predicaments of individuality within the social and political dynamics of late modern societies, in which we can also observe the workings of a regressive modernization. By that, we mean developments that are characterized by a contradictory simultaneity of modernization and counter-modernization. The change in norms and a heightened sensitivity towards instances of discrimination open up the political space but also cause closures and new conflicts. Under such conditions, knowledge, too, becomes fiercely contested: indeed, individuals may enjoy higher education levels and be familiar with a broad range of techniques of acquiring knowledge, and yet, paradoxically, their knowledge of reality continually decreases. The increase in global risks entails a dependency on third-party knowledge, and particularly on scientific expertise.

Similarly, the crisis of democratic representation may also be understood as a consequence of regressive modernization. The political system is perceived as closed and hermetically sealed, even as 'postdemocratic' (Colin Crouch). That said, the counter-movements critical of authority, too, frequently fail to achieve any correction of the problem, and, if anything, they exacerbate it. Plebiscitary demands are apodictically articulated, always displaying a tendency to overstate the case. In parallel to this, a kind of counter-epistemology, ongoing since the 1970s, has popularized scepticism towards modernity and its knowledge systems. Nevertheless, here, too, the critique has radicalized; it has become an end in itself and is now directed against general social reality. In both cases, progressive causes have been transformed and have produced a neo-authoritarian discontent.

In the fourth chapter, 'Social aggrievement', we address the affective tensions and frictions that are stirred up within the individual by the dilemmas of late modernity. Individualization increasingly shifts social conflicts into the self. Individuals become more susceptible to taking offence, they experience disappointment and frustration. As a consequence, negative affects may arise – such as shame, rage, grudge and resentment (*Ressentiment*) – and increasingly develop a life of their own. But what are the triggers that evoke such negative sentiments in some people? We ultimately see three dilemmas at work here: first, the paradox of egalitarian norms, the implementation of which entails an increased sensitivity towards injustices; second, a lack of aspirations, emerging from the incongruity between a legally stipulated ideal state and its deficient realization; third, situations of social anomie in which universally recognized aspirations (such as success) foster forms of behaviour that violate certain social rules. This may result from the over-identification with norms, but also from rebellious or even destructive practices, an overambitious obsession with success, a competitive mindset or a sense of superiority. Since the 1970s, such reactions have been associated with the figure of the narcissist, and today we see them returning once again among libertarian authoritarians. In this context, we regard narcissism, which continues to feature prominently in most current diagnoses of the times, not as a manifest civilizational disease but rather as an indication that the economy of imagination in late modern societies is deeply unsettled.

In the fifth chapter, 'Libertarian authoritarianism', we engage with the question of how to account for the normative disarray in which the ideal of freedom is conflated with profoundly illiberal views and practices. What are the key features of the libertarian-authoritarian personality structure? In what character traits does it surface, and through what types of behaviour is it expressed? Here we draw on the notion that libertarian authoritarianism is a symptom of reified freedom. The authoritarian personality, as conceptualized by Critical Theory, changes its form under the conditions of late modernity. We interpret the libertarian-authoritarian personality, which no longer follows any figure of authority, as a side-effect of the emergence of the liberated and self-reliant individual who is confronted with abstract dependencies and turns against them. In this sense, libertarian authoritarianism represents a demonstrative gesture of dissociation.

Although we do not consider the Critical Theory of authoritarianism to be obsolete, we focus on figures who were only marginal characters during the first half of the twentieth century but who have gained a stronger presence today: namely the above-mentioned 'rebel' who defies the forces that seek to restrict their independence, as well as the so-called 'crank' who loses themselves in conspiracy thinking and regards epistemological secession as a means of self-empowerment. However, the late modern expansion of the zone of humiliation, or offendedness, does not engulf all social spaces equally and, in our view, encompasses particularly those social contexts with a more individualist value system. In this chapter, we seek to

11

comprehensively establish, based on distinct scenarios, the conditions under which contradictory, frustrating experiences can translate into libertarian-authoritarian attitudes and behaviours.

To this end, we illustrate the varying manifestations of libertarian authoritarianism on the basis of three examples. In the sixth chapter, 'The demise of the truth seekers', we investigate the ways in which the figure of the general intellectual, who rises to speak out publicly on behalf of freedom, equality or justice, can get tied up with regressive positions (though, of course, this need not necessarily be the case). The intellectuals we encounter in this study emphatically invoke the freedom of speech or the interest of the majority – albeit only to defend sectional positions. They exemplify a critique of society that has become ill-defined, causing ideological interferences between opposing political camps. What unites the intellectuals we surveyed is their fight against a common adversary: the identity politics of formerly marginalized groups and cultural minorities, scientific expertise or an alliance of state and media elites who have allegedly been forced into line. We conceive of these disconcerting coalitions as a reactive self-hardening against progressive change.

In this chapter, we examine intellectuals' diminishing sphere of influence, engage with distorted freedom struggles, fought not least against the enemy image of 'cancel culture', and elaborate on specific cases that cut across traditional boundaries between political camps. We consider the work of Peter Sloterdijk, which we briefly summarize, to be an important precursor of what cultural scholar Diedrich Diederichsen has termed 'post-ideological *Querfronts*' ('cross fronts', i.e., left–right alliances). This is followed by three specific examples: the overweening intellectual criticism of government measures during the COVID-19 pandemic; the nostalgic class struggle against the identity politics of marginalized groups; and the transition from an erstwhile anti-hegemonic postmodern mindset to libertarian-authoritarian positions. Finally, we contemplate the ways in which the registers of social critique have shifted and changed in recent years – reflections that are instrumental for properly understanding the two subsequent case studies.

In the seventh chapter, 'The re-enchantment of the world', we analyse the protests of the so-called '*Querdenker*' (or 'COVID deniers'). The measures the government implemented to contain the COVID-19 pandemic represented considerable interference with people's everyday lives. Everyone had to wear a facemask when out in public, cultural venues and gyms were closed, and even the individual freedom of movement was temporarily restricted. The government justified the far-reaching measures with scientific evidence on the risk of contagion and the severe disease progression. The '*Querdenker*' not only fiercely criticized the measures as such, but also challenged the knowledge base they were founded on. Furthermore, besides denying the danger of a COVID-19 infection altogether, they frequently detected a large-scale conspiracy behind the measures.

For our analysis, we evaluated an online survey of 1,150 '*Querdenker*' and conducted interviews with forty-five others, attended numerous protest marches and dug through Telegram channels. Many of the people we spoke to are from the remnants of the old 'alternative milieus'. They are prone to new-age practices, indulge in esotericism, practise yoga and seek inner harmony. For other '*Querdenker*', who instead come from the milieu of top performers, a hedonistic lifestyle and the meritocratic principle take centre stage; they are preoccupied with conspiracy theories and sympathize more strongly with the AfD. In their majority, they are people who tended towards the left in the past but are now moving towards the right. They are so alienated from representative democracy that they have no problem with attending the same marches as right-wing populist or even explicitly far-right forces. In a way, the '*Querdenker*' represent the prototype of libertarian authoritarianism: in terms of lifestyle, for example bringing up a child, they support more anti-authoritarian positions, they are not particularly xenophobic and they are critical of hierarchies. At the same time, however, they defend a radical individualist concept of freedom that can quickly take on authoritarian contours. Many of them are obsessed with the idea of punishing those who have restricted (and continue to restrict) their self-determination (such as 'the virologists' or 'the government').

The eighth chapter, 'Subversion as a destructive principle', is based on an empirical study conducted in 2017. The non-governmental organization (NGO) Campact, which specializes in online campaigns on behalf of ecological and social causes, had contacted us in 2016: some subscribers to their mailing list were objecting to a Campact-led anti-AfD campaign in the run-up to the German general election in 2017. They expressed sympathies for the right-wing populist party, and more than just a few stated their intention to actually vote for

13

them. Together with Campact, we wanted to find out why some people dedicated to progressive causes nonetheless develop an affinity for the AfD. For this purpose, we conducted sixteen biographical-narrative interviews with people who had criticized the campaign. Many of our interview partners have always despised authority, they struggle to submit to conventions and frequently come into conflict with their social environment.

Their inclination towards the extreme, the excessive or subversive has turned rather destructive more recently. They rail against refugees, Muslims or Jews, and in some cases obsess about fantasies of violence. Most of them have experienced existential disruptions or crises in their life, for which they blame a corrupted system that restricts their freedoms and gives preferential treatment to 'strangers'. They are reminiscent of the rebels that were studied by Critical Theory, although they exhibit one key difference: their fundamental scepticism towards authorities prevents any kind of authoritarian identification, neither with a powerful leader nor with the nation. The group we refer to as 'regressive rebels' with reference to the studies on the authoritarian personality appear to be the most radical variant of libertarian authoritarianism. They consider the democratic system with all its liberal norms to be so severely suffocating that their – if only verbal – rebellion against it is extremely aggressive. Alongside the type of the regressive rebel, we also introduce the 'authoritarian innovator', who may be regarded as the former's more moderate comrade-in-arms.

How, then, should libertarian authoritarianism be classified? How does it differ from the authoritarianism analysed by Adorno and his colleagues? Is it here to stay? We return to these questions once again in the final chapter. But, just to make it clear from the start: we have little hope that libertarian authoritarianism will disappear any time soon. At the same time, of course, we are not simply left at its mercy, defenceless. Alternatives do exist. We conclude the book by outlining possible courses of action that might not only improve our social coexistence and our relationship with nature, but which could also help drain the breeding grounds of libertarian authoritarianism.

— Chapter 1 —

APORIAS OF ENLIGHTENMENT: THE CRITICAL THEORY OF FREEDOM

Freedom is the guiding trope of modernity.[1] It is the key rationale underlying the bourgeois societies emerging since the eighteenth century, as well as of the rationalization, industrialization, democratization and individualization of all areas of life in these societies. Freedom is the trope on which modern society builds its own self-image. The question of what is meant by the term freedom, and how it is to be realized, is one of the 'fundamental questions' of community and society listed by Greek-French philosopher Cornelius Castoriadis: 'Who are we as a collectivity? What are we for one another? Where and in what are we? What do we want; what do we desire; what are we lacking?'[2] The semantics of the term freedom serves as the basis for negotiating the identity of both society as a whole and that of its members. Moreover, it indicates opportunities for self-realization through social institutions which can grant or deny freedom. Finally, it harbours a promise, an idea, which, through a normative imperative of action, encourages us to compare our social being to that of others.

Correspondingly, formulating a precise definition of the concept of freedom is no simple task: 'There is no word that admits of more various significations and has made more varied impressions on the human mind than that of liberty', noted French philosopher Montesquieu as early as 1748.[3] To this day, the term is usually coupled to two horizons of meaning: firstly, a person's freedom implies the absence of coercion, at least in those areas that are supposed to guarantee a sphere of freedom, such as in one's private life, in science or in art. Secondly, freedom also implies a legitimate social authority which enacts the individual right to freedom and protects it from being violated, in particular the state, as an authority of power and decision-making.[4] Which of the two meanings is dominant in public disputes says a lot about a society's self-understanding.[5] The respective semantics of freedom reveals the *sense* that members of society attach to it. Does individual freedom mean carte blanche for action, within a space protected from outside interference? Or is the freedom of the individual to be realized via social institutions? These specific emphases reveal how the social is substantiated through very varied rationales. The concept of freedom can legitimize state interference in individual independence (e.g., when the liberties of others are being infringed upon) or else contribute to the erosion of social cohesion (such as when individuals selfishly assert their own freedom to act at the cost of others).

Critique of freedom

Rather than defining the modern concept of freedom more closely, at this point we would first like to address its peculiar structure – which is what makes today's synthesis of freedom and authoritarianism possible in the first place. Needless to say, the term freedom is marked by a broad-ranging *plasticity*. It is malleable and receives its force precisely through its intrinsic ambiguities. Whereas negative concepts of freedom emphasize the absence of external obstacles, positive ones underscore the inner intentions that precede free volition as well as the external preconditions required to protect individual freedom.[6] In his *The Principle of Hope*, the philosopher Ernst Bloch, echoing Montesquieu's remark from two centuries before, speaks of the momentousness of words able to harbour highly varied imaginaries: 'The bigger the words, the more easily alien elements are able to hide in them. This is particularly the case with freedom, and with order, of which everybody often has his own idea.'[7] Bloch insightfully observes that its enormous semantic range accommodates contrary meanings, including those which may at first glance appear unrelated to the term.

The concept of freedom proves itself in individual everyday actions, in which we find our notion of freedom either affirmed or denied, or at the superordinate level of political decision-making power which can strengthen or restrict individual rights and liberties. Images of freedom have a *creative* effect; while historically they

16

have been placed in service of planned organization or, indeed, been politically abused, as a normative idea they elude any immediate control or direction. Rather, freedom as a social idea engenders new historical situations and new forms of behaviour. From the plurality of its meanings emerged its open, forward-looking potency, which resulted in its historical concurrence with social progress. This structural composition of the concept of freedom turns it into an essential resource of sense-making in modernity.

This is the backdrop against which a *critique of freedom* needs to be understood, indeed in two respects. On the one hand, it comprises all the both failed and victorious social struggles fought in the name of freedom. Advocating the realization of autonomy entails the critique of the societies which systematically prevent it. The bourgeoisie's emancipation movement fought to implement universal civil liberties, the working class aimed for the elimination of its subordination within a capitalist structure, and the women's movement – like the movements of social minorities – pursued the aim of no longer being discriminated against and attaining the right to lead a free, self-directed life. That is to say, historically, the fight for self-determination and self-realization has always motivated challenges to established social orders.[8]

On the other hand, a critique of freedom also requires the scrutiny of its own preconditions, so as to reveal its aporias and the ways it undermines itself.[9] The reason why the concept of freedom is regarded with a degree of scepticism is its normative nature. The idea of freedom can founder on its own promises, for example, if they are delivered only insufficiently and in fragmented ways; it can set in motion unwanted side-effects, e.g., if, in order for opportunities for freedom to be granted, individual independence is restricted elsewhere. This calls for reflection on the limitations and contradictions inherent in real-life freedom. In this book, we seek to combine both these strands of critique: proceeding from the disturbingly regressive critique that is currently being articulated in the name of freedom, we analyse the aporetic structure of bourgeois freedom that carries a potential for social erosion in late modern societies. When institutions are regarded mainly as a restriction of one's own free will and action, this says a great deal about our society and the social pathologies it engenders. After all, things have not always been this way.

Throughout modernity, freedom was usually spoken of in the same breath as progress.[10] This is particularly noticeable in the Hegelian

17

notion of the 'cunning of reason', according to which history progresses as 'the development of the spirit's consciousness of its own freedom and of the consequent realisation of this freedom'.[11] The philosopher Georg Wilhelm Friedrich Hegel was convinced that reality was inherently reasonable, and that reason was realized both in the action of individuals and in the social world. Here, history is conceived as progress, in whose course the limited forms of realization of the spirit, which is objectified in world history, are overcome – leading to the realization of freedom.[12] For Hegel, only after individuals have reached a mutual understanding about themselves, about what they are and what they want to be, can we even speak of history. He conceives of this form of reflective self-understanding in practical terms: it is sedimented in the rationality of social action. In this sense, freedom constitutes not only an intelligible yardstick for reason, but has its place in the moral organization of society.

Modernity is regarded as the most comprehensive emancipation project in human history. The ability to act on one's own free will is no longer the privilege of a few, but a universal claim of bourgeois society.[13] Consequently, the idea of individual freedom is inextricably tied to the social institutions designed to protect it. As philosopher Axel Honneth points out in his work *Freedom's Right*, '[t]he enormous gravitational force exerted by the notion of autonomy derives from the fact that it manages to form a systematic link between the individual subject and the social order.'[14] In this conception, the modern subject is not already free because it can decide according to its own will, but only once it is able to act freely during socially interactive processes. In modernity, autonomy, which is commonly associated with the independence from external forces, is a social product. The individual is independent not when *detached from* social circumstances, but within them. Conversely, the legitimacy of the social order depends on the degree to which it can guarantee individual freedom.[15]

Alongside the question of institutions providing opportunities for freedom, another aspect also comes into play, which may initially appear at odds with individual autonomy: namely, *domination*. Modern freedom rests on an asymmetrical order in which varying degrees of self-determination are legitimized. This applies not only to eighteenth-century societies. It was quite normal until well into the twentieth century for different social groups to be granted unequal opportunities to realize their autonomy. This pertains to workers who had only limited resources available; women, who were granted only limited participation opportunities (in Switzerland, for example, women's suffrage was not introduced until 1971, and in one of its cantons not until 1990); or migrants, who were largely legally forced (and, in part, still are today) to lead an existence outside of the social community. Freedom and oppression may at first glance appear as opposites, but both are closely connected to the idea of bourgeois freedom. Although people were legally free in bourgeois society, the bulk of the population still had to subordinate their lives to the relentless rhythm of the production line. The bleak reality on the shop floor seemed to contradict the philosophical ideal of freedom, as Theodor Adorno summarizes in his *Negative Dialectics* (1973 [1966]):

> Ever since the seventeenth century, freedom had been defined as all great philosophy's most private concern. Philosophy had an unexpressed mandate from the bourgeoisie to find transparent grounds for freedom. But that concern is antagonistic in itself. It goes against the old oppression and promotes the new one, the one that hides in the principle of rationality itself. One seeks a common formula for freedom and oppression, ceding freedom to the rationality that restricts it, and removing it from empiricism in which one does not even want to see it realized.[16]

Adorno is not insinuating some unfulfilled idea behind a real unfreedom; rather, in his view, the bourgeois concept of freedom sublates an antagonistic principle inherent to the society on whose foundations it emerged. That is how, by eliminating estate-based barriers and privileges, bourgeois society created the *bourgeois*, who always pursue their private interest, and complemented them with the *citoyen*, the citizen invoking liberal basic and human rights. This Janus face is the 'principle of rationality' of bourgeois society which Adorno refers to in the quote above: although it guarantees, for the first time ever, comprehensive liberties, it simultaneously – because this idea of freedom largely means economic freedom – establishes a new system of oppression. Here, we can discern an obvious parallel with Karl Marx's critique of human rights (or 'rights of man') written in 1844: in his review essay *On the Jewish Question*, Marx reconstructs the *droits de l'homme* as the rights of a person who pursues

19

their selfish private interest and exists in isolation from society. For Marx, the universal right to liberty is based on a separation of individual interests; the 'right of man to private property is, therefore, the right to enjoy one's property and to dispose of it at one's discretion (*à son gré*), without regard to other men, independently of society, the right of self-interest'. And he adds: 'This individual liberty and its application form the basis of civil society. It makes every man see in other men not the realisation of his own freedom, but the *barrier* to it.'[17] The institutional framework that was supposed to advance the autonomy of the individual proves in reality to be a means of safeguarding private interests. Since its very inception, Critical Theory has regarded it as its task to point out this discrepancy between the formally guaranteed freedom of the modern individual and its actual potential for self-determination in reality.

Freedom in Critical Theory

In November 1964, Adorno kicked off his final course on the philosophy of history with a lecture that likely fell on sympathetic ears among the students present. He told them that 'it can be said that a direct progress towards freedom cannot be discerned'.[18] A year before, the first of the Auschwitz trials had begun in Frankfurt's City Hall, the *Römer*, which brought the suppressed crimes back into the consciousness of a Federal Republic of Germany still healing its wounds after the experience of World War II. One thing the trial demonstrated was that the 'cunning of reason' did not necessarily lead to individual self-determination but rather – in the form of the Holocaust – to the abandonment of any concept of humanity whatsoever. Given the immediate historical backdrop, the disillusioning realization that Adorno used as the premise to his lecture is more than understandable, in this sense. Modern society was founded on a pathos of freedom which failed to materialize in reality. This is the very point from which Critical Theory's diagnosis of pathology proceeds.

The question of the individual's historical liberation from natural and man-made constraints provided the key normative reference point for the Frankfurt School, which took shape at the Institute for Social Research (IfS – *Institut für Sozialforschung*) in Frankfurt from 1931 onwards under its director, the social philosopher Max

Horkheimer.[19] The institute had been founded in 1923 by Felix Weil, the son of a wealthy business owner who wanted to use his inheritance to support the production of socialist theory. Unlike his predecessor Carl Grünberg, as director Horkheimer set himself the goal of developing a social theory which included the inner workings of psychology alongside capitalist economic structures. The affiliated scholars, such as psychologist Erich Fromm, economist Friedrich Pollock or literary sociologist Leo Löwenthal, dedicated themselves to the emotional state of workers and employees or the state's function for capitalism, before the institute was shut down by the Gestapo in 1933. These studies were continued by the researchers who headed into exile, including Adorno and Horkheimer, whose works would have a significant impact on the image of the Frankfurt School. Both retained their faith in the historical promises of Enlightenment and the French Revolution: Liberty, Equality, Fraternity. Precisely because they held onto these ideals, the fact that they had not materialized led to a bleak, pessimistic perspective on progress. In their view, reality was revealing that individuals were willing to submit to civilizational constraints that robbed them of their individuality. This background, then, explains their critique of freedom in bourgeois society. In 1947, they published their *Dialectic of Enlightenment: Philosophical Fragments* in New York, dedicated to Friedrich Pollock on the occasion of his fiftieth birthday. The title already provides a hint that the two did not associate the project of modernity with an optimistic faith in progress, but that they rather intended to reflect on its aporias, as they clarify in the Preface, written in exile in California in 1944:

> We have no doubt – and herein lies our *petitio principii* – that freedom in society is inseparable from enlightenment thinking. We believe we have perceived with equal clarity, however, that the very concept of that thinking, no less than the concrete historical forms, the institutions of society with which it is intertwined, already contains the germ of the regression which is taking place everywhere today.[20]

This influential study works through two social experiences characteristic of Western societies in the twentieth century: the emergence of capitalist mass democracies and fascism. These two experiences nurtured the realization that the modern concept of freedom also harbours the possibility of regression – or, in more drastic terms: of 'self-destruction'.[21] The contradictory nature of the Enlightenment lies in the fact 'that the self-implementation of Enlightenment changes into its negation', as philosopher Gunnar Hindrichs emphasizes.[22] In other words: the threats of authoritarianism and unfreedom are not looming outside of modern society, but rather develop inside of it, arising from its internal composition. The book appeared at a time when fascism had only just been defeated in Europe. Yet to Horkheimer and Adorno, this did not imply that it had been overcome once and for all. In their Californian exile, they encountered (and studied) people who in their view were susceptible to fascist and authoritarian propaganda even though they did not openly identify with it.

Based on the Greek myth of the Odyssey, which, according to philosopher and sociologist Jürgen Habermas, holds an archive of the 'almost lost traces of a primal history of subjectivity',[23] Horkheimer and Adorno illustrate that the free will guided by reason has always coincided with the will to power. Only thanks to his cunning can Odysseus survive the encounters with mythical beasts during his Odyssey – namely, by pretending to subject himself to them: 'The nimble-witted man survives only at the cost of his own dream, which he forfeits by disintegrating his own magic along with that of the powers outside him.'[24] Although he thereby proves his independence, he makes a great sacrifice by denying himself his wishes and desires. Despite orders to the contrary, Odysseus's companions, beset by hunger, slaughter and eat the cattle of the solar deity Helios on the Island of Thrinacia. Odysseus alone resists the temptation. The wrath of the sun-god is not long in coming: after they embark in order to continue their journey, their ship is smashed in a violent storm. Only Odysseus, who has practised self-denial, survives. The point of Horkheimer and Adorno's reading of the epic of Odysseus is that the domination of the external natural world can only be attained at the cost of conquering one's own inner nature. Consequently, the civilizational birth of the self is inextricably linked to renunciation and formation: 'The human being's mastery of itself, on which the self is founded, practically always involves the annihilation of the subject in whose service that mastery is maintained.'[25]

Although rationalization and the disenchantment of the natural world have thus far enabled an unprecedented scope for freedom, they are based on domination over oneself and others. As a result, then, both humans and nature are robbed of their potentialities: nature is reduced to its utility and exploitability, and human instinctual impulses to self-affirmation. The authors reach the paradoxical conclusion that the origin of the autonomous individual is simultaneously its obliteration. In his 1947 work *Eclipse of Reason*, Horkheimer applies this notion to contemporary industrial capitalism: in his view, the formerly strong and unemotional subject eventually degenerates into a 'shrunken ego'.[26] On the streets of New York – the city where Horkheimer gave public lectures at Columbia University in 1944 – he observed how workers were rushing to their workplaces, united not only by the same fashions, but also in the fact that they were subjected to the same requirements. In industrial late capitalism, Horkheimer asserts, an atomized and heteronomous social character emerges, which behaves in an adaptive manner towards monopolistic corporations, bureaucracy, standardization and social control, even submitting to them.[27]

In other words, the first generation of Critical Theory refused to adopt an optimistic concept of progress. Instead, their works can be read as an early articulation of that 'defeatist and catastrophic attitude'[28] which would begin to spread from the end of the twentieth century onwards. Throughout his life, Adorno would maintain the notion that even though modern society, based on the division of labour as it is, does indeed create material prosperity, at the same time it imposes immense restrictions on the individual scope for liberation. In his last lecture on the *Introduction to Sociology* in 1968, he once again emphatically stressed that he understood society as a 'coercive union in which we find ourselves'.[29] However, we should not misunderstand Adorno: he is neither discarding individual autonomy nor the individual's dependence on others.[30] His concept of a 'dialectic of freedom'[31] always includes both aspects, i.e., self-determination and submission.

A diagnosis in great demand in the 1968 student movement, and which may initially appear rather disenchanting, was advanced by philosopher Herbert Marcuse, a representative of Critical Theory who continued like no other to stick by the idea of liberation. In his 1964 work *One-Dimensional Man*, it sounds as if domination has become virtually perfected in societies based on the division of labour.[32] After all, for Marcuse, the freedom to act independently and critically has not grown but become smaller. Oppression has become subtler: precisely *because* Western industrial societies have abolished direct

23

coercion – as they have managed to satisfy material needs through an unprecedented supply of goods and have largely liberalized sexual morality – individuals lose their ability for critical reflection. Now, they sit in front of their TVs, as the new mass media offer them a pleasant, albeit 'ready-made world'.[33] In mass society, human beings want to be like all the rest, the same cars are parked outside the terraced houses, and the same cans of Coca-Cola fill their fridges. People's thinking and being tends towards one-dimensionality. As Marcuse notes:

> In this society, the productive apparatus tends to become totalitarian to the extent to which it determines not only the socially needed occupations, skills, and attitudes, but also individual needs and aspirations. It thus obliterates the opposition between the private and public existence, between individual and social needs.[34]

Technological innovation, shorter working hours and increasing prosperity reduce the need for instinctual impulse control and sublimation – which Horkheimer and Adorno had considered constitutive of modern societies. Pleasure can be realized more freely and hardly meets any moral barriers. Psychoanalyst Sigmund Freud assumed that the pleasure principle, which is geared towards the unimpeded satisfaction of needs, is kept in check by the reality principle, which adapts pleasure to the requirements of the outside world. In a largely disinhibited society, however, the psychodynamic changes: the pleasure principle, and this is the essence of Marcuse's social critique, is now in the service of oppression. Although the individual may have greater freedom, it is confined by what is demanded by society. The pleasure principle, in a stunted form limited to sexuality, is identical with the reality principle.[35] Pleasure thus loses its emancipatory substance, leading to a repressive desublimation:

> In this new historical form of the Reality Principle, progress may operate as a vehicle of repression. The better and bigger satisfaction is very real, and yet, in Freudian terms, it is *repressive* in as much as it diminishes in the individual psyche the sources of the Pleasure Principle *and* of freedom.[36]

In Marcuse's view, the emancipatory potentialities of desire are replaced with false substitutes (consumer goods, commercial forms of sexual attraction, reified intimate relationships, etc.), which may create a tempting illusion of freedom but simultaneously render the concomitant oppression invisible.[37] For Marcuse, overcoming capitalist society was the precondition for realizing the aspiration for happiness – an idea that corresponded with the basic sentiment of the student movement. In 1967, in his talk on 'The End of Utopia' ('*Das Ende der Utopie*') in the packed-out auditorium at Freie Universität Berlin, Marcuse painted the utopian picture of an emancipated society in which an aesthetic-erotic sensitivity could emerge, a lifeworld that links up work and pleasure.[38]

However, in highly industrialized societies, not only do individuals' libidinally driven possibilities for emancipation recede, but, along with this limitation – and here Marcuse is fully in line with the Frankfurt School's basic premise – regressive potentials are released, too. The result is a 'loss of conscience',[39] a kind of neglect of morality – an observation that shall become more important for our analysis as we proceed. If the conflict-ridden dynamic of individual desire and social requirements, which was institutionally mediated in modern societies, is erased in favour of individual pleasure gains, the moral judgement of the fully libidinally satisfied individuals also regresses. This facilitates the 'acceptance of the misdeeds of this society',[40] because the superego is now only moderately developed. Disinhibited action can no longer be perceived as immoral deviation if moral parameters are absent. As a result, an 'instinctual [...] aggressive energy'[41] is unleashed, potentially turning against any arbitrarily selected object at any time. In a society that is based on competition and exploitation, the unleashing of instincts becomes destructive. The political consequences, which Marcuse only hints at here, had already been comprehensively addressed by his erstwhile colleague and subsequent adversary Erich Fromm.[42]

Fromm had been the head of the social-psychological department at the Frankfurt Institute since 1930 and was for a long time regarded as its most important theoretician.[43] However, in their US exile, Horkheimer, Adorno and Fromm increasingly found themselves in disagreement. In particular, the first two were rather displeased by Fromm's critique of Freud. Although they also critiqued Freud, they did so from the left. Fromm's humanistic conception of the human being, and his emphasis of the spontaneity of human action, contradicted their materialist orientation. After his irreconcilable departure from the institute, in 1941 Fromm published his *Escape from Freedom*,[44] whose German title was *Die Furcht vor der Freiheit* (*The Fear of Freedom*, the title by which the book was republished in English in the UK in 1942). The original English title seems far more appropriate: in this book, Fromm approaches authoritarian dispositions as a flight from modern freedom. This is a freedom which, he argues, induces negative feelings of isolation and powerlessness rather than a sense of self-determination in the individual. Even though his former colleagues accused Fromm of having advanced a revisionist Freud interpretation, he develops an idea in this interpretation that also featured in the *Dialectic of Enlightenment* some years later. To him, the completely voluntary, at times pleasurable 'submission' that distinguishes the authoritarian personality arises from a deficient resolution of the dialectical character of human freedom. In order to understand fascist and authoritarian political systems, the logical task, according to Fromm, is to represent the 'two aspects of freedom'[45] in their eminently real contradictions:

> We see that the process of growing human freedom has the same dialectic character that we have noticed in the process of individual growth. On the one hand it is a process of growing strength and integration, mastery of nature, growing power of human reason, and growing solidarity with other human beings. But on the other hand, this growing individuation means growing isolation, insecurity, and thereby growing doubt concerning one's role in the universe, the meaning of one's life, and with all that a growing feeling of one's own powerlessness and insignificance as an individual.[46]

Fromm observes a parallel between the ontogenetic and social development of the human being towards freedom. Children form their self by stepping out of the primary bonds through which they become aware of both their autonomy and, simultaneously, their vulnerability. To Fromm, the social advancement of increasing individualization is organized in a similar way. In modernity, the individual, who is freed from barriers and constraints, certainly does form a free will, including a critical judgement – but they are thus haunted by new doubts. The bourgeois sense of time, which communist Hungarian philosopher György (Georg) Lukács so insightfully termed 'transcendental homelessness' in his early work *The Theory of the Novel* (1920),[47] is thus substantiated by Fromm on the terrain of social psychology. According to Lukács, the impact

26

of the enlightened immanence of life – resulting from the erasure of transcendental references – on the individual's emotional economy is, at once, both liberating and overwhelming. Like the hero of the novel, which Lukács subjected to analysis, the modern individual roams about in a world that has become confusing and which has turned against their desires and aspirations.

In Fromm's view – and, quite similarly so, in that of Horkheimer and Adorno – this negative release is the outcome of an industrial-capitalist domination of nature, which may be organized in a technological-rational manner and enhance scopes of freedom, but which has irrational consequences for society: '[O]n the contrary, this man-made world has become his master, before whom he bows down.'[48] In Germany, but also in the United States, the market at the beginning of the twentieth century was dominated by major corporations whose monopolistic grip was increasingly threatening the overall economic dynamic. Under the conditions of 'monopolistic capitalism', Fromm notes with a still somewhat Marxist-informed style, the individual is subjected to external constraints. Economic crises or the supremacy of cartels prompted the suspicion in the individual that they were being manipulated by sinister powers of which they were at the mercy.[49] If the social institutions leave the individual behind with a feeling of lacking security and social cohesion, Fromm asserts, then 'this lag makes freedom an unbearable burden'.[50] It is this freedom *from* bonds which, according to Fromm, leads to a desire for submission. Authoritarianism constitutes a regressive attempt to resolve the tension between a threatening outside world and a precarious self.

Fromm's conception marks a turning point in Critical Theory's concept of freedom. Like his former colleagues, he is aware of the authoritarian dangers of negative freedom. Unlike Horkheimer and Adorno, however, he formulates an ideal of positive freedom. The break with his colleagues, who were still very strongly influenced by Marxism at the time, is reflected in his image of the human being: '[The individual] can relate himself spontaneously to the world in love and work, in the genuine expression of his emotional, sensuous, and intellectual capacities.'[51] To Fromm, the antinomies of modern freedom can therefore be resolved regressively, i.e., through authoritarian domination or submission, *or* through a responsive relation to the world. In the appendix to *Fear of Freedom*, he underscores this aspect as a key difference between his social psychology and

Freud's psychoanalysis: [T]he key problem of psychology is that of the particular kind of relatedness of the individual towards the world, not that of satisfaction or frustration of single instinctual desires.'[52] As against instinctual determinism, Fromm posits people's free, spontaneous capacity for relationships. What may read like an implicit reckoning with his former Frankfurt colleagues is simultaneously an expansion of the modern freedom problematic surrounding its intersubjective structures, in which resonance can be either facilitated or blocked.[53]

This brief overview of the concepts of freedom that were advanced by the first generation of Critical Theory has revealed one basic thought in particular: from the outset, in light of a radical disillusionment of the optimistic faith in progress, it regards the project of modern freedom as dialectically structured, causing pathologies and threats throughout its historical trajectory. The antinomies, which individual freedom is exposed to in the social process, are inherent in this freedom itself, '[b]y this I mean, in a very real sense, that we are simultaneously both free and unfree'.[54] In other words, formalized freedom in market societies based on the division of labour involves a contradiction, whereby individuals are legally free but effectively unable to be in charge of themselves.

This idea is facilitated by two internal differentiations within Critical Theory, which must be understood, in historical terms, against the backdrop of early organized capitalism in the twentieth century. The first one refers to the paradox of liberation in a late industrial modernity that created new scopes of freedom through comprehensive liberalization but thereby, paradoxically, engendered an unprecedented conformity of action and thought and ultimately reduced emancipatory spaces. Take, for instance, Marcuse, who emphasized the liberating, unfettering yet essentially destructive potency of liberal freedom. The second differentiation brings into play the constraining character of individual freedom, which is deduced from a peculiar combination of competition and monopoly. Human relationships are organized in a competitive manner, and the world of work is dominated by the power of major corporations. As we have learned from Fromm, this induces feelings of isolation and dependence that encourage a susceptibility to authoritarian modes of response.

The historically developed perspectives of early Critical Theory differ in their nuances. Yet, there is an overall agreement that 'the individual, under the conditions of late capitalism, stands only a slim chance of survival'.[55] Over the past fifty years, however, the individual has summoned up new vitality; in many areas they have become more individualistic (and, therefore, from the perspective of Critical Theory, more conformist) than ever before. According to Zygmunt Bauman, this sophisticated diagnostician of modernity, the '"individual"' – he intentionally puts the term in quotation marks, thus accommodating syntactically the doubt about the individuality of the individual – has already been granted 'all the freedom they might have dreamed of and all the freedom they might have reasonably hoped for'.[56]

A Critical Theory of freedom today must take these changes into account. It may well benefit from the interpretations of modern individuals' immanent tensions, but it simultaneously faces the challenge of synchronizing them with the new social situation. Classic Critical Theory emerged in the face of totalitarianism and developed under the conditions of 'organized modernity'.[57] This modernity was 'a sworn enemy of contingency, variety, ambiguity, waywardness and idiosyncrasy'.[58] It was regulated and standardized from above; its social institutions may not have morally condemned the individual but nevertheless pressed them into an 'administered world' through homogeneous opportunities in life and employment prospects – thereby leaving the individual alienated and isolated. Today, we live in a different society: late modernity is accelerated, transient and geared towards permanent differentiation.[59] Desire, wishes and fantasies no longer need to be liberated. Under these changed social conditions, the idea of liberation as an inherently human potentiality which is only being blocked by external barriers needs to be readjusted.[60] Freedom has become an individual responsibility. The antinomies which hitherto mainly concerned the social difference between institutions and persons, between the public and the private spheres, now need to be fought out by the individual. These tensions now take effect within the individual as a steady flow of conflicting emotional states, seething with energy and urging for discharge. The Critical Theory of the present no longer needs to enlighten the individual about the dangers of a repressive society; its task is, rather, to warn society about the individual rebelling against this same society. If Critical Theory was originally underpinned by its assessment of subjectivity as a source of liberation, the task at hand today is to rehabilitate the public space as a sphere of freedom.

Liberalism and authoritarianism

Against the backdrop of such an extreme historical experience as the transformation of liberal societies into fascist dictatorships, Critical Theory did not regard authoritarianism and liberalism as mutually exclusive opposites.[61] In the Foreword to his work *Negations: Essays in Critical Theory*, Marcuse underscores this certainty which he shared with his colleagues from the Institute for Social Research: '[T]otalitarian violence and totalitarian reason came from the structure of existing society, which was in the act of overcoming its liberal past and incorporating its historical negation.'[62] Whereas liberal societies drew their legitimation from guaranteeing their citizens spaces of freedom, totalitarian societies, by definition, seek to extend their rule into almost all spheres of social life and struggle to tolerate inaccessible domains. This unites them with traditional authoritarianism, which rests on the precedence of the state's sovereignty over the individual will.

In their American exile, the associated scholars of the Institute for Social Research set themselves the task of identifying the junctures that connected liberal society with its totalitarian sublation – not least for the sake of explaining the transition of bourgeois liberty into authoritarianism. To Critical Theory, authoritarian measures represented a dark, and yet by no means alien, excess of liberalism, which, after all, was happy to rely on the state's monopoly on the legitimate use of force when it came to defending the (individual) power of control over private property. Marcuse points out that 'powerful interventions [...] by state authority'[63] were common during the liberal era, whether in the form of restrictions of parliament's jurisdiction; drastic measures against the workers' movement and the trade unions; or the curtailment of social rights, freedom of expression and press freedom. Indeed, the emergence of capitalist societies themselves 'is written in the annals of mankind in letters of blood and fire', as Karl Marx characterized the process of primitive accumulation.[64] 'Thus were the agricultural folk first forcibly expropriated from the soil, driven from their homes, turned into vagabonds, and then whipped, branded and tortured by grotesquely terroristic laws into accepting the discipline necessary for the system of wage-labour.'[65] And later, too, there was no question that if the 'silent compulsion of economic relations' did not suffice to break any popular resistance, the state resorted to 'direct extra-economic force'.[66] Ever since the onset of capitalism, the freedom of private property has always been enforced through authoritarian means whenever the need arose.

In 1934, the year after the Nazis seized power in Germany, the Institute for Social Research's journal published Marcuse's insightful essay 'The struggle against liberalism in the totalitarian view of the state'. Marcuse, who had emigrated the previous year, observes that the 'basic structure'[67] of capitalist economic relations continued to exist behind the ostentatious distancing gesture with which the fascist state dissociated itself from the idea of liberalism and – even more importantly – that an authoritarian dictatorship would always be able, in a case of emergency, to protect the power of disposition over private property far more effectively than parliamentary democracy ever could. To underpin his claim, Marcuse references no less an authority than Ludwig van Mies, one of the major founding fathers of liberal social theory, who had written in 1927:

> It cannot be denied that Fascism and similar movements aiming at the establishment of dictatorships are full of the best intentions and that their intervention has, for the moment, saved European civilization. The merit that Fascism has thereby won for itself will live on eternally in history.[68]

What Mies here describes as the 'best intentions' is the fight against socialism and the international workers' movement. And yet, his acknowledgement of fascism must not be misunderstood: for Mies, authoritarian state power represented the very last resort to protect the capitalist circulation of goods from its foreign and domestic enemies. A year before emigrating, Marcuse had to acknowledge that the liberal liaison with authoritarian concepts of governance was ultimately realized.

In 1932, the right-wing conservative scholar of constitutional law Carl Schmitt delivered an address to the *Langnamverein* employers' association in Düsseldorf, entitled 'Strong State and Sound Economy'.[69] In this speech, he proposed to distinguish between two forms of a 'total state', which made this intervention into a significant

31

reference point for early ordoliberalism.[70] Schmitt regards the first form, an 'especially strong state', as *'total in the sense of quality and energy'*, whereas the second form is merely *'total in a purely quantitative sense, in the sense of pure volume and not in the sense of intensity or political energy'*.[71] It is no surprise that he identifies the second form with parliamentary democracy: for him, this latter may be total in the sense that it 'penetrates all domains and all spheres of social existence', but it is simultaneously weak as a result, as it lacks assertive power to resist the pressure from political parties and organized interest groups. By contrast, the fascist state, which Schmitt lists as the first form of state, has 'undreamt-of new means of coercion' available to it; such a state unites novel techno-military instruments and new technological means of mass propaganda in order to protect its stability both domestically and against foreign powers.[72]

To those closely following Schmitt's talk, the *'stato totalitario'*[73] he outlined must have appeared as an entirely new interpretation of economic liberalism: the formula of 'Strong State and Sound Economy' equated the interest of the state with that of the liberal economic system. While the sphere of 'economic autonomous administration [or economic self-management]'[74] was to be protected from any political intervention, the state authority served to suppress the claims of the *demos*. Schmitt's approach entailed a depoliticization of the economy, paralleled by the simultaneous expansion of the state into social affairs, so as to repress any protest by the workers' movement. Schmitt thus regarded a repressive state apparatus as an appropriate instrument to guarantee the free circulation of goods. In his study *The Ungovernable Society*, French philosopher Grégoire Chamayou succinctly encapsulates Schmitt's project: private self-government is not 'called into question, but on the contrary, extended and sanctuarised'.[75] Authoritarian unfreedom was placed in service of economic freedom. For Critical Theory, these deliberations, which must have evoked a promising outlook among the business elite that had invited Schmitt to address them, was an unmistakeable sign of civilizational regression.

To capture this combination of economic liberalism and authoritarian government, the social-democratic lawyer and scholar of constitutional law Hermann Heller coined the term 'authoritarian liberalism'.[76] He did this in his critical reading of Schmitt in 1933, the same year he escaped Germany, before subsequently dying in Spain.

According to Heller, the most characteristic features of authoritarian liberalism included the 'retreat of the "authoritarian" state from social policy' and the 'liberalisation (*Entstaatlichung*) of the economy' – either of which could be implemented only in a despotic manner, but never as the result of popular will.[77] This form of liberalism is *authoritarian* because the state claims sovereign decision-making power over the people; and yet, it remains *liberal* because it abolishes all and any government intervention in economic matters. It can thus be most simply defined as follows: 'Authoritarian liberalism is *liberalism without democracy*.'[78] This general understanding does not necessarily imply a dictatorship, because authoritarian liberalism, as Chamayou emphasizes, 'applies to all situations where, as well as the scope of political decision-making being restricted by economic prohibition (its *liberal* side), the subordinate means of pressure on the political decision-making is also restricted (its properly *authoritarian* side)'.[79] On this reading, the term does not convey any contradiction but results from the aporias of a liberal concept of freedom that can conceive of freedom only in the sense of individual interests.[80]

The same year as Heller's intervention, Friedrich Pollock, himself a founding member of the Institute for Social Research, noted: 'That which is ending is not capitalism, but only its "liberal phase".'[81] To the concerned observers in exile, authoritarian liberalism represented a historical possibility rooted in the transformation of capital during the twentieth century. In 1929, the United States was gripped by the Great Depression, which would also engulf Europe in the following years. Pollock listed the indicators of the looming crisis: an expansive credit policy of the major banks; an alarming increase in economic concentration (in Germany, the establishment of the I.G. Farbenindustrie AG in 1925 made it into the largest chemical corporation worldwide, followed a year later by the Vereinigte Stahlwerke (United Steelworks), which constituted the largest mining corporation in the world); and the collapse of the price of goods. Given this tendency to form monopolies and cartels, which slackened competition – if not eliminating it entirely – capitalism now almost necessarily required a strong state power that acted repressively domestically and aggressively towards other countries. Alongside Germany and Italy, Pollock also cited the Roosevelt government – which quickly managed to curb the crisis in the US through the New Deal – as an example of a state-capitalist interventionism that did not shy away from dictatorial measures. The bureaucratic institutions that managed their constituents and an industrial mass culture geared towards standardized consumerism radically restricted individuals' scopes of freedom. This inevitably had an impact on the social character of this society.

In the mid-1940s, Adorno and Else Frenkel-Brunswik, Daniel J. Levinson and R. Nevitt Stanford jointly conducted the studies on *The Authoritarian Personality* in Berkeley, California, which would become the single most important document of Critical Theory. In the US society of the New Deal era, researchers had not only encountered self-reliant and self-responsible individuals, but also people with an authoritarian inclination, who clung to a rigid value system and, if necessary, aggressively defended it. They were intent on exploring this phenomenon empirically. One consideration underlying this endeavour was that the personality structure of an individual could heighten the susceptibility for 'antidemocratic propaganda'[82] and that social institutions which systematically restrict the thought and action of the individual can have long-term consequences for the personality disposition. In order to study this subject matter, the Berkeley Group both conducted interviews and devised a questionnaire (the so-called Fascism- or just F-scale). This latter, distributed to 2,000 individuals, consisted of around forty statements by which authoritarian attitudes were to be measured. What distinguished the scale was that it went well beyond conventional attitude surveys, as it elaborately addressed private views and peculiarities of individual lifestyles.[83] In their *Remarks on 'The Authoritarian Personality'*, Adorno and his colleagues explain this research tool as follows: 'All aspects of anti-minority prejudice are so affect-laden, so deeply involved with irrational urges and mechanisms, that a rational approach must necessarily remain superficial and fallacious.'[84] While some of the statements would appear rather outdated today (such as, 'Homosexuality is a particularly rotten form of delinquency and ought to be severely punished'), others could hardly be any more topical (e.g., 'To a greater extent than most people realize, our lives are governed by plots hatched in secret by politicians').[85] These individual phrases were then matched with certain features that were meant to represent more or less essential personality traits:[86] submission to an idealized authority (*authoritarian submission*), the condemnation of those who violate conventional norms and the call for them to be punished (*authoritarian aggression*), opposition to imagination and sensitivity (*anti-intraception*), belief in fate and disposition to think in rigid categories (*superstition and stereotypy*), a binary conception of power (strong-weak/leader-follower, etc.) and fantasies of superiority (*power and 'toughness'*), generalized hostility (*destructiveness and cynicism*), projection outwards of unconscious emotional impulses (*projectivity*), and exaggerated preoccupation with sexuality (*sex*).[87] Adorno and his fellow researchers regarded the combined occurrence of these traits as a sign of an authoritarian *syndrome*.

Apart from selected groups among whom they suspected a pronounced authoritarian inclination (such as war veterans or inmates of California's San Quentin jail), they largely surveyed members of the white middle class who were born in the United States. They concluded that workers *and* members of the middle class both exhibited an identical degree of anti-democratic attitudes.[88] Only individuals with a 'disposition toward liberalism'[89] and a tendency towards progressive values appeared to resist this temptation. Among the remaining citizens, however, there were clearly other internal forces at work that eluded their critical judgement – and which were not necessarily reflected in their everyday behaviour, either.

One key consideration of Critical Theory was that authoritarian social formations need not necessarily be based on external coercion. For they may just as well be met with a voluntary, at times even pleasurable, affirmation by their constituents. In other words, the Frankfurt School saw authoritarianism not merely as a form of domination, but as a psychodynamic switching point that reconnected the individual with the authorities in society. This insight resulted from a collective thought process which had begun shortly after the exiles' relocation to New York in 1934. In the almost thousand-page *Studies on Authority and the Family* (1936), the young Erich Fromm was tasked with the partial study on social-psychological aspects. He observed that some people only appeared to be happy in situations of dependence, whereas others rebelled against each and any precept that might be given, even if, objectively speaking, it was perfectly reasonable. Notwithstanding this variety in reactions to a superordinate authority, in Fromm's reading they each arose from the ambivalent emotional culture of authoritarianism, vacillating between fear and reverence, admiration and hatred[90] – an insight that he would return to in his widely acclaimed *The Fear of Freedom*.

In his early search for the emotional bond that creates cohesion between a subordinate and a superordinate person, Fromm still relied on Freud's drive theory, which he would subsequently repudiate. According to Freud, the civilizational requirement of inhibiting one's instinctual impulses leads to the formation of the superego as a psychological authority. The external authority of social institutions which, if need be, discipline their constituents with coercive means, is naturalized by the superego and transforms into an internal authority issuing precepts and prohibitions. This internalized agency of society, Fromm notes, is then, in a second step, projected onto an external authority, which appears as the personification of morality, wisdom and strength.[91] The relation of authority must therefore be understood dialectically; it is an externalization of the internalized society:

> At times, the super-ego is the internalized authority and the authority is the super-ego personified, at other times their interaction creates a voluntary obedience and submission which characterize social practice to an astounding extent.[92]

If, however, the mastery of instincts (or drive denial) cannot be achieved through a strong ego that knows how to balance inner desires and outer requirements, but only through an emotional attachment to an authority, then eventually social pathologies emerge which are marked by a lust both for being subjected and for the subjection of others. In authoritarian societies, whose members are integrated into an asymmetrical fabric of dependencies, an authoritarian-sadomasochistic character structure thus emerges which is engendered by the 'economic structure', Fromm notes.[93] After all, he continues, the individual in authoritarian society is exposed – just like in bourgeois society – to a profound contingency: the fact that one is unable to comprehend, let alone control, one's own life generates a feeling of dependence. This in turn advances a disposition towards that ambivalent character associated with the lust for both obedience and domination over others – an argument that we are familiar with from Fromm's later works. Insofar as one's own helplessness increases, the sadistic desire also grows stronger. Whether it concerns real objects (here, Fromm mentions the important role of children, women or animals), imaginary enemies, or social minorities, the sadistic impulse strives to dominate all those who rank lower in the social hierarchy.[94] This only appears to contradict a masochistic thought pattern that restlessly searches for fateful connections. This thinking is equally geared towards gaining control over a potentially uncontrollable world – but here, powerlessness is overcome through identification with higher powers: '[L]ife is determined by powers that lie outside the individual, his will and his interests. One must submit to these powers, and the ultimate attainable happiness is to enjoy this submission.'[95] The institute's staff members came to the US at a time when the peak of the economic crisis there already seemed to have passed. Yet Americans nevertheless showed high levels of anxiety. According to Fromm, the less controllable the social situation becomes, the more forcefully the authoritarian character structure is activated in the individual.

Political scientist and scholar of constitutional law Franz L. Neumann, who was closely associated with the Institute for Social Research, would return to this consideration about two decades later. In his lecture 'Anxiety and Politics', delivered upon his being awarded an honorary doctorate by the Freie Universität Berlin in 1954, Neumann, too, proceeded from Freud. He interpreted the repression of instinctual impulses as an impellent of 'neurotic anxiety', which, detached from any real threats, floats freely and seeks to avoid any – including imaginary – danger, so as to protect the individual's self-esteem.[96] One crucial aspect in the resistance against fears of social deprivation is the identification with an authoritarian leader-figure. Through the latter, the authoritarian personality participates in a power that it itself lacks. Neumann thus conceives of anxiety as an effective political emotion that is capable of mobilizing the masses on a pre-rational basis. It is the origin of a 'conspiracy theory in history', which becomes increasingly valid the longer those events that threaten one's own social status remain incomprehensible:

> Just as the masses hope for their deliverance from distress through absolute oneness with a person, so they ascribe their distress to certain persons, who have brought this distress into the world through a conspiracy. The historical process is personified in this manner. Hatred, resentment, dread, created by great upheavals, are concentrated on certain persons who are denounced as devilish conspirators.[97]

A society that appears to people as chaotic and incomprehensible, and at times even confronts them in a hostile manner, ultimately alienates them from social reality. It produces not only masses that passively acquiesce in their fate but also mobilizes a destructive activity that turns against the imaginary threat.

— Chapter 2 —

FREEDOM IN DEPENDENCE

The major promise that modern societies make to their citizens is that they are – or, more precisely, have the *ability* to be – individuals. In pre-modern times, birth and family background determined a person's estate and status, which would remain unchanging throughout their life. The inequality of human beings was regarded as a natural fact, as part of a divine order in which each individual had their permanent place. The daughter or son of a peasant family would also become a peasant. The sons of the smiths would, one day, take over their fathers' hammers and smite the anvil themselves. Only few people were able, through distinguished achievements, to overstep the boundaries of status. In short: social position was passed down by heredity, there was hardly any social upward mobility, no room for emancipation, no escape. The family structure was just as static as the biography of any individual. While from a certain point there were free (mostly male) burghers and townspeople who did possess extensive liberties, peasants largely remained locally bound by serfdom and socage. The desire to be in command of one's own life would subsequently become the collective imaginary upheld by bourgeois movements for liberty. But even the free townsman, liberated from the rule of feudalism, was far from being a free individual who could autonomously determine his life. Each respective status commanded certain norms of behaviour, occupational prospects, taste in art, and choice of partner. Historically speaking, today's late modern individual is both the result and the initiator of social change – and it can only be adequately grasped in this context of its historical state of *having-become* and against the backdrop of its (various) metamorphoses.

In contemporary societies, individuality is expressed in many different ways. It is a mosaic made up of a diverse range of identities, lifestyles and moral values. Yet, all of these elements are united by an overarching pattern: each historical stage of modernity was accompanied by a specific social character that influenced how individuals acted, thought and felt.[1] An ethical, sovereign individual emerged in the liberal-bourgeois modernity of the eighteenth and nineteenth centuries, who was geared, above all, towards respectability: namely, *the bourgeois*. This latter wanted to live a life in accordance with their status, always striving for conformity with their own class. In the – much shorter – period of organized modernity, lasting from the 1920 to the 1970s, an other-directed individual became dominant: *the employee* (or *white-collar worker*) (*der Angestellte*).[2] This figure was the result of a far-reaching 'conventionalisation'[3] aimed at social assimilation and the performance of one's duties. In this chapter, we reconstruct the emergence of the late modern individual since the 1970s. This means speaking of *the creative self-realizers*, complete with their conflicts over freedom.[4] We analyse their interrelations and entanglements, the claims that they make and their preconditions in society. Furthermore, we shall discuss the meaning of freedom and its contradictory side-effects. Understanding the history of the unleashing of freedom is crucial if we want to diagnose the pathologies of contemporary societies – recognizing that the late modern individual, too, can only be free *within* society, and indeed is only able to become an individual *with* society. Then, concluding this chapter, we shall see how the present-day individual is oblivious to their dependency and lives under the sway of a reified concept of freedom that negates any relationship with society.

The birth of the individual

Putting a date on the birth of the autonomous individual is no simple task. Individualization is a continual historical process, and not a fact that could somehow be unequivocally assigned to a certain stage of historical change. The earliest theorists of individualization include two authors who are generally classified as collectivists: namely, Friedrich Engels and Karl Marx, often wrongly identified as dogmatic advocates of *the collective* to which the individuals should submit. This pair did indeed develop a concept of collective socialization, yet they did so with the aim of fully realizing individuality and not restricting it. The two men – one the son of a factory owner from Wuppertal, who went to Manchester to continue his father's business, and the other the offspring of a lawyer's family from Trier – were both highly familiar and involved with that segment of the bourgeoisie which sought emancipation, both in terms of the political sphere and its own lifeworld, and was intent on pursuing individualization. That said, Marx and Engels were also familiar – the latter not least through his relationship with the worker Mary Burns – with the life of the lower classes, whose material destitution prevented them from pursuing any kind of autonomous lifestyle. Against this background of ambivalent experiences, their writings expound a concept of individual freedom that may justifiably be regarded as the vanishing point of their entire theory. In the *Manifesto of the Communist Party*, which appeared in 1848 even before the onset of industrial modernity, they depict the utopia of a social 'association, in which the free development of each is the condition for the free development of all'.[5] As Marx and Engels emphatically insist, the bourgeoisie makes sure that it puts 'an end to all feudal, patriarchal, idyllic relations'. 'It has pitilessly torn asunder the motley feudal ties that bound man to his "natural superiors", and has left remaining no other nexus between man and man than naked self-interest.'[6]

The 'motley feudal ties' that the two are referring to here included the traditional loyalties and duties towards the nobility, customary law and, in particular, physical and social immobility. In sharp contrast to this permanent static condition, Marx and Engels regarded capitalist modernization as a great furnace in which nothing would remain as it had been: 'All fixed, fast-frozen relations, with their train of ancient and venerable prejudices and opinions, are swept away [...]. All that is solid melts into air.'[7]

Marx and Engels, however, considered another feature of modernization essential for the ambivalent constitution of the modern individual: for, in their view, the workers were free in a double sense. They were 'free from all the old client or bondage relationships and any obligatory services, and free also from all foods and chattels, from every objective and material form of being, free from all property'.[8] As free bourgeois subjects, workers may be able to choose their employer, but it is precisely this freedom that harbours a moment of coercion: given their lack of material property, workers are forced to sell their labour power in order to survive. Hence, liberation does not necessarily imply freedom but may also entail a lack of alternatives. As Marx and Engels repeatedly made clear, when the bourgeois idea of individual freedom was realized, this produced severe restrictions for the majority of the population, in outright contradiction with the emancipatory promise of self-realization. Workers in the towns may have been legally free, but their lived reality was marked by daily hunger and a proletarian existence in the smallest dwellings.

For bourgeois individuals in possession of the necessary resources, then, freedom amounted to business calculation. Marx and Engels stress the subjectivity of 'egotistical calculation' so typical of modernity, as well as the 'indefeasible and chartered freedoms' already existing in feudal societies, which were now being replaced by 'that *single*, unconscionable freedom – Free Trade'.[9] For Critical Theory, almost a century later, this commercially reductionist conception of freedom would come to signify a key experience. In his 1936 essay 'Egoism and Freedom Movements' ('*Egoismus und Freiheitsbewegung*'), Max Horkheimer diagnoses 'otherness' (*Fremdheit*) as a new 'anthropological category'. In the generalization of economic relations, the emancipated individual experiences itself merely as an 'isolated subject of interests'; the basic sentiment of that era, he notes, was one of coldness and alienness – and this had severe moral consequences: '[N]othing in the essence of the bourgeois individual opposes the repression and annihilation of one's fellow human beings.'[10] Hence, emancipation harbours the potential for regression. Marx and Engels, moreover, already conveyed a sense of that *dialectic of individualization* which is still posited in sociological theory today: the emergence of the individual is based on the simultaneity of liberation and new constraints.[11]

At the sociological seminar, held at the Institute for Social Research, a young sociologist called Norbert Elias began his position as assistant to Karl Mannheim in 1930. Elias's intention was that he would soon qualify as a professor there, but he never would give his inaugural lecture; like so many other members of the institute, he was forced to emigrate in 1933.[12] To put it mildly, under Horkheimer's directorship, the institute maintained a somewhat distanced relationship with Mannheim. Yet his assistant Elias, living in exile, dedicated himself to a question with which Critical Theory was much concerned against the backdrop of rising fascism. While browsing through a book on social etiquette at the British Museum by pure chance,

Elias discovered his interest in the interplay of civilization and the repression of instinctual impulses. In 1939 he published his work *The Civilizing Process* in two volumes. In it, he illustrates how social differentiation has a civilizing effect on emotional impulses, from which, ultimately, arises the modern individual with its specific drive dynamic: '[A]s the social fabric grows more intricate, the sociogenic apparatus of individual self-control also becomes more differentiated, more all-round and more stable.'[13] To him, the transformation from *external* to *internal constraints* that regulate individual action represents a precondition for the stability of the interdependent, organized society based on the division of labour – a society, of course, which alienates individuals.[14] Only the process of individuation eventually allows the individual to comprehend society as a separate entity with its own internal mechanisms.[15] The Frankfurt colleagues, then, saw not so much the inherent potentialities for the fulfilment of civilizational potential but merely a stunted form of individuality, threatening to vitiate the thin layer of civilizational varnish. In his considerations, Elias likewise proceeds from Sigmund Freud, who, in his work *Civilization and Its Discontents*, published in 1930, deduces the creation of civilization from an externally enforced sublimation of instinctual energy. In other words, activities such as the construction of a cathedral or the enjoyment of an opera prevent people from turning against each other. According to Freud, it is 'impossible to overlook the extent to which civilization is built up upon a renunciation of instinct, how much it presupposes precisely the non-satisfaction (by suppression, repression or some other means?) of powerful instincts'.[16] The essence of individuation, Elias notes, ultimately centres on the translation of sexual instinctual energies into civilized forms of behaviour. Freud – and Elias shortly after him – sees the 'regulation of social relationships' as the cause of the need for such a translation.[17] The amalgamation of separate individual needs into a social coexistence imposes boundaries on the individual subject. The regulated instinctual economy proper to modernity rests precisely on this interplay of individual satisfaction and societal deprivation.

In the course of modernization, not only did professions, hierarchies and private forms of cohabitation change but so, too, the individual's emotional inner life. Social constraints were reduced – and it was only this that allowed the space for reflecting thereby on oneself and controlling one's emotions and drive-economy to open up for the first time ever. People attained a higher level of self-regulation and were able to develop an ego identity that relied less on the collective. They were liberated but simultaneously thrown into a world that had changed and which they themselves had little control over. Following the end of guild coercion, journeymen could now become craftsmen and the offspring of the serf became a factory worker. And yet, the liberties which were now codified as rights initially applied to men only.[18] Some individuals may, to some limited extent, have been able to break through the ossified patterns of life, yet even this came at the cost of being subjected to new dependencies. Still, this observation on the contradictory character of the individualization process does not by any means imply that the modern concept of freedom is merely imaginary and aloof from social reality – an argument that we came across in the preceding chapter. The freedom of social mobility did actually increase in real terms, but it did so on the basis of new instances of unfreedom. Polish-British sociologist Zygmunt Bauman succinctly encapsulated the coercive nature of modern freedom: 'The task confronting free individuals was to use their new freedom to find the appropriate niche and to settle there through conformity: by faithfully following the rules and modes of conduct identified as right and proper for the location.'[19] The general expectation was for individuals to adapt to the norms of modernity, within which they could then '*become* what one *is*'.[20] That is to say, individualization brought about a limited individualism, a new independence from traditions and moral constraints – and needless to say, this could take place only on the basis of the shared rules. Within this framework, new spaces opened up for individual distinction, which was made visible and expressed through a 'distinctive lifestyle'.[21] The individuality of style was, of course structured by class position – a reality that has largely remained unchanged to this day. The upper and middle classes had the resources available to develop unique individualities, whereas the lower classes were condemned to a greater degree of conventionality.

According to sociologist Georg Simmel, it was particularly social differentiation that allowed for an extension of individual latitude: faced with diverse areas of action, the individual was no longer strictly tied to the social legacy or the surroundings of their parents.[22] The advancing division of labour multiplied the number of choices open to them. In this way, an autonomous individual emerged that was able to protect itself against the authority of the monarchy and the church by invoking human and civil rights. But Simmel, who regarded the industrialized German Empire from his urban Berlin context, also discerned countervailing effects: the individual may no longer have depended on other individuals or societal sub-areas, yet they now relied heavily on the 'whole of society'.[23] The totality of relations constituted the framework for the development of individuality – though this did not necessarily have a coercive character. Simmel emphasized that individualization always remains an ambivalent process that cannot be resolved unidirectionally, for it is an 'uninterrupted alternation between bondage and release, obligation and freedom'.[24] For sociologist Émile Durkheim, the socialization of the individual represented the very precondition for individual freedom:

> For man freedom consists in deliverance from blind, unthinking physical forces; this he achieves by opposing against them the great and intelligent force which is society, under whose protection he shelters. By putting himself under the wing of society, he makes himself also, to a certain extent, dependent upon it. But this is a liberating dependence. There is no paradox here.[25]

Society is pervaded by an assemblage of rules and norms, which people usually abide by even though they may be mostly unaware of them. The smooth everyday functioning of society is stabilized by routines that rumble on in the background. Grammar is a precondition for free thought, etiquette facilitates free speech and interaction, laws allow for unimpeded market exchange. In other words, rules enable spaces of freedom. The degree to which these routines ensure a certain stability in everyday life only becomes apparent in crisis situations. As Durkheim explains, the willing renunciation of certain options is what makes social, and thereby individual, freedom possible. The individual's 'submission' is the precondition for freedom.[26]

In early modernity prior to 1800, individualization was still tied to the principles of both freedom *and* equality. Although the rise of individualism has always been accompanied by an anti-modern diagnosis of decadence that entailed a concern about the loss of commitment to the common good, it has also been regarded as a vital source of democratic coexistence. During a trip to the United States in 1831, the young Alexis de Tocqueville interpreted individualism as a virtually 'gravitational force'[27] providing individuals with coherence in their yearning for civil and political rights. Proceeding from Tocqueville, Durkheim went as far as depicting individualism as a secular system of faith, which ensured 'the moral unity of the country'.[28] He would be proven wrong. Even Tocqueville had already suspected that individualism might contain a force that would have a corrosive effect on democratic societies in the long run (more on this in chapter 4).

In parallel with the rise of capitalist societies and their political antagonist – socialism – individualism changed its historical shape. Freedom and equality were no longer conceived as one, and individualism would henceforth instead be closely associated with inequality and difference, with the notion of individual uniqueness. '[I]ndividualist liberalism'[29] conceives of the individual exclusively in opposition to society – fully in line with philosopher Thomas Hobbes, who, in the seventeenth century, defined freedom as the absence of external constraints and as the possibility to realize one's own plans 'as [one] has a will to'.[30] In bourgeois societies, this concept of negative freedom is closely related to the 'deep-seated intuition'[31] to claim a radically idiosyncratic distinction for oneself. In this negative notion of freedom, individual striving can only be conceived in isolation from social bonds and relationships. Still, as liberal philosopher John Stuart Mill emphasizes, this does not necessarily mean that a radically individualist understanding has no awareness whatsoever of the boundaries of this freedom: 'The only freedom which deserves the name is that of pursuing our own good in our own way, so long as we do not attempt to deprive others of theirs or impede their efforts to obtain it.'[32] For Mill, the question of the conditions under which society can intervene in the individual's liberties, and at what point in time, takes centre stage. His answer is somewhat surprising, as it indicates individual self-interest as the only legitimate justification but simultaneously leaves open the question of whether the individual or humanity as a whole must formulate this self-interest: 'That principle is that the sole end for which mankind are warranted, individually or collectively, in interfering with the liberty of action of any of their number is self-protection.'[33] A century after Mill, philosopher Isaiah Berlin coined the widely adopted differentiation between negative and positive freedom. *Negative freedom* denotes the absence of state coercion – or, to put that the other way around: it protects subjective rights from external infringement. *Positive freedom*, in contrast, is essentially an autonomous self-relation. The individual is free in

46

the positive sense as long as their action is motivated by purposes that were defined without any kind of external coercion.[34] Despite the externality of negative freedom, it possesses a propulsive vector which continues to be highly significant for contemporary societies.

Negative individualization

In our view, the relevance of the late modern individual at the heart of our investigation arises primarily from its ambivalent basic constitution. Sociologist Ulrich Beck historicized this individual as the outcome of a continuous process of modernization. To Beck, there are three aspects that play a key role: the liberation from obsolete social forms; the loss of traditional securities; and new forms of social inclusion or, rather, control.[35] The separation from traditional constructs of the family and class relations, from loyalties and disciplining institutions, is part of the precondition for spatial mobility, self-realization and autonomy in one's life. The farewell to what Adorno referred to as the 'administered world'[36] of predefined rules and heteronomous objectives simultaneously marked the birth of the intrinsically motivated individual. This latter no longer abided by a handful of authorities (the father; the boss) but by a wide variety of such figures – although the most important authority of all was now the individual themselves.

Beck thus implicitly refines Norbert Elias's concept of a continuous process of civilization of the individual, in which individuality and socialization are inextricably linked: 'More and more people', Elias had written, 'came to live in increasing dependence on each other, while each individual was at the same time growing more differentiated from all others'.[37] At the same time, Elias notes, individuals always remain related to collectives both in their individuality *and* identity – here, he speaks of 'figuration'.[38] In this figuration, the subject is not separated from 'We'-groups such as the family, professional groups and social milieus. However, during the 1980s, the later Elias perceived a shift from the We–I balance to the I–We balance.[39] The term 'balance' is not the most fortunate choice, here, as Elias is actually pointing to a disequilibrium resulting from a shift in the weighting of its components: while the significance of occupational groups or the family diminishes, the I moves to the fore but remains tied to the We-forms.

Beck makes a similar observation. Although he was noted mainly for his individualization hypothesis (which he formulated in somewhat affirmative terms), already in this hypothesis he anticipated the limits of a process which itself brings about new vulnerabilities. After all, separating oneself from the often-complex family structure and traditional networks comes at the cost of new dependencies on the institutions of a society that is itself becoming ever-more differentiated and standardized. The social forms handed down from the past have been replaced with new modes of socialization, which may not have an impact on the lives of each and every member of society, but certainly do have such an effect on the vast majority. Beck had in mind the social transformations underway since the 1970s and 1980s: in case of unemployment, one now went to the job centre instead of resorting to the family; in 1971, the introduction of the so-called *BaföG* law provided financial assistance for basic and higher education and training independently of one's family background; more and more people lived by themselves or in flat-sharing communities.

The stages in one's biography prescribed by estate-based or class background were replaced by 'secondary agencies and institutions'.[40] Compulsory schooling had not in fact been introduced in Germany until 1919; prior to that, education had in part still been imparted (or not) to children at home. Yet now, childhood was followed by completing the education system, pursuing an occupational career and, finally, spending old age in state-regulated retirement. The individual, in this sense, is only free to a certain extent, as they remain reliant on the labour market and educational institutions, on infrastructures, or on the planning and organization of public transport and traffic management, etc. The result is what Beck called *'institutionally dependent individual situations'*.[41] Beck, a sociologist and lecturer at Munich's Ludwig Maximilian University, did not, however, analyse individualization primarily as a process of loss, but rather as the gaining of (institutionally) dependent autonomy. The loss of traditional bonds, Beck states, must not be understood as a 'demise of society'[42] – for on the contrary, social ties gain even more influence over the individual. In particular, the volatile market in which the individual must assert themselves is beyond any individual control: they are at the mercy of trends, fashions, economic cycles and scenarios of risk and conflict which resist individual resolution or for which no established adjustment strategies exist.

Individuals in late modern societies are thus exposed to a dilemma that can hardly be resolved single-handedly. That is, they harbour huge expectations in their own self-efficacy – but this is precisely what they often fail to experience. Their own occupational biographies have become uncertain; global markets, international politics or climate change are difficult to make sense of, or are altogether beyond the control of any individual action. Even if individuals no longer follow in the footsteps of their parents' standard biographies, and they may at times even reject these lifestyles, many – especially those from the middle classes – nevertheless consider comprehensibility, controllability and security very important. For risk-taking individualists, in turn, the loss of experiences of self-efficacy or a disillusioned future outlook constitute a potential source of frustration. In this context, *negative individualizations* take effect, which restrict the increase in action resources and freedoms. If we hope freely to choose the doctor we want to see, first we need health insurance; to interact on social media, we need electricity and the Internet; in order to receive unemployment benefits, we require proof of our neediness. Seeing as 'the whole' is heteronomous to the individual, the latter is constantly forced to adapt and insist on their self-determination. Indeed, it is this 'very real conflict'[43] between freedom and the pressure to conform, which Marx and Engels had already noticed, that individuals must continually internalize. And yet, it is not until late modern capitalism that it turns into a dominant feature of the societal dynamic.

Over the past thirty years, some of the fundamental prerequisites of modern individualism have been destabilized.[44] This process refers primarily to welfare-state security and the world of work. Wage labour continues to represent the key mechanism of social integration, but its historical form has changed. Social advancement has become more difficult; inequality has been rising since the 1990s, especially at the margins of society; precarious employment conditions have proliferated. The integrated middle classes have shrunk, and a new underclass has emerged.[45] The societal dynamic differs fundamentally from that of organized modernity, whose directedness Ulrich Beck described as the 'elevator effect': although the gaps between the classes remained, the individual classes were all on their way up. The lower and middle classes were ascending in the elevator and harboured quite similar aspirations: a car, a house and going on holiday. The material social advancement of parts of the lower class and the gain in social rights led to a society of 'similar individuals'.[46]

The dynamic of late modernity since the 1980s, by contrast, can more accurately be illustrated using the analytical metaphor of an escalator moving downwards, which the individual has to keep pace with by running up the steps.[47] Whoever aspires towards success or seeks to protect a once-attained status must show flexibility, constantly adapt and readjust themselves.[48] Those who stop moving forward start heading down the escalator. Self-optimization thus becomes the prime imperative of late capitalist modernity. This is also reflected in the restructuring of the welfare state, which was steadily liberalized beginning in the 1980s. Institutionally embedded social rights were tied more strongly to individual performance and, thereby, to conditions – which fundamentally contradicts the idea of a civil right. Social rights became a disciplining mechanism. Individuals became market citizens, customers with rights.[49] To them, the tax- and contributions-funded welfare state appears not as a collective achievement of past struggles, but, at best, as an insurance system with mandatory membership, which is considered with instrumental reason. One simply tries to find the most efficient solution for oneself by optimizing one's claims entitlements and reducing one's costs. In this context, self-exclusion not only weakens the general relations of solidarity but also produces vulnerabilities: many people who, when they were young and productive, took out private health insurance, discover in old age – when their energy and health are declining, their career path is no longer pointing upwards and their children need to be insured separately – the downsides of leaving the public health system. For the costs of private health insurance rise continuously. The way back into the public, solidarity-based system is full of obstacles. The restructuring of the welfare state would have been impossible without a concomitant 'revaluation of values' (Nietzsche). In organized modernity, self-responsibility constituted a precept of emancipation, of freedom. Workers wanted to be able to shape their lives autonomously without getting smothered by the maelstrom of capitalism or being bullied by the factory owner. The welfare state was regarded as the precondition for leading one's own life in a responsible way. The reforms introduced by the 'Red–Green' government (a coalition of the SPD (Social Democratic Party) and the Green Party under Chancellor Gerhard Schröder) shortly after the turn of the millennium (the so-called Agenda 2010, as well as reforms to the pension and health system) were, however, based on a different interpretation of self-responsibility.[50]

The restructuring of the welfare state was dressed in a semantics of provision, activation and prevention, but it ultimately amounted primarily to a reduction of freedom and collective social rights and, thereby, for the lower classes, to negative individualization.[51] The reissued semantics of self-responsibility bear an authoritarian and paternalistic dimension: the objective is no longer the social assurance of a self-determined life. Rather, self-responsibility became a term denoting social disciplining – allegedly in the service of the common good.[52]

The gains in autonomy for the late modern individual may have always been organized along class lines. And yet, *social* freedom, as defined by Axel Honneth, which guarantees 'the material conditions under which all individuals can exercise their freedoms more effectively', has once again come to be linked more strongly to one's position within the social hierarchy.[53] Highly skilled class segments gradually improve their spaces of freedom, whereas the experience for the lower classes is the exact opposite:[54] they are forced to accept jobs below their qualification levels, disclose their financial records or grant inspectors access to their homes. Adorno would have identified such an understanding of freedom as a form of *ideology*. To him, the utopian substance of the theory of freedom is corrupted when it portrays people as if they were absolutely unrestricted in their will and responsible only for themselves. In that case, theory merely serves repression and the justification of unfreedom.[55] After all, at least from the perspective of absolute 'freedom', there are no 'mitigating circumstances' in favour of individual subjects anymore; people experience the merciless side of the state first-hand, should they fail to act self-responsibly.

Negative individualizations also have an impact on the change in the semantics of success and achievement. The achievement (or: performance) principle itself is a highly ambivalent concept.[56] This surely can be used – based on a productivist interpretation – as a tool of exclusion and discrimination ('Whoever doesn't work shall not eat') and, to this day, continues to conceal the ongoing exploitation of workers in reality. Yet, historically it also served as a political means of struggle for the bourgeoisie against the corporative privileges of the nobility. For the middle classes and the working class, all different interpretations aside, this same principle provided orientation and

51

identity. In its very essence, it is reciprocal, synthesizing individual effort and the gain that may justifiably be expected.[57] Technically, then, the achievement principle is also and at all times the result of social conflicts around the issue of what measurement should be applied in the distribution of any gains.[58] It is the product of a negotiation as well as a device of social self-assurance and integration.

Ever since the 1970s, however, late modern capitalism has become pervaded by a cult of success.[59] It is success that determines prestige, recognition and social position, and no longer the work actually performed. Performance (or: achievement), in this sense, has not become obsolete, as it continues to be demanded from everyone, but it is no longer a guarantee for success. The reason is that the latter has become more contingent more generally; the individual has only very limited control over whether they can secure success *through* performance and achievement. Success comes to those who are already successful, in a specious self-referentiality. As a result, the yardstick of performance – exertion, effort, discipline – is shattered, and even devalued. Because those who are not successful are no longer regarded as top performers. Now, these latter include only those who are successful – managers, consultants and celebrities.[60]

Another important reason why the pressure on individuals increases is the fact that the criterion of success bears the threat of a degrading evaluation. There surely are different degrees of success, but it is coded in binary or at least in ordinal terms – and not in gradual terms in the manner of the achievement principle. The question is no longer one of *greater or smaller* achievements, but of success *or* failure. There are winners and losers. Aesthetic and technology markets in particular become winner-takes-all markets, in which success is concentrated among the superstars,[61] in literature usually limited to very few best-selling authors.[62] In the digital economy, network effects and increasing returns to scale enhance the concentration among the tech corporations.[63] And the invasive culture of comparing, rating and ranking engenders new hierarchies of success: the few at the top benefit from the Matthew effect ('He that has plenty shall have more'). The orientation of wages and salaries according to *performance* (an English term that has now been adopted also in German) is a double-edged sword for workers in lower and middling positions: although they can always achieve a bonus, they accept that their performance is – permanently – monitored. Each mistake, each instance of exhaustion and weakness is made visible.

The orientation towards success is a win–win situation only for members of management. This latter group have shown that they will do anything to drive up stock prices, always in pursuit of shareholder value, even if this is to the detriment of workers and/or the company's long-term success. After a few years, they are able to sell their shares, rake in the bonuses and move on. Failure, moreover, is rarely a danger for managers. Whenever they are forced to resign, their departure is usually generously compensated. For most workers, in contrast, failure generates treacherous ascriptions of its own. If someone is *unsuccessful*, not even the effort that was made counts. In the case of failure, the individual can no longer point to an unjust system (capitalism) nor others who are collectively responsible (such as the company). This is where self-responsibility is invoked.

Success often draws on the resources and privileges that the achievement principle was originally supposed to have eliminated. Many members of the elites have not risen to the top solely based on their own achievements, but often come from (upper-class) bourgeois families.[64] But once they have reached the top, this privileged background is often denied in the interest of highlighting their own achievements.[65] *Success* now *appears* as an individual achievement, whereas lack of success becomes the result of individual failure.[66] The latter is further reinforced by the fact that there are ever fewer members of support collectives such as trade unions or political parties, i.e., organizations where people can discuss what connection links their individual problems to harmful developments in society.

Furthermore, the imperative of success, has severe consequences for the individual and societal processing of conflict. To put it more bluntly: the obsession with success harbours an anomic tendency, as we shall see in more detail in chapter 4. Successful action is guided exclusively by the desired goal, which is why it does not feel bound by any 'other norms'. Success 'becomes the epitome of instrumental reason'.[67] While the achievement principle is founded on cooperation based on a division of labour, the advance of a logic of success causes 'resentment'.[68] Indeed, error culture is highly regarded in modern business culture, which has its guiding image in Silicon Valley – it is almost *bon ton* to have failed at least once, so long as one immediately moves on to the next successful project.[69] And yet, apart from that, individual failure is not an option in late modernity. Illness reflects a lack of health-preserving behaviour, being overweight is the result of lacking self-discipline, setbacks at work are caused by a lack of motivation, private problems indicate a lack of social skills, and fears of the future appear as the inability to think positively.[70] Society's problems are turned into individual ones.[71]

Despite its polarized outcome, success is a significant internalized norm, and in certain groups it is paradoxically even more important than general social advancement. Everybody wants to be part of the upper or middle class, for being part of the working class is regarded as a stigma.[72] Workers are those who have failed to make it – the losers. Yet while advancement, particularly in the middle class, can actually be attained through investments in status, through diligence, ambition and the disciplined accumulation of knowledge, and thus ultimately lead to success, the norm of success plays a rather contradictory role for younger people from the lower classes. For the children of the lower 20–30 per cent of society, since the 1980s the promise of social advancement has applied only to a limited extent.[73] Instead of trusting in the uncertain achievement principle, individuals set themselves goals that rank higher in the success hierarchy, but which require more risk-taking – and which are difficult, if not impossible to achieve. When somebody says, I want to be a manager, or a pop star, they are exempting themselves from the achievement principle from the very outset – as a result of which they can no longer fail in achieving.[74] This leaves them with a short cut via artistic performance, casting shows, an existence as an influencer or would-be gangsta rapper, etc.[75] In all this, there is very little room for solidarity.

In late modern societies, competition is no longer restricted to markets of goods. It is omnipresent in people's lifeworld and has become a 'dominant mode of interaction'.[76] The competition for scarce resources is an external constraint for the individual, but that is simultaneously the reason why it turns into an internal urge. 'When the subject's validity depends on the social comparison of current success balances, any prestigious level of ranking and the corresponding status symbols must be permanently displayed and even small competitive advantages must be cultivated', writes sociologist Sighard Neckel.[77] Comparison, rating and ranking are going on at all levels. The sociologist Marion Fourcade, who teaches in Berkeley, California, refers to these processes as an 'ordinalization' rooted in a radically liberal and individualist philosophy. Externally ascribed classifications such as race or gender (Fourcade speaks of 'nominal' features) are supposedly resolved or move to the background. In a seemingly classless, inclusive society based on equality, everyone starts out with the same opportunities in life; but their individual achievement becomes even more visible as a result. It would seem that no one can claim any kind of disadvantages through certain group affiliations anymore, and everybody is ranked in a hierarchy of worth, which is exclusively guided by achievement.[78] This is the essence of the meritocratic promise. But behind this very promise, we find a hidden, symbolically structured power process, for even top marks in school are rewarded only to a limited extent. In formal terms at least, the child of a single mother or a Syrian refugee family certainly has the same opportunities in assessment tests for elite education institutions. But they are unable to succeed because in their home there were not parents listening to Schubert sonatas, and nor did they have the cultivated middle-class everyday conversations that would have pointed them to the particularities of the lighting in Caravaggio's paintings. That is to say, formal equality of opportunities is not remotely identical with real equality of opportunities: 'Under a veil of fairness, precision and objectivity, traditional boundaries and inequalities can be reinforced or created anew', as Fourcade and Alex V. Barnard write.[79] Furthermore, this process signifies a devaluation precisely for those disadvantaged social groups for whose identity symbolic ascriptions were very important: 'What used to be stable, internally homogeneous categories, such as race, now appear as an arbitrary grouping together of the most diverse individuals in a single category.'[80] In short: educated Afro-Americans compete with other educated members of minorities in the labour market. But in the maelstrom of competition, they lose even those particular features that distinguished them as Afro-Americans.

Ubiquitous competition is thus itself a crucial driver of negative individualization. It promises fairness and equal opportunities, but at the same time it heightens inequalities; it levels out symbolic boundaries, but increases identity consciousness; it facilitates successful action, but generates a loss of norms; it mobilizes and activates and simultaneously causes exhaustion; it is a means of emancipation but, at the same time, forces people into conformism; it is a driver of sober social rationalizing, but simultaneously unleashes new emotions. The latter are also a result of the rise in inequality. According to British political economist William Davies, many typical modern indicators of progress such as GDP conceal the cracks in society. Political narratives leave many people angry, because these narratives and the *official* facts on socio-economic development do not correspond to their own subjective reality.[81]

Paradoxes of emancipation

Up until the early 1970s, organized modernity was essentially geared towards an increase in legal and social equality.[82] The members of the lower classes could, for the first time ever, participate as full members of society. The most important status symbol at the time was, of course, car ownership. But washing machines and dryers were also something after which people aspired. When the first colour TV went on sale in Germany in 1967, many people had to take out a loan to be able to afford one. Those who had 'made it' would perhaps install a party room in the basement of their new family home. People effectively wanted to be conformist, be *like all the others*, live a 'standard biography',[83] as this promised security not only in one's lifeworld but also in socio-structural terms.

The conformist lifestyle of organized modernity offered security. But at the same time, it brought an inhibiting constraint for ever more people, which put up a barrier to individual claims. This was reflected in the 1968 movement as well as in pop culture. These lyrics from a Kinks song written by Ray Davies encapsulate this rebellion against conformity: 'And I don't wanna live my life like everybody else. And I won't say that I feel fine like everybody else. 'Cause I'm not like everybody else.'

The 1970s marked a significant turning point – the beginning of late modernity. The appeal of conformism now faded even outside the world of subcultures; free self-development and the free choice of lifestyle became a generalized ideal. Occupation and family roles were supposed to be freely chosen and flexibly arrangeable; people wanted to not only break out of their own milieu, but, ideally, simultaneously participate in multiple other milieus in an experimental manner. Young people leaving home no longer automatically started professional training followed by marriage. They took their time, tried many new things, including different models of romantic/sexual partnership, forms of cohabitation, drugs, drink and tobacco. Some travelled to India, others toured across Europe in a van. Individuality became a new mass phenomenon. At the beginning of this chapter, we listed three historically dominant social characters: the bourgeois of early modernity, the *employee* (*der Angestellte*, i.e., white-collar worker) of organized modernity, and the creative late modern self-realizer. Sociologist Andreas Reckwitz, who contributed substantially to fleshing out this distinction, points out that these characters were in no small part the result of erstwhile 'minority cultural *counter-movements*'.[84] Individualism in late modern societies unites earlier social characters and movements.[85] On the one hand, the ideal of a performance-oriented individual, which is highly rationalized and adapts to the laws of the competitive market, is highly efficacious. On the other hand, many long for sources of social sense-making that contradict a market-conforming rationality – that is, people want to be more than simply an interchangeable component of a machine. The concept of individual autonomy is thus significantly expanded: it is no longer only about being able to shape one's life autonomously but also about doing so more authentically and in accordance with one's own self. Late modern individualism is an attempt to unite different practices and objectives in a flexible manner: the pursuit of hedonism and authenticity on the one hand with an orientation towards performance and achievement and one's professional career on the other.[86] As a result, an emotion-oriented consumer culture has emerged which seeks to dissociate itself from mass consumerism.[87]

In other words, from the 1970s the search for one's *true self* became an overarching societal phenomenon. Numerous changes in behaviour were based on the adoption of cultural practices and identities that were previously limited to non-conformist minorities.[88] Self-realization was suddenly no longer an issue for hippie-like flat-sharing communities but also for previously rather traditional-leaning families. Now there were yoga mats on the terraces in the posh Munich suburbs, too. However, this simultaneously changed the status of the alternative movements. Their breaking out of social constraints did not mean that they transcended the social order. Instead, they quite happily found a place for themselves within it: the anti-capitalist acid changed into alkaline self-realization. Capitalism had successfully absorbed the 'artistic critique' of the 1968 movement – meaning, demands for more self-determination and authenticity, and less standardization and hierarchies – and made it productive for its own purposes.[89] It now seemed as if these goals could only be achieved *through* capitalism and no longer *against* it.

This, in turn, has consequences for what were once emancipatory norms. When embedded in a strongly deregulated work-centred society,[90] they become requirements that have a similarly repressive effect as the standardized world of work did in organized modernity. We would now briefly like to illustrate this point based on the principles of New Work, which have become increasingly influential over recent years, in part turning out as a dystopian form of liberation.[91] New Work is conceptualized in terms of emancipation: self-reliance, self-realization, freedom, personal development, flexibility and participation. Indeed, many workers welcome forms of work that are not organized in a vertical manner. And yet, at the same time, they now have to define performance standards themselves. Workers who might perceive routines as a relief are now regarded as deviating from the creative norm. The ostensible autonomy ultimately turns into a new heteronomy. The appealing idea of a work–life balance morphs into work–life blending – meaning, workers are no longer even *supposed* to separate work and life, but must instead be constantly available, with the current project always on their minds. Another practice cloaked in the semantics of freedom and community is so-called 'desk-sharing', whereby workers *can* freely choose their workstation on a daily basis. Here, we can also clearly see how the supposedly free choice turns into a steel cage. Internal business organization is increasingly guided by the principle of 'musical chairs': inside office buildings, in this scenario, there are fewer workstations than staff members, the aim being to achieve an overall reduction by up to 40 per cent.[92] In larger companies, a certain number of staff are always absent, either because they are ill or travelling for work. Moreover, companies rely on a certain share of their workforce working from home. For the rest, however, a competition for the best seats takes place on a daily basis – and these spots need to be left immaculate after work (i.e., a *clean desk*), as the whole game starts anew the following day. For companies, this brings many advantages, the lower costs for heating and maintenance being only a small part of them. Yet for workers, the practice of desk-sharing is a stressful challenge. They are no longer able to personalize their work environment with flowers or pictures, but become nomads in a uniformized surrounding. Each day, they are 'allowed' to take a seat next to a new co-worker, and thus get the 'opportunity' to meet other people. Of course, there are those workers who take pleasure in such forms of work organization (they see it as a 'challenge'), but for most it is an experience of intense alienation; they have a wide-ranging freedom of choice, but this freedom is highly reified. Workers can choose between variants of exploitation over which they have no influence. The option of spending one's working hours next to one's favourite co-workers, with whom one may have established certain solidarity-based routines to manage the various daily work tasks in a collective manner, has deliberately been eliminated.

Whereas individuality in organized modernity took shape via the cultural pattern of adaptation, which had a repressive effect through its compulsion to conform, individuality in late modernity exerts its pressure through a delicate system of difference. Social inequality and precarity, which have been on the rise since the 1990s, have made it clear, particularly to the middle class, that their position is anything but safe, at least not in the long run.[93] Having once been the driving force, it is now being driven by a lifestyle in which the need for self-realization and emotional satisfaction is alloyed with the urge for success, recognition and attention.[94] The middle class is forced to engage in persistent 'investive status work',[95] even in those areas where anxiety has not yet seeped through the pores of everyday life. Yet, this self-concept harbours contradictory effects; it becomes a 'systematic generator of disappointment'.[96] There are several reasons for this.

Firstly, individuals who have internalized two complementary norms systems – success *and* authenticity – face an irresolvable dilemma. The rationalized lifestyle of a pragmatic pursuit of success surely can be synthesized with the need for self-development or self-realization. It may even provide the material and social resources for this, as conspicuously illustrated by a series of figures that meet with wide identification: start-up entrepreneurs, professionally successful computer nerds, or influencers. However, a failure to balance these inherently conflicting claims can create a sense of inadequacy. If self-realization is prioritized too strongly, this heightens the risk of a socio-economically precarious existence. Conversely, if an individual is exclusively oriented towards their pragmatic, professional career, they might neglect their own self. Self-realization and status work have converged. Yet there remains a trade-off tied to any one-sided pursuit of these principles: the more dominant the one, the more regressive the other.[97]

Secondly, late modern societies are based on the permanent valorization and simultaneous devaluation of cultural practices.[98] What might have been regarded as unique, meaningful and valuable in one moment, can already be ordinary in the next. Through emulation alone, its uniqueness is routinized: if white sneakers today represent an omnipresent lifestyle accessory, their exceptionality will soon be negated through their mass use. The pursuit of a unique life can be rewarding, but simultaneously threatens to sabotage itself. One's own individuality resembles a mimesis of pre-existing symbolic signs, forms or fashions. Exceptionality leads to formal standardization; it produces a homologous habitus, at the heart of which lies the urge for difference.[99] Due to the structural uncertainty of their uniqueness, individuals are thus forced to establish a self-reflective distance vis-à-vis themselves and their environment. In aspiring towards difference, individuals essentially behave in a streamlined way. Simmel may have had precisely this phenomenon in mind when he attributed modern individuality, in its money-mediated adaptation, a certain 'characterlessness'.[100]

Thirdly, the condition of tension outlined here entails a logic of increase and expansion. Self-realization is an endless process in which satisfaction is immediately perceived as a new lack. It knows no limits, not even when it is practised in an anti-consumerist sense – such as in the return to the countryside, leading the simple life, going back-to-nature, etc. It can never get *enough*, there must always be *more*. In particular, individually perceived happiness demands expansion. It is, above all, the reinvigorated discipline of positive psychology, which has come to play a significant role in everyday thinking, that generalizes the notion of happiness as an indispensable objective without any definitive end point.[101] One's own life conduct is perceived as successful to the extent that it engenders positive emotions. The permanent increase in satisfied experiences results from the fluidity of happiness; it dissipates as soon as the pursued condition has materialized.

Fourthly, this logic also has an effect within the process of self-optimization, which bears a 'form of interminability and infinite possibilities for further surpassing oneself'.[102] Not only performance and achievement but also happiness becomes a goal that can be attained exclusively by the individual themselves, and only to a very limited extent using the help of external factors. If happiness or suffering, success or failure, health or sickness are regarded as direct results of individual action, the result is that people become restlessly preoccupied with self-optimizing activities. If 'personal fulfilment has become the central measure'[103] of a successful life, it transitions into its opposite, namely the disciplining and control of the self.[104] This is apparent in the vexing context of 'body work': those lifting weights in today's gyms are no longer only old-fashioned individualists like bodybuilders. Across all social milieus, the body is exercised, hardened and defined – be it at a gym or with a personal trainer. The smartwatch around the wrist monitors our pulse and measures the steps taken each day, recording all and any shortcomings on our part. At night, when people sleep, the smartwatch constantly monitors how well they are doing it. Their sleep rhythm, heart frequency and breathing are turned into long-term biometric readings. If the keen Reformed Christian of the past century still 'felt his own pulse'[105] by keeping a religious account-book, so as to record and monitor his sins, today this is done by an algorithmic device. This can then be made immediately visible on social media through the sharing function, that is, once atonement has been made in the form of a lengthy run. It is an exhortation to others – and to oneself. Digital self-tracking constitutes permanent self-optimization.[106]

Fifthly, comparison, which is an inherent feature of self-optimization, brings us to the aspect of omnipresent competition. There is competition between businesses, in markets, and, of course, between individuals. The spheres of competition have expanded; all life is geared towards optimization, investment and the creation of one's own 'entrepreneurial self'.[107] In industrial modernity, individuality referred to stability: the welfare state security net, professional qualifications and, ultimately, the trust that individuality would be rewarded or at least would not have a negative impact on one's personal record. The sweet nectar of uncertainty tasted best when drunk from the chalice of social security. In late modernity, however, individuality is a never-ending game. One is always in motion, there is no rest, no arriving, no 're-embedment'[108] in reliable structures. One cannot *not* participate in this game. There is no option to *not* live one's life in a competitive mode. Every individual *must* be competitive, *must* invest in themselves and *must* be autonomous. Today, people who systematically evade this obligation – a refusal that was once publicly displayed by punk culture – are a relic of days gone by.[109]

To summarize: in contemporary societies, self-management has moved to the centre of individual aspiration. The appropriate investment of resources (including emotional ones) is regarded both the precondition and the result of a successful individualism – it is no coincidence that bookstores have endless stocks of self-help books on display. Since the contradictory norms structure – composed of performance-oriented rationalism and authentic self-searching – produces a sense of personal inadequacy, practical contradictions or irresolvable dilemmas, individuals confront this situation through control (of emotions, the body or one's biography). Which is to say, they internalize the external requirements.[110] Time and again, new appeals arise which eventually become norms; most recently, for example, mindfulness and resilience.[111] All of these newly asserted claims are reactions to problems arising from previous norms. For example, the incorporation of self-realization into the world of work has led to a situation in which workers dedicate themselves to their jobs so intensely that they end up suffering burnout and exhaustion.[112] Almost twenty years ago, Honneth had still expected that the requirements of individuality, the instrumentalization and standardization of self-realization would overwhelm people, such that an 'emotionally fossilized set of demands' would eventually create suffering, feelings of guilt and passivity.[113] There are many indicators that, for example, burnout and other psychopathologies can be attributed to the excessive burden resulting from this system of requirements. We shall see this in more detail further on. In recent years, however – and this is the topic of this book – there has been mounting evidence that it is precisely this 'emotionally cold' system that generates simmering negative emotions.

Reified freedom

In sum, then, the individual in Western societies is freer than ever, at least in formal terms. Or at least, this is the case if we understand freedom, along the lines of Bauman, to mean experiencing 'no hindrance, obstacle, resistance or any other impediment to the moves intended or conceivable to be desired'.[114] One achievement of modern societies is that they have put fundamental liberties into concrete effect. We can freely express our opinion, but we must factor in the consideration that other people also exercise their right to do so. Likewise, we can pack up and travel wherever we want to or quit our job at any time. Horkheimer pointed out that '[i]n the actual struggles for freedom the primary concern has been a better life, or life in general'.[115] Only in modern societies did freedom become synonymous with the good life, freedom of action and having the freedom to choose from a wide variety of options. Yet, if the major freedoms and democratic rights are today taken for granted, the outcome of this can be quite paradoxical. It leads, on the one hand, to indifference towards the democratic public and the democratic order; and, on the other, to a reduction of the concept of freedom, in its most simplistic form, to the ability to do whatever one pleases.

This libertarian concept of freedom has its most substantive philosophical incarnation in Robert Nozick's book *Anarchy, State, and Utopia*,[116] published in 1974. In opposition to John Rawls's influential *A Theory of Justice*, a standard reference for the liberal justification of state redistribution, Nozick posits an unfettered negative freedom that grants individuals inviolable and almost unlimited rights.[117] Nozick thereby goes beyond the liberalism of John Stuart Mill, for whom, as we have seen, there were certainly reasons for limits to such an unlimited freedom. Nozick shared with neoliberal thinkers such as Friedrich August Hayek an opposition to redistribution by the state.[118] Essentially, however, Nozick adopted a position far more radical than that of the neoliberals, for, in his theory, the state has a right to exist only in an absolutely minimalist form. It should never be permitted to interfere with the life of the individual, but merely serve to protect individual freedom and personal property. Least of all should it be permitted to expect any kind of behaviour from individuals such as acting in solidarity with the rest of society. Compared to this understanding, even an author like Hayek was virtually a partisan of the state. In his view, it could even be conducive to improving the functional mechanics of markets.

In Nozick, we find an atomized and yet unrestrained individual, who has regard for (almost) nothing and no one except for themselves: 'Peaceful individuals minding their own business are not violating the rights of others.'[119] In Nozick's view, the only legitimate restriction is the inviolability of the individual freedom of others. Nozick's book became greatly influential in libertarian philosophy and simultaneously marks a shift in the meaning of the concept of freedom, which is once again gaining influence in parts of society today. Freedom is now no longer primarily conceived as a protection (and thus dissociation) from the state's authority but also as freedom from social norms in general. From this standpoint, the state regulation of everyday life, such as the obligation to wear a seatbelt or a helmet, represents a restriction of personal freedom just like the social imperative of non-discrimination. An individual adhering to these kind of notions of freedom rejects 'any source external to oneself as a guide to one's action'.[120] Here, as Tocqueville had already feared, individualism ceases to be a democratic virtue, but signifies the end of all virtues, for it attacks both private and public ones and destroys them – producing 'loneliness' and 'selfishness'.[121] It is thus unsurprising that it was during the 1970s, precisely when the libertarian concept of freedom was gaining popularity, that narcissism as a social phenomenon was discovered (see chapter 4).

In our view, the problematic aspect of modern individualization is not rooted in a profane egotism, but in an individual denial of the dependency on social institutions. It is a *reified freedom* that invokes radicalized claims concerning the scope of individual freedom. The concept of reification was developed by György Lukács, who in his work *History and Class Consciousness* (1923) merged the theory of commodity fetishism that Marx developed in *Capital* with Weber's analysis of capitalist rationalization. According to Lukács, reification is marked by the fact that social relations take on a 'phantom objectivity', which is 'so strictly rational and all-embracing as to conceal every trace of its fundamental nature: the relation between people'.[122] When we look at our pay cheque, the human interactions which we engaged in at work have disappeared. The algorithm that rates our performance has coercive power over us, and seemingly develops a life of its own. It is no longer clear to us that at some point people who were set precise objectives programmed and trained this algorithm. This also applies to our private lives. In dating apps, interpersonal contacts are established – or swiped away – exclusively on the basis of external features.

According to Lukács, who developed his theory on the basis of a highly rationalized organized modernity, reified relations pervade society in the form of impersonal mechanisms such as commodity exchange or law. The logic of the market and of calculation appears to the individual as a 'second nature' of powers beyond their own control.[123] They are no longer able to experience the world as a more or less rational man-made totality. Lukács observed that people accepted as unchangeable the power of the large corporations and of the bureaucratic apparatus. They perceived their occupational activity and their interhuman relationships in the form of commodities.

This is a fantastical form, in which social relations appear to the individual as reified.[124] Indeed, at the time wage earners had little choice, if they wanted to make ends meet for their families, except to turn up each day on the factory floor. However, they largely accepted this compulsion as a fact of nature, and not as a social agreement that could generally be subject to alteration. Lukács's key argument is precisely that the reified world appears 'without mediation as the true world'.[125] In this *true* world – which is not by accident also and simultaneously the world of commodities – freedom becomes an individual quality, an abstraction, where it really should be a social relation. 'Possessive individualism' becomes the dominant mode of socialization.[126] Reified freedom *belongs* to the individual; it is no longer a relation to others.

Lukács's book is now over a century old, and yet, it offers – so to speak – an original approach to the libertarian idea that denies the sociality on which freedom depends. Jürgen Habermas has pointed out that the 'mechanism of reification' in late capitalist societies changes and is reflected in a 'fragmented consciousness', which, in his view, has been robbed of all its synthesizing power because of one-sided rationalizations – with severe consequences for the 'assimilation' of everyday consciousness.[127] Everything seems to exist in isolation: failure at work, wars, ecological crises; none of these are attributed to the capitalist economic system. Like early Critical Theory, Lukács had identified a profound feeling of powerlessness deriving from the reification of social relations, especially among the proletariat; in late modernity, however, top-performing individuals have in part learned to use reified relationships strategically. The influencer who puts their entire private everyday life on display on Instagram like a commodity is but one of many such examples.[128] Individuals who tend towards a reified notion of freedom identify with late modern capitalism, embrace its norms and enthusiastically throw themselves under the 'wheels of the juggernaut of capital'.[129] They are, so to speak, 'excessively' individualist (*individus par excès*).[130]

As we will go on to see, while Critical Theory focused particularly on *suffering* as a social pathology of capitalist individualization, we would like to concentrate more on a different consequence, which in our view is key to explaining libertarian authoritarianism; the active *affirmation* of capitalist norms of freedom. Indeed, even the 'one-dimensional man' of organized capitalism identified directly 'with *his* society and, through it, with the society as a whole'.[131]

However, this identification occurred in the context of advanced industrial societies, where, according to Marcuse, the striving for self-realization was systematically repressed.[132] Today, the scenario has fundamentally changed; largely emancipated individuals identify with the society that promises them comprehensive individual self-development and self-realization and actually redeems this promise, at least in part. Many people perceive capitalism not as a machine of one-sided rationalization that prevents the pursuit of authenticity but, on the contrary, as *the* system that enables individual self-realization.

In his review 'On the Jewish Question', Marx had already launched a polemic against such a form of libertarian individualism: 'The liberty of egoistic man and the recognition of this liberty, however, is rather the recognition of the unrestrained movement of the spiritual and material elements which form the content of his life.'[133] Such individuals see regulatory, redistributive intervention into capitalism as an interference with freedom, *their* freedom. That said, reified freedom need not necessarily prevail. Its counterpart is social freedom, in which individuals mutually recognize each other within their dependence. But, as we shall argue in the final chapter, this also depends on the strength of movements based on solidarity.

So, if dependencies that confront most people in everyday life are denied through the identification with a libertarian concept of freedom, this is by no means merely an illusionary act. It is rather a result of *real*, *actual* individual freedom, in which autonomy and dependence are inextricably linked. Here we can again take up our observation about individuals' increased dependency on institutions: although they are liberated from standardized biographical patterns, there are great limits to their ability to act in a truly self-determined way in the volatile market in which they have to assert themselves. They are dependent on developments beyond their control. Inevitably, this leads to irresolvable contradictions in the subjective consciousness. Although social requirements and individual claims are geared towards the expansion of the spaces of freedom, the expanded spheres of individuation are pervaded by external forces. One's own actions do not necessarily serve freely self-determined purposes. The root cause of this contradiction is already implied by the '*principium individuationis*' that continues to apply even in late modern societies: Adorno pointed out that the isolated individual must 'insulate itself against the consciousness of its own entanglement in general'.[134] This 'self-insulating' is a key element of the libertarian notion of freedom. In the practice of libertarian freedom, the conditions on which this freedom is founded are ignored; it aims at a purely external liberation of the individual's capacity for action.

— Chapter 3 —

THE ORDER OF DISORDER: SOCIAL CHANGE AND REGRESSIVE MODERNIZATION

It has never been easier to pursue a lifestyle in accordance with one's individual preferences. And yet, even in contemporary societies, individuality remains a contentious issue. It is constantly being challenged, undermined and adjusted. Today's individual is autonomous, and yet, even within this autonomy, they are fragile; educated but structurally overwhelmed; moralistic but normatively anxious; reasoning yet highly emotional. In this context, the offence dealt to freedom, the topic of this book, results from the fact that individuals have developed more elaborate needs but cannot realize their aspirations in late modern societies (or can only do so in fragmented ways).

As they approach epochal transitions, social orders can reach certain points at which they 'tip over', as Andreas Reckwitz argues.[1] Considering the multi-faceted crises afflicting contemporary societies, he suggests that late modernity has long passed its peak, and that we are moving towards a new era. He tentatively terms this era 'post-late modernity', with the prefix 'post' indicating a futurity that remains vague.[2] Seeing as this new era is only beginning to take shape, its specific contours cannot yet be identified. It thus remains difficult to assess whether this indistinct state of transition will eventually precipitate a new configuration of the social order. Surely, in future it must be possible to find a term for a diagnosis of the times that is not limited to doubling up the post-temporality to modernity.

Our concept of *regressive modernity* refers to the modus operandi of the most recent stage of social change. In this, we can observe a 'dialectic of modernization and counter-modernization' at work,

68

as Ulrich Beck noted as early as 1996.[3] Progress and regression(s) are interwoven – indeed, inextricably linked – in one and the same process.[4] This – at times, confusing – dynamic is illustrated by the process of globalization and indeed in the context of European integration, in which economic, political and cultural spaces were opened up. At the same time, welfare-state systems of social security were dismantled, and social rights restricted, under the banner of competition-oriented austerity. European integration may have brought improvements with regard to workers' mobility, but it has also weakened the system of workplace 'codetermination' for German workers.[5] Although the integration process creates opportunities for participation as a result of the various openings it offers, it simultaneously entails exclusion through closures in other fields. In platform companies and tech corporations, for example, diversity is strongly promoted, while precarious employment (particularly for migrant workers) is widespread.[6] These developments, riddled with immanent contradictions, do not constitute regressions to past forms of social coexistence. Societies are dynamic: new developments and advances respond to old problems. Yet solving these problems often also creates new ones. Such inherent side-effects can call social progress itself into question. In that case, they appear as decline or decay. From our perspective, however, we are dealing with a synchronicity of the asynchronous.[7]

Horkheimer and Adorno considered this synchronicity to be a structural feature of modernization: 'The curse of irresistible progress is irresistible regression.'[8] Admittedly, they wrote this bleak phrase in 1944, against the historical backdrop of fascism. After 1945, the prospects for the future became somewhat brighter again, and faith in linear progress became dominant. Now, the regressions that accompanied progress only marginally entered into public consciousness. Needless to say, this optimism has dwindled in late modern societies. The increase in social regressions prompted Claus Offe, more than a decade ago, to bid farewell to the goal of irresistible progress. The task from now on, he stated, is to consolidate existing achievements. Offe had little hope for future developments. All the sociologist could do now was raise awareness of the looming 'regressive potential'.[9] In contrast, his colleague Peter Wagner can still discern social advancements taking place even today, such as the reduction of formal domination and a dismantling of hierarchies; but, in his view, the increase in the individual freedom of choice has produced such profound social inequalities and instances of exclusion that the normative ideal of progress has exhausted itself.[10]

By contrast, we remain wholly committed to the notion of social progress, even though our analysis proceeds from its contradictory dynamic. In our view, advancements *and* regressions have become considerably more radical over the past decades, which injects renewed topicality into Horkheimer and Adorno's anthropogenesis. The individual's offended freedom is not only but primarily a result of the simultaneous expansion and restriction of the degrees of freedom.

The pitfalls of normative progress

In one of his essays, historian Reinhart Koselleck recounts the following story that allegedly took place in a rural area in the south of what is today the state of Lower Saxony during the late nineteenth century. Children were traditionally not permitted to eat at the table with their parents, but had to eat their meals standing up. On the day of their confirmation (i.e., the Protestant religious initiation around age 14), they received a slap in the face and were henceforth treated as adults – and were thus allowed to sit at the table with their parents. But later, from a certain day onwards, the youngest son was allowed to sit with the grown-ups – yet without any confirmation or slap. When asked by his perplexed wife what was going on, the father replied: '*That's progress for you.*' It was obvious that progress was underway. But it was unclear to the father as to why and how.[11] Today, the opposite seems to be the case: there are many reasons to continue fighting for progress – but, sadly, we can no longer see it.

Such a disillusioned view, however, ignores the internal dynamic of late modern societies. After all, we are experiencing a broad *progressive* change in social norms, not only among the younger cohorts.[12] Many forms of discrimination are no longer considered legitimate (even though the struggle for new norms can at times overstate the case in moralistic terms). The social and political space in general is becoming more open and egalitarian. Exclusions resulting from ascribed attributes such as gender or ethnicity are less acceptable than twenty years ago. In 2021, freshly elected German Chancellor Olaf Scholz regarded it his obligation to provide equal gender representation on his cabinet, though he was harshly criticized for failing to extend this representation to other groups and lifestyles, too.[13] The normative edifice is more progressive overall, but at the same time the furious interjections are growing more vocal.

By applying the concept of *regressive* modernization, we seek to expand Beck's theory of *reflexive* modernization. In industrial modernity, society's objectives, according to Beck, were more or less clear-cut: social integration and emancipation. The means of attaining this goal were also essentially undisputed: technological progress, economic growth and social reforms. However, in Beck's view, the key institutions of industrial modernity – the nation state and democracy – are fundamentally transformed in the process of reflexive modernization, indeed because of the deployment of the means we have just mentioned. Although these institutions do not disappear, Beck tells us, their effectiveness is limited and they become more hybrid. Above all, then, Beck was concerned with the *side-effects* of the accomplishments of industrial modernization and economic growth, including new civilizational risks such as environmental pollution.[14] In late modern societies, the means thus become more disputed and the goals more uncertain. *Reflexive* turns to *regressive* modernization. Societies fall back behind once-attained standards in individual social fields. Progress shows signs of regression. Such instances of regressive modernization can be observed in four areas in particular, each of which we shall delve further into: firstly, the changes in the political horizon and social alternatives; secondly, the problem of side-effects; thirdly, the transformation of emancipatory norms; and, fourthly, the metamorphosis of social movements.

The utopian horizon has largely turned rather sombre – in times of climate change and global pandemics perhaps more so than ever. Even before Beck, Jürgen Habermas had already observed a dwindling of utopian energies. Two interrelated developments marked the starting point of his diagnosis: the crisis of welfare state-regulated capitalism and a corresponding loss of emancipatory thinking. The reforms-oriented optimism of the 1960s had faded. Utopian visions gave way to disorientation, and the *future* now evoked negative associations.[15] This pessimism has further radicalized over recent decades: on the issue of climate change, we would today settle for even somewhat mitigating the inescapable challenges faced. Only few people continue to hold on to the dream of a fundamentally different world.[16] In his often-quoted witticism, according to which it is easier to imagine the end of the world than the end of capitalism, Marxist cultural critic

71

Fredric Jameson alludes precisely to this aspect.[17] One reason why the struggle around morality and social norms has gained such intensity today might be that the collective imagination lacks any vision of a social alternative.

While the *fundamental* alternatives and utopian visions have disappeared, there is suddenly an abundance of options *of the same kind* that can be realized in the here and now. In the early days of organized modernity, in 1922, pioneering US car manufacturer Henry Ford had written that '[a]ny customer can have a car painted any colour that he wants so long as it is black'.[18] Today, every car is customized. It is no longer a question of ordering a black or a red Volkswagen Golf but rather of selecting from dozens of colours, engine and transmission types as well as from infinite interior designs. This new complexity is also reflected in individual life trajectories and personal relationships. After finishing high school with *Abitur* (the German university entrance qualification), the question is not *whether* one will take up university studies, but *which* of the many study programmes best matches one's personal inclinations and preferences. Commercial dating apps like Tinder produce an inability to decide or commit oneself.[19] Never before has it been possible to choose from among so many potential partners, while the number of singles has risen by 25 per cent since the year 2000.[20] These singles may have superficial social contacts, but the danger of social isolation is growing. The sheer abundance of options makes all decisions somehow provisional.

The enthusiastic search always has a playful feel to it. Experiences are collected like an infinite number of beads for a necklace – which then becomes too heavy to wear. Zygmunt Bauman considers the 'state of unfinishedness, incompleteness and undetermination' to be a reason for the rise in alienation and the increase in anxieties:[21] according to Bauman, the world appears as 'an infinite collection of possibilities: a container filled to the brim with a countless multitude of opportunities yet to be chased or already missed. There are more – painfully more – possibilities than any individual life, however long, adventurous and industrious, can attempt to explore, let alone to adopt.'[22] Slovenian philosopher Slavoj Žižek has identified three problems concerning the freedom of choice in contemporary societies. The first is the *choice without alternatives*. I can choose freely, but only on condition that I make the *right* choice. My decision is limited to the 'empty gesture of pretending to accomplish freely what is in any case imposed on me'.[23] Furthermore, secondly, the choice we have is often only between two *equable* alternatives: consumers are led to believe that there is a broad variety of choices, but, ultimately, this is only the choice between two variants of the same thing – Coca-Cola or Pepsi.[24] The Audi Q3 is based on the exact same in-house module as the Volkswagen Tiguan and the Škoda Kodiaq, which are all produced by the VW group. And thirdly, although truly *free* choices are still possible, they are increasingly perceived as frustrating precisely because of the aforementioned factors. The selection of a subject of study, for instance, has enormous consequences for one's subsequent path in life, and yet, it has to be made based on insufficient prior knowledge.[25] The manifest abundance changes over into a feeling of being overwhelmed, and the objective freedom of choice turns into the subjective inability to choose. Yet, at the same time, because late modern societies promise an ever-greater degree of freedom, the vast number of options cannot be reduced, either. Regressive modernization thus means we have no real alternatives even as we are confronted with far too many options.

A second problem that contemporary societies face is the fact that negative developments are often the unintended side-effects of emancipatory modernization. Advances for one group can entail regressions for another. Take, for example, the (needless to say, still far from adequate) increase in gender equality.[26] Although the glass ceiling continues to exist, many forms of discrimination have become less pronounced or are at least being seriously challenged. Executive bodies without the participation of women appear as relics of a different era, and companies have great difficulties in justifying the employment of female staff at lower rates of pay than their male colleagues (though the gender pay gap remains considerable in overall economic terms). The current situation is a result of liberalization processes that have partially dissolved traditional gender roles and forms of family life. Alongside the advances in the emancipation and labour market participation of women, however, new sub-stratifications have taken place, as social liberalization was accompanied by economic liberalization: 'progress that bears retrogression within it' – and usually affects the lower classes.[27] Due to the erosion of the male breadwinner and married housewife family model, middle-class families today require household assistance, such as a nanny for children or a carer for parents in old age. Groceries are delivered to the home, and everyday errands are outsourced to new types of service workers. The expansion of education has given rise to a new upper middle class which, given its open-mindedness and sustainable lifestyles, dissociates itself from the old middle classes and, even more so, from what are regarded as profanely materialistic underclasses.[28] In parallel, a growing low-wage sector is emerging and, along with it, a visible class society.[29] While elements of democratic inclusion have been implemented, at the same time social rights, particularly those of workers, the unemployed and the poor, have been curtailed. For these latter groups, the two-fold liberalization signifies a reduction of their positive freedom.[30]

That said, neither is this a zero-sum game in which progress for one group signifies regression for another. The adverse effects are not necessarily reducible to a regression within that same area of social change; for it can also bear its effects in a *different area*, which is nevertheless somehow related to it. Advances in dimension A lead to regressions in dimension B, whereby A and B may mutually influence one another but are partially autonomous in both the normative and the structural sense. It would therefore be unjustified to reverse the regression in dimension B to the detriment of the advance in dimension A – these regressions cannot simply be one-sidedly dissolved. To take the example that we mentioned already: solving the problem of precarious service work by reinstating the married housewife family model, and reducing women's participation in the labour market and labour supply to such a level that only well-paid standard employment relations would be 'left over', would be neither possible nor normatively desirable.

This brings us to a third problem and back to the observation made at the beginning: the change in social norms may be progressive overall, but entails aversive reactions and new conflicts. Dutch sociologist Cas Wouters, a student of Norbert Elias, concurs with the latter in holding that the process of civilization is based on the formalization of social interaction and etiquette. But Wouters points out that over the course of the twentieth century, strict rules of conduct were increasingly perceived as repressive. The range of emotions and forms of behaviour considered acceptable grew broader, and the term social etiquette itself increasingly required justification. Seeing as most forms of social etiquette are embedded in social hierarchies, their 'informalization' from the 1960s onwards also entailed a reduction of power and privilege.[31] Thomas Mann insisted that his children should address him formally, using the German '*Sie*' instead of '*Du*', whereas today parents frequently let their children call them by their first names. At the dinner table, no one needs to wait for permission to speak from the highest-ranking person present any more. At a party, both men and women can dance with whomever they like. And, perhaps with the exception of the late Queen Elizabeth and the Pope, nobody can still expect to be bowed to.

When Wouters made these – surely accurate – observations in the 1990s, little did he know what ramifications for social coexistence they would entail. Given that informalization rests on the levelling of social hierarchies, it enhances the aspirations and demands of previously weak groups; the 'power balance' in society changes.[32] Groups who were previously excluded from higher (discursive) positions now voice their legitimate claim to rise to that level. The political field becomes more pluralistic, but there is also a rise in conflicts.[33] At times, the normative advances can prompt resistance because they are frequently accompanied by a moralistic overshoot of 'positional fundamentalism'.[34] Irrespective of their actual views, individuals are equated with certain positions, for instance when so-called 'old white men' are ascribed a reactionary stance. The oft-voiced criticism of such 'moralizing', however, misses the essence of the conflict. Of course, the new actors bring along not only their own views but also the scars they have received and their idiosyncrasies. But most importantly, groups need to share their power. Those 'whose moral standard was discursively hegemonic thus far', as sociologist Armin Nassehi notes, 'now dwindle to become just one group among others themselves'.[35] For them, democratization signifies not only a loss of power but also a symbolic devaluation. In order to preserve their power, they resort to traditional social norms or to a conservative identity politics based on the vertical hierarchization of lifestyles and identities. Because this protest has morphed into an outright *Kulturkampf*, the impression is created of a reactionary backlash.[36] This may indeed be true for countries such as Hungary or Poland, but the situation is different in the West. Even where right-wing populist parties do win elections, they are only rarely successful in reversing advances in normative liberalization. Although we have indeed recently witnessed a major backlash concerning abortion rights in the United States, the country has simultaneously made substantial progress in the inclusion of ethnic minorities and in gender equality. Movements such as #MeToo and Black Lives Matter react to everyday sexism and deeply rooted racist structures, while they simultaneously articulate the demand that the norms of equality be implemented *at long last.*

But things get even more complicated: normative advances – and this is the fourth problem – contain a regressive modernization resulting from the metamorphosis of social movements. Up until well into the first half of the twentieth century, the struggle for emancipation was fought in the name of an oppressed majority against a powerful minority. The interests of the majority – above all, the working class – were equated with the common good and universalist principles. It was not until the second half of the twentieth century that the focus shifted to minorities as victims of oppression. Universalism today means acknowledging and granting equal rights to minorities. And here, again, the textbook example comes from the US: although the labour movement had won a certain degree of social security through the New Deal, its principles were anything but universalist, as it failed to fight against other forms of discrimination with the same ferocity, or even accepted them: for instance, the disadvantages placed on women in the labour market, the married housewife family model and racist exclusion.[37] The new social movements therefore, from the very outset, dissociated themselves from the trade unions as well. They fought to end all forms of discrimination, for a *social* opening and more social mobility, and thereby came into conflict with parts of the old working class. The latter saw their livelihood coming under threat from the *economic* opening of global markets pushed for by economic elites.[38]

Ultimately, a coalition formed in favour of greater social openness, which Nancy Fraser has termed *progressive neoliberalism.* The US sociologist's diagnosis has been widely adopted (but also harshly critiqued), because it provides an explanation for the rise of right-wing populism. Equal rights, diversity and empowerment, Fraser explains, were blended with an agenda of economic liberalism – to the disadvantage of less flexible, less mobile groups who depend more strongly on social security systems.[39] She criticizes progressive neoliberalism, or left-liberalism, for aiming primarily at more diversity in management structures and executive staff, even as it accepts the vast increase in material inequality with a shrug. White industrial workers threatened by downward social mobility responded to this with regressive demands for a new closure. Politicians like Donald Trump promise them a neo-protectionist economic policy and aggressively discard the issues raised by the LGBTQ+ movement – an approach that appears to be developing towards classic authoritarianism. Over the course of this volume, we will also come across another regressive reaction to progressive neoliberalism: a circle of public intellectuals complains that the consideration of minorities as such has today become a repressive norm (see chapter 6). They allege that previously permissible forms of behaviour are condescendingly chided, that people are being forced to use gendered language, and that it is no longer possible to freely speak one's mind. Here, the emancipation of minorities is perceived as a restriction of one's own freedom of action and opinion.

Offended knowledge

In organized modernity, reality went largely uncontested. It was regarded as comprehensible, solid and materially palpable, just like a wrought iron factory gate. It was understood as a shapable reality, which could be bent to one's will through detailed plans and in accordance with reason. Yet, following the transition to reflexive modernity or late modernity, reality increasingly appeared to elude human knowledge. This was due to several factors, some of which we shall look at in more detail later on. At this point, we would first like to address the issue of offended knowledge, which is related to what Beck identified as the increased awareness of risks – a side-effect of industrial modernity.

In late modern societies, Beck noted in 1986, 'the social production of *wealth* is systematically accompanied by the social production of *risks*'.[40] By using the category of risk, Beck introduced a new approach to social reality. Risks are contingent by definition; there is no predicting whether or when exactly they might materialize. Risks in industrial modernity were usually sensorily perceptible and tied to the place of their production. Starvation and poverty were tangible or visible, the water of the river Wupper in the city of Wuppertal was frequently deeply coloured with chemicals during the nineteenth century, and it was unthinkable, up until the 1930s, to swim in the Rhine downstream from the chemical plants based in Basel without developing blisters and skin rashes. However, over the course of the twentieth century, Beck argues, risks took on a qualitatively new form, becoming increasingly invisible, while their materialization became more temporally and spatially contingent. Beck was thinking in particular of industrial toxicants and radioactivity. The fact that the nuclear disaster at Chernobyl occurred shortly after his book was published lent additional plausibility to his argument. Today, we may think especially of viruses and CO_2 emissions, which also elude direct sensory perception. At the same time, this scenario produces new asymmetries of knowledge: although individuals are generally better educated than in the past, the total social knowledge has likewise expanded vastly; and yet, we as individuals know increasingly less about the world that surrounds us.

Recognizing, measuring and eventually managing risks thus requires 'scientific *expansion*'[41] and, along with it, a growing number of experts. Risks are open to varying definitions and readings, and only through interpretation do they become social reality. However, the knowledge-dependence of the risks of modernization does not lead to a fact-based objectification of public debates; rather, they become highly politicized and *de-rationalized*. Numbers and statistics introduce objectivity to the world; they are the opposite of feelings. Yet, abstract figures must be interpreted and conveyed in the form of arguments. Assumptions of causal relationships do not automatically emerge from statistical data. Ultimately, they must be *'believed'*.[42] This inevitably leads to conflicts. The 'increasing encroachments of science on the world', as Adorno noted in 1965, represent 'a mortal threat to freedom'.[43] Surely, Adorno was not an early *Querdenker*. But, by using this wording, he nonetheless anticipated a problem that the sociologist of science Alexander Bogner has recently termed the 'Epistemisation of Politics'.[44]

The interpretation of scientific data is always accompanied by the normative question of how we want to live. In any society, there are actors and affected groups with antagonistic interests that influence their respective definitions of risks. A tobacco company or the Hotel & Catering Association will assess the dangers of smoking entirely differently than the Federal Association of Respiratory Physicians will. Political decisions taken with the aid of scientific expertise contain a normative core, despite their rational legitimation. Social conflicts are initially sparked by the objective-sounding question of how great a particular risk is, and, from there on, how great it is for which social groups. This inevitably prompts questions of responsibility: who is liable and pays for the damage in the event that the risk does materialize? The pluralization of risks is therefore paralleled by a pluralization of definitions of risk that designate both victims and perpetrators (or relativize such ascriptions). The corresponding conflicts are fought out by weaponizing numbers, 'used as a way of silencing dissenting voices'.[45]

Beck assumed that a 'grass-roots *developmental dynamics that destroys boundaries*' was set in motion in global risk society, which '[forces together] the people [...] in the uniform position of civilization's self-endangering'.[46] Today, this diagnosis is more accurate than ever. Be it climate change or the coronavirus, both represent global phenomena that are indeed creating a collective threat for humanity. And yet, this does not lead to a shared subjective awareness, but to interpretations that are extremely polarized both within and between nation states. There is no '*solidarity motivated by anxiety*'.[47] Instead, what we can observe is individuals' anxious feeling of being overwhelmed, combined with a humiliation of their knowledge-sovereignty. This has its root cause in the increase in complexity and the related increase in the individual inability-to-know. Ignorance constitutes the flip side of the constant production of knowledge, as we become more aware of what we do not know. At the same time, non-knowing can also emerge from media or communicative filters, selections or distortions, from scientific errors, a repressed unwillingness-to-know or an inability-to-know.[48] As diverse as the forms of unawareness (or non-knowing) are, the ultimate result is a profound 'uncertainty on all sides'.[49] This has direct implications for the normative integration of society. This is the reason why French historian Pierre Rosanvallon speaks of a dawning 'society of distrust'.[50] Beck, too, already noted that the 'relations of definition' really constitute relations of domination.[51]

The production of ever-more comprehensive stores of knowledge and, potentially, insights requiring subsequent correction, constitutes an attack on the autonomy of late modern individuals. They are left epistemically weakened. Although many people obtain more and higher educational qualifications, at the same time they become increasingly '*dependent on external knowledge*'.[52] Threats and dangers are generalized, anyone can be affected at any time, and yet the reach and degree of the consequences elude individual perception. Due to the complexity of risks, the reasoning rationality of enlightened individuals loses its authority; they are stripped of their sovereignty *and* left to fend for themselves. Although they depend on knowledge institutions, they are at the same time, as critically reasoning individuals, 'forced to mistrust the promises of rationality of these key institutions'.[53] The individual is confronted with its antitype: experts. The latter not only constantly generate new knowledge, but increasingly gain a monopoly on the assessment and interpretation of new insights. They thus become authorities on the conduct of one's individual life, for instance by establishing what healthy food I ought to eat, where and by what means of transport I should travel, and where I am allowed to be and whom I can meet during a pandemic. This is why, given today's complex civilizational risks, experts can easily become scapegoats.[54] The more thorough the permeation of day-to-day reality by science and technology, the greater the likelihood of the expert's authority being challenged. In reaction, individuals stage epistemic resistance against these experts in order to reclaim their own sovereignty. Not only are political decisions called into question, but also the underlying facts that they are based on (see chapter 7).

Democracy and counter-democracy

The crisis of democracy has been debated for some time, and is being addressed from a range of perspectives. One feature of this debate is that the diagnoses of crisis are often more dramatic than the actual threats. However – with the exception of a few who consider even the faintest light, amidst the encroaching darkness, to signal the resurgence of democracy – there is today widespread agreement that the political system is indeed in bad shape. In our view, this is the result of a structural shift in politics which has led to a rise in *affective* tension. Late modern society, in which rationality, reason and control have deeply pervaded the social fabric, is at the same time a society that is based on *affective, emotional excitement*. Many 'long to be affected and to affect others in order to be considered attractive and authentic themselves', Reckwitz writes.[55] His colleague Hartmut Rosa considers the affective tension to be the result of the structural pressure for constant increase, escalation and acceleration. The drive to make available, control, dominate and commodify just about everything essentially constitutes a *'hostile relationship'* to the world, which produces tensions – and, according to Rosa, deeply engulfs the political sphere.[56]

Diagnoses of 'post-democracy',[57] which have become increasingly fashionable ever since the 1990s, assume that even though outwardly the institutions of parliamentary democracy continue to exist, citizens and trade unions are losing political influence. According to this argument, democracy is being hollowed out from the inside.[58] In his 1999 work *The Ticklish Subject*, Žižek described a form of post-political governance in which there are no longer any great visions or major conflicts. Instead, domination is legitimized through a proclaimed lack of alternatives and the discursive manufacturing of consensus: long-standing ideological distinctions have largely disappeared, and political authority is replaced by expert knowledge and the illusion of ubiquitous opportunities to participate in decision-making.[59]

Growing inequality, however, has since destabilized particularly the established democracies across the world.[60] The (erstwhile) major parties have lost touch with their constituencies and no longer serve as transmission belts for the interests of political milieus. Decisions are increasingly prepared and pre-empted by experts, commissions and lobbyists. Furthermore, many decisions are immanently asymmetrical, with the interests of the upper class and upper middle class mainly attended to.[61] The result is a crisis of representation. Parliamentary democracy is growing more detached from the democratic ideal, and although citizens may not be alienated by the concept of democracy as such, they certainly are by its current form.[62] Instead of 'welfare state and mass loyalty', the new formula of our day has changed to 'liberal society and citizen disaffection'.[63]

However, the crisis of representation is also a paradoxical consequence of regressive modernization processes, as democracy has indeed become more inclusive over time. Political scientist Philip Manow thus speaks of a 'democratisation of democracy'.[64] According to Manow, historically, representation has always entailed the exclusion of social groups (for instance, originally it excluded the plebs). Especially from the 1970s onwards, however, more and more groups were included in the democratic process. As a result, representation proves an almost impossible task, given that the rules, norms and resources of legitimation have become extremely complex. So, the image of a depoliticized democracy – an understanding which has hardened, thanks to declining electoral participation (which, incidentally, has partially recovered since the emergence of populism) and a decreasing commitment or affiliation to large organizations – is somewhat inaccurate. Not only have the opportunities to participate increased overall, but democratic demands have also become more radical. Considered in isolation, these demands are surely progressive in character, but as a whole, they have contributed to democratic regression. Civic initiative and local referendums have become more widespread as a complement to parliamentary procedures – and have thus also complicated the latter.[65] Rosa notes another aspect: the problem of 'desynchronization'.[66] Particularly the major crises in recent years – from the euro and migration crises, to the coronavirus pandemic and on to the war in Ukraine – required prompt political decisions.[67] Yet, on structural grounds, parliamentary politics can hardly be accelerated. It requires processes of opinion-forming, exchange and reaching compromise. Due to the pluralization of democracy, it has been slowed down even further and become more chaotic and contentious, as conventions and moral values have become more plural, too. That is precisely why the search for consensus or agreement is not facilitated or accelerated through the Internet and social media, but essentially undermined by them.

Correspondingly, what matters for our analysis here is the social aspect of democracy, the change in civil society engagement and democratic norms. We proceed from Pierre Rosanvallon's concept of *counter-democracy*, which subsumes the politically active civil society and institutions monitoring the state. To the French historian, active civil society primarily includes social movements and NGOs, but also discussion forums and online communities. Bodies and institutions such as the German Federal Audit Office, the Federal Data Protection Officer or ethical review commissions also evaluate government actions.[68] According to Rosanvallon, counter-democracy serves three functions: the monitoring of democratic procedures, a veto on democratic decisions, and the quality assessment of the results of democratic processes. He thereby opens up a different perspective on democracy. We usually consider the latter to be an electorally legitimized system of governance that produces collectively binding decisions. Rosanvallon, by contrast, shifts the focus to an institutionalized distrust that monitors democracy from within with a lesser or greater degree of suspicion. In other words, democracy is systematically accompanied by distrust – which democracy itself cultivates. In the process, counter-democracy does not *oppose* democracy but supports it 'as a kind of buttress'.[69] Rosanvallon is particularly interested in the unconventional forms of politics, whose relationship with electoral democracy he identifies as the crucial cause of current conflicts. Corresponding initiatives develop a 'sort of *counter-policy*', which may seek to control and restrict government bodies but no longer to conquer the latter themselves.[70] This was already a feature of the 'New Social Movements' that emerged from the 1960s onwards. According to a succinct summary by protest researcher Dieter Rucht, they pursued 'projects within society' rather than regarding 'society as a project'.[71]

Rosanvallon sees destructive mechanisms at work in counter-democracy. In his view, the strengthening of civil society paradoxically causes a fragmentation of the political space, which eventually dissolves the 'signs of a *shared world*'.[72] Some movements, he tells us, have cultivated a politics of generalized distrust, which, by definition, is inherently negative.[73] What we are witnessing is a kind of negative 'sovereignization' through distrust-saturated obstruction, which Rosanvallon calls '*regressive direct democracy*'.[74] This structural change took place against the backdrop of a secular trend: the erosion of the membership in large-scale organizations such as political parties, trade unions and religious congregations. During the 1970s, the two major political parties in Germany, the (conservative) Christian Democrats (CDU) and the (centre-left) Social Democrats (SPD) each had more than one million members. Today, these numbers have fallen by over half. Trade union density has seen a similar decline: while one in three workers was a union member back then, today it is only one in seven. This development certainly has something to do with individualization, the decrease in long-term loyalties, and the increase in temporary commitment and sequential organizational affiliation. Yet, it is also the result of changes in the political system, where parties no longer act as milieu-specific organizations.

More than fifty years ago, the scholar of law and Critical Theory Otto Kirchheimer analysed the rise of what he called the 'catch-all party'.[75] He argued that these parties were replacing the parties of ideological mass integration, which had been common since the interwar period; these 'catch-all parties' instead pursued a de-ideologized pragmatism for the sole purpose of gaining political power. The parties generally remained distinct, but they were no longer easily distinguishable with regard to economic policy and their understanding of the state. Although Kirchheimer may have painted his picture with rather broad-brush strokes, its predictive power is undeniable. Because the 'catch-all parties' are no longer able, given the pluralization and differentiation of society, to provide coherent representation, but instead find it difficult to forge consensual synthesizations, eventually it is no longer the representation of followers' interests that takes centre stage but the maximization of votes. Parties morph into cartels for gaining government power.[76]

In Germany's current coalition government, liberals, Greens and Social Democrats have managed to agree on a form of economic liberalism which they frame with a narrative of a new social 'progress'.[77] They see themselves primarily as a coalition of the centre – just as the Grand Coalition (Conservatives and Social Democrats) claimed before them. With the exception of the (far-right) AfD and (left-wing) Die Linke, all parties represented in the German parliament (*Bundestag*) adhere to the median voter theorem: they target those voter groups who embody the ideal centre of society. Specific appeals to their traditional constituencies are made only infrequently, as they take these groups' votes for granted.[78] What ultimately emerges as a result is an unofficial coalition of the 'extreme centre'.[79] This centripetal dynamic amounts to a cartel of consensus. Belgian political scientist Chantal Mouffe writes on this phenomenon: 'All those who oppose the "consensus of the centre" and the dogma that there is no alternative to neoliberal globalization are presented as "extremists" or disqualified as "populists".'[80] In the context of the politics of consensus, conflicts are fought out in a moralistic mode that revives a fundamental us–them distinction.[81] However, this pacifies the political conflict only briefly, whereas in the long run it leads to the mutual de-legitimation of political opponents – both within and outside the centre. This has disastrous consequences for democracy as a whole. Precisely because democracy has become so universal, it lacks a non-democratic Other (which, incidentally, might now return in the form of Putin's Russia). During political disputes, political opponents *within* democracy quickly become enemies *of* democracy, which creates a rising 'inner heat'.[82]

Kirchheimer closed his article with the realization that the demise of the old ideological mass parties would be difficult to avoid. At the same time, he feared that we might one day 'regret the passing [...] of the class-mass party'.[83] Indeed, the development towards a highly professionalized, mediatized, ideologically pragmatic cartel of

84

parties has deeply alienated erstwhile followers and fomented further distrust.

The formation and consolidation of a consensus of the extreme centre produces normative disorder in parts of the counter-democracy, as clear-cut alternatives no longer exist. To many people, politics now appears hermetic and decoupled from the realities of life. Moreover, given the increase in civilization-induced risks and complex threat environments, the impression is created of a democratic 'de-sovereignization', which in turn engenders feelings of powerlessness and helplessness as well as aversive affects. The technocratic tendency of politics blurs the boundaries between political value judgements, scientific expertise and supposed factual constraints, as was the case, for instance, with the bailout of the banks during the financial crisis of 2008/9, the central banks' bond-buying programmes, or COVID-19 pandemic-related measures. To many, the government, science and politics all appear as a 'game being played by insiders'.[84] A general suspicion begins to gain currency.

The protest formations which correspond to this scenario refuse to adopt any ideological position, sometimes quite decisively. Participants instead self-identify as independent and sceptical citizens. Their negative critique, as is typical of counter-democracy, is free-floating and no longer tied to any positive vision of society. They are mistrusting individuals, who adapt the performative forms of protest typical of social movements (such as pickets, vigils and 'walks'), appropriate elements of left-wing semantics of critique (such as the clientelism ascribed to political actors, usually tied to an antagonistic us–them distinction) and simultaneously develop an affinity for alternative media and conspiracy theories.

If normative disorders have gained so much ground in counter-democratic movements, this owes a great deal to the exhaustion of left-wing critique.[85] Whereas up until the 1980s counter-democracy was dominated by a range of diverse left-wing forces, now the situation has changed entirely. Trade unions have become politically powerless; nor do they today offer any orientation in terms of theory or a critique of domination. Counter-cultural milieus that determinedly opposed the omnipresent commodification transformed into vegan lifestyle communities of highly skilled professionals, who no longer live in shared apartments but sit on designer chairs in luxury flats while churning out their newest concepts for start-ups. In 1968, the protests against the Vietnam War reinforced an anti-authoritarian revolt. In 2021, the United States, Germany and other countries withdrew from Afghanistan after twenty years of war – that is, two decades without any noteworthy protests by the anti-war movement. Progressive critique has today selectively entered the state apparatus, moving into the 'mainstream'. For those who have become wary of domination and the government, the traditional left no longer represents a political home. Precisely because they have been repeatedly disappointed by left-wing organizations, their revolt often arises from a strong anti-institutional impulse. For example, there were left-wing populist attempts to update classical social critique with an agenda of a nation state-based 're-sovereignization'. While such initiatives doubtless had progressive intentions, corresponding projects – such as, in Germany, the movement '*Aufstehen*' – proved to be inherently contradictory and fizzled out. It is a bit like a blanket that is too short: it is impossible to reverse a regression (reduction of labour regulation) at the cost of other advances (international integration and freedom of movement). Yet internationalist responses to the crisis of democratic capitalism remained ineffective as well. After the ideas corresponding to the left-wing critique of globalization faded, so did this critique's status of a 'material force'.[86] Instead, the theme of re-nationalization began to convey a regressive imagery. In Germany, the term '*Heimat*' (home, homeland) has suddenly become charged with a modernized aura of an authentic, embedded life – as opposed to the supposedly unbound cosmopolitans.

Today, ever more political actors have internalized the various late modern normative disorders. They often – and particularly in their self-description – elude the classification as either left- or right-wing. In fact, the Green Party, too, which recruited many of its members from the alternative milieu and was founded by local grass-roots initiatives, eco-farmers, feminists, peace activists, etc., self-identified as an 'anti-party party' and, at least in its early days, also included advocates of ethnic nationalism such as Baldur Springmann. During the Occupy protests in 2011, a majority of supporters rejected being classified as left- or right-wing.[87] These protests represented a new phenomenon in the sense that social and systemic critique was merged with individual democratic demands in an anti-institutional practice.[88] The distrust towards the institutions of parliamentary democracy was particularly pronounced among Occupy supporters.[89] The same pattern could be observed at the 'Monday vigils for peace' that were held during the first Ukraine crisis in 2014.[90] In this protest movement, which distanced itself from the 'old' peace movement, a certain indifference towards the participation of right-wing actors or conspiracy narratives was part of the political DNA from the outset. The *Querdenker*, whom we shall turn to in greater detail below, thus have a precursor in the political landscape. In contrast to the now-'old' New Social Movements, there is no common normative frame of reference of a better world, but merely a meagre overall narrative for collective action: that of opposition itself – opposition to the establishment, to power. Their followers share a profound anti-institutional affect of self-empowerment. This impulse often leads to the yearning for dis-intermediation, i.e., the cancellation of all organizational or representative bodies that can pool their interests and objections and achieve compromises. Instead, plebiscitary demands are expressed apodictically – with grass-roots democracy, populism and authoritarianism all moving in close vicinity to one another.

Counter-epistemology

Knowledge was not the only thing to become increasingly uncertain in late modern risk societies, for the sciences themselves were also thrown into epistemological disorder. In parallel with the newly forming counter-democracy, a *counter-epistemology* emerged from the 1960s onwards, initially arising from the critique of science and technology. It was a reaction to the advancing scientification of the world: from the perspective of Critical Theory (and, since the 1960s, from that of the anti-authoritarian student protest movement, too), nuclear energy, arms production, cybernetics and planification all represented key elements of a *'fusion of technology and domination'*.[91]

Even in the nineteenth century, the critique of domination was accompanied by a critique of socially accepted knowledge and scientific methods. But even the greatest political and ideological antagonists nevertheless agreed – at least in principle – that they shared the same reality. Marx and Engels drew on the bourgeois sciences, immersed themselves in the works of Adam Smith, David Ricardo and Charles Darwin, and studied not only economic works but also the natural sciences, anthropology and geology. What fundamentally distinguished them from the authors of the texts they studied was their respective interpretation and assessment of social reality. Free-market liberals read it from the perspective of factory owners and merchants, Marx and Engels from that of workers. The struggle was about changing social reality in accordance with one's own ideology. Yet there was hardly any epistemic disagreement concerning the reality of reality. Similarly, the positivism dispute between representatives of Critical Theory and proponents of Critical Rationalism primarily concerned the question of the correct methodology of the social sciences, the purview of theories and the validity of value judgements. The dispute was about the assessment and the character of the world, not about its reality.

From the 1970s onwards, however, a counter-epistemology took shape that was aimed against modern rationalism and core elements of what it conceived of as Enlightenment and scientific expertise. Horkheimer and Adorno had analysed the myth *within* the project of Enlightenment, precisely because they maintained faith in this project. The new counter-epistemology considered the Enlightenment *itself* to be an outdated myth.[92] This was not a coherent theoretical current, but represented disparate variants of postmodern thinking and the emerging critique of science.[93] It proceeds from the point at which social reality is rejected as a whole, transforming the fissures which are inherent to truth claims and deeply entrenched certainties into a positive sign. Such counter-epistemologies share a fundamental doubt, which seeks to provoke, and which opposes genealogies of the origin of individuality and constructs of social totality or permanently assigned denotations of linguistic signs. Postmodern theories are frequently accused of promoting obscurantism and irrationalism, even of subverting reason as such. What they all have in common is – put in negative terms – the 'elusiveness of "reality"' ('*Entzogenheit des "Realen"*');[94] in positive terms, they exhibit a radical pluralism.[95] The fact that they have managed to gain considerable influence even beyond academic institutions is likely because 'modernity itself' has increasingly appeared to many 'as a profoundly problematic and, indeed, a failed project', as Swiss historian Philipp Sarasin writes.[96] Another reason is the status of knowledge and the producers of knowledge in modern societies.

In premodern societies, truth was formalized in the role of the priest or magicians who had privileged access to higher knowledge. In (late) modern societies, experts embody *propositional* truth: whereas truth was established through performative rituals in premodern societies, and pertained less to specific objects, '"[p]ropositional truth" [...] is valid by virtue of its correspondence with facts'.[97] At least, if we go by the ideal image of expertise. In late modern risk societies, however, experts can, in a way, once again assume the role of an oracle with privileged access to knowledge – for the simple reason that knowledge is increasingly specialized and organized as collaborative practice, making it ever-more incomprehensible for the layman. People *have to* trust, otherwise they get caught up in the maelstrom of epistemic resistance, which will be further discussed at various points throughout this volume.

Even before Beck described the accumulation of risks and their consequences for knowledge, postmodern thinking had more fundamentally called into question the status of knowledge. To French philosopher Jean-François Lyotard, who may be regarded as the trailblazer of postmodernity, the modern meta-narratives of truth, rationality and progress had lost their meaning. According to Lyotard, there was no longer any unambiguousness, but instead only differences, fissures, hybridities and, along with them, a vast variety of language games, knowledge forms and lifestyles.[98] Michel Foucault demonstrated that notions of normality and truth are the results of discourses and practices which discipline and stabilize domination, even beyond vertical hierarchies. From the philosophical perspective, subjects are engendered by social *dispositifs*, but the historically specific form of this process is contingent.[99] And French media theoretician Jean Baudrillard claimed that, in the age of electronic media, reality disappears behind the simulation of linguistic signs which ultimately refer to nothing but themselves.[100]

Postmodern theories struck a chord: the modern promise of social progress had begun to crumble and rebounded on itself. Further authors such as Gilles Deleuze, Félix Guattari and Jacques Derrida also popularized the suspicion towards unchallenged stores of knowledge and their object, namely, reality. By deconstructing the social system as an infinite variation of codes and signs, they also transcended the distinction between reality and its signs-based representation. They cultivated a form of critique that 'elevates social dynamization to an end in itself' and, in its 'pure negativity', rejects any kind of positive, constructive formulation, as the latter, so the argument goes, always also contains 'closure and quiescence'.[101] Postmodern theory's system of thought therefore raises no claim to coherence (on the contrary, the latter is even decidedly rejected for the most part), but celebrates diversity instead. Postmodern theorists sought to deconstruct unquestioned knowledge, the optimism in progress of their time, although they were not some kind of early *Querdenker*, as some critics may today suggest.

Another form of counter-epistemology is the critique of science, which pertains not to the individual but to the possibility of truth and knowledge as such. The most important representative of this counter-epistemology was Austrian philosopher Paul Feyerabend, with his almost anarchist approach.[102] He was regarded as an important theoretician of science who challenged the certainties of established paradigms. His critique concerned the rationalized and scientificated society in modernity and instead pleaded for a methodical relativism which explicitly included alternative methods of knowledge generation such as myths, cosmologies, astrology, Reiki, etc. For Feyerabend, the freedom of epistemological choice constituted an indispensable precondition for an open society. From today's perspective, Feyerabend's interventions appear problematic, however. Bogner considers his approach as the intellectual build-up to today's conflicts around knowledge, as Feyerabend not only had high regard for alternative sciences, from anthroposophy to Hopi medicine and on to creationism, but also saw any knowledge as a 'hypothesis', regardless of how it was obtained.[103] Yet, if all forms of knowledge are regarded as equal, people may have a real freedom of choice, such as whether to believe in the existence of a virus; but what is lacking for meaningful mutual communication is a shared understanding of reality.

For relativists like Feyerabend, holding on to a scientifically founded truth is above all related to a claim to power. There is no 'better knowledge', only ideological coherence and correspondence. His fundamental critique – one that certainly appears accurate and appropriate – according to which science must substantiate its claim to validity, ultimately leads to an 'epistemic tribalism' along distinct notions of reality.[104] In a somewhat different yet no less radical manner, sociologist of science Bruno Latour subsequently took a position against ossified factual truths. In his view, all facts are ultimately socially constructed, which makes it necessary to give 'things' a voice in democratic debates, too.[105]

Paradoxically, the social-constructivist critique of science, whose original objective had been to expose the natural sciences' myth of rationality as a claim to domination and truth, provided the epistemic instruments for today's science-sceptics. They use these instruments to cast doubt on undeniable knowledge, indispensable for the continued existence of civilization, such as knowledge of the reality of climate change.[106] Through its objective of democratizing knowledge, in emphasizing the equal status of different forms of knowledge counter-epistemology has produced (unintentional) regressive side-effects. Indeed, in its 'abandonment of the notion of better knowledge', it fostered the legitimacy of post-truth knowledge.[107]

Alongside the popularization of a counter-epistemology, the edifice of social norms changes, too. This has far-reaching consequences for the protest against a social reality which has become questionable itself. Sustainability scholar Ingolfur Blühdorn attributes the rise of today's neo-authoritarian movements in part to a metamorphosis of emancipatory norms such as autonomy, self-determination and authenticity.[108] While Fraser considers the consequences of the coalition between progressive forces and neoliberal free-market policies, Blühdorn immerses himself in the semantic depths of society's repository of utopian imagination. As we have already seen, the change in contemporary societies' norms is closely interwoven with individualization. Individuals no longer seek to emancipate themselves primarily from social domination, hierarchies or predetermined roles, but instead strive for distinction and singularity. Furthermore, this notion of individuality then attributes new meaning to emancipatory norms as well.

The initiators of the more recent emancipation movements challenge the concept of the enlightened individual that had begun its rise in Immanuel Kant's Philosophy of Enlightenment: the idea that a subject possesses a consistent identity and strives to be reasonable and responsible, principled and rational, autonomous and authentic. According to Blühdorn, this traditional notion of the subject was confronted with a new subject that is spontaneous and emotional, follows alternative rationalities and possesses several identities which are all part of the subject's uniqueness. Even though modern norms such as autonomy and authenticity continued to form part of a progressive vocabulary, Blühdorn tells us, they are now decoupled from the belief in reason and, in particular, disconnected from the horizon of social transformation.[109] Autonomy and authenticity, he asserts, are no longer regarded as the outcome of another, better society, but as the result of self-optimization within the existing order. Consequently, according to Blühdorn, the logic of the emancipatory project has been hollowed out, it has lost its impetus and – unintentionally – given way to a regressive appropriation of originally progressive norms.[110]

Paternalistic governmentality

At the end of the 1970s, Greek philosopher Nicos Poulantzas had feared the rise of a new 'authoritarian statism', in which the state would display an increased interventionism into socio-economic affairs and curtail civil liberties.[111] At the time, the expansion of the state's powers was regarded as a conservative response to the widely diagnosed crisis of non-governability, which, in turn, was blamed on rampant public spending, inflation and social conflicts.[112] Yet Poulantzas's prediction did not materialize. Instead of statism, the economic path chosen was that of neoliberalism, promising – through authoritarian government measures – to free the economy from the shackles of collective rights.[113] What followed were deregulation and market expansion, the privatization of previously public responsibilities and the commercialization of public services, tax cuts and a restructuring of the welfare state.[114] In contrast to the claims of their cruder adepts, however, the objective of neoliberalism's intellectual founding fathers was not the complete deregulation of markets nor the total retreat of the state, but rather the protection of the markets from democracy and the masses. The aim was to fortify them against democratic interference and to *encase* them, not least by creating supra-national organizations.[115] The neoliberals fiercely opposed a social-democratic state, but also rejected a laissez-faire order, instead favouring a regime that simply guarantees the existence of free markets (see chapter 1). It is therefore no surprise that Milton Friedman and Friedrich August von Hayek, two of the most prominent neoliberal theorists, did not shy away from cooperating with Chilean dictator Augusto Pinochet and approvingly observed and supported his authoritarian liberal economic policy. The authoritarian aspect of neoliberalism was also reflected in how it addressed poverty and unemployment. In the United States, a so-called *workfare* system was established in the 1990s, which tied the eligibility to receive government benefits to the obligation to accept job offers.[116] In Europe, a kind of carrot-and-stick politics of 'supporting and demanding' (*Fördern und Fordern*) soon followed suit. While such policies were commonly legitimized with reference to self-responsibility or republican/civic values (such as the duty to contribute individually to the common good), the traditional welfare state was derided as paternalistic. In fact, today's state actions are no less paternalistic, only in different ways than in the past. The state no longer decides *for* the individual, but supports the latter to make their own – albeit predetermined – *right* choices. The individualist lifestyle is interwoven with an underlying paternalism whose authoritarianism operates not through direct violence but via the illusion of a diversity of lifestyles and identities.

From this perspective, paternalistic governance occurs not via coercion and disciplining but in the form of what Michel Foucault refers to in his later works as 'governmentality'.[117] At the heart of his analysis is the concept of government, by which, however, he understands not the group of people in charge of a country's daily political affairs, but rather techniques and methods of exercising power and leading the population in a comprehensive sense. In his concept of governmentality, Foucault unites the terms govern (*gouverner*) and mentality (or mindset: *mentalité*). This combination allows him to flesh out indirect power technologies and the underlying stocks of knowledge, but also techniques of the self and of self-governance. Foucault thereby anticipated the soft strategies of neoliberal governance that have proliferated considerably over the past thirty years.[118] The term 'libertarian paternalism' in fact denotes an explicit strategy that many governments worldwide draw on.[119] *Nudging* thus constitutes a practical application of behaviourism and behavioural economics: people are to be prodded in their everyday lives in order to make *correct* decisions. However, this occurs not by way of explicitly formulated prohibitions and precepts but via the design of the architecture of everyday decisions. After all, one particular sign of what we would consider liberal rather than libertarian paternalism is the formal retention of freedom of choice: that is, it must always remain possible to decline the *nudge*. Liberal paternalism refrains from restricting individual freedoms but is sceptical of the adequacy of individuals' autonomous reasoning for making the right choices. In this sense, images of cancerous lung tissue on cigarette packets are merely there to 'remind' people that smoking is unhealthy. Hotels kindly inform their guests that other guests actually use their towels several times over. And our smartphone lets us know how much time we've wasted on social media platforms.

At the same time, under conditions of liberal paternalism, the individual is confronted with a liberalization paradox.[120] For deregulation, privatizations or public–private partnerships have often meant that juridification occurs to a greater and not lesser extent. It is precisely the weakening of vertical state authority that requires it to safeguard its fields of action on all sides and in all directions, so that every individual can participate to the same degree or responsibilities can be unequivocally assigned. Individuals find themselves confronted with a growing number of regulations, which may not directly restrict their freedom of choice but surely do condition it, slow it down and impose limits on it. Ultimately, the individual in late modern society may be freer than ever before, but constantly encounters boundaries in everyday life.

In this chapter, we have seen that progress can be accompanied by regression. And yet, instead of a relationship of cause and effect, it is rather a complex set of concurring and interacting developments. Progressive causes can overshoot and prompt unintended side-effects, which may be the case, for example, when radical variants of the critique of power and science transition into and/or facilitate a dangerous relativism. Similarly, norms can lose their emancipatory substance when they are synthesized with the requirements of the capitalist present. In this scenario, the forms of governance also change. Today, these forms appeal more strongly than in the past to the self-responsibility and inner acquiescence of individuals. Instances of regressive modernization have an impact on individuals, too, leaving them exposed, in the crossfire of conflicting appeals, to being offended and aggrieved.

— Chapter 4 —

SOCIAL AGGRIEVEMENT: ON THE SOCIAL CHARACTER OF AVERSIVE EMOTIONS

Undoubtedly, in late modernity there are many people who lead their lives in greater accordance with their notion of self-realization than ever before. And yet, the conditions based on which they seek to harmonize their lives with their wishes and preferences are slipping from their grasp. Behind the claim to self-efficacy, there is a creeping awareness of one's own powerlessness. It remains uncertain whether one will be able to really develop the potentialities which one detects within oneself. And even if the individual is able to model their lifestyle to match their inner inclinations, they can never be fully satisfied. In the moment of abundance, many experience themselves as inadequate. Yet this is attributable neither to inflated expectations nor to an increased sensitivity.[1] Rather, it is that late modern socialization confronts individuals with irresolvable dilemmas: while the margins of freedom are becoming ever-more generalized across different milieus, many individuals face barriers in everyday life. The dependence on institutions, which has grown as a result of the increase in risks, leads to frustrations that prepare the ground for the late modern self taking offence.

The classical offended figure in cultural history is the handsome Narcissus, who brusquely rejects all displays of affection from others.[2] Yet, when he kneels down to quench his thirst at a pond, a casual glance at the surface unleashes an insatiable desire within him. He falls in love with the refracted mirror image which he can make out on the surface of the water. Fate takes its course, eventually culminating in the sudden realization: 'Iste ego sum!', 'That's me', as Ovid writes in his *Metamorphoses*.[3] The realization that he himself is the adored Other leads the mythological Narcissus not to engage in grandiose self-aggrandisement, as the pathological interpretation of Narcissus according to Freud would suggest, but to his death.[4] The recognition of the self-referentiality in the mirror image reveals the failure of the relationship. This love must necessarily remain unrequited. In other words, the myth conveys the profound vulnerability that accompanies excessive self-consciousness.

The continual refinements and reinterpretations to which the Narcissus myth has been subjected make it a vehicle of a self-experience that appears to lie deep inside our *condition humaine* – one which has been processed ever since the dawn of the modern era.[5] The fateful dilemma of being simultaneously both the one *and* the Other allows for a narration of the double structure of desire and failure. The self takes form within an impossible relationship, which strives for identity but is simultaneously unable to incorporate the object of desire. It is precisely this self-referentiality, which denies any external ties, that demonstrates the dependence on a (social) counterpart: 'It is precisely the dependence on the Other that is both concealed in narcissism and, simultaneously, reveals itself in a peculiar manner', notes psychoanalyst Martin Altmeyer.[6] Even in the ancient myth, the self-relation alludes to an authority that grants recognition. As Narcissus's tears hit the surface of the pond and cloud the contours of his mirror image, he blusters in furious despair: 'Where do you fly to? Stay, cruel one, do not abandon one who loves you!'[7] The self-relation turns out to be object-less, and ultimately becomes a generator of negative, even destructive emotions, culminating in self-effacement. Narcissus experiences temporary fulfilment only in the fleeting illusion of his own reflection – that is, in the moment which he will later recognize as delusional.

Narcissus has become a myth of modern culture, which seeks to substantiate itself through him: as the classicist Almut-Barbara Renger puts it, 'he creates and incarnates the *Zeitgeist*'.[8] Narcissism proves compatible with social sensitivities, especially when embedded in pathologizing interpretations of the culture of the self: self-interest, relationship-phobia, isolation, obsession with success and competition, consumerist attitudes, media self-referentiality, or fear of failure and the shame associated with it – in all these cases, the self-loving Narcissus, removed from his ancient context, incarnates the negative side-effects of individualization.[9] As a diagnostic tool, this figure pushes towards the semantic disambiguation of disparate cultural phenomena. But here we would like to highlight the ambiguous two-sided structure of Narcissus, who represents both the promises and the curse of individual liberation. What the myth illuminates is 'the subject's narcissistic interest in freedom',[10] which allows them to deny painful dependencies by demonstrating their own independence.

Contours of social aggrievement

Asked in a 2021 interview why so many people struggle to practise individual self-restraint even though it might appear appropriate in a social emergency such as a pandemic, philosopher Peter Sloterdijk responded: 'The desire for instant gratification, preferably at no cost, has become so intense that the reintroduction of reasonable restraint is perceived almost as counter-revolutionary over-burdening. Any renewed liability at first causes anger and exasperation.'[11] The virtue of contentment – that ascetic readiness to postpone one's own pleasure, which Max Weber construed as an essential feature of a modern individuality influenced by the spirit of Protestantism – appears, in Sloterdijk's view, to have given way to the precept of ostentatious gratification. Individuals want everything at once, and they want it all immediately. He warns that this cultural development, which deforms the self, leads to destructive consequences: hedonism is paralleled by an increased excitability, which releases destructive energies in situations of disappointment. Desire becomes a relation to the self, with an anomic effect: if the social world is merely a mirror of one's own emotions, then it becomes the target of anger once it disappoints this identification.

As early as 1979, sociologist Christopher Lasch advanced a similar diagnosis: 'The modern propaganda of commodities and the good life', he writes in his widely acclaimed book *The Culture of Narcissism*, 'has sanctioned impulse gratification and made it unnecessary for the id to apologise for its wishes or disguise their grandiose proportions. But this same propaganda has made failure and loss unsupportable.'[12] Lasch wrote these lines shortly after the peak of industrial modernity, which, with its standardized mass products and increased opportunities for prosperity, created new desires. He, too, diagnosed an obsession with one's own desires that was not limited to consumption. Back then, a whole generation engaged in self-searching by attending self-awareness seminars, yoga retreats, or aerobic classes, etc. Authoritarian toughness or rigid hierarchies disappeared from the everyday reality of many – but domination did not. It now appeared in more subtle forms, for instance, as educators, therapists, or as an abstract bureaucracy. The parallel existence of disinhibition and increased social control, Lasch's later widely acknowledged diagnosis tells us, makes people susceptible to narcissistic pathologies.

Even though the two descriptions were advanced at several decades' distance from each other, they refer to a similar starting point: the social world becoming a mirror of the self, which tolerates no rejection. And both Lasch and Sloterdijk conclude that this causes feelings of offendedness that paint a rather bleak picture of the state of society. Is the social phenomenon of narcissism returning? Or is it that it never went away, but is simply becoming more noticeable again? Is it the reason why so many people are unwilling to adjust their behaviour during a global pandemic with countless victims? Are they *mere egoists*? Is that the explanation for the protests and, at times, frivolous rule-breaking? This would be a fairly simple conclusion, but an unduly simplistic one, too.

Studies that consider psychopathologies as the secondary consequences of social structures shift the perspective: now, the spiritual suffering offers insight into social contours. This form of social diagnosis is not new, but has a long tradition behind it: around 1900, a rising number of neurasthenia cases were being registered, which people at the time attributed to the acceleration of a modernized society. People were restless, easily agitated and simultaneously permanently exhausted. The reason why such diagnoses continue to enjoy great popularity to this day may be that mental health problems illustrate cultural uneasiness in particularly drastic terms. In this reading, we live in a depressed, exhausted, fatigued, nervous, or egoistic society. At the same time, such diagnoses are problematic because they divide social conditions into those of normality and those of its pathological disruption. They often contain a nostalgia for the supposedly good old days when, for instance, we were not yet slaves of our smartphones. Many pathologizing descriptions thus breathe the stale spirit of cultural conservatives' narratives of decay. All these shortcomings aside, we would like to proceed from the same basic thought in this chapter and present an interpretation of individuals' inner lives, their suffering and emotions, in correlation with social change.

Beginning in the last third of the twentieth century, it was precisely the social emphasis on *individual* suffering that marked its *social* character. We have already depicted the heightened awareness for the individual and their feelings which, during the 1970s, erupted in a 'psycho-boom' and the popularization of New Age thinking and the esoteric.[13] Societies are now more strongly oriented towards the autonomy of their members, while traditional ties lose their significance. Social inequalities, however, are not thereby eliminated but rather 'redefined' as individual risks, writes Ulrich Beck in *Risk Society*. This has far-reaching consequences:

> The result is that social problems are increasingly perceived in terms of psychological dispositions: as personal inadequacies, guilt feelings, anxieties, conflicts, and neuroses. There emerges, paradoxically, a *new immediacy of individual and society, a direct relation between crisis and sickness*. Social crises appear as individual crises, which are no longer (or are only very indirectly) perceived in terms of their rootedness in the social realm.[14]

The insight that individualization does not entail an increased distance between the individual and society, but rather the transposition of society into the self, helps explain the new desire for spiritual self-tracking in which the social roots of one's own suffering are blocked out. This change in the relationship between the individual and society, then, demands that sociological observation should pay close attention to individual anxiety, to the 'weariness of the self'. Particularly in this context, as French sociologist Alain Ehrenberg notes in *La Société du Malaise* ('The Uneasy Society'), the spiritual suffering turns into a 'form of expressing [...] the conflicts, tensions, or dilemmas of a social life oriented towards autonomy'.[15]

In what follows, we refer to late modern subjectivity as *susceptible to taking offence* and having an *affinity for taking offence*. We do this based on the premise that social conflicts are contained in a refracted form within the individual. Our intention is not to advance a narrative of decay, but rather to embed and translate social tensions into inner arenas of struggle.[16]

The phenomenology of aversive emotions

The specific origin of the offence caused differs from one individual to another, as does the extent to which they feel offended.[17] As varied as the reactions to denigrating situations may be, what they all share is that some external factor triggers a negative emotional dynamic with a highly independent and destructive character. What once had its origin outside the self now becomes a system with a dynamic of its own. The traces of the social world are erased, the individual themselves appears as the generator of states of inner unhappiness; this unites offendedness and narcissism: both arise from a failed connection, which must be erased in order to suppress a profound despair. Instead, aversive emotions are now attached to new object worlds, in which individuals experience that which was supposed to be denied: the profound feeling of dependency. A closer inspection of such emotional states of rejection reveals the hidden structures that set them in motion. Georg Simmel referred to feelings as 'social' because they emerge in relationships and (in our case, negatively) connect individuals with one another.[18] The demonstrative gesture of detachment, in particular, implies social structures and interactions.

One initial and somewhat blurred set of emotions associated with experiences of humiliation is *shame*. It is a state of bashful embarrassment or timid diffidence that is painful to tolerate. We are all familiar with it. Experiences of embarrassment burn a lasting stain into our memories. Remembering an embarrassing moment usually makes one want to curl up and die once more. What is clear, here, is that the individual feels monitored by a superordinate authority whose gaze reveals aspects of the self that are supposed to remain hidden.[19] Simmel was the first to conceive of shame as a social emotion resulting from a 'representation of the *social group* in ourselves'.[20] At the heart of shameful embarrassment, Simmel notes, is the individual's own subjectivity, which is perceived as deficient, yet this inadequacy is only discernible when contrasted with an internalized authority. The ashamed individual recognizes themselves as inadequate through their awareness of their otherness, they feel that their integrity has become vulnerable. The admonitory gaze is so potent because one is fully aware of one's incorrect conduct. This is what makes for the enormous power of this emotional state: shame means subordinating oneself to the 'evaluating glance' of negative

100

classification – namely, by applying it to oneself. As a result, shame sublates the separation from the powerful object.

As Sighard Neckel diagnoses in his insightful study *Status und Scham* ('Status and Shame'), processes which increasingly address individuals in their self-responsibility now expand the spaces of social shame: 'In parallel with the "individualization" of the culturally shaped personality patterns, social conditions and forms of subjective perception [...], the possibilities of social shame potentially grow as well.'[21] Status deficits become perceivable as personal failure by being attributed to individual decisions: 'The individual is forced to explain a personal deficiency to themselves, because collective interpretive patterns of social inequality lose their validity.'[22] Individualist culture has led to increased feelings of guilt. That is to say, guilt is closely connected to shame; although guilt is supposed to be averted through the act of shaming, it remains present precisely as a result thereof.[23] The more unbearable the feeling of being shamed, the greater the tendency to escape this state through 'projective identification': the source of one's own embarrassment is now scrutinized for weak spots and humiliated in return.[24] In a way, we may speak of a retaliation by the individual, as a destructive dynamic is set in motion. In our studies, we spoke to people who had harboured progressive attitudes for many years but developed xenophobic positions following denigrating experiences such as old-age poverty or unemployment (see chapter 8). They avert their shame – towards their family, their social environment, but also towards themselves – by disparaging others.

What the ashamed individual usually does not dare to verbalize is fully openly articulated in the state of *grudge*.[25] This emotion of angry discontent is also located outside one's own self. The grudging, or aggrieved individual, according to psychoanalyst Heinz Weiß, looks 'reproachfully from the bottom to the top'; they identify an injustice and demand its rectification.[26] In the case of grudge, the inner injury is also transferred to an Other who is blamed for this humiliation. Hence, grudge inherently contains a tendency towards distinguishing between a victim and a perpetrator. While the reproachful glance provides the Other with the power to act, in the sense of offending and inflicting harm on others, the individual constitutes themselves as a suffering object. In the case of grudge [*Grollen*], a profoundly portentous state of the world is revealed that cannot be articulated any other way – and which calls for justice.[27]

After all, it is characteristic of the grudge that one is keen to no longer endure the intolerable status as victim, but to reverse it by mobilizing hostile emotions. The suffering experienced is supposed to overcome the dichotomy of victim and perpetrator. The anger encourages the individual to reclaim the capacity for action and interpretation over the offensive situation: now it is the perpetrators who come under pressure to explain themselves.

In the emotional state of grudge (or rancour), situations are subjected to a moral evaluation so that one may gain a handle on them: the grumbling articulation of one's own powerlessness condemns the perpetrator and reverses the asymmetrical relationship. The rhetoric of victimhood is often pervaded by 'connotations' which place 'events in an overarching system of meaning' in order to attach relevance to the injustice suffered.[28] The emotional structure of grudge frequently harbours an element of self-referentiality: 'The corresponding individuals demonstrate their uniqueness not through outward grandiosity, but through the outrageousness of the injury they have suffered', as psychotherapist Reinhard Haller observed in conversations with his patients.[29] Here, the grudge becomes conceivable as an emotional device of self-positing, which, however, contains a crucial flaw: it can be applied only in the relational dynamic between victim and perpetrator. In other words, the tragedy of the grudge lies in the fact that an exchange is desired but simultaneously one clings on to one's own suffering – meaning that reconciliation is pursued only for appearances' sake.[30] This circumstance also helps explain the expansive character of the emotion that repeatedly assails the affected anew, of grudgingly resisting an illegitimate superior power. Correspondingly, time and again, some intellectuals intervene in public debates with controversial remarks (most of all against 'gender asterisks', trans people or people of colour), face criticism, and subsequently feel that their freedom of speech has itself been offended (see chapter 7). The drive towards generalization here is often accompanied by a polarizing, pointed emphasis in which moral roles are clearly assigned.

An amorphous and deeply unsettling emotional state can thereby be more clearly pinpointed. What is being processed here is the perceived powerlessness from which the grudging individual seeks to wriggle themselves free by identifying a culprit, and thereby at the same time controlling them.[31] Correspondingly, it becomes clear why scepticism towards ambiguities is an inherent feature of the aggrieved, grudging individual, for they undermine the definiteness of assigned guilt and thus their own self-affirmation. Given its logic of increase and expansion, grudge can take on delusional forms, and, in extreme cases, evolve into a 'pre-stage of paranoid hatred'.[32] In such a case, the world is read through the polarized interpretive grid of the grudge; it is divided into the powerful and the powerless. This is the target at which the anger is directed, the indignation is channelled into protest. Such emotions motivate political action – albeit a kind driven by an authoritarian impulse.[33]

Rage in particular has in recent times been interpreted in political terms.[34] The '*Wutbürger*' ('angry citizen'), who is wrongly equated with that rage, became emblematic of a new political style: they 'boo, shout, hate'.[35] Where populist rhetoric insinuates a gulf between a morally upright people and a corrupted elite, rage erupts out of the certainty of being on the right side.[36] Unlike anger, which has an eruptive and uncontrolled element, rage is directed at an object that is meant to be harmed (which, in the context of self-loathing, may well include one's own ego, too). The enraged individual reflects the Old Testament notion of God's wrath, intervening into worldly affairs in order to dole out punishments. While grudge glances upwards with bitterness, rage reverses the perspective.[37] This unites the latter with contempt, in which one disparagingly condemns the social Other.[38] This is why violence is an intrinsic feature of rage, in the sense of what sociologist Heinrich Popitz refers to as a 'power of action', which seeks to harm and injure others.[39]

Psychoanalyst Heinz Kohut locates rage at the far end of a range of narcissistic anger, through which a fragmented self seeks to affirm itself in the face of injuries suffered.[40] With its destructive energy, rage can be interpreted as an attempt to restore a damaged self whose sovereignty must be expressed all the more emphatically the more deeply the offence suffered has built up. We have spoken to men who once saw a privileged life ahead of them but today lead a rather bleak existence. They develop fantasies of taking revenge on the elites or bluster about mass shootings and labour camps.

In his book *Rage and Time* (2006), Peter Sloterdijk attempted to appreciate this emotion, with reference to the ancient idea of Thymos, as a positive force of life. According to Sloterdijk, it is a cultural hallmark of 'victorious cultures', who constitute their 'feeling of sovereignty' via an aggressive resistance against their adversaries.[41] In the constricted perspective of rage, pride and sovereignty, a narcissistic pathos of superiority is openly verbalized and situated in a universal history of civilization: disinhibited emotions that were made into taboos in modernity have historically been an indicator of strong cultures, Sloterdijk notes. Sloterdijk's philosophical defence of rage can be interpreted as historiography of civilizational aggrievement, when he explains the rise of political Islam 'from the excess of vitality of an unstoppable giant wave of unemployed and, socially speaking, hopeless male adolescents'.[42] It appears plausible to interpret Sloterdijk's tract as a cultural expression of offendedness (particularly that of *men*) that is transferred to an image of the enemy who is constructed as inferior and of lesser value.

Similar to rage and grudge, *resentment* (*Ressentiment*) is marked by its fundamentally reactive character. It requires an external offence to trigger a seething sense of rejection that is pervaded by envy and the thirst for revenge. In his work *On the Genealogy of Morality* (1887), philosopher Friedrich Nietzsche referred to resentment as a peculiar form of action; he regarded it as one that 'is basically a reaction'.[43] The smouldering aggressive energies are not acted out, the impulse for revenge is inhibited, the offence suffered continues to fester within the individual's emotional economy. Resentment, Nietzsche continues, is a feeling harboured by those 'who, denied the proper response of action, compensate for it only with imaginary revenge'.[44] Nietzsche now describes precisely this enforced inaction, in somewhat Darwinian terms, as a peculiarity of the weak as opposed to the strong and victorious.[45] As a result of the feeling of powerlessness which it entails, resentment develops a dynamic of its own. Revenge *cannot* be carried out; an instinctual discharge eludes the individual. That is why this negative emotional state occurs again and again.

As with grudge, in the case of resentment the identification of some external cause of one's own powerlessness is used as a mechanism of relief: the cause of one's suffering lies outside the self, it has a beginning and can therefore – that is the tacit hope – come to an end, too. But unlike grudge, which rebels against injustices, resentment constitutes a generalized feeling of malice that has no specific adversary. It matters not so much who or what is identified as the cause, but rather that a relationship with a harmful object can be established in order to address the unredeemed impulse of revenge. In his work *Ressentiment*, first published in 1912 and subsequently in an extended version in 1915, philosopher and sociologist Max Scheler concludes, similarly to Nietzsche, that the suppression of vengeance engenders 'indeterminate groups of objects'; in its tireless search for causality, resentment ultimately remains peculiarly object-less.[46] The humiliation suffered is transferred to an unrelated Other, resentment creates the emotionally efficacious illusion that there is a kind of perpetrator who caused it on purpose. This tendency towards projection can turn into an inexhaustible paranoia whereby the world is perceived through a template of humiliation and offence. Philosopher Thomas Bedorf has more closely located resentment in the emotional world of populism. He references Horkheimer and Adorno, who attributed this emotion a tendency towards 'stereotyped schemata', which are openly flaunted in antisemitism: 'For the ego, sinking into the meaningless abyss of itself, objects become allegories of ruin, which harbour the meaning of its own downfall.'[47] What matters is that the allegories of one's own predicament, of which the two authors speak, are indeed in flux but at the same time adhere to the 'imperative of reification' by personalizing guilt.[48] This makes resentment susceptible to authoritarian thought patterns. In our interview conversations, we also encountered longstanding antisemitic prejudices, conspiracy theories about 'Bilderbergers', the Rothschilds or George Soros (see chapters 7 and 8).

Unlike Nietzsche, however, Scheler conceived of resentment primarily as an emotion of the modern era. In pre-modern estate-based society, there was a rigid hierarchy of status, which made questions of the individual's social worth irrelevant: according to Scheler, a subordinate feels no urge for revenge when being chided by their master. In his view, the precondition for resentment is that 'the injured person always places [themselves] on the same level as [their] injurer'.[49] From this perspective, the societies susceptible to resentment are those which may publicly and legally recognize equality but exhibit a highly unequal distribution of power, education and wealth: 'while each has the "right" to compare [themselves] with everyone else, [they] cannot do so in fact.'[50]

From Scheler's conclusion, which we shall turn to in the following section, we may deduce two insights regarding the emotional structure of resentment: firstly, the relational comparison eliminates the asymmetry of the gaze, which can be directed from the bottom upwards, from the top downwards, or at eye level. Secondly, Scheler deciphers aversive emotional states as a quality of the social. Resentment may be unique in its form of expression, but the dilemmas and tensions which it processes are social in nature.

Here, we have only presented a small snapshot from the range of emotions associated with suffering (or sensing) offence. In chapter 2, we saw that authors who can be seen to represent more recent Critical Theory (such as Axel Honneth, Alain Ehrenberg, Thomas Fuchs, Sighard Neckel, Hartmut Rosa or Greta Wagner) point out the imperative of individual self-realization, which structurally overwhelms the individual. Instead of being able to self-develop freely, they experience themselves as powerless in the face of omnipresent competitive relations. They become depressed, exhausted, passive, suffer burnout, or seek self-enhancement through the use of pharmacological substances. Under certain conditions, however, powerlessness can lead to an aggressive rebellion. Over the past years, aversive emotions have been at the heart of this rebellion, which have one thing in common: they are directed against some object in a confrontational fashion. Emotions such as rage, grudge and resentment surely are regarded as socially unacceptable and have a destructive effect; but they also motivate people to act. We interpret these emotions as reactions to lasting disappointments, which the individual is no longer capable of processing because the cultural tools that they have internalized produce precisely the frustrations that they are supposed to prevent.

The expansion of the zone of aggrievement

We shall now turn to exploring the social dilemmas that can trigger aversive emotions in the individual (even if they do not necessarily have to do so).[51] These latter are symptoms of a regressive modernization in the course of which social progress is accompanied by unintended negative consequences for individuals. The contradictory dynamic of individualization we have outlined can cause aversive emotions and deviant forms of reaction when confronting the individual with irresolvable contradictions. In late modern societies, three aspects are gaining currency that could already be observed during previous transformations in modern societies: firstly, the paradox of egalitarian norms; secondly, aspirational deficiencies; and, thirdly, anomic normative structures. These aspects also prepare the breeding ground for libertarian authoritarianism.

A first driving force of frustrations and disappointments can be discerned in the paradoxes of equality in modern societies. During his trip to the United States, Tocqueville registered 'contrary tendencies'.[52] With passionate interest he observed the social coexistence of the young democracy in which he lived for almost a year – although he had to acknowledge that it was precisely the norm of political equality, recognized by all members of society, that threatened the democratic ideal. The partial levelling out of positions of status did not even come close to eliminating the reality of inequality. It unquestionably persisted, albeit with one difference: in modern societies, social differences are regarded as legitimate because, 'according to the paradigm of equality [...], all areas of society and positions are generally open to everyone', notes sociologist Hans-Peter Müller.[53]

This is indeed a tricky situation, albeit not so much for democratic society per se as for its members, to whom the ideal of equality necessarily had to appear as an unredeemed promise: 'To the extent that equality seems to have become ubiquitous, so, too, has the arsenal of disappointment proliferated'.[54] The more universally the egalitarian norm applies, the further the gaze of comparison wanders, as it is no longer bound within limited social circles. Obviously, this gaze inevitably detects differences. 'There is, in fact, a manly and lawful passion for equality which excites men to wish all to be powerful and honoured', Tocqueville notes:

> This passion tends to elevate the humble to the rank of the great; but there exists also in the human heart a depraved taste for equality, which impels the weak to attempt to lower the powerful to their own level, and reduces men to prefer equality in slavery to inequality with freedom.[55]

In egalitarian societies, a mode of comparison is deployed in which everyone is compared to everyone else. For this reason, the ideal of equal opportunities especially releases negative emotions, in function of the perception of real differences. The grudging individual seeks to emotionally realize the normative promise of equality that is implemented only deficiently in reality.[56] At the same time, the aversive emotions cannot openly erupt, for the egalitarian ideal insinuates that the differences observed have emerged on the basis of an equal endowment of resources and opportunities for access. As a result, the emotion continues to fester on the inside, as long as the norm creates infinite impulses for frustration.

Tocqueville analyses further effects that can be triggered by the ideal of equality and which themselves threaten to undermine it. In particular, he notes that increasing equality not only encourages comparison but also engenders a sensitivity to even minimal differences: 'The hatred which men bear to privilege increases in proportion as privileges become more scarce and less considerable, so that democratic passions would seem to burn most fiercely at the very time when they have least fuel.'[57] If the major differences disappear, the smaller ones become even more clearly visible: 'More equality increases the awareness of inequality.'[58] This sensitive mode of perception leads to a humiliation of one's own normative perception. The outcome here is, once again, a series of constant disappointments, which, far from weakening the validity of the norm, instead fuel the urge for assimilation, the egalitarian passion, as Tocqueville writes. The fact that supposedly secondary issues such as gender-neutral language conventions are being demanded is most certainly related, in some measure at least, to an increase in the social awareness of inequality.

And yet, the discontent which social assimilation may entail need not necessarily arise from a heightened sensitivity to differences – for it may also be based on a real loss of power. The emergence of new norms leads to the punishment of previously accepted behaviour. The slave driver is no longer allowed to treat humans as his property, parents are no longer authorized to subject their children to corporal punishment, and men are no longer permitted to sexually harass women. The progressing equalization limits the actions of privileged status groups and restricts the social power that they had once monopolized. Norbert Elias defined power as an 'expression for the special extent of the individual scope for action associated with certain social positions'.[59] This power to influence other people or even control or use force against them not only diminishes: high-status individuals' power to act now relies on the acceptance of others. Society itself has become more powerful than them. The powerful are forced to readjust their actions to prevent potential norm violations. The powerful individual experiences this as a painful disruption. Their rage is directed against those groups who now participate in the previously monopolized power, meaning, all those whose fate they are no longer able to (co-)determine. Elias notes (see chapters 3 and 6) that power conflicts are the result of changes in norms that have far-reaching consequences for the acceptance of the social order, because they alter the figuration of established groups and outsiders.[60] Losses of power 'in relation to rising outsider groups' especially trigger 'bitter resistance, a scarcely realistic longing for the restoration of the old order and not merely for economic reasons'; the affected groups indeed 'feel themselves lowered in their self-esteem'.[61] Consequently, the established groups stigmatize the former outsiders. Against this backdrop, Nietzsche's assumption that resentment exclusively represents an emotion of weaker groups was not entirely accurate. In modern societies, the strong groups are just as much deprived of the opportunity to react to the limitations they suffer to their social power. They are now equally forced to control their indignation. For not only do their actions run the risk of being sanctioned, but so, too, their emotional reaction to being sanctioned. This is the reason why Scheler describes resentment as a manifestation of 'declining life'.[62]

The second trigger of frustration in modern societies is hinted at by Scheler in the above-quoted statement. It is the unresolved tension between a morally founded *ideal* state and its factual *realization*, which is already inherent in the idea of equality and becomes a key feature of modern capitalist socialization. Whereas Tocqueville discerns the origin of this destructive force in the universal implementation of the norm of equality, Scheler locates it within the modern 'structure of society'. This latter, according to Scheler, is marked by a 'discrepancy between the political, constitutional, or traditional status of a group and its factual power'.[63] Although negative liberation turns all members of society into formally free and equal citizens, it does so only in order to universalize capitalist commodity exchange that is founded upon the actual inequality of ownership structures. What Marx described as the legal condition of an economic structure is the starting point for Scheler to analyse the emotional dynamic that this configuration engenders and maintains. Indeed, his considerations start off from the individual's inner states, yet his ultimate aim is to describe the *'system of free competition'* as the 'soul of this society'.[64] According to Scheler, modern resentment has its origin in the universal implementation of value comparison, a relational judgement whereby one's own value is determined through comparison with the Other. In the estate-based social order, Scheler writes, a peasant will never compare themselves with a feudal lord or a knight, but with wealthier peasants from their 'own sphere'.[65] The moral and normative equalization of the conditions of life, however, leads to a change in the mode of comparison: everybody compares themselves with everyone else. Unlike Tocqueville, Scheler attributes this to the situation of economic competition. 'The aspirations are intrinsically *boundless*', detached from social circles or intrinsic qualities, finding discharge in a dynamic of economic progress motivated by the uninterrupted accumulation of capital. An inner drive towards value accumulation turns into a functional condition of capital accumulation. Here, Scheler anticipated a development which has produced status differentials through ranking and rating. Let us recall, for instance, the discontent which Marion Fourcade observes, caused by ordinal classification systems which may formally have an inclusive effect but indirectly reinforce traditional boundaries and inequalities (see chapter 2).

The accelerated economy of comparison causes a social order that facilitates aversive affects (against oneself as well as against others). In his study *Suicide* (1897), Émile Durkheim observes the phenomenon of a negative 'liberation of desires' in periods of accelerated economic dynamics, which coincides with an increase in auto-aggressive modes of behaviour.[66] People not only become depressed, lethargic or suicidal, but also turn into each others' enemies. From Durkheim's perspective, they are 'victims of their exaggerated aspirations',[67] of their restless and unfulfillable desire: 'Thus, the more one has, the more one wants, since satisfactions received only stimulate instead of filling needs.'[68] Satisfaction is impossible if the object of desire is not something specific but, above all, always *more*. In the economic sphere governed by the law of accumulation, anomie, violence and rulelessness ossify into a 'chronic state'.[69] If the world in which people live is deeply immoral, then they need to adapt to these adverse conditions in order to survive. In this sense, Durkheim notes, the economic sphere engenders an 'excessive individualism'[70] which affirms a purely negative freedom.[71] Egoistic and inconsiderate modes of behaviour arise on the basis of normatively unregulated relations of competition: 'Egocentric utilitarian calculation and the insatiable narcissistic desire for psychological gratification', Neckel remarks in this regard, 'fuse in the common emotional state of regarding moral claims merely as obstacles to the pursuit of private interests – a monotheism of the ego between money and feelings'.[72]

If the enormous energy inherent in the aspirational drive cannot be sensibly invested, this will inevitably cause frustration. Reacting to this with rage is but one way of affirming one's own sovereignty in the face of a situation of offence; in other cases, negative emotions are not vented and build up inside. The shame of failing to meet the expected standard leads to profound self-doubt.

Especially in a social atmosphere of uncertainty, in which hopes for social advancement are frustrated by status barriers, the individual's aspirations are confronted with their own powerlessness and transformed into bitter feelings of being disadvantaged. When the individual's own 'superiority' – and this is Scheler's term for the spiritual counterpart of economic surplus value – cannot be realized through action, the powerless individual attains it through the 'illusory devaluation' of their object of comparison.[73] Rather than feeling ashamed, the blame is shifted on to others. The power differential which grants individuals unequal opportunities establishes an illusionary value system in the individual who is disadvantaged or threatened by social decline, a value system in which the promise that they are deprived of by reality may instead be redeemed. It may go along the lines of, 'I might be the social loser, but I am the moral winner'. Resentment offers an imaginary opportunity to block out social dilemmas and tensions. In the case of hostile disparagement, positive characteristics of the object of comparison are re-interpreted as negative ones: those who are successful have enriched themselves with insatiable greed; they have managed to socially advance only by dubious means, etc. In other words, the individual doing the comparing posits their own – in their view, true – ranking system. Here, Scheler describes a normative secession with remarkable accuracy. We shall come across a similar phenomenon in the context of libertarian-authoritarian discontent (see chapter 8). That said, Scheler wrote down these thoughts on the basis of a stable norms-economy which, even in the illusion of resentment, awakened 'that obscure awareness that one lives in a *sham world*'.[74] The self-deluding individual is secretly aware of their self-deceit, which is why this provides only very limited relief. If the norms themselves, whose irrefutable reality convinces even the most wrathful individual, begin to wobble, then the self-awareness loses the basis for reflection. The illusory world of unilaterally constructed norms takes on a life of its own.

Anger, resentment, envy, or grudge are therefore anything but subjective emotional states. Rather, they are a social 'relational

111

structure' that is put into effect by the 'compulsion to compare and relate' in capitalist society.[75] If the mechanisms of evaluation develop in an atmosphere of uncertainty, in which claims to equality are tied to unequal opportunities for their realization, 'affective societies' of rejection emerge.[76] Alongside vertical hierarchies, these latter create a hardened emotional order, in which individuals relate negatively to one another. It is therefore unsurprising that aversive emotions have become the starting point for many critical social diagnoses in recent years. For instance, Indian author Pankaj Mishra observes a *'ressentiment*, [...] [which] poisons civil society and [...] is presently making for a global turn to authoritarianism and toxic forms of chauvinism'.[77] Mishra explains the rise in negative emotions, fully in the spirit of Scheler, with reference to two parallel developments: on the one hand, inequalities are rising in the context of a globalized world in which people with strongly differing pasts are thrown into one and the same present, and in which the unequal distribution of power and wealth engenders new unjust hierarchies; on the other hand, procedures of comparison are multiplying within digital communication networks which, in turn, become generators of envy, loathing and malice.[78] Now everyone can see who is wealthy and who is not. And the former, at least, sometimes ostentatiously put their condition on display. For Mishra, the actually existing material differences in reality – which persist despite the worldwide promise of growing prosperity – and the *subjective* sensitization to difference are the factors at work in the recurrent excitement cycles of envy, resentment and anger. And this social situation is simultaneously the precondition for a libertarian authoritarianism which, in the face of perceived barriers, affirmatively demands redemption of the promise of an autonomous life.

Yet, it is not socio-economic inequality that leads to a culture of disappointment but rather the already mentioned modern game of social selection and assimilation in which two competing ideals – egalitarianism and meritocracy – are conflated. Success is now no longer to be gauged exclusively on the basis of the performance delivered; and this has disastrous consequences for the affect-dynamic when individual professional success fails to materialize despite the efforts made or when people are inhibited in their actions. In chapter 2 we saw how performance-based fairness loses its validity in economic reality and is replaced with other distributive principles: 'Risk, success, and inheritance'.[79] In his study *The Tyranny of Merit: What's Become of the Common Good?*, US philosopher Michael J.

Sandel returns to this thought as he identifies the 'primary source of populist anger' not in the 'explosion of inequality' in society, but in the collective 'faith in the possibility of upward mobility'.[80] The American dream not only harbours an unbroken suggestive potency, but it also produces frustrations, such as when the path from rags to riches fails to work out. The discrepancy between collective imagination and individual reality changes over into a 'tyranny of merit', causing arrogance and self-exaltation in the winners, and shame and disappointment in the losers.[81] While some look down condescendingly, the others look up with envy and resentment. To avoid any misunderstanding: here, Sandel is by no means lamenting an inflated sense of entitlement but rather the fact that society is failing to redeem its promises. If, however, the social order is divided by interdependent feelings of disparagement, this can engender new forms of social clamour. Sandel observes that populist protests not only erupt in reaction to social injustices, but as a 'protest against humiliation',[82] which concern the individual's self-worth. These protests contain a nervous moment of radicalization, which need not necessarily erupt in a manner aimed at the top of society – *au contraire*. What is noticeable is that the rage of the disadvantaged is directed against objects of comparison that are ranked below them in the social hierarchy, at minorities, outsiders and foreigners.[83] The regressive rebels, for example, often had to acquiesce in experiences of decline – even though they had done everything right (see chapter 8). They have completed decent levels of schooling, etc. But success never materialized. Instead of calling into question the unjust system, they now shift their attention to asylum seekers, whom they regard as having invaded Germany's social security systems. While they consider those they perceive as strange or foreign to be lazy, they themselves have always had to work hard for everything. The anger of one minority towards another seeks to suppress feelings of inferiority by denigrating others instead of being subjected to such treatment themselves. Libertarian authoritarianism, too, is not a protest against the norms of meritocratic society but a reified identification with them, which leads to a projective resistance against those who, in the eyes of libertarian authoritarians, fail to comply with these norms. In a society of winners, failure is not communicable.

As fascism was still raging in Europe, sociologist Robert K. Merton was investigating quite similar phenomena. Beginning in the late

113

1930s, he concerned himself with social groups who were only poorly integrated into US society and, in extreme cases, had become criminals. He regarded this behaviour as anything but individual pathological deviance. Rather, he concluded that people were under such social pressure that they hardly had a choice but to behave in an unadapted manner. We have already seen that Merton observed an excessive obsession with financial success, particularly among those who were disadvantaged in social competition. They resorted to illegitimate means to attain goals regarded as desirable by society. In this sense, for Merton, too, it was not the unequal distribution of wealth that encourages deviance and crime among the disadvantaged but a highly contradictory configuration that is marked by a 'conflict between cultural goals and the availability of [...] institutional means'.[84] Merton refers to this 'breakdown' in the cultural structure as anomie, given that the values themselves encourage forms of behaviour that in fact undermine them.[85] In the 'superstar economy',[86] for example, success is the only thing that counts, not the effort. Particularly the superstar, with their ambivalence of closeness ('they're one of us') and elusiveness ('they're so different from us') can initiate negative emotions or non-conformist modes of behaviour. As miraculous as the success of the superstar may be, the paths to success for oneself are similarly dismal. The anomie inherent in society's set of norms constitutes the third trigger of frustration which engenders modes of reaction to escape this stress-inducing situation.

But how is it possible for an intelligible, i.e., not directly visible, system of rules to exert such compelling power over individuals? Heinrich Popitz, who regards behavioural standardization as a restriction of the possibilities of how one could or should act, provides a clue in this regard. He defines a social norm based on four characteristics: 'A behaviour that we can expect as future behaviour; a behaviour that corresponds to certain behavioural regularities; an obligatory [...] behaviour, one that runs the risk of being punished in the case of deviance.'[87] In essence, social norms first and foremost guarantee that people will act in a certain way in recurrent contexts or situations. The social order ultimately rests on an 'effort of abstraction', whereby situations are compared and classified.[88] For example, knowing that it is customary in many Western countries to shake hands when you meet other people makes interaction with others a lot easier – although, perhaps not so much anymore. Deviance from this behavioural expectation not only causes irritations that illustrate the fragility of the social realm to the individuals concerned, but also has the effect that deviant behaviour is deemed intolerable or even punished. One disturbing phenomenon that could be observed during the pandemic was that previously expected behaviour was suddenly disapproved of. The extended hand was generally met with sceptical looks (see chapter 7).

Merton, however, mainly observed deviant forms of behaviour that were motivated by adherence to social expectations. For example, members of the group which he analyses as 'gangsters' often came from immigrant families who were deprived of the legal means for social advancement. They were neither able to work in qualified professions nor even to send their children to renowned schools. Nor did an existence as a day labourer lead to prosperity or success. In their view, crime was the only way to conquer a higher social position.[89] Paradoxically, norms can thus contribute to the erosion of the social order, if parts of society are structurally blocked from access to resources and prevented from abiding by conformist modes of behaviour.

An anomic configuration can arise either when social structures collide with social norms or when norms are renewed or contradict one another. As Merton describes, in the first case a person is exposed to tensions which grow out of the disparity between a norm and the subjective chances of its realization. Children from households receiving social benefits are likely able to share many such devastating experiences.[90] The pressure weighs not so much on society as a whole but rather on social groups that have no or only limited means to pursue or meet normative or standardized expectations and claims. Erich Fromm went so far as to claim that the 'self-esteem' of a person depends on success (which necessarily leads to tensions).[91] Besides this, the plurality of norms can cause tensions as well. Individuals move within different circles with distinct values, responsibilities and requirements: every 'individual is always [...] a member of *various* societies', Popitz notes.[92] A complex, differentiated society, in which a person has several roles, is therefore always prone to '*norm conflicts*'.[93] Although the punk rocker wearing a business suit will likely remain an exceptional case, we all know situations in which we not only change what we are wearing, but also our modes of behaviour, our speech, and our demeanour. When differing responsibilities or requirements collide, this need not necessarily lead to an anomic state. Contradictory appeals, however, can expose individuals to situations in which the adherence to one norm might entail the violation of another. In late modernity, in which contradictory expectations are increasing, and in which both traditional and progressive norms continue to coexist, the contradictory appeal becomes a key element of subject formation. The basic structural dilemma cannot be resolved, but requires constant processing (see chapter 2). Indeed, we need to work 40 hours a week in order to make ends meet, but at the same time we are supposed to live our lives according to our dreams – otherwise we must surely be doing something wrong. We will see shortly that the potential forms of reaction to this frustrating situation include not only rebellious deviance but also exaggerated perfectionism or apathetic withdrawal.

In the norm conflict, the individual becomes aware of their dependency, of being part of not only one but of several social units. These situations increase in number when societies modernize, for the socio-economic change also entails a change in the collectively shared norms. Modernity, based on rationalization and standardization, was a society of discipline that presented its members with entirely different expectations than late modernity, which selectively shed some of the more suffocating normative corsets. Generational conflicts therefore by all means reflect disputes over norms given that each regard completely different behavioural standards as obligatory. Alongside pluralization, asynchronicities and changes of norms can lead to irritations and blockades in the social structure. Social change always entails a moment of uncertainty, as other people's behaviour loses its predictability. Until new regularities have been asserted, there is (an at times unintended) non-conformity on the part of those holding onto the now-obsolete norms. Well-practised modes of behaviour are inert, as they constitute internalized structures. Their progressive replacement is therefore often accompanied by a rigid conservatism in certain social sectors. The more the norm loses its validity, the more strongly they try to preserve it. The resistance against gender-neutral language, for instance, on the one hand represents a reaction to the uncertainty regarding behavioural routines (it is no longer clear what is acceptable to say and what is not), and, on the other, a refusal to accept the new expectations. In this sense, the current conflict around gender-neutral language can be understood as a conflict between progress and freedom. Gender-sensitive conventions aim at inclusivity, yet they are perceived by previously established groups as a restriction of their freedom. In part, the actual practice of egalitarian language does have an exclusionary effect: those who have not yet internalized the new norms are rebuked and morally devalued. The reactions to this include, alongside a nuanced criticism, a resentful resistance. Politician Sahra Wagenknecht, for example, rails against the demands from 'ever-smaller and ever-more obscure minorities' (see chapter 6).[94]

Individuals react differently to anomic tensions and dilemmas. Although feelings of discontent, disappointment or frustration are increasing for everybody, the forms of behaviour seeking relief vary. Merton lists five distinct forms of reaction, which differ with regard to the recognition of norms and the means of their fulfilment: conformity, innovation, ritualism, retreatism and rebellion. Whereas people who behave in a conformist manner have access to sufficient resources to attain a recognized goal, all others must perform an act of adjustment. In the case of *ritualism*, they surrender some of their claims because they have repeatedly been disappointed. Yet they compulsively cling on to institutional norms.[95] Here, individuals react to humiliating situations with schematic explanations, exaggerated perfectionism or rigid behaviour patterns.[96] The pressure of an accelerated society based on progress and innovation makes individuals feel that they are lagging behind an unstoppable logic of increase and expansion.[97] Their position is never secure, they must permanently optimize their performance, as they are always moving on 'slippery slopes':[98] one must constantly work to reduce one's personal flaws, try out new exercise programmes, pursue further education in one's free time, etc. Refusing to pursue 'self-improvement', according to Edgar Cabanas and Eva Illouz, is essentially regarded as a sign of a mental dysfunction.[99] In particular, the perfectionist changing of one's own self, such as we have described above, is an expression of an 'over-conformity' which seeks to avert the looming failure through adaptation.[100]

In the case of *retreatism*, individuals react to disruptions in their personal life by abandoning previously highly valued aspirations *and* the related institutionalized modes of behaviour.[101] During personal crises, people often retreat to their 'inner citadel'.[102] Some of our interview partners are so embittered that they leave their house only if they really have to (see chapter 8). Others fall out with their families or their friendship circles (see chapters 6 and 7). That said, depression, cynicism or indifference are not necessarily a symptom of social decline; they can also reflect an 'anomie of prosperity', as Merton points out with reference to Durkheim.[103] The more individuals themselves are responsible for their 'investive status work', the more they will perceive inadequacies in themselves, even if they are rising socially. What depression illustrates, Ehrenberg writes, is that '[a] society of individual initiative and psychic liberation [...] encourages the practice of self-modification and, in so doing, creates problems with the structuring of the self'.[104] The transition to late modernity did indeed modernize a norms system that had been geared towards discipline and the performance of one's duties, but it also left behind a social vacuum blocking individuals' capacity to act freely.

According to Merton, *innovation*, by contrast, occurs 'when the individual has assimilated the cultural emphasis upon the goal without equally internalizing the institutional norms governing ways and means for its attainment.'[105] The psychological suffering created by the imbalance between aspirations and opportunities for realization may, in extreme cases, result in the nihilist attitude of no longer feeling bound by any kind of norm. In Merton's studies, it was the groups of criminal individuals in particular who resorted to illegitimate means to realize the cultural goals of which they were deprived. At the same time, the term innovation which he chooses already points to the moment of new creation contained within the destructive subversion of institutional norms. Innovators devise new forms of action that undermine routines and institutions which they no longer trust. Doubt is hard to find among these groups, blockages and inhibitions are compensated through a self-heroic gesture of deviance. By no means does this apply only to delinquent milieus. In *The Corrosion of Character*, sociologist Richard Sennett observed that the uncertainties associated with de-standardized biographies and professional careers reward an innovative processing of one's own uncertainty: 'The true victors do not suffer from fragmentation. Instead, they are stimulated by working on many different fronts at the same time; it is part of the energy of irreversible change.'[106] Success-oriented personalities who are able to flexibly adapt to new situations at times even perceive a kind of 'rebellious enthusiasm for innovation'.[107] It is the bluffers and impostors who abandon the ideal of authenticity and enact their identity in an 'as-if' mode.[108] We happily immerse ourselves in the artificial Instagram world of influencers with their simple advice on how to achieve success and their displays of wealth – even though we secretly know that it has most likely been arranged only for the moment in which they are making this video.[109] The big car is only rented, the luxury mansion belongs to someone they know.

The conflict between cultural values and socio-structural conditions, however, can ultimately also provoke reactions that are oriented towards the development of new norms. In the *rebellion*, neither the cultural values of society nor the socially recognized modes of behaviour for realizing these values are still shared.[110] In contrast to resentment, which curses that which it actually desires, the rebellion curses the desire itself.[111] Society is now regarded as an impediment to the satisfaction of one's own aspirations. Rebels tend towards secession, and create their own organizational forms, to which they attach meaning via a 'new myth'.[112] When society confronts individuals with irresolvable tensions, they circumvent these by escaping into new communities. While Merton was most likely still thinking about the socialist movement, today's rebellion manifests itself in a radical far-right variant. In chapter 8 we shall take a closer look at the modes of authoritarian reaction that are marked by innovative and rebellious practices.[113] The corresponding individuals want to overthrow the system, but they do not advocate any utopia of a different society. Instead, they yearn for the retrotopia in which everything is restored to how it allegedly once used to be in the past.

The imaginary presence of narcissism

The 1970s saw the popularization of sociological diagnoses that focused on the emotional socialization of individuals. A profound preoccupation with the self and one's own world of emotions was regarded as an indicator of regressive cultural trends. In 1976, Tom Wolfe's essay 'The "me" decade' appeared in *New York Magazine*; in 1977, Richard Sennett published his work *The Fall of Public Man*; and in 1979 there followed Christopher Lasch's above-mentioned book *The Culture of Narcissism*. What they all share is that they proceed from a common observation: social emancipation, which had been taking shape in alternative milieus at least since 1968 and which had blown open the tight constraints of traditional institutions, did not produce enlightened human beings. Rather, it generated self-centred individuals who were oblivious to history and lived only for

the moment while constantly chasing the spectre of boundless gratification; people whose behaviour was determined by affects, who were
unable to cope with setbacks, and, simultaneously, were terrified of
sickness and death. In short: pathological narcissism was generalized
into a social code, which allegedly marked an epochal turn. These
diagnoses, which initially circulated in the Anglo-American world,
drew their success from the fact that they articulated a culturally
conservative position in the language of a radical critique of society
inspired by psychoanalysis – which allowed them to appeal to an
existing social discontent across different milieus.

It is not modern industrial society as such that encourages pathological character structures, Lasch writes in his preface, but rather
a 'culture of competitive individualism, which in its decadence has
carried the logic of individualism to the extreme of a war of all
against all, the pursuit of happiness to the dead end of a narcissistic
preoccupation with the self'.[114] Here, Lasch has in mind people
who defend a permissive sexual morality, view traditional loyalties
with suspicion, have a strong need for acknowledgement of their
uniqueness, regard their fellow human beings as rivals, and yet
distrust the concept of competition in workplace contexts and instead
extol cooperation and teamwork.[115] In other words: educated people
who strive for self-realization but sense an inner void, loneliness or
a lack of authenticity. Lasch discerns the cause for this emotional
suffering in a shift of social control which has led to what he refers
to as 'warlike conditions of social life'.[116] The erosion of vertical
authorities such as the state, the churches or, in particular, the middle-
class family as the most immediate unit of socialization entails new
forms of control which now abide by the abstract authority of
success and admiration.[117] The fight against hierarchies and paternalistic father figures, Lasch asserts, was thus ultimately beside the
point. By removing the moral barriers of traditional institutions, the
emancipation movement paved the way for the universalization of
competition.[118] The principle of relentless competition now extends
into the individual – a hypothesis which we already found in Beck's
argument – and produces a feeling of emptiness and dependency
within them.[119]

A few years before Lasch, Sennett had already concluded that shifting
the view to one's inner world represents a highly efficacious strategy
for denying dependency. He criticized the anti-authoritarianism of
the 1968 movement and the desire for emotional self-exploration; the

title of his concluding chapter, 'The Tyrannies of Intimacy', was no accident.[120] For Sennett, human relationships have been fundamentally restructured by changes in the relationship between the self and the world, which now proceeds from one's own stock of emotions and experience. In the public sphere, Sennett writes, until well into the nineteenth century, it was precisely the absence of emotions that enabled the experience of otherness. In modern civilizations, social relationships are forged only given the premise of distance. In the theatre, in the café or during one's Sunday walk, one encountered people whose family one did not know and whose social rank one could only vaguely guess at. They were strangers, but with whom one could easily strike up a conversation precisely because there was an existing etiquette governing how it was to be done, what the topic of conversation might be, etc. According to Sennett, the encroachment of intimacy upon the public sphere has curtailed such spaces of encounter. '[E]rasing the line between self and other', Sennett states, 'means that nothing new, nothing "other", ever enters the self.'[121] The end of restraint, which, during the 1970s, was raised as a progressive demand in opposition against rigid conventions, yielded contrary consequences. Sennett concludes: 'The closer people come, the less sociable, the more painful, the more fratricidal their relations.'[122] He notes that a culture that structures reality according to intimate feelings mobilizes narcissism.[123]

We have already seen that this transformation was marked by a *normative* liberalization. This revaluation of values, however, did not occur on the basis of stable institutions, cross-class socio-economic security, or increased participation opportunities for the lower classes. That was precisely the reason why the new values would develop their emancipatory potential. The alternative movements rebelled against an ossified moral shell that had been overtaken by reality (see chapter 2).[124] However, the *economic* liberalization that soon followed attached a negative connotation to individual liberation. Welfare state institutions became fragile, inequalities became more visible, people had to assume greater self-responsibility and were exposed to greater competition (see chapter 3). At the same time, as mentioned earlier, this did not mean that society retreated but rather that it expanded into the individual's inner world. Self-realization was tied to socio-economic self-responsibility and thus produced systematic disappointments. It was against the backdrop of this double liberalization that Lasch and Sennett formulated their – from

121

today's perspective, conservative – social critique. In retrospect, it is conservative because these two US sociologists were unaware of the dialectical tension of liberalization: social regressions went hand in hand with real advances. They saw only the regression, not the 'emancipatory substance'. And yet, the parallel existence of these two moments is precisely what leads to an expansion of the zone of aggrievement.

The narcissist as a social figure is present in our own day, too, even though their presence among the broader population cannot easily be verified empirically.[125] In 2009, US psychologists Jean M. Twenge and W. Keith Campbell published the volume *The Narcissism Epidemic*, which, given its alarmist title, resonated well beyond the expert audience, just like Lasch's book had thirty years earlier.[126] The difference was that they were intent on empirically proving the much-debated phenomenon in American everyday culture. In their studies, they ascertained, based on the Narcissistic Personality Inventory (NPI) – a measurement tool that records the non-pathological and primarily grandiose variants of narcissism (such as cockiness, striving for dominance or the urge to be admired) – that self-referential personality dispositions among students increased significantly between 1979 and 2006: the presence of narcissistic characteristics among the youngest cohort rose by 30 per cent.[127]

The reasons that the psychologists indicate for the rise in narcissistic personality dispositions are particularly interesting because they differ little from Lasch's diagnosis. To Twenge and Campbell, one key factor is a new education culture that promotes self-esteem over achievement: according to the authors, children receive too much praise and too few challenges.[128] Appreciation and affirmation turns them into little tyrants – a conservative critique that continues to resonate widely even today, especially among those generations who raised their children based on strictness and discipline. The celebrity system of the mass media, which promises a routinization of the exceptional, a universalization of fame and success, is listed as a second reason for the increase in exposed self-displays.[129] Other studies indicate popular casting shows as a cause of self-referential individuation; in other TV programmes targeting a young audience, a shift was detected from community-oriented to individualist values geared towards individual fame.[130] Further investigations have observed an increase in self-centred and anti-social terms in song lyrics. According

122

to DeWall et al., the pronoun 'I' and expressions associated with aggressive emotional states ('kill, hate, annoyed, damn, fuck') appear more frequently.[131] This is in some aspects related to the third cause of the rise in narcissistic traits listed by Twenge and Campbell: social media.[132] Of course, it remains controversial whether social media really do cause narcissistic characteristics; it is conceivable that individuals with a tendency towards grandiose self-elevation are active online more often, which, in turn, reinforces the corresponding personality traits.[133] The final trigger cited by the two authors is the ubiquitous availability of credit cards in the United States, which facilitates the imagination of a higher social status and pretentious consumerism, whereby self-elevation and the denial of reality are interlocked.[134] Twenge and Campbell paint a stereotypical picture of an entire generation, and indeed we can virtually see the caricature they evoke: a spoiled youngster, preoccupied only with themselves and taking selfies, and whose brand-name items are all financed by credit rather than paid for with hard-earned wages.

But is this really the essence of today's reality? Is narcissism a cultural phenomenon of individualist societies? Other studies contradict this notion, and even find a slight decrease in narcissism.[135] What matters is not only the specific definition of narcissism, but also whether it is regarded as a permanent personality trait or as a dynamic pattern of reacting to external circumstances which may vary over one's life and, indeed, be unevenly distributed across social classes and cultural milieus. Further inquiries show that society is divided into different zones of aggrievement which can be distinguished by socio-cultural socialization, political views or social classes.[136]

The social figure of the narcissist articulates the imagination of an uneasy society, rather than a manifest civilizational disease; it reveals and illustrates inner states that are difficult to verbalize and, thereby, a gruelling experience of time.[137] Corresponding explanatory approaches gain plausibility when norms lose their validity, or when a conflict develops between aspirations and the subjective opportunities for their realization. The image of the narcissist condenses regressive modernization processes whose unredeemed promises cause trauma. It is likely precisely the ambivalent emotional world of narcissism, between self-elevation, aggrievement and rejection, that provides a palpable frame for capturing the normative disorder.

— Chapter 5 —

LIBERTARIAN AUTHORITARIANISM: A MOVEMENT FOR A REIFIED FREEDOM

In 2017, we conducted a study to investigate the authoritarian downsides of civil-society engagement. At the time, we encountered people who had long been advocates of progressive social change or who had been active members of progressive citizens' initiatives, trade unions, social organizations or other kinds of associations, but now considered right-wing populist parties a more effective form of political participation (see chapter 8). In the course of an investigation of the so-called *Querdenker* protests during 2020, the first year of the pandemic, we observed people who were once active supporters of the peace movement and had cultivated an ecologically conscious lifestyle, and who were now taking to the streets to protest a 'health dictatorship' and a manipulative 'cartel of elites' (more on which in chapter 7). In public debate, we heard critical intellectuals who had once advocated a more just society and who now bewailed their being suffocated by the demands of cultural minorities (see chapter 6). Today, these particular groups of people, whom we shall turn to in greater detail in the following chapters, only constitute a fraction of society. And yet, many people have probably had one of the following (or similar) encounters: an uncle who perceives the admission of refugees into the country as a threat to his German identity; a friend who suspects a global conspiracy by Big Pharma behind the vaccination campaign during the pandemic; or a professor who invites a politician from the AfD to their lecture and then claims their freedom of speech is being violated when students protest.

Given their fundamental scepticism towards externally imposed restrictions and their insistence on their unimpeded self-development as individuals, these people appear, at least at first glance, as the self-reliant citizens that individualism has supposedly produced. They want to make independent choices for themselves and wish to comprehend and make sense of the world that surrounds them. However, in the articulation of their uneasiness, the insistence on the individual entitlement to negative freedom advances a destructive potential which is discharged in various expressions of dissidence, ranging from frivolous to aggressive. How can we explain this normative disorder in which political ideals once regarded as incompatible enter into a fateful union? How was it possible for the normative ideal of freedom to be fused with profoundly illiberal views?

Political scientist Wendy Brown regards the electoral successes of right-wing populism in the United States as the outcome of a neoliberal expansion of the private sphere to the detriment of a democracy that provides public goods such as economic and social security to its constituents.[1] From this angle, freedom and authoritarianism do not stand in contradiction but represent complementary aspects of an authoritarian neoliberalism. 'In short, expanding the "personal, protected sphere" and curtailing the reach of democracy in the name of freedom develops a new ethos of the nation.'[2] Yet for the idea of negative freedom to morph into aggressive nationalism, Brown notes, additional affective energies are required, which arise from a 'desublimation of the will to power'.[3] As Brown expounds with reference to Nietzsche and Marcuse, the neoliberal marginalization of the social dimension is accompanied by normative nihilism, indeed by a loss of conscience, and produces a kind of disinhibited freedom. It is a destructive freedom, which is 'joyous in its provocations and animated by aggrieved, vengeful reactions against those it holds responsible for its suffering or displacement.'[4]

At the same time, Brown's quite plausible explanation fails to grasp what we fleshed out as the core of libertarian authoritarianism in our studies, for the latter does not primarily identify with a nation or an authoritarian leader figure. The superior external authority is replaced with the self, in the sense of an autonomous subject. We conceive of *libertarian authoritarianism* as the symptom of a reified concept of freedom that serves to repel the acknowledgement of social dependencies. According to this notion, freedom is not a condition shared throughout society but rather an individual asset (see chapter 2). Sociologist Wilhelm Heitmeyer has also observed

125

a new type of authoritarianism, which he has termed 'anomic'. According to Heitmeyer, it is the result of emancipatory rather than oppressive processes of socialization.[5] We go one step further in our diagnosis. Although in late modernity the norms of autonomy and self-realization become increasingly more significant and individual scopes of freedom do actually grow in reality, this does nothing to reduce social dependence or control. Critical Theory pointed out this antagonistic character early on: '[S]ociety has enlarged, not individual freedom, but its control over the individual.'[6] We have seen that the dialectic of autonomy and assimilation has become more aggravated in late modernity: the orientation of individual lifestyles towards self-determination and self-experience is no longer coupled with demands for a different social order, but instead amounts to an assimilation to the norms of an individualist, competitive society.[7]

To summarize, there are two particular irresolvable contradictions of late modern subjectivity that make people susceptible to libertarian-authoritarian attitudes under certain conditions: on the one hand, individuals want to be addressed as *self-determined* subjects more than ever, while, at the same time, they have no control over the social conditions on the basis of which they are supposed to develop their competitive autonomy. On the other hand, late modern individuals see themselves as *critical* subjects who want to appropriate knowledge independently and question the knowledge of others. But here again, they encounter external boundaries: reality is becoming ever-more complex and increasingly difficult for the individual to see through. While these critical subjects are becoming ever-more distrusting, they are at the same time forced to trust anonymous experts (see chapter 3).[8] In other words, the libertarian-authoritarian protests are staging a rebellion *against* late modern society, but *in the name* of its most essential norms: self-determination and self-realization. It is this contradictory unity of identification and subversion that libertarian authoritarianism feeds on.

The libertarian-authoritarian personality structure

The Frankfurt School's theory of authoritarianism emerged against the historical backdrop of organized capitalism and the twentieth-century fascist dictatorships. In order to understand and explain the libidinously charged attachment to leader figures and the aggressive hostility towards weaker groups and outsiders, the structures and affective economies of modernity were studied. The standardized production of mass consumer goods corresponded to a self-ideal that rested on discipline, orderliness and diligence (see chapter 2), and was reproduced through strict educational methods. Experiencing violence from parents and teachers was a common feature of childhood socialization. The individual was integrated into the vertical hierarchy of bureaucratic institutions, which demanded considerable emotional impulse control. It was suspicious of emotions, as they were considered a sign of weakness. Efficiency and bureaucratic control merged with an orientation towards individual performance and social advancement. There were mass products that boosted consumption: the (washing powder manufacturer) Persil promised clean clothes, and housewives would use Dr Oetker products in the kitchen. Likewise, the democratization that followed after 1918 raised individual aspirations. Next came the chaotic years of hyper-inflation and economic crisis.[9] Critical Theory was extremely wary of the bureaucratic apparatus that restricted scopes of freedom – as the individual price of an 'administered world'[10] consisted of tormenting feelings of powerlessness and dependence (see chapter 1).

From the perspective of Critical Theory, authoritarianism offered a fateful way out for individuals: in blind submission to a personalized authority, perceived as overwhelmingly powerful, modern humans sought to rid themselves of their shackles. In order to deny their dependence on society, they voluntarily submitted themselves to a new incapacitation. 'It may well be the secret of fascist propaganda that it simply takes men for what they are: the true children of today's standardized mass culture, largely robbed of autonomy and spontaneity'.[11] Fascism benefits from this libidinous structure, Adorno notes.

Seeking a better understanding of these mechanisms, the Frankfurt sociologists studied Sigmund Freud's works on group psychology, as mentioned earlier. In his later work *Civilization and Its Discontents* (1930), the psychoanalyst describes how the individual comes into conflict with the requirements of an increasingly complex society, which they are only able to resolve by internalizing social norms through the development of a superego. Civilization and drive repression are ultimately synonymous. Freud therefore regards the individual urge for freedom not as a modern cultural asset but as an archaic residue which can erupt into rebellion against an inhibitive culture: 'The urge for freedom, therefore, is directed against particular forms and demands of civilization or against civilization altogether.'[12] Here, Critical Theory returns to the notion that it is precisely the rationality of cultural socialization that engenders irrational impulses: 'As a rebellion against civilization, fascism is not simply the reoccurrence of the archaic but its reproduction in and by civilization itself.'[13]

To Freud, the masses' attachment to a leader figure is the expression of a modern yearning for the primal father who rules over the primal horde with absolute power.[14] Freud wrote this against the backdrop of a patriarchal society in which the father figure still exercised 'socializational authority'.[15] These rules were not to be challenged – unless one was keen to get a beating. For sons (but not so much for daughters), submission also entailed a promise, as this turned them into part of this authority. The aggressive omnipotence of a leader figure, with whom the authority-abiding collective identifies, now resolves the ambivalence of modern subjectivity, just like the identification with the father: the desire for sovereignty in the face of dependence is projected onto this external figure, just like the ostracized aggression against the leader figure is projected onto weaker groups. For Freud, this figure emerged to a significant extent from narcissistic idealization: one loves the leader just like the narcissistic object, 'on account of the perfections which we have striven to reach for our own ego, and which we should now like to procure in this roundabout way'.[16] Erich Fromm, too, who was rather sceptical about the adoption of Freud by his Frankfurt colleagues, presents the authoritarian personality in sadomasochistic terms: 'He admires authority and tends to submit to it, but at the same time he wants to be an authority himself and have others submit to him.'[17]

A similar premise guided the empirical research of the Berkeley Group, whose findings were eventually published in the studies on *The Authoritarian Personality*. To recap: the F-scale was designed as a tool to record the attitudes and character traits of the authoritarian personality (see Introduction and chapter 1). Its development was geared towards the ambivalence of obedient submission and projective aggression described earlier. While the items on the sub-scales 'conventionalism' or 'authoritarian submission' were supposed to measure a pre-reflective obedience towards unquestioned authorities and social norms, those of the sub-scales 'authoritarian aggression', 'binary power thinking' or 'destructiveness' were designed to detect fantasies of omnipotence that were accompanied by aggressive hostility.[18]

The crucial question, however, is whether the twentieth-century theory of authoritarianism can still help us understand contemporary authoritarian phenomena that are happy to do without a commanding authority figure. Does the 'Obsolescence of Psychoanalysis',[19] which Herbert Marcuse observed as early as the 1960s, mean that the Critical Theory of authoritarianism is obsolete as well? Critical Theory saw the escape into authoritarianism as a regressive surrender of freedom through the establishment of new ties, be it to personalized authorities or to rigid value systems.[20] Alongside this traditional authoritarian personality, which can still be encountered today, a different type is coming to the fore more strongly.[21] It is oriented towards individual freedom, which is conceived of as a self-relation rather than a relationship with one's social environment: such reified freedom is to be consumed, experienced, invested, and ultimately denotes a raw, negative (economic) freedom that is pitted against all and any inhibiting state or other societal authorities. Marx, for his part, had mocked such a shallow liberal concept of freedom: 'It is the exclusive realm of Freedom, Equality, Property and Bentham.'[22] A similar notion is returning today (or, depending on one's point of view, has survived, without interruption, to this day). In the libertarian authoritarian personality type, people do not identify with an external authority but with their own ego.[23] Although they may temporarily form communities (such as for a collective protest against restrictions of freedom), they are not merged into a social group in the long run. They remain a loosely connected crowd of individuals. That is the reason why we speak of a *libertarian* para-type of the authoritarian. But how far are these individuals indeed authoritarian? After all, they explicitly reject any interference from above. What distinguishes them from mundane egoists?

In our view, it is, firstly, the hostile dismissal of anyone they consider to be flouting the individual right to freedom. Yet it is not only this aggressive rejection of other positions that substantiates their *authoritarian* character. They simultaneously harbour a grudge towards any superordinate authorities and project their rage onto weaker groups (women, trans people, migrants, Jews, etc.). Hence, they are *libertarian authoritarians* because they no longer feel obliged by any socially compelling norms, have shed all previously internalized consideration for others and are obsessively focused on an external threat. If classic authoritarianism was characterized by the simultaneity of aggressiveness and adjustment,[24] in the sub-type we studied this configuration appears to have dissolved in favour of the demonstration of one's own sovereignty. Libertarian authoritarians rebelliously defy any external authority.[25] They are assimilated only in the sense that they have thoroughly internalized the norms of competitive society.

The interesting question, then, is whether and – if so – in what way the psychodynamics of the personality structure has changed. With a view to twentieth-century authoritarianism, Critical Theory assumed that the juxtaposition of submission and empowerment is caused by an ego weakness. The ego of the authoritarian personality, which generally mediates between the superego's internalized adherence to norms and the libidinal desire of the id just as much as between the self and the outside world, is unable to achieve this synthesis.[26] This explains the exaggerated commitment to convention and the aggressive disregard for deviation and dissenters. It was precisely during organized modernity, which was based on emotional self-control, that the equilibrium of the psychodynamic lost its balance. Subsequent studies (the best-known of which are the ones conducted by Herbert Marcuse) identify the cause of post-1945 inner-psychological changes in the devaluation of the family as the key site of socialization. Although life in the nuclear family was certainly still marked by authoritarianism and violence during the twentieth century, it simultaneously constituted a private protected space. In welfare-state mass society, then, the scope of social institutions increases, which refers, among others, to mass media, schools and peer groups. In the afternoon, children watch *Tom & Jerry* on TV or stroll about outdoors with their friends, and only sit at a table with their parents at dinner time. The 'society without the father'[27] prevents the conflictive friction in which the ego is formed: '[t]he Ego Ideal is rather brought to bear on the Ego directly and "from outside", before the Ego is actually formed as the personal and (relatively) autonomous subject of mediation between him-self and the others', Marcuse writes.[28] He thereby seeks to explain the emergence of an assimilated mass of people who submit to an expanded reality principle. If Freud considered the reality principle a civilizing function of the ego, in Marcuse's reading it develops, in advanced capitalism, into an instrument of control which entails a 'surplus-repression': '[W]hile any form of the reality principle demands a considerable

LIBERTARIAN AUTHORITARIANISM

degree and scope of repressive control over the instincts, [...] the specific interests of domination introduce *additional* controls over and above those indispensable for civilized human association.'[29] Freud deduced the reality principle from material scarcity; there simply were not enough resources in pre-industrial societies to satisfy all individual needs. The individual had to restrain their desires but learned to prioritize and developed a conscience as a result. According to Marcuse, this is different in capitalist welfare-state societies. Here, there is an abundance of goods, though, at the same time, the merit principle is dominant. Individuals constantly have to prove themselves. Rigid behavioural norms become liberalized, while lust and passion are simultaneously constricted to the areas of consumption and sexuality. Desire is disinhibited *and* suppressed at the same time, and it is precisely this 'repressive desublimation', as Marcuse terms it, that leads to a loss of conscience (see chapter 1). Individuals in Western industrial societies tended towards authoritarian, anti-democratic attitudes because they had lost that mediating and deliberative self that can maintain a critical distance.

Today, we encounter a different form of the authoritarian personality. Late modern individuality is based not on the welfare state, mass consumption and self-control. Rather, it is built on deregulated self-responsibility, on the consumption of unique commodities and experiences as well as on an inflated demand for self-realization. It is no longer only the extent of repressive desublimation alone that precipitates aggressive impulses. Instead, contradictory social requirements are internalized. Gunnar Hindrichs points out that the 'rationalism of bourgeois society has absorbed hedonism'.[30] As a result, the ego is confronted with an insoluble dilemma: it needs to follow competitive society's rational logic of increase and escalation and is simultaneously supposed to incarnate an authentic, self-directed subject. But, still more: regardless of how much an effort individuals make (which, as self-responsible individuals, they are both committed and forced to do), they cannot satisfy the internalized expectations. This surely owes in part to the logic of increase and escalation inherent in the social norms themselves (success is insatiable, competition is all-pervasive, the search for one's self is potentially never-ending, etc.). But another reason is that they encounter structural obstacles which prevent them from living up to these norms (see chapter 2). Although one does everything to meet expectations – completing *Abitur*,[31] earning a degree – success fails to materialize nonetheless:

131

those countless applications do not lead to the desired job. Or, one sees oneself confronted with a paternalistic state that imposes barriers and restrictions on individuals – which one never agreed to but is expected to adhere to through one's own inner understanding (see chapter 3). The essential moment underlying the metamorphosis of the authoritarian character, however, is the shift of the process of socialization into the individual itself, which leads to inner tensions and humiliations (see chapter 4). The aggressive demonstration of one's own independence is simultaneously a *symptom* of late modern individualization and a *protest* against it.

What exactly does this mean? Although increasingly more people received rights and, to a limited extent, resources in order to meet society's expectations in late modernity, at the same time, the attainment of these objectives remains beyond their own control. Aversive emotions and forms of deviant behaviour are also increasing alongside contradictory or anomic configurations (see chapter 4). For example, the emphatic reference to the German Basic Law (*Grundgesetz* – Germany's equivalent of a constitution) during the COVID protests indicates not a rigid value conventionalism but rather a claim to individual entitlement to attaining society's objectives: I, as an autonomous subject, am entitled to freely shape my own life. The individuals who vocally lay claim to this consider that they have been cheated out of it. The promise of unrestricted self-realization turns into an experience of being offended when society fails to redeem it in the ways desired. Hence, the psychodynamic of libertarian authoritarians is not so much made up of a lack of integration of social norms into the personality structure. Rather, the entirely self-reliant ego is unable to cope with resolving potentially irresolvable conflicts. Although the individual is increasingly burdened with ever-more mediating responsibilities, they are unable to perform this mediation because these tensions are beyond the individual's capacity to process them. The ego of traditional psychoanalysis synthesized libidinal, or drive-based desire and internalized self-denial. The weakened ego of Critical Theory ceded unlimited control to the authorities of the id and superego. This is not fundamentally different in our day. Yet, today, it is becoming clearer that the cause of this weakness of the ego lies outside the instinctual dynamic, namely in a society that rests to equal degrees on disinhibition *and* abstinence, on freedom *and* dependence. The resulting libertarian authoritarian personality combines two opposing movements, 'so that centrifugal forces that go beyond society – especially those of hedonism, but also those of an authority that seeks friction with its opposite – can be mitigated'.[32] The individual seeks to improve and develop itself, realize its aspirations, satisfy its needs – and therefore defies society's authorities who fail to deliver on these promises.

Libertarian authoritarian personalities are no longer committed to a figure that promises relief and empowerment. The identification with external authorities is abandoned because the external world is a source of frustration. Libertarian authoritarians posit themselves as sovereign subjects instead. Through narcissistic self-overelevation, the dependence experienced is denied. They cultivate a reified concept of freedom that wards off any relationship with society. In this sense, the libertarian variant of the authoritarian personality can also be described as a relation of ostentatious social isolation. The blocked self-realization leads not so much to conflicts *in* reality but rather to a rebellion *against* reality. In extreme cases, these people construct an imaginary world of illusion in which abstract processes are given clear-cut forms. They regard Angela Merkel's refugee policy as a 'great replacement' or the COVID-19 vaccination campaign as an attempt by Bill Gates to control them through secretly implanted microchips (see chapter 7 and 8). These personalized substitute objects then serve as a surface for the projection of their aggressions. Within their paranoid activity, which struggles to cope with any kind of contingency or ambiguity, the world is decoded according to a standard pattern. As a result, reality becomes controllable – namely by one's own self.

Variants of libertarian authoritarianism

So, is the Critical Theory of authoritarianism obsolete? More than seventy years have passed since the original studies on *The Authoritarian Personality*. Society has changed, and, along with it, the social preconditions for people to develop anti-democratic, authoritarian attitudes. That said, the general approach itself is still apt even today. It proceeds from the assumption that the way in which capitalist societies integrate their members itself entails an authoritarian tendency. These societies control, discipline and direct individuals. In such societies, some people develop anti-democratic

133

character traits which may resemble one another, recurrently manifest themselves, and condense into a full-fledged syndrome. Alongside this general syndrome, which the historic study referred to as the 'potentially fascist personality', the research team identified six 'subsyndromes' or sub-types in which certain symptoms are particularly strongly developed or combined in characteristic ways.[33] These latter included the '*Surface Resentment*', in which stereotypes of prejudice are adopted from outside 'as ready-made formulae' (but which does not represent a full-fledged 'type' in the narrower sense); the '*Conventional*', who anxiously seeks external recognition and in whom the fear of deviating is dominant; the '*Authoritarian*' type, who vacillates between submission and aggression and is afraid of showing weakness (or, indeed, being weak); the '*Tough Guy*', in whose case repressed id tendencies gain the upper hand in a destructive form; the '*Crank*' and the '*Manipulative*' types, both of whom have retreated to an illusionary inner world of conspiracy theories or into a formulaic schematism that appears to be void of any emotions whatsoever.[34] The most frequently found types at the time were the '*Authoritarian*' and the '*Conventional*'.[35] They have certainly not disappeared today, but other types, which were rather peripheral and seemingly outlandish back then, are now becoming more visible: the *Tough Guy*, or '*Rebel*', who destructively direct their id-tendencies outwardly, and the '*Crank*', who replaces reality with an imaginary surrogate. While these last two figures played no significant role in the further adoption and refinement of the theory of authoritarianism, we consider them essential, namely as precursor types of libertarian authoritarianism.

In his work *Eclipse of Reason*, Horkheimer already pointed out as early as 1947 that the demanded 'renunciations of instinctual urges' in the civilizing process can trigger resistance within the individual. At the time, however, the 'hatred of civilization' was not so much triggered by the restriction of individual needs as by the broken promise of society to grant material security in return.[36] During the years of the world economic crisis, people worked hard, made many sacrifices, and practised restraint – and yet, not even that protected them from poverty. Just like Robert K. Merton, Horkheimer discerned a rebellious potential in this gulf between essential promises and frustrating reality. Yet the German social philosopher still considered the 'rebel' to be a progressive figure; after all, this type 'does not shrink from persistently confronting reality with truth, from unveiling the antagonism between ideals and actualities'.[37] However, the rebel can also have a regressive side. The authoritarian revolt during the mid-twentieth century entailed the resistance against the overpowering authority instead of an identification with it. In those cases, observed by Adorno, the resistance became a constant reaction to an inhibitive outside world: these people defied every figure of authority, even if it was conducive to their own interest. In trying to overcome their powerlessness in the face of an overpowering authority, they posited themselves in the position of that authority. The rebellion constituted an act of 'defiance'[38] against powers that obstructed independence, as Fromm put it. Adorno had in mind people like the Nazi Ernst Röhm. The long-standing head of the SA referred to himself as a rebel and wanted to establish a fascist popular militia, before Hitler had him assassinated for allegedly plotting a coup d'état in 1934.[39] The rebels develop a projective hostility towards weak authorities who assert their power only insufficiently. This 'negative transference [of dependency]'[40] was even more conspicuous the more strongly the tabooed feeling of one's own powerlessness had to be fought. One distinct feature which Adorno identified was a destructive disinhibition in the individual's actions, a tendency towards excess, or an inclination to violence. This was accompanied by a conscienceless nihilism, which was expressed through an indifference to individual existence.[41] The adherence to social norms appeared to have lost all and any meaning. To the Berkeley Group around Adorno, the rebel was rather marked precisely by the blanket rejection of a collectively shared value system, an attitude accompanied by a profound distrust of those institutions and officials who represented that system. An ostentatiously professed 'no' became the compelling action imperative, instead. Adorno attributed this rebellious stance to a failed development of the regulating ego and restricting superego, which he thought led to an unleashing of ambivalent libidinal energies vacillating between lust and aggression.[42] Yet, as Marcuse emphasized more than a decade later, in certain cases the 'instinctual hostility' may also result from the internalized system of norms itself: in his view, the identification with the competitive system's 'ego ideal' can, under certain conditions, cause an aggressive will for power which tolerates no inhibitive authority.[43] Given such demonstrations of sovereignty, one must not forget that the rebels back then did not entirely denounce authoritarian attachments.

135

They certainly submitted themselves – at least temporarily – to those who guaranteed the development of their individual power: in other words, the hostility towards authorities was at times accompanied by submission to the object of their hate.[44] In our studies, we mostly encountered the more civilized version of the *Rebel*. For example, they may refuse to pay the radio licence fees, possess a *Reichsbürger* passport or keep a food depot to be prepared for the coming uprising. That said, we did actually also encounter people who were in contact with the armed *Reichsbürger* scene or had temporarily been members of the (overtly Nazi party) NPD, fascinated by military drills and nihilist radicalism (more on this in chapter 8).

This brings us to another supporting act which has today taken on a larger role: the so-called *Crank*, as this type was referred to in the past. Of course, we would no longer speak of a *Crank* today, yet the type of conspiracy theorist that this term denotes is all too familiar to us. These people reacted to frustrations by breaking with the reality principle. A form of privation that was imposed on them drove them into complete isolation: 'They have to build up a spurious inner world, often approaching delusion, emphatically set against outer reality.'[45] They had lost touch with reality because it no longer seemed tolerable to them. In this context, Adorno reports of a woman in her fifties who indicated during an interview that she was a member of a secret order but that she could say no more about the matter. She did not care too much for her fellow workers but felt superior to them. Although her colleagues at work were unaware, she explained, she was gifted with special talents. She read a lot, and after her husband's death she started to write herself. Yet she hardly ever showed the stories she had written to other people. When she spoke about 'race questions', about Afro-Americans or migrants, she gave free rein to her xenophobia and antisemitism: 'Japs, Jews, and N[*] should go back where they came from.' She lost herself in antisemitic conspiracy theories. Ever since she had had an experience of awakening, she believed in her own 'individualistic religion', her 'inner voices'.[46]

For this woman, epistemic secession represented a tool for self-empowerment. Although the group identified by the research team as *Cranks* were driven by paranoia, which allowed no turning back or reflection, this paranoia simultaneously provided them with a sense of being sovereign subjects. They were caught in a state of total dependence on the self-fabricated imagination, and yet – paradoxically – they felt free. The humiliations suffered led to the formation of a binary mode of perception that knew only good or evil and thereby provided their aggression with an object. The *Crank* was 'highly projective and suspicious', prejudice was vital to them.[47] Their fragile integrity was held together by the image of an external enemy, in which persistent, mostly antisemitic or racist stereotypes were revealed. A 'magical belief in science'[48] combined fragments of scientific knowledge into a unified worldview. That is to say, science, which is guided by methodology and empiricism, served as the very means by which the *Crank* could create an imaginary reality. To this day, conspiracy theory adherents operate with 'half-truths'; they cherry-pick their material while omitting essential elements.[49] What matters is the production of a semantic definiteness that provides an explanation for the opaque and frustrating outside world. Adorno observed a desire for taking revenge in return for the deprivation suffered, which fuelled the creative imagination, but which simultaneously prevented any kind of reconciliation. Here, the compulsion to repeat resurfaces, which characterizes many aversive emotions (see chapter 4). For only in their illusory reality can the subject retain their sovereignty. Through their enraged gaze at vulnerable groups and minorities, the *Crank* constituted themselves as a powerful authority. From this position, the *Crank*, instead of being the object of social contempt, became the authority that passed judgement themselves. This type of *Crank* from the past refers to people with a deficient social integration whose 'isolation is socially reinforced by their virtual exclusion from the economic process of production'.[50] In other words: people who cancelled out the anomic pressure weighing on them through an imaginary inversion of reality. In our conversations with *Querdenker* and regressive rebels, we came across similar narratives (see chapters 7 and 8). Time and again, we heard accounts of experiences of awakening or revival – which had nothing to do with religion but caused a transformation of perspective: one sees everything differently now, one is able to connect the dots and one is aware that there is a master plan behind it all.

Indeed, these two types, the modernized version of which we will get to know in more detail in the following chapters, manage largely without a leader figure, but not entirely without 'secondary bonds'.[51] In this case, the personalized authority is replaced with 'an idea, an abstraction' that serves a similar function.[52] Marcuse noted that such ideas could include '[t]he National Purpose or Capitalism or Communism or simply Freedom' – albeit with the limitation that, given their abstract generality, they were only partly suitable for libidinal, narcissistic identification. And yet, this is precisely what we can observe in libertarian authoritarianism: the reified freedom imago represents a projection surface for unsatisfied desires and wishes, which, once they are unleashed, can develop a regressive, aggressive energy. Social philosopher Oliver Decker, who is conducting the Leipzig Authoritarianism Studies together with his team, also assumes, with reference to Marcuse, that the authoritarian identification in post-war Germany was tied to an abstract object: according to Decker, the economy became a 'narcissistic filling'. The (West) German economic miracle served as a defence against a narcissistic humiliation – caused by the lost war and the defeat of fascism. Henceforth, it was the capitalist norms and ideals that stabilized self-confidence and allowed for a positive identification with the nation.[53] In her analysis of neo-authoritarianism, philosopher Eva von Redecker indirectly updates this thought: in her view, a new authoritarianism is engendered by the structure of neoliberal socialization as such, which may guarantee legal equality in formal terms, but which simultaneously materially dispossesses people. Neo-authoritarians identify, in a regressive manner, with the logic of ownership and property, precisely because they are being stripped of it. In their rage against cultural minorities, Redecker explains, we are seeing the discharge of a lost 'freedom of the wounded owner defending his phantom possession and refusing any social contract that does not restore it to him'.[54] The authoritarian build-up shifts from the economic sphere to that of cultural identity: whiteness or masculinity. A similar observation can be made with regard to libertarian authoritarianism, even though this latter does not necessarily identify with essentialist identities as is the case in the neo-authoritarianism of right-wing populism (see chapter 6).

In our view, the aggressive disinhibition of libertarian authoritarianism can be understood in the sense of an identification with the norms of a competitive society, which harbour a destructive, aggressive and excessive potential. We have seen that the competitive worldview can coincide with narcissistic fantasies of superiority and authoritarian mindsets. The rebel type, in its libertarian variant, does not negate the social authority against which it is staging a revolt. This

138

type's protest is based precisely on the affirmation *and* destruction of social norms. The origin of the rebels' destructive behaviour, in reference to Merton, is the identification with universally recognized objectives (autonomy and self-realization, performance and success), which come into conflict with the social reality of those who are moving down the social escalator. The combination of subjectively experiencing external blockages and a simultaneous lack of power to act entails the danger of radicalization not only because this constitutes a violation of individual aspirations, but also because it aggrieves the integrity of the fragile self that seeks stability within these norms. Indeed, libertarian authoritarians did relate two very distinct stories of humiliation and taking offence. What unites them all, however, is that they perceive their self-determination and sovereignty as impaired by state intervention, the elites or cultural minorities. In this sense, they question not the society that has repeatedly led them into dead ends throughout their individual biographies, but they aggressively project their humiliations onto substitute objects. In the process – similar to right-wing populism – a marginalized masculinity asserts itself, disquieted by the feminization of labour and the progressive changes in norms.[55] Erstwhile members of the alternative milieus see themselves threatened by refugees who were admitted into the country in 2015, the fallen intellectuals see themselves suffocated by a 'cancel culture', and the *Querdenker* are taking to the streets against global elites. And, even today, the hostile projection entails expressions of racist, misogynist and antisemitic stereotyping.

Alongside the rebel, the sub-type Adorno referred to as *Crank*, with its affinity to conspiracy-theory thinking and prejudice, is also returning more forcefully today. The conspiracy theory adherents we observed renounce the reality principle in order to escape social pressure. Their ego balances tensions out by modelling reality in accordance with the respective desires. Conspiracy theories or paranoid explanations of the world compensate for the reality of barriers and deprivations by creating a spectre of sovereignty based on exclusive stocks of knowledge: in this view, the world process is systematically directed by dark powers, whose existence is known only to privileged individuals – who can 'see' or are 'awakened' or 'revived'. Coronavirus sceptics not only question the danger of the COVID-19 disease but, along with it, the state's authority to enact measures that restrict the individual's freedom to act (see chapter 7). In this sense, the conspiracy theory adherent can be understood as a symptom of epistemic conflicts, with broken promises and experiences of humiliation being channelled via corresponding narratives. As we have seen, the risk and threat scenarios in late modernity multiply, while experiences of contingency and their own inability to know are increasing. The position of the omnipotent leader figure has been taken by exclusive knowledge which subjectively generates agency – regardless of (a lack of) objective verifiability of this knowledge. The immersion in alternative knowledge further reinforces the outward isolation, though it can create internal group cohesion. The paranoid worldview thus advances a dysfunctional social integration by associating individuals not with society but with a temporary community of like-minded individuals. In this context, knowledge – or, rather, counter-knowledge – serves the function of creating a community which constructs a collective universe of meaning and accommodates the narcissistic illusion of sovereignty. The followers participate in a supposedly 'better' knowledge through which reality can be properly decoded.

One essential question is why some people drift off into imaginary worlds or embrace the aggressive revolt against all superordinate authorities, while others do not. Although we shall not be able to present any conclusive answers to this question, we do believe that we have identified certain socio-cultural milieus which are – to varying degrees – susceptible to a regressive processing of social tensions.

Social spaces of aggrieved self-affirmation

If we want to understand why people who see themselves as critical and autonomous individuals stage a destructive protest against any form of social constraint, taking a closer look at the internal differentiations in socio-cultural lifestyles might be helpful. Contemporary societies are developing fairly unevenly not only in terms of social structures, but also with regard to binding values and behavioural norms. All social milieus develop their own distinct lifestyles, complete with their own everyday norms and web of relationships. The milieus' members identify with these and thereby distinguish themselves from other groups.[56] Historian Sven Reichardt therefore understands social milieus to be 'lived "interpretive communities"'.[57] Their expressive lifestyles not only convey competing normative values. They also correspond to different socio-structural positions.

140

Ostentatious claims to exclusivity and status, for example, are considered typical features of the conservative milieu of the upper classes, whereas feelings of being left behind are more characteristic of the precarious milieu of the lower classes. Internally, these milieus are, of course, anything but fully homogeneous. They are marked by an 'internal diversity and distinctness of lifestyles'[58] – and, we may add, of moral values.

Most individuals we studied come from milieus whose primary feature is a 'striving for autonomy and self-realization, as opposed to social patronization, restriction and alienation'.[59] In other words, they come from progressive social milieus which few would suspect of authoritarian attitudes. Although we cannot say with any certainty whether libertarian authoritarianism is particularly widespread within these milieus, its existence among these milieus might give us an idea of the changes within the social space. Thus, our aim is not to redefine social milieus in terms of authoritarian thought patterns; that would in fact constitute a comprehensive research project in its own right.[60] Based on the metamorphoses especially of progressive social milieus, we can approach the socio-cultural sources of libertarian authoritarianism heuristically, which allows for identifying *spheres of aggrieved self-affirmation*.

Existing milieu studies highlight the diversity of expressive lifestyles in correlation to the respective availability of resources and therefore provide a suitable starting point for our inquiry. The most comprehensive – albeit not undisputed – studies are the milieu studies conducted by the Sinus Institute from the 1970s onwards. They were developed for commercial target group research and consider preferences in taste, lifestyle and consumption patterns.[61] In the 1990s, sociologist Michael Vester and his colleagues returned to the results of the Sinus studies, but mapped out a different landscape of social milieus that was largely based on the theory of French sociologist Pierre Bourdieu. Their aim was to explore, based on quantitative surveys and 'two-generation interviews' (in which parents were interviewed together with their children), the way in which lifestyles become individualized and to what extent this is influenced by socio-structural position.[62] In this context, they were particularly interested in 'the modes of behaviour concerning social dissociation and exclusion, the stance regarding social inequality and the forms of social cohesion or anomie'.[63] The elective affinities matching these milieu characterizations and the normative dilemmas that we believe

141

heighten the likelihood of drifting towards libertarian authoritarianism are, quite simply, astonishing.

Most individuals we interviewed come from the middle class, often have a medium to high level of education as well as an alternative, individualist self-image. They are influenced by a milieu metamorphosis that has now been underway for several decades, whose origins lie in the now-modernized and no longer coherently existing alternative milieu, whose members were once united, following the protest year of 1968, by a shared 'commitment to and demands for self-realization and personal development, individuality and authenticity'.[64] This alternative milieu was once characterized by an independently organized infrastructure as well as its own characteristic lifestyles and rituals, based on emancipatory value orientations.[65] In particular, its members included academics in professions with considerable social prestige, but also school pupils and university students who would later move into higher income groups. After 1980, the political mission and the rigorism of alternative lifestyles receded. The alternative milieu was replaced by what Vester calls a 'postmodern milieu', often a blend of the aesthetic avant-garde and social climbers from the culture, media, technology and service sectors.[66] Instead of utopian field trials of alternative lifestyles, an individualism charged with avant-gardism now became dominant. Members of the postmodern milieu 'enacted their self-understanding as aesthetic avant-garde' and understood their 'urge for experience, consumption and variation as an egocentric privilege without any restricting responsibilities'.[67] Norms such as autonomy or authenticity acquired a new meaning: autonomous subjectivity no longer implied an emancipatory horizon, but a quest for spontaneity and uniqueness, which was to be realized within the immanence of Being.[68] Libertarian authoritarianism, in our view, is also – albeit not exclusively – a movement of avant-gardists who have lost their political home.

Indeed, a closer look at the social milieus of contemporary societies reveals that the individuals we studied, in their normative self-image, are neither conservative in the traditional sense nor geared towards normative re-orientation. They comprise, firstly, primarily *former* modernizers, whose everyday behaviour is guided by individualist or hedonistic values, albeit often with a simultaneously internalized exclusive status awareness. If we position this group on the map of the Sinus studies – which represents the social position on the vertical axis and the cultural orientation and lifestyle on the horizontal axis – it seems appropriate to first take a look at those milieus that are positioned in the middle to upper layers on the vertical axis and in the centre to centre-right on the horizontal axis indicating the lifestyle (see Figure 1). These are the upper social milieus, which Andreas Reckwitz associates with the lifestyle of *'expressive individualism'*:[69] people who strive towards self-realization and simultaneously exhibit a pronounced status-oriented and materialist mentality. Secondly, however, we observed a highly heterogeneous range of individuals who are located between middle to precarious positions, but who are also part of a milieu that is less conservative, conformist or performance-oriented and far more strongly oriented towards values like individualism and pleasure. The goal of self-realization is pursued through an experience-oriented lifestyle, despite limited material resources. Members of this milieu ostentatiously dissociate themselves from the deontology of the traditional petty bourgeoisie and working-class milieus.

In the higher social positions, there is the 'post-materialist [or "liberal-intellectual"] milieu', which comprises around 7 per cent of the German population.[70] This is where the critical-humanistic educated elite is concentrated, who, for the most part, have higher-education degrees and middle to high incomes. This milieu encompasses an above-average number of freelancers, but also highly skilled white-collar workers or upper-level civil servants. Its members express liberal and cosmopolitan values and pursue post-materialist lifestyles: 'They seek to create free spaces for themselves (including to elude factual constraints), strive for time sovereignty and deceleration.' The desire for individual sovereignty is reflected, among other things in the appropriation of new knowledge. They cultivate 'a critical, reflected stance towards the media and its content' and 'prefer to proactively look for information and background knowledge by themselves'. Members of the post-materialist milieu substantiate their social position with their achievements and – despite their orientation towards social justice – emphasize the principle of self-responsibility.[71] 'Their distinct work and performance ethic', Vester and her colleagues wrote of the 'progressive educated elite' more than twenty years ago, 'is connected to the sense of self-realization and self-display, but also to the progressive-elitist urge to explore new and unconventional paths and start modern trends'.[72]

143

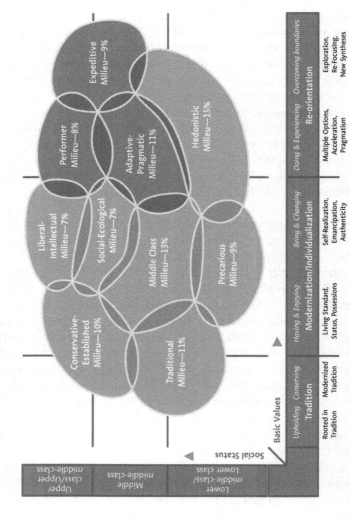

Figure 1: Sinus Milieus in Germany 2020/21
Source: Sinus Institute (2021), *Die Sinus-Milieus in Deutschland*, Heidelberg.

Today, the last-named elitist and avant-gardist self-orientation is more strongly embodied by the 'performer milieu', which comprises around 8 per cent of the total population.[73] These people also have higher education degrees and middle to high incomes. They frequently have middle to executive management positions and see themselves as the 'modern elite'; and yet, these latter define themselves through 'consumption, design preferences and lifestyle' rather than pursuing the classic educational ideal. The conspicuous pretentious consumption is accompanied by a 'strong orientation towards efficiency, competition and one's professional career', which is associated with 'striving for self-realization and an intense lifestyle'. The competitive individualists advocate open competition; individuality and freedom are the most important values to them. Their basic orientation is summarized in the Sinus studies as follows: 'Everyone is responsible for their own fortune; everyone must know for themselves what they can perform and achieve.' The performers are confident of their achievements and display this pride via material status symbols.

The 'socio-ecological [or "neo-ecological"] milieu' can be regarded as the residue of the former alternative milieu, as its members exhibit a socially critical and engaged self-image. This milieu represents about 7 per cent of the total population. Its average age of 51 years is fairly high, with its members from the old alternative milieu now working in non-executive high-skilled professions. Apart from this group, this social space is dominated by other individuals with emancipatory moral values. They often combine their post-material claims with civil society engagement and counter-cultural communities: 'Many have very specific ideas about what is right and good, make an effort to set an example for a sustainable lifestyle (diet, housing, energy, mobility) and seek – at times with a pronounced sense of mission – to convince others to follow suit.' According to their own self-image, they are tolerant, multicultural, ecologically minded, show solidarity and dissociate themselves from materialistic and competitive ideals. They posit a decelerated lifestyle, which is marked by a 'striving for authenticity, wholeness and balance', in opposition to the performance principle. The guiding values are 'freedom, responsibility, self-realization [or "self-actualization"], as well as mindfulness [...] and sensuousness', often dusted with spiritualism and the esoteric. They reject an exclusive, pretentious status consciousness and 'mainstream' taste alike; instead, they yearn – frequently with a tendency towards nostalgia and idyll-mongering – for authenticity and naturalness. Needless to say, this holdover of alternative culture has long lost its leading social role as dominant counter-culture. In middle to lower social positions, we find the 'hedonists', who make up around 16 per cent of society. They are relatively young and have basic to mid-level education qualifications. It is a heterogeneous milieu of skilled workers and foremen (or forewomen), clerks and mid-level staff.[74] Vester and his colleagues identified this milieu with a juvenile urge for distinction, marked by 'radical anti-conformism and individualism'.[75] In contemporary society, the attitude of individualist obstinacy is not necessarily limited to a transitional phase in life and can also represent a constant basic orientation. These people want to live their lives 'spontaneously and without restrictions'. They strive for an intensification of experiences, which follows an inherent logic of increase and escalation: it is not so much a matter of *what* is actually experienced, the important thing is to generate *new* experiences. This restless search is underlain, however, by a yearning for 'social acceptance', which sets it apart from the self-assured basic orientations which were possible to observe in higher social positions. The site of their self-realization is not a regulated – at times exhausting and meaningless – wage labour, but their free time, in the sense of a 'refuge for unprogrammed living'. Here, it is possible to play out all that which the world of work – based on duty performance as it is – cannot provide: 'as few restricting responsibilities as possible, if any, and no stress; adjustment where necessary, freedom where possible'.[76] Their inner normative economy is adjusted in accordance with these precepts. An orientation towards social advancement and short-term sacrifice in favour of long-term goals can only rarely be observed. The metamorphoses in the social space point to a rather differentiated history of individualization. During the nineteenth and twentieth centuries, individualism constituted a progressive demand raised by social liberalism, which sought to create a collective general framework in order to increase the individual's opportunities in life. The reified concept of freedom, which is today virulently asserting itself in many social milieus, has only very little in common with the former. Here, freedom no longer means being able to lead an independent life, free from state interference, and to move within a context of collectively established rules and norms. Instead, it signifies an overelevation of one's own autonomy which denies its dependence on society – and can become authoritarian as a result.

146

Triggers for an authoritarian drift

We concerned ourselves with the question of why some people from these milieus develop a tendency towards libertarian authoritarian positions under certain conditions – a question that can hardly be answered definitively. After all, libertarian authoritarianism is neither a reaction by *all* members of these milieus nor it is the *only* possible way to react to frustrating or immanently contradictory situations. The disposition for developing aversive affects varies individually and is rather difficult to objectify. Furthermore, negative forms of reaction are by no means necessarily as regressive or destructive as in the case of libertarian authoritarianism. The dilemmas of modernization have always mobilized a wide range of affects and actions, and there is a broad spectrum of possibilities between the two extremes of apathy or aggression. That is to say, whoever seeks to relate authoritarian attitudes and behaviours with specific social spaces is confronted with a series of pitfalls. Although it is not the membership in a certain milieu that leads to libertarian authoritarianism, many libertarian authoritarians in our study population come from the social milieus mentioned.

We were keen nonetheless to understand why the individuals we studied are more vulnerable in their reaction to the dilemmatic configurations of late modern socialization and develop inclinations towards libertarian authoritarianism under certain conditions. For while the vertical social positions vary, libertarian authoritarianism appears to be a phenomenon which predominantly emerges along those basic orientations based on self-determination, self-realization or hedonism. One possible explanation might be that these social milieus are more thoroughly affected by regressive liberalization (see chapter 3). Although not all of the depicted milieus exhibit an intrinsic orientation towards performance or achievement (take, for example, the socio-ecological or the hedonistic milieus), but the members of these groups, too, want to lead a self-directed life (be it in an alternative niche or in their free time). Experiences of anomie come in widely varied forms in everyday reality. We encountered, in particular, the following preconditions which facilitate (but do not necessarily mean) the development of libertarian authoritarian attitudes in anomic configurations.

Disruptive setbacks: our conversation partners frequently reported a momentous event in their lives that had caused them to undergo a radical inner conversion. This might include biographical ruptures such as the loss of one's job, or sickness, or state interventions like the restrictions on movement during the coronavirus pandemic. The self-directed life is confronted with a sudden restriction. One can no longer travel freely, no longer indulge in carefree consumption, etc. In order to protect one's own self-image, it is proactively defended against the external threat. Some might recall the TV images of the second pandemic winter (2021), when people who were denied access because they had no vaccination certificates stormed Christmas markets. In extreme cases, this perceptual pattern radicalizes, emancipating itself from its original catalyst and generalizing into an affective world experience. In this case, the grudge is tied to a general suspicion towards superordinate authorities.

Narcissistic resilience: Experiences of dissonance can also lead to changes in the self-image. Some people, especially those from the socio-ecological milieu, see themselves as tough individuals who emerge even stronger from great misfortunes. Resilience is commonly regarded as psychological adaptability that allows for enduring and coping with crises.[77] In the cases we studied, a resilient self-perception, in contrast, led to a subjective dissociation from the social world. This may also affect people who attribute themselves a great deal of resilience, who believe in the self-regulating forces of the human body, who can decide what is good for themselves, who display a strong desire for self-reflection and cultivate techniques of self-care (such as yoga or a healthy eating). This self-image is often accompanied by a striving for a naturalness that needs to be protected from harmful outside influences. These people draw their faith from lifeworld competence, which requires no mediating authorities or external knowledge, from a pre-rational intuition that provides explanation without requiring an explanation itself. Here, resilience transforms into a narcissistic self-empowerment, while feelings of powerlessness or dependence can be blocked out.

Limits to the critical mind: a complementary variant of self-empowerment feeds on an absolutization of the enlightened mind, the desire to fully comprehend the world and be able to critically assess existing stocks of knowledge. This is what provides people from the post-materialist (or liberal-intellectual) milieu with their self-confidence ('having something to say', 'having a critical opinion', etc.). They generate their knowledge from carefully curated sources, and challenge the knowledge of others on this basis. What can cause an identity crisis under certain conditions is not so much the revision of knowledge as one's own *inability-to-know*. Palpable limits to one's own critical judgement are experienced as a painful humiliation, which is compensated through anti-scientific resentment. In following the logic of increase and escalation that underlies this aversive affect, the critique threatens to develop a momentum of its own. The corresponding individuals become renegades who cultivate a rather instrumental relationship with the objects of their critique. What matters is not so much *what* is being critiqued, but that something *is* being subjected to critique. Critical reasoning becomes detached from its specific substance and turns into an end in itself. What all these respondents share is the tendency to provoke and to be suspicious, the latter of which can, in extreme cases, turn against everything and everyone. This empty demonstration that one is relying on one's own judgement serves the self-assertion as a sovereign subject of knowledge.

Inability: while the feeling of dependence constitutes a general world experience for people in precarious milieus, high-performing individuals use social institutions to realize their value orientations; to them, the volatile and competitive market harbours a potential for self-realization. They successfully adjust themselves to a world faced with which they are powerless. If, however, this adjustment comes to nothing, if success fails to materialize despite all efforts, the identification with the norms of competitive society changes over into a feeling of inability or inadequacy. All of a sudden, people in secure positions experience themselves as vulnerable, unable to realize their competences. A common reaction in this case is a regressive negation of dependence, which questions not the norm itself but rather those deemed to be receiving unjustified gratifications. Their rage towards these latter provides them with purpose and agency. For example, we spoke with open-minded and socially engaged people who developed xenophobic positions after an experience of social decline. This apparent abandonment of their erstwhile attitudes becomes clearer when we reflect the value systems on which their self-relation and relation to the world is based: these systems are relational norm repositories, which actuate a competitive mode of social comparison and facilitate negative emotions such as envy and prejudice. At the same time, they entail an inherent exponentiation dynamic, which not even the top-performers can keep up with. Trying to meet the norm leaves individuals with a feeling of powerlessness.

Paradoxes of liberalization: discontent, according to Alexis de Tocqueville, does not only result from disrupted norms. The French historian came to a different conclusion: namely, that it was precisely the advancing implementation of egalitarian ideals that led to a greater sensitivity for inequalities (see chapter 4). This also applies to the individualist normative economy in contemporary societies. Never before have the members of the upper and middle social positions been as free as today – and that is precisely why the perception of shortcomings in individual freedom is rising. In this context, Zygmunt Bauman saw the danger that freedom would become the de-politicized demand of a privatized individual.[78] We have termed this phenomenon 'reified freedom'. Instead of the major questions pertaining to political freedom, the main point of concern is the maximization of individual freedom in everyday life. These individuals dream of a house in the countryside, want to work from home, shop around the clock – or, better yet, have the groceries delivered.

If we consider the metamorphosis of the milieus against this backdrop, the aforementioned can be localized socio-spatially, too. The place of the alternative milieu, which combined an emancipatory idea with individualist values, was taken by the so-called 'postmodernists', who continued to adhere to the norms of autonomy and self-realization and self-determination but regarded this as an utterly individual affair:[79] a self-image that is by all means compatible with the 'entrepreneurial self'.[80] Ingolfur Blühdorn notes that although the transcendental substance is lost, the inscribed logic of disinhibition is not (see chapter 3): one wants more freedom in the here and now (especially given that it can only be realized in fragmented ways).[81] Liberalization can thus prompt a countervailing development, namely emotionally charged conflicts around private freedom, particularly in times when individual scopes of freedom are being restricted by the government.

Normative hardening: another aspect concerns the changes in social norms and their continuity. When the social space becomes more open, even if only partially, the dominant value systems change as well – and this plays out unevenly across generations. The US political scientists Ronald Inglehart and Pippa Norris take the change in moral values as a starting point to explain the rise of right-wing populist parties in post-industrial societies.[82] According to these authors, disruptive liberalization threatens the identity of that generation oriented towards traditional values, i.e., the family, religion or the nation. When liberal values dominate the public discourse and political decisions, the overarching social norms structure can disintegrate and activate authoritarian values in older generations without higher education – resulting in the onset of a cultural backlash (see chapter 3). Although the individuals in our study sample have fairly little in common with the traditionalist and conservative voters of right-wing populist parties, non-simultaneities between generations can cause normative hardening.

The reason is that the people we studied feel part-restricted in their personal integrity and everyday life as the result of a change in moral values. A middle-aged generation in higher social positions, still strongly oriented towards individualization and consumerism, is now confronted with a younger generation that has internalized a profound awareness of climate change and is advancing a sharp critique of the older generation's hedonistic lifestyles. Moreover, segments of the older representatives of the liberal-intellectual milieu, who identify with an exclusive discursive position on behalf of – wholly progressive – values, are being challenged precisely because of their claim to opinion leadership. One possible response to this is the radicalization of one's own basic orientations, which can morph into authoritarianism. In order to justify their consumerist attitude, some of them become climate change deniers.[83] Others give free rein to their frustration over rules and regulations, for example, by interpreting trigger warnings or sensitive language conventions as a politics of exclusion. A logic of increase and escalation develops, in which formerly socially established individuals can manoeuvre themselves into a marginalized position: the exclusive position is defended through closure and radicalization, whereby self-assertion is followed by self-exclusion (see chapter 6).

—— Chapter 6 ——

THE DEMISE OF THE TRUTH SEEKERS: FALLEN INTELLECTUALS

'It could have been our moment to shine', noted Hans Ulrich Gumbrecht in the *Neue Zürcher Zeitung*. Yet then he remarked, with some disillusionment: 'But never before in the two-and-a-half centuries since the public sphere emerged as a forum for all people in society, have we intellectuals appeared as pathetic as we did in the summer of 2020.'[1] When the literary scholar and journalist wrote these words, the world was just letting out a sigh of relief after its first spring under COVID-19. The pandemic had brought 'rising uncertainties', and scientists were confronted with a new and extremely dynamic phenomenon. We may easily think that confusing times call for clarification and explanation. And surely, there was a mass of intellectual interpretations on offer: philosophical jargon seeped into public debate, and there was talk of 'biopolitics', 'necropolitics', the 'state of exception' and even the 'disruption of reality'. So, what exactly was Gumbrecht complaining about? He observed two rival phenomena: while European intellectuals were retreating 'obediently into ethical-moral support for social distancing and the obligation to wear a mask' during the pandemic, rather than critically scrutinizing the government's actions, at the same time 'academic intellectuals' were establishing 'a terror regime of opinion dictatorship at American universities'. In that case they had displayed true Jacobin exuberance – knocking down monuments, renaming buildings and ostracizing some of their colleagues, who in some cases were even sacked.

These two phenomena lead Gumbrecht to conclude that intellectual discourse has become 'tautological': 'With stubborn seriousness, they merely reiterate what has already been established as the harmonious majority opinion anyway.' For Gumbrecht, who counts himself among the ranks of intellectuals (speaking of 'We intellectuals'), this represented something new. According to Gumbrecht, the intellectual has assumed three functions in history: from the progressive educator at the universities, via the revolutionary stirring up the masses, and then on to the intellectual advocate for the weak and underprivileged. All three roles have now been made obsolete by social progress, Gumbrecht claims. The focus in the universities is more on pragmatic professional training than on searching for the truth and new insights. The welfare state lures the working class into making their peace with capitalism. And oppressed minorities have long started voicing their demands independently. In Gumbrecht's view, philosopher Peter Sloterdijk is the only one who is still able to open new 'horizons' of thinking – such as in his strident criticism of the SPD's tax policy in 2009 – rather than obeying the 'ethical seriousness' of the majority opinion. With the exception of Sloterdijk, Gumbrecht finds himself missing a 'libertarian' or 'contrarian' 'risky thinking' among his colleagues. Yet, he also overlooks something: namely, that his reasoning is itself a symptom of a late modern metamorphosis of intellectuals, albeit of a different one than he is criticizing.

'The' intellectual is commonly regarded as a widely educated person (and, historically, usually imagined as a man), who uses their privileged access to knowledge to make themselves heard in *public*. This brings to mind the *'Manifestes des intellectuels'* in the context of the Dreyfus affair, the impassioned 'I accuse!' (*'J'accuse!'*) which writer Émile Zola directed at the French president in 1898 to protest the conviction of Jewish army officer Alfred Dreyfus for high treason.[2] In those days, the modern 'public sphere as an authority of critique' of the state was established.[3] When we think of intellectuals, we usually have in mind writers, scholars, artists or journalists who advocate for universal norms and who speak on behalf of a superior morality, of oppressed minorities, or even of humankind as a whole. Intellectuals, who are themselves powerless, are commonly located on the side of counter-power.[4] Seeing as they usually do not belong to a specific social class or stratum with partisan political and material interests, they have often been referred to as 'socially unattached intelligentsia', who have a clear view of reality.[5] In other words, intellectuals are often depicted as outsiders who possess 'insider knowledge' about society.[6] Just like referees, they observe the game and know exactly when they have to show a red card.

This 'universal' or 'general'[7] concept of intellectuals – the educating sceptic or the critically intervening interferer – had a major influence on how they were perceived until well into the twentieth century.[8] Intellectuals embody change and progress. Our view of intellectuals is doubtless influenced by a certain progressive bias: scholarly custodians of conservatism, who promote constancy instead of progress, order instead of change, are less frequently identified with this type.[9] At the same time, conservative voices played a vital role in the intellectual foundation of the Federal Republic (i.e., West Germany) following World War II – which is also why they were sometimes portrayed as opponents of intellectuals, as authority-obeying 'Mandarins', if not downright 'counter-intellectuals'.[10]

In highly differentiated risk societies, the notion of the general intellectual who issues an 'incompetent yet legitimate critique'[11] appeared to become obsolete during the final third of the twentieth century.[12] All of a sudden, there was a high demand for experts on specific subject areas who were able to predict and calculate certain risks. Natural scientists warned of the dangers of acid rain and chlorofluorocarbons (CFCs). Their expertise became political, as it affected all of humanity. Writers like Günther Grass or Martin Walser, who had once been regarded as the 'conscience of the nation', may not have fallen silent, but they faced increasing competition. Specialists were now needed instead of generalists. In some segments of the liberal-intellectual milieu, however, a contrary development has occurred in recent years: the general intellectual has returned, albeit, at times, as a *regressive opponent* of social change.

In this chapter, we explore intellectual discourses that thwart the modern equations of 'universalism equals progress' and 'particularism equals regression', resulting in indistinct political interferences. In an initial approach, these disorders could be described, in reference to Diedrich Diederichsen, as 'post-ideological *Querfronts*',[13] in which the semantics of political norms changes and certain concepts are inverted. The intellectuals we shall encounter in the following emphatically invoke, for instance, their independence or universal values – but defend sectional positions. They feel patronized by their antagonists and consider threatened their freedom to speak their mind. Invective is often their device of choice.

We may interpret Gumbrecht's observations as paradigmatic of this altered mode of critique, insofar as each of its diverse variants develops in explicit dissociation from common foes: the identity politics of previously excluded groups and cultural minorities, scientific expertise, or government and media elites allegedly forced into line. We interpret what is often disparaged as 'grumbling' ('*Raunen*') in the skirmishes of public discourse as a reactive self-hardening against progressive change. The corresponding intellectuals form ideological coalitions in order to compensate for their loss of power. Before we inspect this context in more detail, we shall first address the social transformations that are changing and, in part, limiting the sphere of intellectual influence.

Crumbling foundations

'Lamenting the demise of the intellectual',[14] a practice which Gumbrecht also joins in with, is itself nothing new. At least since the 1980s, intellectual doubt was accompanied by a fundamental self-doubt regarding their opportunities for intervention and their efficacy.[15] Hans-Peter Müller has identified several reasons for this crisis of identity:

> Firstly, the utopian faith in a different society was lost in the 1970s; at the same time, secondly, modern certainties and ultimate justifications were eroding; in parallel with these developments, thirdly, occurred the already mentioned rise of experts; and the media transformation (first through TV, later through the Internet), fourthly, and the restructuring of universities, fifthly, eventually transformed the typical forums of intellectuals.[16]

In the twentieth century, for a long time the horizon of left-wing critique was the overcoming of capitalism and the building of a different, socialist society. When the book *The Gulag Archipelago* by Russian dissident Aleksandr Solzhenitsyn appeared in 1974, broad layers of intellectuals were in shock. Instead of a free association of equals, the plans for the construction of a new world had ultimately given rise to a repressive system of re-education and labour camps in the Soviet Union.[17] A new generation of intellectuals emerged, embodied particularly by the *nouveaux philosophes* around André Glucksmann and Bernard-Henri Lévy, who popularized scepticism towards potentially totalitarian ideologies. In this climate, Jean-François Lyotard in

1983 erected the 'Tomb of the Intellectual' in an article for the left-liberal newspaper *Le Monde*.[18] A tombstone, at least, for the 'activist' intellectuals, we should add, who were keen to fight for the interests of the revolutionary classes.[19] Indeed, the *nouveaux philosophes* did side with oppressed groups and particularly advocated for human rights; but rather than create a new world, they wanted to realize a better world within the existing one.

When Eastern Bloc socialism collapsed in 1989, the utopian space finally narrowed completely. At the end of the twentieth century, there was a 'widespread sense that not only is capitalism the only viable political and social system, but also that it is now impossible even to imagine a coherent alternative to it', Mark Fisher noted in 2009.[20] This British cultural theorist referred to the corresponding attitude as 'capitalist realism'. Part of the intellectual protest lost not just social utopias, but its own normative standards, too. Although ideals such as freedom, equality and justice retained their validity, they have since been de-coupled from a 'future-oriented theory' (such as socialism)[21] and are now no longer linked to the concrete hope for a different society but aim at an immanent improvement of life under capitalism (see chapter 3). That is not to say that progressive doubt has disappeared; but it is no longer sparked primarily by the socio-economic conditions of social coexistence.

Alongside disillusionment with utopias, an epistemic doubt has been on the rise ever since the 1970s that has shaken the foundations of intellectual activity. In the 1980s, there were intense disputes over postmodernity, which, according to Müller, was an 'indicator' that the self-image of intellectuals was also being destabilized.[22] Linguistic signs no longer had a fixed meaning, and narratives of origin, stable identities, or the systemic view of society were being radically called into question.[23] Instead, postmodernity asserted a pluralism of lifestyles, forms of knowledge and values. As mentioned before, intellectuals thus also lost their normative standards, after having previously issued their assessments on the basis of stable normative points of reference (such as reason, progress and truth).[24] According to Zygmunt Bauman, the social function of intellectuals in postmodernity is shrunken, reduced to the role of 'interpreters'. They are no longer able to appeal to shared ultimate justifications. They are left interpreting distinct forms of knowledge and normative discourses in order to create a shared ground for a public communication between 'autonomous (sovereign) participants'.[25]

Furthermore, intellectuals now faced competition over their supposed 'better knowledge'.[26] In highly differentiated risk societies, with their tangles of problems that are almost impossible to unravel, intellectuals lost their knowledge privilege to the advantage of experts.[27] As early as the 1970s, Foucault referred to the 'specific intellectual', who, in their own workplace – universities, labs, hospitals or psychiatric wards – struggles precisely against the knowledge-based power of which they are simultaneously the tool.[28] Instead of issuing universal statements that are backed by an abstract nominal knowledge, the specific intellectual, given their special knowledge, points out the '"regime" of truth'.[29] Although experts today are not necessarily calling into question systems of domination, they are – due to their special knowledge – ascribed a special political responsibility which was formerly delegated to intellectuals.[30] Foucault, for instance, considered physicist Robert Oppenheimer to personify a transitional figure between the universal and the specific intellectual, who was persecuted because of his 'specific knowledge' about nuclear physics but simultaneously embodied 'the fate of the world' and, therefore, the universal.[31]

In terms of the places where we would usually find intellectuals, the universities are clearly one of their key domains. Although universities may no longer automatically deliver upon the promise of cultural excellence, the spirit of an educational elite combining their ethics of science with an interest in public affairs does live on inside them.[32] The establishment of the democratic – albeit, at the same time, highly specialized and bureaucratically organized – mass university during the second half of the twentieth century had itself challenged this elitist self-understanding of the scholarly intellectual.[33] Instead of debating among a small circle of students, the professor now had to manage a growing number of educational climbers. From the 1980s onwards, the possibilities for imparting an attitude of political and public reflexivity, in addition to the reproducible specialized knowledge, were further curtailed.[34] The university reforms initiated at the beginning of the new millennium moreover subject research and teaching to 'an economically inspired governance'.[35] Academic thinking is currently being challenged by business-minded, utilitarian approaches, by the dependence of research on third-party funding, and by a selection mechanism for academic publications that is based on standardized ranking systems.[36] This transformation can trigger status fears that are compensated through an exaggerated identification with lost knowledge privileges.

A similar, albeit contradictory, change is taking place in the media. 'Whoever wants to be regarded as an intellectual', cultural scientist Thomas Macho wrote in 1992, 'must commit to becoming a writing being – *homo scriptor*'.[37] It is no surprise that the rise of audiovisual media such as television from the 1960s onwards eroded this self-understanding.[38] Debates on TV talk shows now feature slick 'media intellectuals', who represent much of what is regarded incompatible with classic intellectual virtues: rather than fighting for universal values, they present themselves; instead of issuing well-founded social critique, they seek to break taboos; rather than alternative interpretations, they mainly provide entertainment.[39] As Jürgen Habermas has critically noted in this regard: 'Ideally, it is about reasoned exchange, not about the orchestrated concentration of audience's views.'[40] The media logic replaces the argument with eloquence. Such reservations continue to have an effect even today. Philosophers like Richard David Precht or Markus Gabriel are not only eyed with suspicion by their colleagues from the discipline because of their omnipresence in the media, but also because they have something to say about everything and everyone.

If TV was tentatively encroaching upon the intellectuals' classic stomping grounds, since the 1990s the Internet has been comprehensively digging up this terrain. In the increased media competition, the forums that were dominant in the past – print and TV – have lost their leading role. Review sections are shrinking, and the struggle for the limited amount of line space is intensifying.[41] At the same time, Twitter and Facebook, among others, create a parallel public sphere in which the asymmetry between speaker and spoken-to is erased. This alone leads to 'the critics' authority taking offence', including among intellectuals who 'used to pass sovereign judgement and addressed a rather vaguely conceived readership'.[42] Readers suddenly not only respond, but they actually present their own views in lengthy discussion threads. This *democratization* is paralleled by a *re-feudalization* of the digital public sphere by private tech corporations.[43]

People can now engage in low entry-threshold communication and networking – yet they can do so outside of the arena marked by democratic norms. The universalization of digital communication channels, in particular, has, paradoxically, facilitated the 'creation of sectional forms of community'.[44] Habermas discerns a regressive potential in this: the erstwhile 'great emancipatory promise is being drowned out by the desolate cacophony in fragmented, self-enclosed echo chambers'.[45] Although the supposed polarization resulting from such echo chambers has not received any unequivocal empirical verification, the digital monopolies certainly do raise new problems for freedom of speech.[46] Indeed, ever since the epidemic of fake news and hate speech, the departments for 'content moderation', i.e., well-intentioned censorship, have been massively expanded. The tech corporations are turning into private legislators.

Twisted freedom struggles

'There's no law against posing the question …' is a phrase that kicks off many a conversation about the freedom of expression. According to a study by the Allensbach Institute in 2021, only 45 per cent of respondents felt that they could freely voice their opinion in Germany – an historic low since the survey was first conducted in 1953.[47] Although the extent of freedom is increasing for ever-more groups, the majority simultaneously senses a growing pressure towards conformism.[48]

This feeling of being patronized is today often articulated with reference to so-called cancel culture, a diffuse phenomenon that is charged with all kinds of negative associations. Despite the inflationary focus upon this theme in public debate, it is in fact quite difficult to define the exact meaning of this term, which has been spread from the English-speaking world also to other countries.[49] If we consider the cases in which the term is commonly used, we mainly find situations in which remarks by well-known personalities cause protest, in the wake of which an exclusion (of the person) or removal (of the remark) is demanded, which is in fact heeded in some cases. For example, a video produced by the German Research Foundation (DFG) with stand-up cabaret artist Dieter Nuhr was temporarily deleted because he had made jokes that discredited science and were perceived as racist. During a literary festival in Hamburg, an event with his colleague Lisa Eckhart was cancelled due to allegations that her satirical pieces were antisemitic as well as trans- and homophobic. Each of these decisions was preceded by controversial discussions on social media. Using hashtags with the names of those concerned (such as #Nuhr or #Eckhart), digital protest collectives were organized.

Up to this point, the procedure largely corresponds to the long-familiar strategy of political scandalization, whereby norms violations are exposed and collective affects are released in order to reinforce or restore social cohesion.[50] Now, we can frequently observe a kind of scandalization of the second order. The original protest is problematized by other observers as a symptom of the said cancel culture: it is allegedly no longer possible to say anything without being morally chided, defamed, discredited or threatened in one's professional existence, or, in short, without being cancelled by left-liberal or 'woke' speech watchdogs. From this perspective, the actual scandal is not so much the jokes of the comedian or cabaret artist but their public denunciation. Interestingly, this form of 'scandalizing the scandal'[51] has historically served as an effective device for intellectuals to challenge state power.

Historian Ingrid Gilcher-Holtey has traced how the roles of prosecutor and defendant were reversed during the 1962 affair concerning the news magazine *Der Spiegel*. The federal prosecutor had launched an investigation against *Der Spiegel* after an article on the German army (*Bundeswehr*) it had published allegedly constituted high treason. The magazine's chief editor Rudolf Augstein and other editors were arrested. A storm of protest erupted and the affair quickly turned into a crisis for the government, with the then-defence minister Franz Josef Strauß from the Bavarian branch of the Christian Democrats (CSU) ultimately being forced to resign.[52] The debate at the time amounted to a public negotiation of collectively shared norms and rules: which principle should take precedence – freedom of the press or military secrecy?

Despite these structural similarities, two aspects stand out: firstly, the various cancel culture scandals often seem peculiarly staged and exaggerated. Individual episodes are depicted as a 'culture'. All of a sudden, the matter at hand is the social climate as a whole. And this dramatization – and it is more than questionable whether the cases really do constitute a culture – suggests, secondly, that a renegotiation of social values is precisely what is meant to be prevented.

In our view, the feeling of being patronized and the curtailment of the freedom of opinion are primarily side-effects of the progressive change in norms (see chapter 4). The evolution of norms is never free of conflict. Currently, we are witnessing a conflict between previously established groups and outsiders, similar to that observed by Norbert Elias and John L. Scotson in the 1960s.[53] On the one hand, there are aspiring outsiders who are demanding the further adjustment of behavioural norms. Although, at least in theory, everyone was entitled to a life without being insulted or discriminated against, in reality this long applied only to one small group: white, hetero-sexual men. By insisting on gender-sensitive speech, the inclusion of non-binary gender identities, or the sanctioning of racist discrimi-nation, previously excluded groups are now claiming this right for themselves, too.

On the other side are the established groups who have claimed cultural sovereignty up to this point. Their routines and conventions corresponded to social expectations; they ordered a 'gypsy schnitzel' ('*Zigeunerschnitzel*') in a restaurant and perhaps had a 'Moor's head' ('*Mohrenkopf*') for dessert. Such terms were not necessarily used with discriminatory intent. Rather, due to an 'epistemic limitation',[54] privi-leged status groups were unable to notice certain moral problems: they had simply never had the experience of being discriminated against because of their origin, gender or skin colour. The outsiders' growing power of interpretation is now penetrating the everyday world of the established groups; suddenly the menu includes 'paprika schnitzel' and the supermarket shelves are stocked with 'chocolate marshmallows'. Hence, it is not surprising that more than half of the respondents (55 per cent) in the study cited said that they did not pay heed to political correctness in their speech *intentionally*, as it annoyed them that others were trying to impose language rules on them.[55] In other words, the subjective right to freedom of expression invokes a general norm so that the particular claims to power of the established groups remain untouched.[56] It is not freedom *as such* that is being defended here, but rather the established groups' freedom to continue to define the bounds of what can be said.

Disputes about new norms can entail regressive effects – on either side. Parts of the liberal-intellectual milieu react to the 'loss of majority status advantages' and the associated 'loss of orienta-tion'[57] with authoritarian resentment. Indeed, the fight against the gender asterisk is being pursued most tenaciously in the feature sections rather than amongst the general public. Two examples: in a column for *Zeit Magazin*, the author Harald Martenstein vehemently opposed gender-neutral language ('I will never use gender asterisks unless threatened with torture; the threat of jail is not enough'[58]), and the journalist Anna Schneider points out the socially explosive power of the gender asterisk in an article for *Die Welt* ('Whoever talks about gendering cannot remain silent about polarization'[59]). Time and again, we come across the same narrative that seems to have taken on a life of its own immune to external factors: the revision of language or behavioural rules based on inclusivity threatens either individual self-determination, social cohesion or civilization as a whole.[60]

Interestingly, the resistance against cancel culture displays a number of aspects that the Berkeley Group observed in classic authoritarianism and which we observed in libertarian authoritarianism as well. A reified right to freedom, which rejects the social negotiation of interests, inclinations or forms of behaviour, is posited in opposition to regulations or prohibitions. Those who flout the right to self-determination are aggressively condemned, one's own impulses (such as the accusation of illiberalism) are projected onto the opposing party, the notion of sensitivity is resisted (and identified with sectional special rights), and discourse is fixated on sexual topics (such as the rejection of non-binary gender identities). On the surface, a universal right to freedom of expression is demanded, but behind this lies the (not necessarily conscious) intention to protect the freedom of expression from its generalization in practice so that sectional special rights remain untouched.

At the same time, the activism of emerging minorities is not entirely free of regressive elements, either. In heterogeneous milieus, 'militant group identities' take shape that tie the interpretive power over a situation to emotions, particularly to being offended.[61] Moreover, at least in the more extreme cases, the counter-epistemology, which criticizes the mechanisms of exclusion behind universalist truth claims, can itself morph into a new politics of exclusion. Now, the exclusion is directed against all those who had previously exercised a cultural interpretive power which excluded others. Established male intellectuals – the 'old white men' who had in the past regarded themselves as advocates for minorities seeking emancipation – feel offended by disinvitations and alleged 'speaking bans'. The fact that marginalized groups are now themselves rising to speak – and, even worse, in opposition to these intellectuals – can trigger a grudgeful activism that frequently leads them to change political camps. The blanket equation of an individual 'person' with a political 'position' by parts of the emerging cultural milieus creates the very opponent they want to fight (see chapter 3).[62]

In our view, the increased sensitivity to subtle forms of discrimination in everyday life – so-called 'wokeness' – is a paradoxical side-effect of inclusive equalization which Tocqueville already noticed. Women, trans people and cultural minorities today not only have more rights than ever before, but any violation of these rights has 'institutional consequences'[63] – a fact that further raises the awareness for deficient implementation and existing inequalities. In other words, the cultural positional struggle that is being fought out in the debates about cancel culture is a reverse effect of normative progress.

In modern mass democracies, the intellectual had enjoyed an exceptional epistemic and normative position. They were the ones who could see through social structures and criticize them. They gave a voice to the marginalized and the unheard. And it is precisely this model that is now in crisis. The oppressed, the excluded minorities, are raising their own voices and exposing the fact that the intellectual's superior knowledge, complete with its universal claim to reason, is itself part of a power structure. Correspondingly, precisely the milieus that have positioned themselves through their ability-to-know-better are losing their symbolic power – and thus cling onto this claim all the more doggedly. Although the excluded and discriminated have no privileged access to an abstract morality or truth, they draw their moral legitimization from subjective experience, on the basis of which they denounce injustice and demand justice.

Excursus: Sloterdijk's meditations

An important precursor for an intellectual discourse that engenders indistinct interferences between ideological camps is the work of Peter Sloterdijk, whom Hans Ulrich Gumbrecht praises for his 'risky thinking' in the essay quoted at the beginning. Although Sloterdijk has always remained somewhat spurious in academic institutions,[64] *Bild* newspaper[65] calls him 'Germany's most important thinker'[66] – and not without reason. As the brilliant stylist that he is, he has won himself a broad audience, from the upscale villas in Hamburg-Blankenese to the chip shop in the ex-industrial Ruhr area. The young Sloterdijk, who for a while wore the orange-coloured robes of the Bhagwan movement, would hardly have imagined this.

The atmosphere of the 'meditative province'[67] that Sloterdijk experienced with his spiritual teacher Bhagwan Shree Rajneesh, who later called himself Osho, is still present in his work to this day.

Osho's ashram in Pune, India, where Sloterdijk stayed at the end of the 1970s, was both a place of spirituality and anti-metaphysical hedonism. The aim was a cleansing from internalized constraints; in therapeutic meditations, people cried without restraint, danced uncontrollably, even to the point of unconsciousness. The commune caused a public stir due to sexual excesses, which also involved violence and abuse. But, no matter how far removed from civilization Osho liked to portray himself as being, his teachings were, at the same time, in tune with a capitalist, indeed consumerist, orientation. The ashram developed a flourishing business model, running numerous dance clubs in major German cities, among other things. Osho adorned himself with expensive watches and owned a large fleet of Rolls-Royce limousines. This disturbing blend of non-conformism, meditative self-awareness and hedonistic consumerism was nevertheless very much in line with the new needs of late modern subjectivity, which Sloterdijk translated into an influential counter-epistemology. He himself says, in hindsight, that he opted for 'dual citizenship' and has kept his 'passport to the second world' of the Indian ashram to this day.[68]

This autobiographical note is anything but insignificant. In Sloterdijk's works, the legacy of Osho's cosmos of thought remains present, albeit in a concealed form. In his popular 2013 work *You Must Change Your Life*, he attempts to understand people from the viewpoint of a 'transcendent pole'. Although the faith in God has dwindled, we cannot deny a 'vertical tension' within ourselves: we continue to direct our gaze upwards.[69] In the restlessness that defines our lives, we orientate ourselves towards goals that we cannot possibly achieve. Although we are constantly optimizing our self, we can never satisfy ourselves. For Sloterdijk, this is an indication that the pursuit of transcendence persists even in secularized societies. His aim is to imbue our mundane life with spiritual meaning. This realization will prove significant in our subsequent analysis of the *Querdenker* movement (see chapter 7).

The defence of uninhibited, unbridled life, the unabashed 'cheekiness' of an 'essentially plebeian reflection', which he formulated immediately after his return from Pune in the *Critique of Cynical Reason* (1987 [1983]), still characterizes Sloterdijk's thinking today.[70] His style is evocative, metaphorical, and, at times, provocative.[71] However, over the last twenty years, his sometimes frivolously formulated scepticism towards systems of rules has become detached

THE DEMISE OF THE TRUTH SEEKERS

from its plebeian core; it is now directed downwards, and no longer upwards. In 2009, his trenchant interjection '*Die Revolution der gebenden Hand*' ('The revolution of the giving hand') sparked a heated debate on tax policy in the newspapers' feature sections.[72] The problem today, he contended, is not so much the persistence of wealth inequalities, but rather the 'hatred of the losers' that is directed against the 'generosity of the givers', as he had already set out in his 2010 book *Rage and Time*.[73] A society of equals produces a 'jealousy of all against all'[74] – a rather idiosyncratic, nihilistic interpretation of the equality paradox which Tocqueville had observed.

Sloterdijk uses ironic exaggeration as a device to illustrate the defective developments in modern societies. Although Sloterdijk remains the rebellious, provocative cynic to this day, his once fluid and reflexive positions have more recently shown a certain tendency towards hardening. In 2016, he publicly criticized the Merkel government's migration policy. In an interview with *Cicero* magazine, he asserted that Germany had 'surrendered itself to being overrun in an act of renunciation of sovereignty'.[75] Admittedly, Sloterdijk has never shied from coarse language, but here he was more or less directly adopting the slogans of right-wing populist movements, which were garnering considerable support at the time. And yet, Sloterdijk is not a right-wing intellectual; he constantly revises his points of view and is very hard to pin down, given his vast oeuvre that runs to thousands of pages. However, his principle of making the unspeakable sayable through exaggeration makes him a representative of a counter-epistemology that can tip over into the extreme – but need not necessarily remain there.[76]

Intellectual *Querfronts*

Faced with today's cultural conflicts, one might easily feel like a helpless bystander witnessing an impending traffic accident. At first, there are just small signs of drifting off the straight and narrow. Yet once the vehicle has picked up speed, there is no turning back, it heads off-road at the next bend and eventually there is a loud crash. We watched as the once-renowned journalist Matthias Matussek climbed onto swaying beer crates at a right-wing populist rally to call for resistance; and we watched as the singer Xavier Naidoo descended deeper and deeper into obscure conspiracy theories (from which he has since distanced himself); and we also watched as the Italian philosopher Giorgio Agamben established a think tank of the anti-vaccination (or 'anti-vaxxer') movement during the pandemic to end the state of emergency.

But what reason can there be for socially integrated, even successful people to lose themselves so deeply in imaginary worlds of illusion that they would rather accept losing everything – their professional success, their friends, their family – than question their own belief in conspiracies? Our intention in the following section is not to compile psychological profiles. Rather, it is to reveal the mechanisms through which the critique of social grievances can spin out of control and turn into generalized distrust.

Our three case studies criss-cross traditional political bound-aries. Left-wing libertinage is combined with the resentment of cultural diversity, and criticism of the government meets with conspiracy thinking – frequently causing political disorientation. In this confusing situation, intellectual *Querfronts* (or 'cross-fronts') are taking shape which are creating new chains of association and subverting the distinction between left and right.[77] Historically, the term '*Querfront*' referred to a 'political alliance of convenience between right-wing and left-wing groups' in 1930s Germany.[78] After the establishment of the Weimar Republic, forces of the so-called 'Conservative Revolution', such as Oswald Spengler and Arthur Moeller van den Bruck, propagated a nationalist socialism.[79] In the early 1930s, Reich Chancellor Kurt von Schleicher attempted to consolidate his position of power by reaching out to right-wing Social Democrats and anti-capitalist forces within the Nazi party and proposing cooperation.[80] Ultimately, a *Querfront* government failed, but the idea of *völkisch* (i.e., ethno-nationalist) socialism lived on within parts of the broader Nazi movement. This current was embodied by figures such as Ernst Röhm and the Strasser brothers, until Hitler had its leading representatives murdered in 1934.

Admittedly, the current situation has nothing in common with these historical alliances of convenience. There are, without doubt, various figures scouring the political arena in their quest to revitalize the idea of the *Querfront*: either as a political model, as is advocated by a number of authors from the New Right journal *Sezession* and the left-wing online magazine *Rubikon*, or within their own political biographies; cases of the latter include publicist Jürgen Elsässer or former radio presenter Ken Jebsen, both of whom have gone astray.

Here, however, it is merely that old antagonisms are being cemented along new fronts, with no influential political alliances in sight. Furthermore, we consider rather implausible those assessments that conclude from such *Querfront* phenomena that there exists some deeper elective affinity between left-wing and right-wing positions.[81]

Our interpretation of intellectual *Querfronts* concerns the – as yet, undefined – border zones of critique in which the transfer of ideas takes place in an uncontrolled manner, heading in all sorts of directions. Russian semiotician Yuri M. Lotman, a scholar of literary sign systems, defined the border as a permeable zone that not only separates but also connects both adjoining sides, without eliminating the differences. For Lotman, the distinct systems of signs that circulate within a culture are always related to each other; one sign comprises many meanings. By analogy with the concept of biosphere, he terms this cultural web of meanings the 'semiosphere'. The borderland is the 'domain of bilingualism', the zone of contact where different meanings converge and are translated: 'Since the boundary is a necessary part of the semiosphere and there can be no "us" if there is no "them", culture creates not only its own type of internal organization but also its own type of external "disorganization".'[82] Lotman's concept can also be applied to the ideological sphere.[83] Here, too, positions are formed in contradistinction from others; and here, too, there are processes of ideological exchange that throw established systems into confusion and disorganization. In the case studies discussed in this chapter, our main interest concerns precisely such intellectual border zones, in which the entire assemblage of political emblems is set in motion, producing new ideological blends. Here, we can observe the transfer mechanisms that lead to new coalitions – and indeed, to a libertarianism with an intrinsic tendency towards authoritarianism.

Before, finally, we turn to the three case studies, we would like to briefly address a few patterns that can frequently be observed in the aforementioned revaluations, alliances and transfers of ideas. Firstly, new coalitions are formed using the familiar tactics of *scandalization*. This creates an alignment based on moral outrage: although one may disagree with the positions of someone critical of the hijab, a right-wing populist AfD politician, a satirist using antisemitic stereotypes as a provocation, etc., the subsequent harsh climate of rejection they are subjected to is itself regarded as morally intolerable. By generalizing an individual case into a social grievance, patterns of social critique are redefined. Liberal intellectuals defend the right to intervene and take a public stance, albeit now in order to advance illiberal positions. Secondly, such coalitions are usually created via a *common adversary*: anger is directed against a negative signifier, such as gender theory, identity politics, the elites or science. And indeed, this reorganizes the political space, as once-disparate groups are now held together by their *shared* opposition: a sexism that presents itself as libertarian; a xenophobia that appears hedonistic; and a critique of the state that drifts into decisionism.[84] Finally, the *staging of a rupture* is frequently used to substantiate one's turn to the opposite camp. Similar to narratives of religious conversion, a critical experience triggers a conversion, a moment that separates the wrong views before the awakening from the correct ones afterwards.[85] Old alignments are dissolved and an ideological repositioning takes place.

Overshooting doubt

As the coronavirus pandemic began to drag on, an initial intellectual *Querfront* started to take form. It did so as a permanent crisis appeared to set in, as it gradually became clear that even the massive restrictions on everyday life would not bring about a swift end to the pandemic, but that they themselves were having detrimental social effects: isolation, loneliness, exhaustion, depression or unemployment. Intellectuals now raised their voices and pointed out society's plight – and did so on behalf of all those who were stuck self-isolating at home. Surely, their scandal-raising had its share of moral excess. Still, what was called the 'artists' objection'[86] did also advance plausible arguments in exposing the pathologies of a scientistic politics that sought to overcome the crisis based on scientific models.

The element of moral excess was apparent in the videos of the #allesdichtmachen social media intervention in April 2021. It brought together fifty-three actors, including Ulrike Folkerts, Wotan Wilke Möhring and Ulrich Tukur – in other words: a broad assembly of celebrities from popular national prime-time TV shows. Jan Josef Liefers, beloved by viewers for his role as the blasé Professor Boerne in the crime series *Tatort*, accused 'the' media of being forced into line and sardonically addressed his audience: 'Despair all you like. But do not doubt.'[87] Volker Bruch, who became famous as the lead actor in the series *Babylon Berlin*, sarcastically called on the government to step up the alleged scaremongering: 'Make us more afraid. This fear is just what people in this country need right now.'[88] The artists' action conveyed the criticism of the pandemic measures into a diffuse liminal space in which fact and fiction became blurred. In some of the videos, the actors appear to be prisoners of a totalitarian dictatorship, where any criticism of the government is prohibited, or rather, tolerated only when hidden within fulsome praise – even though they are real people who are addressing the equally real federal government. In other videos, an exaggerated compliance with the rules is used to articulate resistance against the system.[89] The intervention failed to achieve its goal of popularizing doubt and instead prompted an intense backlash, as a result of which some actors deleted their posts. It also attracted unwanted allies such as the right-wing conservative former president of the German domestic intelligence service Hans-Georg Maaßen[90] and AfD politician Alice Weidel, who took to social media to congratulate the artists. The *#allesdichtmachen* campaign converted the discontent of artists, who were affected by the lockdowns more than almost any other professional group, into a 'diffuse anger';[91] the corresponding narratives referred to sinister centres of power that patronize and control life and art. Artistic freedom thus became a script with multiple meanings; one that could be translated – not only, but also – into a conspiracy narrative.

On 26 February 2020, shortly after Europe's first COVID-19-related deaths were reported in Italy, Giorgio Agamben wrote about the 'invention of an epidemic' in the left-wing daily *il manifesto*.[92] Agamben's theory of the state of exception, which he developed in his *Homo sacer* series, bears considerable influence in the humanities departments. It proceeds from the assumption that the logic of sovereignty represents a crucial control principle of modern statehood. Time and again, this creates spaces of lawlessness that lead to people being excluded. According to Agamben, the Nazis' concentration camps were ultimately a contingent inherent feature of Western politics from the start.[93] So, as Benjamin Bratton made clear in a blog post for Verso Books, while Agamben's – highly controversial – article identified a 'tendency to trigger a state of exception as the standard paradigm of governance',[94] this was hardly the result of him having 'suddenly changed' his position.[95] Agamben's contributions on the politics of the pandemic vividly illustrate how a critique evoking some kind of dark machinations among the powers-that-be may well morph into conspiracy thinking. In the Foreword to his book *Where Are We Now?*, written in June 2020, Agamben asserted that 'the powers that rule this world have decided to use this pandemic – and it's irrelevant whether it is real or simulated – as a pretext for transforming top to bottom the paradigm of their governance'.[96] Intellectual scepticism is taking on a life of its own. It has become a decoding system that deciphers erratic and uncontrolled events according to a uniform template, seeking to reveal the ruling powers' true intentions.[97] Concerns about a new type of state generalize into a suspicion of an imminent 'Great Transformation' (with a capital G).[98] As is the case in many of the conspiracy theories surrounding the pandemic, which we will discuss in more detail in the following chapter, fascist dictatorship and the 'sanitation terror' of today are interpreted merely as two despotic modes of governance. Philosophers themselves 'are witnessing' transformational events, and do so in the guise of savvy seers with an exclusive claim to interpret reality. It would seem that, faced with a deeply uncertain situation, *they* are able to expose the true order of power.[99] Here, intellectual doubt merges with an eschatological concept of the political: 'What is certain is that new forms of resistance will be necessary, and those who can still envision a politics to come should be unhesitatingly committed to them.'[100] However, Agamben was certainly not the only one to descend into 'diagonalism' during the pandemic. Another widely known case is that of former left-liberal feminist Naomi Wolf.[101] Following her bestselling book *The Beauty Myth* in 1991, she was at the height of her career when, in the 1990s and early 2000s, she served as advisor to US President Bill Clinton and Democratic presidential candidate Al Gore. Over the past fifteen years, there have been increasing reports that Wolf does not take facts and the truth very seriously in her books and articles. During the Occupy protests, she claimed that the United States was on its way to becoming a police state. Subsequently, she repeatedly warned that the US was descending into a dictatorship or downright fascism – during Barack Obama's presidency, mind you. Her drift into the realm of conspiracy theories had thus begun long before the start of the coronavirus pandemic. But, until then, and despite growing doubts about her credibility and integrity, she had remained part of the liberal public sphere. The pandemic, however, led her (and many

170

others) into a whole new field of conspiracy narratives and rhetorical escalations. Not only did she deny the dangers of the infection: by that point, she also regarded the virus as a Chinese bioweapon or, alternatively, suspected that Big Pharma was pulling the strings. The vaccination certificates needed for access to cultural institutions or restaurants and for international travel, which discriminated between vaccinated and non-vaccinated people, were indeed questionable, at least from the perspective of equal political rights. For Wolf, however, they were much more than that. They marked the onset of a 'tyrannical totalitarian platform' and 'slavery forever'.[102] This escalatory rhetoric first landed her on right-wing populist host Tucker Carlson's *Tonight* show on Fox News – and eventually made her a regular guest on the 'War Room' podcast hosted by Steve Bannon, the former advisor to Donald Trump and mentor of the American far right. What Wolf and Agamben have in common is their *determined* negation of the present. They do not formulate a purely negative critique of the existing social order, but rather translate scepticism into a hope for the 'dawn of a new era'.[103] Such critical voices from the liberal-intellectual milieu – who translated the diffuse uncertainty into absolute scepticism, in which arbitrary thinking gains sovereignty over the facts – have been key to popularizing a general suspicion. In some instances, the imaginaries of an unrestricted sovereignty even involve fantasies of political purging and purity.[104] Libertarian thinking, which exclusively recognizes its own authority, tends towards authoritarianism here, but without being authoritarian itself.

Nostalgic activism

A second *Querfront* has emerged in debates surrounding struggles for emancipation which frequently operate with the charged and, ultimately, vague term 'identity politics'. At first glance, one might say that this usually refers to activism by groups who are defined by certain characteristics or who self-identify accordingly: gender identity, skin colour, sexual orientation. Marx and Engels had declared, with revolutionary emphasis, in the *Communist Manifesto* that all 'previous historical movements' had been 'movements of minorities, or in the interest of minorities', but that the 'proletarian movement' was 'the independent movement of the immense majority, in the interests of the immense majority'.[105] But minorities – or at least particular groups – are, critics claim, once again at the centre of attention today. People define themselves not by a characteristic that they share with all other people but by characteristics that set them apart from others,[106] and they fight for the recognition of this uniqueness and against being excluded or discriminated against by the previously privileged majority.

At least in certain parts of the traditional left-wing milieu, this new grammar of political conflict is rejected. The basic argument usually runs as follows: the focus on minorities' particularistic demands has debased and supplanted the general interests of the majority.[107] Wage-earners and déclassé groups no longer feel represented by a left that fights against cultural discrimination instead of against economic exploitation. Instead, they now turn to right-wing populist parties.[108] The reaction patterns which these disappointed intellectuals ascribe to the traditional working class, however, apply to themselves at least to the same extent.

In modern mass democracies, left-wing intellectuals had a prominent role: they spoke, in the name of universal norms, on behalf of disadvantaged groups or even of humanity as a whole, thereby in fact establishing the universal. This role is coming under pressure in the decentralized public sphere of late modern societies: suddenly, marginalized groups are speaking for themselves and, in the process, actually criticizing the established intellectuals who hitherto represented them. Moreover, they no longer necessarily refer to a general or universal, but articulate particular, sectional standpoints and interests. Faced with this situation, individual representatives of the erstwhile vanguard are counterattacking – and yearning for past times when things stood in better order. This also makes their statements compatible with right-wing narratives.[109] This regressive flipside of a nostalgic class struggle is particularly evident among some prominent representatives of the *Aufstehen* movement, launched in 2018. Dramaturge Bernd Stegemann, alongside politician Sahra Wagenknecht (then of Die Linke), had a major influence on the political profile of this movement. He contends that identity politics harbours selfish motives that have made it easy for capitalism to co-opt it: 'When everybody makes their own self the centre of their attention, other sectional claims can no longer be reasonably opposed.'[110] Stegemann, in contrast, proposes to revitalize the positive universalism of class consciousness, which is to be forced back into the political sphere with the help of the 'crow bar of populism'.[111] The aim here is to link up the basic economic antagonism between capital and labour with the populist contrariety between the people and the elite:

> [I]n the current situation, any populist movement, regardless of whether left-wing populist or right-wing populist, has one positive effect: the elites are being jolted out of their hubris and forced, for the first time in decades, to publicly admit to their feudal structures.[112]

This nostalgic impulse also includes Stegemann's adherence to an image of the public sphere as a sphere governed by arguments, not feelings. This reflects a certain affect against emotions, difference and the allegedly oversensitive 'woke' consciousness. Correspondingly, Stegemann considers the key achievement of the public sphere to be the establishment of a 'form of public communication that accommodates complexities'.[113] Here, he states, the chaotic polyphony can be transformed into a common dialogue, which, however, requires the universal equality of all members. The Viennese philosopher Robert Pfaller follows a similar line of argument, emphatically defending 'mature citizenship (*citoyenneté*)' in his book *Erwachsenensprache* ('*Adult Language*') (2017).[114] The public sphere and, therefore, civilized manners, he notes, are based on the 'ability to tolerate distance'.[115] It is not without reason that this argument may sound familiar: it was originally advanced by Richard Sennett and is used by Pfaller to measure the pathologies of 'postmodernity' against a now-perished ideal.[116] However, this bourgeois public sphere is a 'retrotopia',[117] a now-gone place of longing, a past which once guaranteed inner cohesion through homogeneity. This place was marked by a normalizing idea which conceived of universalism as equality and thus averted the destabilizing dangers of the personal, the particular or the different.

Like Stegemann, Pfaller regards 'postmodern identity and language policies' as 'propaganda' for a neoliberal redistribution, this time from bottom-to-top, which makes a 'politics of equality' impossible. Here, we find a version of the radical critique of 'progressive neoliberalism' popularized by Nancy Fraser – and yet, it is so drastically exaggerated that it ends up in regressive waters.[118] In the case of Stegemann's fellow campaigner Sahra Wagenknecht, this criticism tips over entirely into a 'normalism' of the plebs.[119] In her 2021 book

Die Selbstgerechten ('*The Self-Righteous*'), she indulges in endless invective against a supposedly dominant 'lifestyle left' primarily preoccupied with 'lifestyle issues' and 'moral point-scoring', which values 'autonomy and self-realization higher' than 'tradition and community', and which is now – and here one can sense the offence taken from challenges to the claim to sole representation – wrongly identified with the progressive project of social change.[120] Ultimately, however, it is not the longing for stability and security that is conformist, Wagenknecht asserts, but the unique (or 'singular') striving for individuation. Here the semantic alliance with conservative milieus advocating traditionalist values is finally obvious.

With the conflict presented this way, the forms of protest associated with identity politics appear symptomatic of a paternalistic governmentality, said to have emerged as a result of the 'lifestyle left' hijacking the state. This latter is said to be hell-bent on stripping people of the last remaining pleasures of everyday life: cigarette packets are labelled with warnings; women are advised against high-heeled shoes and skirts; warnings are issued against nasty jokes, while disparaging ones are banned altogether.[121] Pfaller interprets this heterogeneous assortment of behavioural norms as a 'cultural puritanism' that no longer expects or trusts adults to be adults.[122] In his view, this 'top-down sensitivity' represents a neoliberal form of rule, which merely distracts from the 'brutalization of social conditions'. Hence, rather than fight unemployment and poverty, people choose to vent their indignation at the lack of a third toilet door.[123]

This taking of sides in favour of the hedonism of the common people and the vertical class struggle is not problematic per se. However, because both are posited in a binary and antagonistic relation to identity-political claims to recognition, they foster a resentment whereby idiosyncrasies and sensitivities are either devalued as mere oversensitivity or aggressively rejected as an instrument of power. Moreover, we once again find the libertarian impulse to refuse to bend to any expectation to show consideration for others. By depicting prohibition and renunciation as forms by which identity politics imposes its cultural domination, one's own stereotypes and aggressive impulses can be projected onto a fairly powerless object of comparison. Here, the political struggle is not waged against the powerful, but against the unruly claims of cultural minorities, which Stegemann refers to as an 'epidemic plague' for the public expression of opinion.[124] The nostalgic class struggle radicalizes into a populist-hued cultural struggle.

Partisans of the sign

A third border zone in which ideas coalesce and re-combine can be identified on a completely different terrain: that is, on the battle grounds surrounding so-called 'postmodernity'. Postmodern thinking's originally subversive impulse to radically deconstruct the pillars of modernity (reason, progress and enlightenment) has led some intellectuals to favour ultimate justifications which seek to give some underpinnings that will steady the destabilization of the present.[125] The questions of how postmodernity should be assessed and what the term actually means remain strongly contested – and the specific demarcations of left-wing versus right-wing ideas are heavily disputed. Jürgen Habermas, for example, in 1980 labelled the French authors Georges Bataille, Michel Foucault and Jacques Derrida as 'young conservatives', alleging that they were advancing anti-modernist positions under a modernist guise.[126] The fact that representations such as 'difference' or 'identity' are currently finding their way into the conceptual toolbox of the right ought to be understood not so much as unmistakable proof of postmodern-ism's supposed right-wing origins. It is rather an indication of the metamorphosis of counter-epistemology (see chapter 3).[127]

The shifting of concepts – leading them to a diametrically opposed political place – is well-illustrated by the erratic trajectory of the journal *Tumult*. The first issue was published in 1979 with the subtitle *Zeitschrift für Verkehrswissenschaften* ('Journal for Transport Studies') as a collective project of the Merve publishing house, which was orientated towards French post-structuralism. According to the editor at the time, Dietmar Kamper, the motivation behind the magazine was to 'test new writing and presentation techniques'.[128] Instead of a grand narrative based on absolute explanatory principles, the medium of the magazine itself was intended to de-potentiate the unquestioned power of the author and of language so as to provide a forum for artistic and subversive forms of social critique. The announcement of the 1978 Merve volume *Das Schillern der Revolte* ('The Shimmer of Revolt'), whose author collective largely overlapped with the *Tumult* editorial team, stated:

Conclusive theories and unambiguous strategies, or counter-strategies, are useless, when the totality develops into a system of delusion and the fields occupied by power become increasingly labyrinthine. Small wonder that it is now high time for the testing of new and different forms of disrupting the system of power, such as diagonal thinking (*querdenken*), reversing the rules of the game, concealing one's identity, breaking into laughter.[129]

A changed approach, which sought to explore the ever-more ramified branches of social power, required new forms of intellectual intervention that abandoned Marxist orthodoxy. No matter how devious the ways of power were, the means of subverting it were likewise diverse. So, according to *Tumult* co-founder Frank Böckelmann, the title 'in contrast to "riot", "revolt", "rebellion", [expresses] an unintentional, indistinctive flowing together and apart'.[130] In rejecting ultimate political justifications, they opened their minds to marginalized perspectives. These included right-wing traditions of thought, too.[131] Not only did they invoke an imminent change of era, but they also wanted to revitalize the notion of heroism. They read Carl Schmitt's *Theory of the Partisan* or wandered through the German undergrowth with Ernst Jünger's *The Forest Passage* in their backpacks.[132] But, at the time, an effort was still being made to harness the grumbling for an anti-hegemonic, deconstructive social critique.

The changing of the magazine's subtitle to *Vierteljahresschrift für Konsensstörung* ('Quarterly Journal for the Disruption of Consensus') in 2013 heralded a political reorientation. The actual rupture in the editorial team occurred in the winter of 2015/16, prompted by a dispute over their stance on the refugee issue. Under chief editor Böckelmann – once a founding member of the alternative-left group Subversive Action[133] – the post-structuralist magazine cultivated a right-wing spirit. According to Böckelmann, the title *Tumult* now implied a 'rejection of the delusion of feasibility: of that hubris according to which we can simply invent the world and construct our own identity at a whim'.[134] While the title originally emphasized that any attempt at social stabilization will always remain uncertain, fragile and riddled with irritations, it is precisely this radical suspicion of modern structural order that has become an effective lever for criticizing political institutions from the right. Scenarios, which the magazine had in its early years referenced in order to celebrate the 'dissolution of constrained security'[135] (as in, dissolution, chaos, catastrophe or war), are now regarded as threats to one's identity, indeed, to society's cultural substance itself. The magazine is staging a right-wing 'insurrection of the signs',[136] namely against these same rights being hollowed out and their meaning being perverted in late modernity. Here, we can cite just a few such examples.

One stated reason for the magazine's re-foundation was a hermetically sealed consensus which had allegedly closed itself off to political alternatives:

> The launch of the quarterly journal is a response to the growing pressure of consensus, caused by globally connected, powerful producers of meaning in both old and new media. They, in alliance with the world economy that is dominated by financial capital, as well as with servile science and research institutes who carry out their preparation work, orchestrate a new conformism in public opinion.[137]

According to this bleak diagnosis, critical thinking has been banned from public communication. Corporations striding the global stage decide what should be said and what can even be said at all. Academic intellectuals submissively concur. Thus, as the two editors explained a year later, the democratic concept of consensus conceals a mechanism of political closure: 'All this raving about diversity and openness; but the idea behind this seems to be rather more a matter of ensuring peaceable passengers.'[138] The only alternatives permitted are those which do not transcend the political order: 'Refugees welcome. Those caring helpers giving the new arrivals a warm applause have no interest in Syrian, Pakistani, or Somali ways of life, faces, or even history.' Böckelmann wrote these words in winter 2015/16 against the backdrop of large-scale volunteer engagement by civil society in the effort to manage the large number of asylum seekers. He continued:

> Any arrival is equally suitable as an object of humanitarian commitment. The display of pure goodness is the epitome of indifference – including towards oneself. To make no distinction amounts to an applied nihilism.[139]

Reminiscent of the subversive spirit, the magazine developed a polemic moral critique similar to that formulated by the philosopher Arnold Gehlen in his 1969 essay *Moral und Hypermoral* ('Morality and Hypermorality'). The helpers were ultimately accused of selfish motives of self-elevation, allegedly degrading refugees as merely shapeless 'objects' of benevolence. In the polemic against the widespread popular commitment to helping asylum seekers, however, the unmentioned Other is also assigned a particular place: that is, a place within the difference between various separately, or rather, hierarchically ordered 'ways of life'. This notion ultimately leads to the ethnopluralist idea that a people must preserve its cultural identity in its assigned territorial space.

Although (or rather, because) its range of authors now include mainly ultra-conservative to right-wing authors such as Matthias Matussek and Uwe Tellkamp, the magazine has not abandoned its subversive original concept. Its objective is to shatter established certainties and moral concepts – but primarily those of liberal society. Inclusive values (community spirit, equality or solidarity) are identified as a power structure and fought against with a gesture of mutiny. In so doing, the magazine is cultivating an intellectual self-image that is reminiscent of Jünger's libertarian 'forest rebel', who, given his self-sufficient position, is able to stage his resistance even in the face of a catastrophic reality:

> The name of this journal, *Tumult*, was and still is a synonym for the uprising of the singularities [...]. We seek to provide a space for figures and figurations that defy universalization and globalization or emerge over the course of such defiance.

Böckelmann and Ebner wrote these words in autumn 2015 with reference to the postmodern media theorist Jean Baudrillard.[140] The intellectual becomes a partisan of the signs, subverting the political order from a subaltern position using the arsenal of semantic warfare. They are the victim of an overly powerful order and, at the same time, a tragic hero who perseveres even in a 'lost position'.[141] The singular individual becomes the trailblazer of authoritarian protest. The rebellious posture of social critique remains, as does the subversive transgression of rules – but they now proceed from a regressive standpoint.

Registers of critique

During periods of social transformation, not only does the social order become destabilized, but the order of critique is also shaken

178

up, thus affecting the way in which social reality is perceived, problematized and judged. Due to the non-simultaneity of regressive modernization, the *registers of critique* shift, move or cross-cut one another.[142] They can be politically charged in a different manner or re-combined in new ways. Libertarian authoritarianism is one of these new varieties of critique.

Firstly, the normative dimension of the *universalist/particularist* dichotomy is reassessed. While particularistic norms were usually attributed to the ruling classes, with their property and ownership rights, in classic social critique, the universalistic norms of the Enlightenment were commonly associated with classes and social movements in search of emancipation. If this distinction was already starting to become blurred during the 1970s, it seems to have indeed turned into its opposite today: the right to particularities and idiosyncrasies is a key demand of progressive identity politics that is directed against the general (public). By contrast, as we have seen, the insistence on universalism becomes a device for maintaining power. Instead of pluralism and diversity, libertarian authoritarians exclusively adhere to just one principle – their own.

Likewise, the weighting of the contrasting pair *knowledge/ opinion*, which concerns the epistemic dimension of critique, has more or less been inverted. Instead of the distanced observation that guides social critique, allowing for the generation of verified knowledge about social inequalities, the subjective space of experience and feeling, which makes social suffering experienceable in concrete terms, is given a new centrality. The gesture which critique makes – talking *about* people – is problematized by the people themselves. Rational cognition is replaced by affect-inducing emotion as the new basis for describing social injustices. This applies in the cases of both 'woke' identity politics and the equally 'awakened' *Querdenker* movement.

Furthermore, critique usually addresses the inclusion of social groups via the opposing pair of *opening/closure*. The demand that no one should be denied universal access to resources as well as opportunities for action and employment is seen as progressive, in contrast to elitist communities that seek to restrict opportunities for social participation. Today, we are seeing attempts to ensure social participation via the exclusion of people or opinions: individuals are disinvited from participating if they have made disparaging remarks, certain words are banned from everyday use, etc. Such closures are intended to open up the public sphere to those who were previously discriminated against and had no access to it.

This latter is linked to a further dimension of critique that focuses on the area of social interests in terms of the *minority/majority* opposition. Today, cultural minorities in particular appear as drivers of social progress, including against the interests of established groups. They articulate particular claims and demand special rights, be it language regulations or quotas, but are nevertheless guided by norms such as universal equality and inclusion. The professed fight for the general interest of the majority, in contrast, is often used to defend exclusive privileges and claims to power; the fight against the gender asterisk and the third toilet door is pursued in the name of the majority.

The *state/individual* dichotomy is also being rebalanced: traditionally, progressive movements were generally suspicious of state institutions and defended individual freedom, whereas conservatives advocated a strong state and conformist lifestyles. Today, however, state institutions are themselves the site of emancipatory struggles, often including the use of instruments aimed at the regulation of individual behaviour.[143] Conservatives and right-wing forces, on the other hand, are defending individual self-determination against state regulation.

Finally, another closely related dimension is concerned with the social regulation of power and is articulated along the *freedom/ unfreedom* dichotomy. While progressive critique, with various nuances, argues in favour of a free society that is to be guaranteed by a tamed market, conservative or right-wing positions usually envisage a traditionalist, i.e., unfree society and liberal, deregulated markets.[144] Within this reference system, entirely different positions are now emerging: progressives are demanding the standardization of everyday life and see new opportunities for emancipation in economic flexibilization, whereas conservatives are insisting on their right to free self-determination.

Today's conflicts over freedom thus entail forms of protest in which regressive and emancipatory elements coalesce. These shifts in the registers of critique will be our focus in the following two chapters.

— Chapter 7 —

THE RE-ENCHANTMENT OF THE WORLD: 'DIAGONALIST' PROTESTS

Ms Weber is a student of educational sciences. She describes herself as a spiritual and intuitive person, and she believes in God and the energy of the universe. Attaining peace and a society in harmony mean a lot to her. She considers herself a cosmopolitan and someone very open to people of other religions or ethnicities. During the interview, she apologizes each time she fails to use gender-neutral language. At the beginning of the pandemic, she returned from India, as she feared dying there all by herself. She took classes in meditating for world peace and soon joined the *Querdenker* scene. In fact, her partner organized several rallies. Before going to a demonstration, she always listens to her inner voice to decide whether she really feels drawn to the protest. When she gave her first ever speech at a protest rally, she did not prepare it; it simply came to her, in the sense of 'divine inspiration'. Interpersonal human socializing is just as important to her as physical contact. In her view, children are being deprived of both during the pandemic, as they can experience neither shared activities nor physical closeness or affection with others. To Ms Weber, this is more than a matter of doing children potential harm, but a real 'crime'. She regards the media and the government as 'forced into line'. For her, the fact that the state is acting oppressively, as she puts it, is to be interpreted as a sign of fear, as an indicator that something is very wrong. In her past activist involvement in environmental protection and veganism, she explains, she experienced state repression for various actions that did not conform to government policies. She harbours a fundamental distrust of democratic institutions. Regardless of how much importance she attaches to empathy, she sees no problem in

181

the fact that the demonstrations she attends are open to far-right forces.

In this chapter, we attempt to explain why people like Ms Weber have joined the *Querdenker* movement, why their pronounced sensitivity towards themselves and their environment can turn into negative affects – and how this ties in with libertarian authoritarianism.

The pandemic era: conflicts over freedom, and the birth of a movement

At first, many trusted that the situation would not get *that* bad. But, as we know today, it did: in March 2020, the first – though not the last – social distancing rules and restrictions on gatherings were introduced. From April, compulsory mask-wearing was added, too. When the coronavirus eventually came to dominate everyday life, there was a sentiment of a 'collective loss of control'.[1] Many people felt that their self-conception was under attack – a perception ultimately shared by liberal society as a whole, which had been confident that this would remain a virus for *Others*.[2] The sense of offendedness, however, went even further: the state, which had made its presence felt especially among the underclasses in recent years, suddenly intervened very noticeably into the lives of *all* citizens.

Compared to previous pandemics, the comprehensive restrictions on outdoor activities and gatherings marked a major interference with civil liberties.[3] Not only were schools, kindergartens and public institutions closed, but restaurants, sports clubs and cultural institutions had to shut down as well. The pandemic, moreover, met with heightened risk awareness compared to the past: as recently as the late 1960s, the so-called 'Hong Kong Flu' had claimed tens of thousands of lives. Yet, during the decades following World War II, contagious diseases were still a normal part of everyday life. Over the half century that followed, the approach to dealing with sickness, death and old age changed. The erstwhile fatalism gave way to a special consideration for the old and the sick[4] – though not everyone in society may have agreed. What matters, as far as we are concerned here, is that the pandemic-related measures manifested a normative advancement in the relation between economy and health. While economic aspects were generally prioritized during the eighteenth and nineteenth centuries, policies related to COVID-19 were now primarily guided by the concern to protect vulnerable groups.

Given that, according to Ulrich Beck, future catastrophes must be constantly anticipated in the 'risk society', its normal state and its exceptional state overlap.[5] During the pandemic, then, there was no more state of normality. Crisis situations – particularly those in which time is of the essence in reacting to a dynamic development – provide the executive branch of government with the opportunity to extend its powers. In Switzerland, where democratic legitimation through federal and direct democratic mechanisms constitutes a vital political principle, the Federal Council (Bundesrat), i.e., national government, declared an 'extraordinary situation' in accordance with Switzerland's epidemic control law. The executive branch was now able to introduce measures by emergency law without consulting the regional authorities in the country's provinces (cantons). The German parliament (Bundestag) confirmed an 'epidemic situation of national scope', which gave the government additional powers. While there was a relatively broad consensus across the centre-left and centre-right parties in Germany initially (the parliamentary groups of both the AfD and Die Linke abstained), the National Council and the Council of States in Switzerland resolved to temporarily dissolve parliament. The restrictions on contacts and gatherings and outdoor activities thus constituted not only a dramatic interference with people's everyday lives, but also with democratic procedures, at least at the beginning of the pandemic. Over subsequent months, deliberation as well as parliamentary and federal negotiation processes were gradually restored. In Germany, many decisions were made in consultation with the minister-presidents (state governors); all along, passionate debates ensued in the Bundestag on what parliament's role should be.[6]

The pandemic caught the state off-guard. It had to constantly adapt its measures. Recommendations and guidelines were changed time and again, often without sufficient explanation. During the first weeks, for example, the public was advised not to wear masks. This was based on medical justifications, though most likely another factor was an insufficient supply of masks.[7] Subsequently, the obligation to wear a mask was introduced – without any more developed public discussion having taken place.

That is to say, there certainly were reasons for criticism. And it was indeed levelled, albeit within certain limits. In the early days of the pandemic in particular, there was a kind of present-day TINA ('There is no alternative') politics.[8] The state acted with what can be described as 'benevolent paternalism' (see chapter 3).[9] Although the debate was by all means controversial, there was a broad consensus not to question the danger of the virus or the need for special measures. Disputes mainly circled around the extent of restrictions on freedom ('team caution' versus 'team sense-of-proportion'). Many critics, however, perceived the tentative, short-term, repeatedly corrected government policies not only as erratic but as downright arbitrary. At this point, the AfD seized the opportunity – after an initial phase of restraint – to boost its profile as the only opposition to an alleged 'digital health dictatorship'.[10] In Switzerland, the SVP also spoke of a 'dictatorship' – even though two of its members served on the Federal Council.

The unfolding of the pandemic was accompanied by an accelerated process of politicization.[11] What might previously have been regarded as more or less apolitical matters (such as the supply of food and other basic goods) or even been ignored (e.g., the precarious status of many essential workers), now became a focus of public debate. The fact that many sites of self-fulfilment (gyms and health clubs, bars, nightclubs, cultural venues) temporarily had to close down appeared to some as a kind of coup d'état against the performance-oriented individual. Distrust was on the rise. In this sense, it was not surprising when rumours started circulating in the *Querdenker* scene that people like Klaus Schwab were seeking to take advantage of the pandemic to implement their hidden agenda. In spring 2020, Schwab, then director of the World Economic Forum and, during the 1990s, a leading proponent of neoliberalism, demanded a 'Great Reset'.[12] In his vision, such an adjustment was meant to ensure that economic action would no longer be guided primarily by the interests of shareholders but by such principles as justice and sustainability. There would be good reason to regard this as little more than flowery rhetoric. Yet, in the *Querdenker* scene, Schwab's statements triggered intense discussions, and the suspicion emerged that capital was plotting to eliminate freedom.

Another important factor contributing to the general politicization were the side-effects of the risk management policy, inevitable in a functionally differentiated society. A lockdown not only reduces social contacts but has consequences for all kinds of areas of society, ranging from disrupted supply chains and the cancellation of school classes to psychological problems and social isolation – side-effects that require additional interventions or corrections of previous policies. Despite the strengthening of its executive power, the government was no longer seen as an authority really in charge of things, but rather as itself volatile. Of course, politics always also constitutes a form of experimentalism; but for many people, there was a growing impression that long-term strategies or even social progress had disappeared entirely from decision makers' agenda. Austerity, which had long been professed as an inescapable economic 'factual constraint', was abandoned overnight. Olaf Scholz – at the time German finance minister – who had previously positioned himself as a staunch advocate of austerity, now veered towards an expansive financial policy (famously speaking of using a financial 'bazooka'). At the same time, clientelism was thriving: members of parliament from the conservative CDU/CSU enriched themselves in mask-procurement deals. This raised questions about the integrity of politicians more generally. Surprisingly, however, such behaviour caused less polarization than the conflicts around (scientific) knowledge.

The already existing need for scientific expertise grew exponentially during the pandemic. Virologists gained immense media visibility. Scientists like Melanie Brinkmann or Christian Drosten virtually became celebrities and had a great deal of influence on a government politics that aspired to be 'evidence-based'. Some decision makers conveyed the idea that 'all has been said once the scientist has spoken'.[13] However, there was hardly any consensus among researchers. Their interpretations and risk assessments differed and were soon heavily contested. Knowledge and values came into conflict with one another.[14] Politics rapidly became more epistemicized, while science was itself politicized (see chapter 3).

The implementation of the restrictions on personal freedom coincided with the beginning of the protests.[15] The first took place in Berlin, where 'hygiene demonstrations' were organized by the left-leaning circles associated with the *Volksbühne* theatre. Before too long, the stronghold of critics of the pandemic policies shifted to Stuttgart, the capital of the state of Baden-Württemberg. There, the initiative '*Querdenken 711*' (referring to the Stuttgart area phone code 0711) became an epicentre and springboard of the protest movement that was soon known throughout the country as '*Querdenker*'. In

Switzerland, the critics initially called themselves the 'Corona Rebels' and were active particularly in Central Switzerland and the capital Bern. That said, the scene fairly quickly branched out into a series of different initiatives. We use the term *Querdenker* from the German context here, as it has been established in the scholarly debate (including internationally, in English often referred to as 'lateral' or 'diagonal thinkers', though the German term is retained here[16]).

The movement comprised many disparate ideologies and currents, yet they all managed to find a shared frame of reference as their lowest common denominator: questioning the danger of the virus and, consequently, the proportionality of the measures taken. This 'frame' proved an effective mobilization strategy.[17] The reiterated shared ideals were freedom, democracy and self-determination. The self-conception was that of a critical segment of the *demos*, the popular sovereign, which was reminding the state apparatus of its obligation to serve the common good, thus following the tradition of '*J'Accuse*'. Demonstrations took place in many towns and cities across Germany from spring 2020 onwards. The protest actions did not occur continuously, and the centres of gravity shifted. By early 2022, the hotspots had moved – over the course of the debate on the vaccines – to the states of Saxony and Bavaria, while the movement had continuously become more radicalized.[18] In this chapter, however, we focus primarily on the early stages, given that the fundamental anatomy and distinct origins of the movement were particularly visible during this period.

From the outset, the *Querdenker* constituted a highly ambivalent movement. One of the most commonly chanted slogans at marches was 'peace, freedom, no dictatorship' ('*Friede, Freiheit, keine Diktatur*'). The participants were very heterogeneous, at least during the first few months: affluent families with their children, aged hippies, anti-nuclear activists, esoterics, and, incidentally, right-wing forces of different stripes.[19] The hand-made placards on which they expressed their dissatisfaction ranged from sober criticism ('NO to obligatory mask-wearing'), to rhetorical escalation ('Hands off our children', 'NO to the corona dictatorship'), and on to the loss of all restraint ('Lock them [politicians and virologists] up already', 'Nail Christian Drosten to the "Cross of Merit" of the Federal Republic of Germany'). At the same time, the word 'Love' appeared throughout – as opposed to the government's cold rationality. The demonstrations often displayed the peace movement's rainbow flags with the

Pace logo, yet with the pre-World War I flag of the German Empire flying right next to them. Many of the protesters saw the country as heading straight for dictatorship, drawing parallels with the Nazi era. Some even wore yellow star badges like those once imposed on Jews. This was widely criticized as inappropriate and antisemitic as it amounted to relativizing the Nazi terror. Countless marches and gatherings were strongly emotionally charged, and even at peaceful rallies there were incidents of violence or at least heated situations on the margins.[20]

The demonstrations were often organized as happenings: drums, dance and performance helped simulate a kind of late modern hippie ambience. An imagery of merging with the crowd and with nature accompanied these almost carnivalesque events.[21] The protest was often staged with an immense lust for provocation, including frivolous disinhibition. Although the 'hygiene demonstrations' in Berlin and the self-proclaimed 'democratic resistance' were dominated, at least initially, by liberal and leftist forms of critique of biopolitical control, a 'murmur of conspiracy theory' was nonetheless clearly noticeable by this point.[22] Furthermore, the fact that the movement did not dissociate itself from right-wing forces, instead displaying an indifference and at times even an openness to such groups, was recognizable right from the start. If, in the beginning, what united the various sub-currents was simply criticism of government measures, the subsequent combination of internal processes of cognitive alignment, the dissociation from other forms of critique, and external pressure, soon created a collective identity as *true* democratic resistance.[23]

Hamburg-based criminologist Christine Hentschel observed at a very early stage how the significance of the German constitution (*Grundgesetz*, 'Basic Law') as the movement's frame of reference shifted. While the aim was initially to defend constitutionally protected basic rights, the constitution soon became the 'symbol of a lack of sovereignty' – an assessment also shared by the *Reichsbürger* (or 'sovereign citizen') movement.[24] On 29 August 2020, demonstrators in Berlin attempted what was described as the 'storming of the Reichstag', which houses parliament. In spring 2022, over the course of the so-called 'Monday walks', the *Querdenker* transformed from a movement *open to* right-wing forces to an *openly* far-right movement, at least in parts, with right-wing extremists taking a leading role in numerous places. The violence increased; politicians were now being threatened outside their homes.

The character of the *Querdenker* movement

Ms Schönle is a 52-year-old freelance psychologist, coach and family consultant. She feels in tune with nature and is a flexitarian. For her, 'lateral thinking' is the precondition for performing her job and even for leading her life in general. When she was three years old, her parents separated. Despite her early age, she learned that both sides had their own truths. She heeds this insight to this day. Her leading principles in life include responding to her inner voice and acting accordingly. In the past, Ms Schönle had faith in the state, and she considers herself to be an 'extremely democratic person'. She had already concerned herself with inequality, discrimination and anti-racism when she was an adolescent. In the past, she has voted for the Green Party and, at times, the SPD. Yet, during the pandemic she was very disappointed with the Greens, as they did nothing to stop what she considers a hollowing out of democracy. Her ultimate moment of awakening came when she was reading a policy paper published by the ministry of internal affairs. She saw the measures it outlined, particularly the obligation to wear a mask, as 'abuse', and the supposed scaremongering as 'psychological terror', especially towards children. After reading this document, she decided to quit supporting a system that exploited fear. Ms Schönle claims that several people from her circle of friends actually died a few weeks after receiving their second vaccination dose. Although the causes of death are unknown to her, she explains, she certainly knows no one who has died from COVID-19. She believes that the pandemic is being used to implement a political agenda. In her eyes, scientists who disagree are being vilified. And yet, she emphasizes, it is of paramount importance to hear different positions – and one should also 'have a bit of faith in one's intuitions'.

Ms Schönle is one of the *Querdenker* with whom we conducted extensive interviews. Since autumn 2020, our Basel-based research group has studied the movement in Germany and Switzerland. Some 1,150 individuals participated in an online survey and completed a detailed questionnaire.[25] Despite the large number of participants, however, we must assume that we were unable to conclusively document the full range of the *Querdenker* movement in our study. Staunch right-wing conspiracy theorists most likely abstained from participating altogether, as they might consider such a study as corrupt from the outset. Furthermore, we cannot rule out the possibility that the more 'progressive' part of the movement participated disproportionately in the attempt to present it in a more positive way. Therefore, the empirical findings we discuss here cannot straightforwardly be transferred to the *Querdenker* movement as a whole; rather, further in-depth research is required.

In our study, we pursued a broad empirical approach: alongside the online survey, we conducted and evaluated ethnographic observations, digital communications, and more than forty qualitative interviews.[26] This mixed-method approach allowed us to reconstruct and correlate the attitudes and forms of critique of the *Querdenker* movement and of the Corona Rebels in many different ways.[27]

The participants in our survey came from almost all social strata, yet the majority were from the middle classes. Some 31 per cent had completed *Abitur* (higher education entrance qualification), 34 per cent had completed a university degree – far more than among the German population as a whole (here, 18.5% have a university degree, in Switzerland 29.6%). Almost one in four were self-employed – again, a markedly higher proportion than this group represents among the German (9.8%) and the Swiss (12.8%) populations as a whole. In Switzerland, more than 40 per cent of respondents had voted for the Social Democratic Party (SP) or one of the two green parties in the last general election; 33 per cent had cast their vote for the right-wing conservative SVP. Asked about whom they would vote for in the next election, 43 per cent now favoured the SVP, and 34 per cent did not want to give their support to any party at all, but only to individuals, or, alternatively, said they would cast their vote for a potential future protest party. The total suggested share for the SP and both green parties, however, dropped to 18 per cent, less than half of what it was before. This same political drift was even more pronounced in Germany: in the general election of 2017, 15 per cent of study participants had voted for the AfD, whereas 27 per cent were intent on doing so in 2021. Some 61 per cent of our respondents planned to cast their vote for alternative parties, such as 'Die Basis' ('The Grassroots'). While 40 per cent had voted for Die Linke or the Green Party in 2017, only 6 per cent were willing to do so again in the next election. In Baden-Württemberg in particular, the decline of the Green Party was dramatic, losing the support of a crucial pillar of its original founding milieu.[28]

The *Querdenker* are profoundly alienated from the institutions of liberal democracy: essentially, they have not an inch of trust in the government, supra-national institutions such as the EU or UN, or political parties. They wholeheartedly reject the so-called 'mainstream' media who allegedly silence or omit critical voices, or else disparage them;[29] to them, 'the' truth is disseminated exclusively via social media. The justice system, civil society initiatives, private businesses, environmental groups and the police still enjoy a modicum of trust, albeit at a relatively low level.

The vast majority of respondents believe conspiracy narratives – those individuals with a lower level of education more so than those with more qualifications. They are firmly convinced of the existence of secret organizations that exert decisive influence on politics and think that the government is withholding the truth from the public. In their view, politicians are no more than 'puppets' of these organizations (only 8.5% do *not* agree with this statement). The *Querdenker* surveyed have no doubt that politics is working hand-in-glove with the media. The statement that Bill Gates is seeking to implement a mandatory vaccination globally is rejected by fewer than 10 per cent of respondents. The only conspiracy theory that they somewhat doubt is the one which holds that the government planned to use the vaccination campaign to implant microchips in people. Interestingly, statements implying that studies on climate change are falsified drew little support; this owes to the fact that many respondents come from ecologically informed, green and alternative milieus and do not adhere to conspiracy theories in all matters.[30]

Furthermore, most respondents are neither openly xenophobic nor Islamophobic, and they display no conspicuous chauvinistic or social-Darwinist attitudes. Instead, they often advocate explicitly anti-authoritarian positions: they are not yearning – in 2020, that is – for decisionist governance nor for a strong leader like Russian president Vladimir Putin (only 4% in favour). Some 64 per cent of respondents say that children should not be taught to obey author-ities. Around 94 per cent agree with the statement that the state is increasingly patronizing the population, and 80 per cent think that freedom of speech is under threat. The majority considers the AfD to be a normal political party like any other. Incidentally, we detected a latent tendency towards antisemitism: the statement that 'Jews have too much influence on politics' is explicitly *rejected* by only 55

190

per cent.[31] This is not surprising, considering that many conspiracy theories contain antisemitic codes.

At the same time, the majority of our study participants displayed a markedly spiritual, esoteric and anthroposophical mindset, which places holism, naturalness or faith in one's own body centre stage. This persuasion, which prioritizes natural immune defences and seeks to increase the role of complementary medicine, also entails vaccine scepticism. The findings suggested a crucial line of conflict here, even before the development and approval of the COVID-19 vaccines: 85 per cent did not even want to get vaccinated in the event that 100 per cent secure vaccines should become available. Correspondingly, 90 per cent expressed their concern that the government might introduce compulsory vaccination and a vaccination pass.[32]

We further investigated the findings from our survey in more than forty qualitative interviews.[33] We established contact with our first interviewees during our demonstration ethnographies. But the majority of respondents are survey participants who agreed to a qualitative interview in addition to completing the questionnaire. Given this self-selection of study participants, we may once again assume a progressive bias, given that far-right extremists or highly paranoid conspiracy theorists most likely consider us, as university employees, to be part of a corrupt 'establishment'.[34] We furthermore proceed from the assumption that our interview sample includes fewer respondents from the hedonistic milieu (usually associated with lower socio-economic strata), given that scepticism towards public institutions is particularly high among these groups, and they also have less free time. Some declined to speak with us because our university allegedly collaborated too closely with the two pharmaceutical corporations based in Basel. On the other hand, many of those who did agree to a conversation often left the impression on us that they regarded the interviewer as a kind of audience with whom they were eager to share their enlightenment. The vast majority of our conversation partners came from the alternative milieu, including naturopaths, radical (free-market) liberals, sympathizers of the Green Party or Die Linke, or anthroposophists. While they voiced a critique of domination, through their involvement in the *Querdenker* movement they frequently drifted from a more or less left-wing worldview towards the right – and became libertarian authoritarians.

The strong desire to talk was noticeable throughout. In our interviews, we frequently encountered a blend of an urge for justification and a pronounced sense of mission.[35] The interviewees emphatically presented themselves as progressive, informed and critical individuals who were not going to be fooled by anyone. They question the facts presented by the government because they are committed to truth, self-determination, democracy and the rule of law.[36] The majority consider themselves to be courageous citizens, resisting state intrusion and a totalitarian threat, as Mr Hoffmann emphasizes:

> In my view, this whole course of action, all the measures, are geared towards restricting the citizens of this country more and more. Based on, essentially, unverified claims. So. Well, phew, when I hear and see all this, it really makes me want to fight back. Not fighting in the sense of violence, but I do feel obliged to stand up against it.

In many interviews, the conversations started off with a form of self-legitimation: referencing *alternative* studies and statistics, respondents begin by criticizing the measures to contain the pandemic as disproportionate. This critique often takes a detour, to first account for the *reality* of the pandemic. The following statement shows how strongly the critics assert that they are arguing purely on rational grounds, and not making value judgements: 'All I'm saying is that it's just not proportionate, and my argument is based on facts, because I know the statistics' (Mr Vukovic). As autodidact experts mounting independent research, they base themselves on a counter-knowledge opposed to that of 'mainstream' experts and media: 'But I've always been like that with everything, in that I always immediately question everything, you know, I'm just not the kind of person who sees something and goes: "Woaaah, wooowww, surely all that has to be true"' (Ms Egli). It is noticeable that the critique often oscillates between abstract statements on freedom or democracy and the utmost specificity. Arguments are mechanically strung together; the autodidact laymen-experts explain why certain study results cannot possibly be correct. Informed by their own views and by accounts from their circle of friends or family, they possess a different, superior knowledge, which makes them particularly suspicious and untrusting. Distrust, however, is not the opposite of trust, but merely the negatively coded counterpart thereof. It equally reduces complexity.[37]

In particular, it was the restrictions on their subjective freedom that enraged many *Querdenker*. Ms Schuster explains her exasperation:

I can't really remember anything that has ever triggered such resistance in me as I feel right now about all these measures. [...] Of course, I've become far more critical now. But I've not yet familiarized myself with that many, with other matters, because there's nothing in which I've ever felt restricted in any major way before. Up until recently, I managed to make good and free use of my personal responsibility and my margins of freedom. I mean, I just never had the experience of feeling like a little child being bossed around from above, concerning matters that really are no one else's business.

To many of the respondents, the rules for social distancing and mask-wearing represented an outrageous paternalistic intrusion, which contradicted their understanding of social interaction. The vast majority of our interviews feature recurrent patterns of critique, which – albeit varying according to the specific account – all exhibit a similar logic. Official information about the coronavirus is doubted and criticized as distorted. Here, we can see a familiar register of critique based on the opposition between knowledge and opinions. In response to official knowledge and the power of the experts, they offer their *own research*, their own *getting-to-the-bottom-of-things*. Ms Fischer sums this up as follows: 'My hobby is thinking for myself.' People in technical professions, in particular, frequently point out their ability to interpret numbers. At the same time, they emphasize that the world of cold statistics is insufficient to develop an adequate picture of reality. They can feel that something is not right. Their personal intuition serves as a defence against abstract sciences that are impossible for an individual to verify. Mr Krugmann points out: 'Right from the outset, given my medical professional expertise and my knowledge of statistics, [I was] sceptical whether the whole thing was really what they were telling us [...]. From the very beginning, I felt like, hey, this doesn't add up.'

Another often-recurring critique is directed against alleged scare-mongering by the government, designed to create collective hysteria and facilitate the implementation of new forms of control – indeed, a total surveillance: 'If there really is a pandemic or some dangerous situation – say, a war breaks out, or whatever, what do I know', Ms Berger stresses, 'then the government's job is to calm people down, not to scare them even more.' Here, we frequently find the combination of the state/individual and security/freedom registers of critique: the state has no right to restrict individual freedom without justification, in exchange for a hypocritical promise of security. The counter-position of opening/closure is also invoked: the government's measures are seen not only as fundamental closures in terms of people's lifeworld but also as a means to restrict the freedom of speech. Ms Weber, the student of education, explains, for example, that an 'open discourse [...] simply is not taking place. People who have a deviating opinion are immediately assigned abusive labels. [...] As in, "these conspiracy theorists".'

Not all, but the greater part of respondents are indignant and feel slighted when they are widely referred to in public as conspiracy theorists because of the critique they voice. Most *Querdenker* see themselves as a minority that is being disrespected by the majority. Most of them make recourse to outwardly positive registers: opening instead of closure, defending individual margins of freedom, protecting minorities. And yet, they couple these registers with the conviction that there is a deliberate government-led conspiracy going on. This assumption turns the progressive registers into a blanket suspicion, into animosity.

Virtually all interviews we evaluated contain passages of conspiracy theory thinking, with claims being made that the government measures are not about the health and safety of the population but something very different, of a much greater magnitude. Over the course of the conversations, specific conspiracy theories are indeed cited, though often introduced in a rather vaguely worded manner – as if to test the interviewer's reaction. Take, for example, Mr Gerber: 'Well, the measures and this whole coronavirus phenomenon is of course, as I said before, only a phenomenon, it is not the cause.' Behind the scenes of the main stage of reality, there is a back stage that remains hidden from everyday public life: *nothing is what it seems*.[38] Mr Zurbriggen sees this concept of reality as a productive form of appropriating the world, even as a pillar of his positive identity: 'I consider myself a conspiracy practitioner, because I have long concerned myself with structures. Systemic structures. How does the world really work, in this or that sense, how does the government operate?' Mr Zurbriggen is the only one of our respondents who openly self-identifies as a conspiracy theorist. At the same time, all of them display a conspiracy theory mentality.

The *Querdenker* frequently see themselves as awakened, or, as Mr Flückinger puts it, as 'only just really woken up'. In the case of Ms Schönle, it was after she read the policy paper issued by the ministry of internal affairs, and for Mr Scholte, too, things had 'clicked' at a certain point. The fact that they are now able to see through the main stage affords them a sense of superiority. Like a section of the group of respondents whom we termed intellectuals, they think of themselves as a vanguard, whereas everyone else remains 'asleep sheep' who naïvely accept being locked up in their homes and monitored (Mr Gerber). They, conversely, speak the truth and mercilessly call things out as they are. In this sense, conspiracy theories can also be interpreted as a device of self-distinction: during the pandemic, no one was able to show their tattoos anymore, nor to present their body in the gym or post hip cocktail bar pics on Instagram, etc., but the awakened still stood out from all the asleep sheep – in other words, as a means of making oneself special again.

Another recurring aspect are the social groups in whose name the government is denounced. Although the question of protecting vulnerable people is largely ignored in the interviews, the *Querdenker* claim to represent defenceless minorities who are unable to speak for themselves. Particularly older people who were no longer allowed to see their families, and, again and again: children. There must be no more scaring the children, masks inhibit children's development, children do not want to wear masks, etc. As Ms Peters puts it: 'I can't believe that we're supposed to fiddle something together here that dangles in front of our children's mouths.' It was noticeable that this type of argument often reflected a kind of *functional solidarity*: the legitimate interests of other groups are referenced in order to challenge policies which one rejects. The problem with this line of argument is not really the concern to protect child welfare – many of the measures do indeed remain disputed. It is rather the projective character of this defence: the respondents in question transfer their own aversive sentiment to children's reality of life. Reference to children also always serves as a 'moral weapon' that lends credibility and weight to the objections expressed.[39] Children represent innocence and naturalness, and thus they must be protected from government intrusion, such as vaccinations. The concern for children's well-being is often conveyed in quite drastic terms (with reference made to 'child abuse' and even 'rape') and underpinned with anecdotal evidence regarding loneliness, depression or suicide. There is no question that the strain caused by the restrictions took a particularly heavy toll on children.[40] But now those who claimed to protect children from being frightened became the greatest scare-mongers of all: mask opponents and vaccine sceptics spread horrific scenarios, attempted to enter schools and harassed the pupils who wore masks.

While different evils are weighed against one another in a calculated manner, the reference to vulnerable groups serves as a moralistic argument for advancing one's own agenda. This is the case, for example, when Ms Fischer criticizes the dedication of intensive care beds to coronavirus patients:

> And if you're out of luck and all the intensive care beds are occupied, and then you show up at hospital after an accident, in need of an intensive care bed, and if things go badly, you won't get one, even though they're all empty right there in front of you. Things like that have happened. I find it absurd to simply pick an individual disease and say, 'this one is really important now and has to be treated with priority', whereas other ailments, diseases, accidents don't have this special status. To me that's playing God, and only an inhumane society could possibly tolerate something like that.

Furthermore, respondents repeatedly complain that the measures are artificially drawing out something that is simply a part of life: death. In their individual risk assessment, between living with restrictions and endangering their (and others') health, some prefer the latter. Such is the case of Ms Bächle: 'I would just say, at some point: "Hey, what the hell." I'm not willing to walk around with a mask and lock myself up forever. I just want to enjoy my life, and should I end up catching the disease and dying, then so be it.' Incidentally, this is the only instance during our interviews in which Ms Bächle reflects on the interconnection between self-protection and protecting *others*. That said, neither is she a mundane egomaniac; she simply believes that the harmful side-effects of the pandemic-related policies for young, poor and old people outweigh the risk of contagion. It is not so much social Darwinism that underlies this risk calculation we encountered time and again during our conversations, but rather a kind of natural Darwinism which puts vibrant life in the community centre stage. Ms Hubacher explains:

> We're all going to die from something eventually, that's part of it all, as sad as it may be. And older people at some point simply no longer

196

have the kind of immune system that helps them get through infections [...]. Does that person even want to go on living for another twenty years in total isolation and being allowed to receive visitors only with gloves, masks and protective overalls, or do they perhaps want to decide for themselves? No, I'd prefer living perhaps no more than three more years, but at least with having visitors and celebrations – and enjoying it.

The threat coming from diseases of civilization, such as, in our case, a global pandemic, is reframed as an inescapable force of nature. If the consequences of civilization are conceived as a force of nature, then any form of risk management policy constitutes artificial interference. To interpret this historical amnesia purely as denial, however, would not be accurate either, as the rise of civilizational dependencies does increase the dependencies on nature as well. What is ignored, then, is the fact that human–nature relations are socially produced, too.[41]

Another feature we encountered in many conversations was a rhetoric of urgency, of imminent danger. Respondents saw themselves as victims, as excluded and persecuted by a dictatorship they felt compelled to stand up to. In these moments, the aforementioned comparison with the Nazi era was invoked, an analogy used to elevate their heroic stance and demonize the powerful. In this sense, Mr Hoffmann interprets mask-wearing as a 'gesture of submission', which he carries even further rhetorically: 'It might well become the new Hitler salute'. In their escalating critique that knows no normative or historical measure or restraint, those protesting compare themselves to the victims of the 'Third Reich': 'Essentially, we are like the Jews back then, no?', Ms Jost rhetorically asks. However, the involvement of the AfD does not bother them, and certainly not that of the Swiss SVP, as they consider these parties to be equally excluded, just like them.

The political imaginary of the coronavirus critics we surveyed, and their forms of protest, suggest that many are from the erstwhile alternative milieu or its modernized offshoots: their ostentatiously paraded non-conformism, the residues of anti-authoritarianism and cosmopolitanism, the constantly reiterated claim to self-realization, authenticity and holism all support this notion. A considerable number of our respondents grew up in households that were ecologically oriented and/or involved with the peace movement, and some attended alternative schools. Furthermore, our respondents are committed to pushing back the reach of institutions and authorities, informalizing everyday forms of interaction, meditative self-care and spiritual techniques, and they syncretistically combine these aspects with elements of New Age and anthroposophical thinking.[42] Every so often, respondents speak of meditation, yoga, as well as spiritual and physical healing – in other words, of practices that are aimed at consonance and equilibrium in their relationship with nature. It may appear rather paradoxical at this point of the analysis, but precisely these elements turn out, as the argument put forward in this chapter shows, to be key elements of *libertarian* authoritarianism.

Further research on the movement as a whole is certainly needed. But the *Querdenker* we surveyed largely belong to the respondent groups of performers, hedonists and the socio-ecological milieu introduced above, whom we consider to be particularly prone to sensing that their freedom is being offended. Alongside individuals with jobs that are marked by human interaction, we also met executive staff and countless people with high performance standards. Our survey sample includes engineers, technicians, educators, IT workers, software developers, artists, food and catering business owners, freelance and self-employed creative workers, but also many life coaches, social workers, massage therapists and alternative practitioners. At the same time, interestingly, production workers or low-skilled workers were just as scarcely represented in our sample as members of the bourgeois upper class[43] – a finding that has been confirmed in the same form or similar by other studies. In a study based on a reduced milieu conception (education, stratum, values), researchers demonstrated that the 'alternative milieu' is more socially and ecologically oriented and open to other cultures, etc., while it simultaneously attaches the least importance to combatting the pandemic compared to all other milieus.[44] A study on 'value milieus' during the coronavirus pandemic, funded by the Bertelsmann Foundation, found that it was the hedonistic 'individualist materialists', the risk-taking 'easygoing socially connective people', the 'performance-oriented self-starters' and the 'unconventional self-realizers' who most fiercely criticized the restrictions on freedom, emphasized self-responsibility and refused to be vaccinated.[45]

Epistemic resistance

Mr Baumgartner works in a scientific-technical profession. He has to evaluate studies for his work all the time, and he is thus only too familiar with analytical thinking. His wife works as a psychologist; his father, with whom he has had only little contact for a long time, is a physician, just like one of his (half-)sisters; the other is a lawyer. He points to his family background to explain his passion for medical and legal issues. His wife was an Antifa activist when she was a student, later they both got involved in local politics and ran for the district parliament on the Green Party ticket. Mr Baumgartner considers himself a progressive. He has encouraged his children, who attend a Waldorf school, to join the Fridays for Future movement.

From the very outset of the pandemic, the government's measures appeared rather bizarre to him, indeed somewhat suspicious. This motivated him to attend the initial demonstrations. In their own social circles, the Baumgartners are soon accused of marching with conspiracy theorists. Yet, Mr Baumgartner and his family insist that they saw mostly 'normies' at the rallies, and surely no 'Nazis' among them. Perhaps some *Reichsbürgers*, but they realized very quickly that this was not their scene, Mr Baumgartner claims. He has a gradually growing impression that the media are reporting the demonstrations incorrectly – so, he starts counting. To him, the 'false' reports on attendance numbers mark a key moment:

> And here I have to say, I was really shocked by this. The way that the public service broadcasters [...] were reporting on TV. And from this moment on, I said, you always have to get to the source. [...] Never believe anything, regardless who said it [...]. And then I, or we, attended the one or other demonstration. Anyway, that was something like an initial spark, when we realized [this], and the damage it caused was far greater than that of the virus itself.

Ever since, Mr Baumgartner obsessively ploughs through studies and searches for mistakes. The government, science, private business, the media – he warily keeps a sharp eye on all of them. He criticizes the implementation of the measures in the Waldorf school as a politics of division – as opposed to dialogue and harmony. He no longer considers the Green Party to be a serious electoral option: 'I can't say, "I'm for environmental protection, but the basic rights only apply for certain people from now on", or so, that doesn't work.' Today, he is an active member of the Party 'Wir2020' ('We2020') that was co-founded by *Querdenker* activist Bodo Schiffmann. He also has a keen interest in alternative medicine and grows wormwood in his garden, with which he was able to treat himself and his family 'without any problems' during the pandemic. For that same reason, the Baumgartners also keep the horse wormer ivermectin in stock. In his view, the failure to widely introduce such treatments is costing lives.

Late modernity is marked by an increase in knowledge, but, consequently, in ignorance, too. The coronavirus did not correspond to the familiar pattern of reality; rather, its intrusion challenged the knowledge which many people live by.[46] That is one important reason why its existence was disputed especially at the beginning of the pandemic. However, the scientific process of knowledge generation, particularly in an exceptional pandemic situation, also means that analyses are always provisional. Furthermore, as Ulrich Beck has pointed out, certain data and interpretations concerning risks imperceptible to the senses have to be, more or less, simply believed, and in fact 'immunized against the objections that are always possible'.[47] This was also true during the coronavirus pandemic, for example with regard to the basic reproduction number (the so-called 'R-value') published daily by the Robert Koch Institute (RKI). But precisely because the risk of infection could not be sensed directly, the virus at the same time appeared just as omnipresent as the aerosols that spread it. The viral risk thus became a kind of 'modern séance'.[48]

As we have mentioned, in our interviews the respondents initially appear as rationally arguing, autodidact experts, who are not hostile to science per se but merely sceptical of a certain variety of modern science.[49] They cite discipline-specific publications and use the respective jargon. And yet, as they boastfully vaunt their familiarity with technical jargon, what they are offering is more of a kind of proto-rationalism. Evidence is never cited in combination with any methodically informed analysis, but serves, in the sense of a subversive disconfirmation, as a defence against 'official' knowledge. The focus is usually on disproving studies that confirm the need to wear a mask or to reduce social contacts, rather than on seeking novel insights.

The increasing abstraction of science is accompanied by a profound devaluation of experience-based knowledge. And the *Querdenker*, too, noticed this during the pandemic. In their view, the empirical facts were giving political action an 'obligatory character'. Some feared the creeping rise of an epistocracy.[50] To them, the fight against science therefore also signifies a fight for certain values – and for freedom. Therefore, the *Querdenker* put up *epistemic resistance*.[51] Just as during any major international tournament there suddenly seem to be millions of armchair football coaches in Germany – claiming to know far better than the managers on the touchline – now laymen virologists post their own expertise scrutinizing the expertise of others on Twitter or in Telegram groups. Such posts are often compiled in collaborative detective work and widely circulated.[52] The *Querdenker* adopt a perspective of observers of the observers:[53] their focus is not on the reality of the pandemic but on its processing by science and media coverage, concluding that the latter have been 'forced into line' and are spreading a 'propaganda of fear'. They themselves, by contrast, have long seen through all this and have ways of glancing behind the veil of illusion.

By contrast, our interview partners were conspicuously indifferent towards the coherence and consistency of their own critique. Everything is connected to everything, and sinister elites secretly control the world. While they consider the contradictions in reality to be mere fissures in the conspiracy matrix, they show no desire to resolve any contradictions in their own line of argument. Although individual conspiracy theories may in parts exhibit internal coherence, they are invoked in a virtually random, structurally incongruous manner.[54] Correspondingly, the theories circulating within the scene in part contradict one another: the virus is either harmless, or being used by Bill Gates to implant microchips into humans worldwide, or it is a biological weapon from a lab, etc. As a result, these narratives may appeal to all kinds of worldviews – including far-right ones – which can coexist without any quarrels over their specific substance. Distinctive elements function as recognizable cues that produce narrative coherence. Many participants would probably refuse to position themselves on a left–right axis of political camps, as they derive their identity from rejecting the 'mainstream'.[55] The *Querdenker*'s main concern is critique *as such*, the act of dissenting.

This form of critique as an end in itself is not directed at specific shortcomings, but at the big picture, at the epistemic structure of social domination. In order to better understand the reasons why parts of the movement have given up believing in a shared frame for the interpretation of reality, it seems worth taking a small detour and inspecting sociological perspectives on social domination.

The French sociologists Pierre Bourdieu and Luc Boltanski have engaged with the critique of domination from two distinct perspectives. In his lectures *On the State*, delivered between 1989 and 1992, Pierre Bourdieu explored the question, among others, as to why 'the social order is so easily upheld'. Bourdieu's starting point for this statement is the 'paradox of symbolic power', the 'power that is exercised in such an invisible way that people are unaware of its very existence'.[56] The state appears, here, primarily as a producer of symbolic forms. Through institutions such as the school system, it asserts 'cognitive and evaluative structures' which establish 'a consensus about the meaning of the world'. Bourdieu refers to the corresponding acts of cognition and cognitive structures as *doxa*. The term denotes 'a kind of belief that is not even perceived as belief'. It affords the state a 'magical' ability to induce obedience. This is true at least until disruptions occur that shake up these interpretive frames. The result is the emergence of *heterodoxies*, i.e., deviating interpretations, whereas the *doxa*, which was taken for granted up until then, suddenly appears as *orthodoxy*, as no more than the majority opinion, which must now be explicitly substantiated.[57] There is a selection process in the political public sphere that restricts critique to the 'finite space' of legitimate discourse. The appointment of talk show panellists or members of expert commissions, for example, ultimately amounts to a 'form of censorship' – although Bourdieu might have worded this slightly more cautiously today, given the excessive use of the term.[58] Eventually, the *doxa* is restored.

That said, Bourdieu was not in the least a progenitor of the *Querdenker* movement. The sociologist critiqued the mechanisms of advanced class societies by exposing their internal rationale. In the case of the *Querdenker*, however, we are dealing with a kind of critique that lacks any factual analysis of mechanisms and functional requirements. This latter critique is instead underpinned by a resentment that surfaces mainly in the suspicion that behind visible phenomena there are always sinister motives. And this paves the way for conspiracy thinking.

Considered objectively, conspiracy theories represent a form of heterodox, socially stigmatized knowledge.[59] Not least, they are an expression of a somewhat distorted critical perspective on domination. None of these theories may be true in the narrower sense of the word, yet their adherents claim an attitude of *truthfulness* for themselves, based on which they challenge the socially established *truth*. Their critique constitutes a performative act, namely that of casting doubt on this truth.

This is where the considerations of Bourdieu's student Luc Boltanski come into play. In contrast to his mentor, Boltanski is not primarily concerned with issuing a critique of domination but with understanding the specific forms of critique as such – hence, pursuing a *sociology of critique*. His aim is to reconstruct how critique works, the ways in which people put their argument forward, which normative foundations, etc., they draw on. His perspective helps us to understand better the performative character of the *Querdenker* movement. Political conflict during the pandemic mainly concerned the question of how dangerous the virus really was. The main approach here was of an epistemic nature, the object of critique was the very knowledge that served as the basis of political action. Boltanski generally assumes that 'the organization of social life must confront a radical uncertainty as regards the question of *how things stand with what is*'.[60] Here, the sociologist differentiates between 'reality' and 'world': 'reality' refers to a socially recognized and institutionally protected construction. By 'world', Boltanski understands, in the words of Ludwig Wittgenstein, 'everything that is the case' but cannot be sensed directly. The 'world' can override 'reality' anytime, such as through a virus that has existed for a long time but has never infected humans before and has therefore remained unknown. Such situations expose the fragility of 'reality' and show that the 'world' is in fact not at all what it seems. As long as 'reality' remains unchallenged, it usually eludes actors' attention. To Boltanski, too, domination thus rests on its 'miscognition' in everyday life.[61] But particularly in those moments in which routines change (or when they are *being* changed abruptly), mechanisms of domination become visible. *Querdenker* suspect a different reality behind the visible 'reality'. Ms Egli, for instance, speaks of a curtain: 'I open the curtain to see what's behind.' During the pandemic, she asked herself: 'Who benefits, that's the questions that lead you behind the curtain, but this curtain is still too thick for me at this point.'

Ms Egli and many other *Querdenker* want to see behind the veil of domination, which they otherwise experience only in its specific consequences. In fact, it is quite likely that the latter have caused the *Querdenker* movement to resonate particularly well with individuals from a middle-class background. As well as the lower classes, whose personal freedom the state already greatly interferes with (e.g., when applying for benefit payments), the pandemic restrictions also affected those parts of the middle and upper classes for whom the state had previously merely provided the infrastructure for them to pursue their varying degrees of freedom.[62] The agreement on what is considered reality turned out to be very fragile during moments of crisis, and transform into a fundamental uncertainty. In this context, Boltanski's reflections, which he presented as early as the Adorno Lectures in Frankfurt in 2008, read like a predictive analysis of the *Querdenker* movement. Once fundamental epistemic doubts begin to emerge, Boltanski notes, 'existential tests' become necessary, which draw their 'examples from the flux of life', examples that 'make [reality's] bases unstable and challenge it'.[63] Many sceptics formulate such a test with a rhetorical question along the lines of, 'Do you know anyone who's had Covid and who had a severe spell of disease?'. Ms Egli, for her part, just like Ms Jost, knows not of one but several cases of people committing suicide because of the pandemic. To her, the pandemic-related policies are just 'not logical', which must be because there is some kind of 'cover-up' going on.

If the suffering from reality – in this case, from the restrictions on freedom – is not alleviated and the impression hardens that criticism is being systematically ignored, this can lead to what Boltanski calls an urge for 'general unmasking' that is manifested as a *general suspicion*. It now 'suffices for a truth to be accredited for it to be suspect'. This critique, which is motivated by the 'drive of suspicion', 'can be called alienated in the sense that it is not determined by anything other than the forces that appear to resist it.'[64]

Whoever harbours a general suspicion perceives reality as a hermetically sealed conspiracy, held together by media and police. The alienated critique that proceeds from this notion tends towards an 'elaboration of fictions', which it relies on in order to continue its own evolution. The critique, Boltanski concludes, seeks satisfaction in the 'critical gesture itself'.[65] Indeed, we frequently encountered precisely this attitude in our interviews: the doubts expressed about the existence of the virus, the critique of anything considered mainstream, the repeatedly invoked topoi of 'thinking for oneself' ... as we have said before, the *Querdenker* critique is not least a performative act. Yet when the critique is merely a performance, there is no need for a principle of reality anymore. From this arises the temptation to deny reality as such, which gives *Querdenker* the freedom to overstep the norms associated with it. In their view, the 'fake pandemic' or 'plandemic' – a common phrase at the demonstrations – is merely a fabrication. To put it in Boltanski's words, they are fighting against the reality of this 'reality'.

The *Querdenker* see themselves as heroic figures in a fight for the truth, as genuinely critical exposers of lies, who unwaveringly stand up for the common good and are willing to risk the consequences. Essentially, they imagine themselves in the rhetorical tradition of *parrhesia*, the ancient virtue of speaking the truth, which also embraces the personal risk that comes with failing to keep a secret.[66] Many were open to conspiracy thinking even beforehand, but the invisible risk then heightened their general uncertainty about what is really going on. Against the backdrop of an alienation from the political system, rapidly increasing overall complexity, uncertain future prospects and social humiliations, the *Querdenker* self-stabilize through self-heroization.

Conspiracy spirituality

What Mr Leimgruber tells us sounds like the plot of a spy thriller. President John Magufuli of Tanzania, he explains, resisted the international COVID-19 regime. Magufuli believed that the virus could be defeated by praying. Then he died, although his cause of death remained disputed. Was it COVID-19? Or really a heart attack? At any rate, he was dead now – like 'all the other Africans', Leimgruber continues, who refused to play along.

> What a coincidence. We've had a heart attack. But here, they say, in our newspapers it said that he had likely died from Covid [...]. It was not a natural death. At the time, four major African politicians died within a month-and-a-half. He was the most prominent of them. All of them rejected the coronavirus.

Mr Leimgruber does not know who is responsible, but he seems convinced that it must be some major corporation or NATO.

However, for him, that is not even the point. If someone puts up resistance or declares their disagreement, 'then the system itself takes care of them'. Leimgruber has long bid farewell to the system at the time of the interview, as he joins us online from South America for the interview. In the past, he was an extremely materialistic person, he tells us. He had a decent job with a financial services provider and his main interest was money. At some point, however, none of this satisfied him anymore. He quit his job and travelled to India with his then-girlfriend. A friend, who has died since, gave him the first spiritual book he ever read. His comment on the fatal accident that killed this friend at age 29 appears rather sober: 'It was time'. Ever since his spiritual awakening, he has been an esoteric omnivore, and he is currently training to be a 'healer'. He repeatedly mentions that others often consider him 'very intelligent'. Thanks to this trait, he is able to grasp the true essence of things. Mr Leimgruber seems very friendly, he is keen to make a good impression, and talks a lot about 'love'. But this may not have always been such a central aspect in his life: during the interview, he mentions in passing that the has only just been released from prison. He had pursued an argument with police over a minor issue so forcefully that they took him straight into custody for a few days.

Historically speaking, the alienation from the rationality of highly differentiated societies, which is so conspicuous in the *Querdenker*, is not an entirely new phenomenon. The motives of a healthy lifestyle, Eastern wisdom or cosmic love, which we discern in many of our interview partners, have a precursor: the *Lebensreform* ('life reform') movement, or just *Lebensreform*, which was immensely popular in Germany and parts of Switzerland especially during the first quarter of the twentieth century.[67] The *Lebensreform* approaches' cult of a natural way of life drew on earlier Romantic ideals. Romanticism originated in Europe as an antidote to the Enlightenment around 1800, again mainly in the German-speaking world.[68] Romantic thinking refuses to subordinate emotions to rationalism, elevating them to a genuine form of cognition. Ideals such as authenticity, autonomy and originality, which have been generalized into social expectations and requirements in late modernity, are highly regarded. In addition – and in contrast to late modernity's expressive individualism – one central motivation for many is a yearning for community, introspection and a traditional, or 'natural way of

206

life'.[69] Indeed, we do not believe, as has been suggested during recent debates, that we are currently seeing the direct heirs of Romanticism taking to the street in the form of the *Querdenker* movement. The Romantic-inspired *Lebensreform* movement certainly forms part of the German-speaking world's cultural legacy, though one that is accessible only in the depths of very specific mentalities. But even though there may not be a direct continuity, we find a similarly positioned, albeit modernized, critique of a highly efficiency-oriented society that has lost its resources of meaning.[70] This was already the case in the historical vaccine-critical movements, which are still quite instructive when reflecting on today's vaccination scepticism.

Vaccinations are among the greatest achievements of modern societies. Beginning in the late eighteenth century, medical research made dramatic breakthroughs. The ability to immunize people against specific diseases helped to establish medicine as a discipline in its own right. At the same time, however, vaccinations were rigorously enforced by doctors and the state. Vaccinations constituted state interference with the individual's body, which, in the nineteenth century, was even more invasive and also riskier – particularly for the lower classes, as vaccination campaigns in working-class districts were often conducted under unsanitary conditions. The vaccine united social progress *and* biopolitical paternalism. During vaccination campaigns, society reached an understanding on nature and sovereignty; but the issue encapsulated conflicts between the state and the individual, social risk assessments and individual fears.[71] The first movements of vaccination critics in the late nineteenth century were cross-class; they were based on different currents, including *Lebensreform* followers alongside social democrats and liberals, all of whom emphasized individual self-determination.[72] Nevertheless, they resonated particularly well with the lower classes, who saw vaccinations as just another form of disrespect for their bodies as well as an extension of the paternalism of a state that ordered them around in other areas of life, too.[73] Although the early opposition to vaccines certainly featured a number of anti-rationalist aspects, it was also a plebeian form of critique of domination, directed at an authority that forcibly implemented biopolitical interventions.[74] Smallpox was most certainly an extremely dangerous disease, but the vaccination also had considerable side-effects. It was not until the second half of the nineteenth century that the harm from vaccinations was substantially reduced. As the risk diminished, vaccination acquired an even greater significance for the twenty-first-century individual. Vaccine readiness revealed citizens' level of trust in the government's health policy.[75]

The question of whether *Lebensreform* represented a progressive or a reactionary movement remains controversial to this day. At any rate, it was a reaction to organized modernity, to the rationalization of life in industrial society, what Max Weber referred to as the 'disenchantment of the world'. *Lebensreform* was a kind of spiritual counterpart to the capitalist way of life: vegetarianism, abstinence from alcohol and naturopathy formed the basis of a *natural* way of life.[76] The so-called New Social Movements from the 1960s onwards, too, emerged as a – partly Romantic-based – response to the modernization of society.[77] The characteristic focuses of the 1970s alternative milieu included the critique of alienation, of traditional authorities and of the lack of authenticity in objects, humans and emotions.[78] Besides, according to Sven Reichardt, the unempathetic seriousness of the theory-heavy student movement kindled a desire for warmth and empathetic styles of interaction within the subsequent alternative scene.[79] The rationalization of the late modern world was accompanied, eventually, by an increasing desire for the world's *re-enchantment*. The focus now shifted to intuition, spontaneous sensuousness and real-life experience. On the other hand, the failed attempt to revolutionize the world led to a focus on changing one's own body and inner self. It is the origin of the trend towards wellness and fitness, the focus on optimizing the body.[80] This trend was flanked, as many will remember, by a 'psycho boom'.[81] Spiritual, cosmological, mystical and psychotherapeutic elements were combined in the wildest fashions. Those seeking meaning quickly veered towards paths of spiritual religiosity, (re-)discovering Buddhism, Hinduism, neopaganism, nature religions and shamanism.[82] From this perspective, *Lebensreform*-related motives and a negative conception of freedom are not opposites but mutually complementary.

Today, these kinds of influences can be found in one specific worldview in particular, whose practices and style of thinking we frequently encountered during our research: anthroposophy. It occupies a special position among the alternative currents within the *Querdenker* movement. In following its originator Rudolf Steiner, anthroposophy explicitly conceives of itself as a scientific worldview, and its impact is significant in other social sectors, too, such as in the education system, namely in the form of Waldorf schools.[83] Steiner's doctrine is an eclectic blend of pantheism, anti-materialism, supernaturalness, notions of reincarnation and a race-based history of humankind.[84] He adopts a vertical perspective, focusing on the connection between humans and the supernatural. That might be the reason why Peter Sloterdijk considers him to be a 'perfectly normal genius'.[85] With a view to the *Querdenker*, it is particularly intriguing that Steiner attributes anthroposophical knowledge a higher, indeed absolute status: only 'insiders' can access the supernatural and non-democratizable knowledge.[86] Furthermore, both anthroposophy and Steiner's educational model are marked by a strong 'anti-statist self-understanding',[87] which proceeds from the perspective of the individual. Anthroposophy is thus primarily an anti-state rather than an anti-authoritarian ideology. During the pandemic, it was not so much the anthroposophically influenced institutions and associations themselves that served as incubators of the *Querdenker* movement. Instead, an elected affinity was revealed: people with a generally critical attitude towards the state more often send their children to Waldorf schools, and then they start campaigning against vaccinations and mask-wearing there.[88] Anthroposophical institutions generally exhibit a lower vaccination readiness.[89] Another reason is the profound distrust of pharmaceutical corporations, who are accused of exaggerating the benefit of vaccinations in their hunt for profit.[90]

In Germany, the popularity of anthroposophy is related to the establishment of the alternative milieu and its subsequent developing into the socio-ecological milieu. Anthroposophy 'appears as an integrative alternative as opposed to a society dominated by functionally differentiated fields', explains theologian and historian Helmut Zander, 'in which, for example, doctors are only concerned with the body, and no longer with the soul. In contrast, anthroposophists see and experience a "holistic" world.'[91] There is a vast demand for such complementary perspectives. In train station bookshops, you can find not only a broad variety of coaching and self-help and advice literature; the share of spirituality and esotericism in total sales is in fact about 10 per cent.[92] Likewise, alternative medicine is also widely established. In 2021, there were around 47,000 alternative practitioners active in Germany, performing some 46 million treatments annually. Homoeopathic 'remedies' – for which there is no scientific evidence of their effectiveness beyond the placebo effect – generate a turnover of more than half a billion euros per year, with women and academics making up the bulk of users.[93]

In addition, anthroposophy is both a source and a historical component of the amorphous esoteric and quasi-religious movement known as New Age, which comprises not only meditation, yoga and various occultisms, but esoteric-influenced forms of psychotherapy, too. Variants of such practices were mentioned in almost all of our interviews, though it should be added that yoga, for example, has changed from an esoteric to a widely adopted practice. Historically, the New Age movement – just like the *Lebensreform* – certainly had progressive roots, but in the second half of the twentieth century the occult element largely drowned out the progressive ones. At the same time, its followers often regard themselves as highly individualist, tolerant, inclusive and open-minded. British sociologist Paul Heelas describes the movement as a Romantic-influenced critique of capitalist modernity, which, however, propagates a spiritually charged consumerism in order to achieve self-realization, similar to what we find in the teachings of Osho. This is a paradoxical arrangement indeed:[94] in late modernity, esotericism is commodified, and the Romantic critique is reified as consumerism.[95] The eclectic reference to higher powers, the union with nature or contact with the otherworld becomes what Adorno mockingly referred to as a 'parody of transcendence'.[96] No wonder that Sloterdijk – the antipode of Critical Theory – popularized this commodified transcendence in his widely read books.

The offshoots of the New Age movement are also today referred to as the *holistic* milieu.[97] Here, holism signifies the notion that everything material and immaterial in the universe is 'interconnected'.[98] There are many similarities between the holistic milieu and the *Querdenker*: holistic actors are less xenophobic and more liberal with regard to drug and abortion policies than the population in general, yet they condemn tax fraud and child abuse in much stronger terms. Although the milieu has its own rock stars and authorities, the structure is not hierarchical but more network-like. However, there is a new alloy forming within the *Querdenker* scene: the holistic milieu's esotericism and spirituality are being combined with conspiracy theories, forming a conspiracy spirituality.[99] The majority of the individuals with whom we spoke assume that a small group of people want to seize control over humanity as a whole, but, at the same time, humanity is *awakening*. While the New Age movement

210

has a higher proportion of women, conspiracy theory scenes are usually more male-dominated.[100]

In a study from Austria, the authors distinguished between a holistic core milieu and a more infrequently practising marginal milieu. Individuals from the core milieu show a more pronounced tendency towards direct democratic, green or left-liberal positions. Individuals from the marginal milieu, who concern themselves primarily with occult practices and alternative medicine and who consult fortune-tellers, astrologists or dowsers, are more authoritarian and are more likely to tend towards right-wing populism.[101] This distinction provides useful bearings for the specific differentiation in our own empirical sample. We also identified an esoteric core group among our respondents: these individuals often earn a living in physical or psychological (therapeutic) services or in white-collar occupations that afford them enough free time. They mainly belong to the socio-ecological milieu, though in part also to the hedonistic milieu, as well as – albeit to a very slim extent – the group of performers. Those in the latter group often feel offended by the coronavirus restrictions, particularly regarding their outward-facing freedom. Many of them are certain that *their* healthy body would weather an infection without any problem. In the socio-ecological milieu, by contrast, a healthy immune system is rather more attributed to spiritual-natural and physical exercise. What we observed in all respondents was that the faith in their own resilience coincided with a lack of awareness of the needs of vulnerable groups.

The esoteric core group is more female, closer to nature and more drawn to direct democratic principles. This group is closer to the political party 'Die Basis' than to the AfD.[102] As esoteric individualists, they may be performance-oriented, but they also criticize the false promises and illusions of late modern competitive society. They seek self-realization within themselves; for them, esotericism means an inner freedom, but it is precisely this spiritual inwardness that makes them oblivious of social dependencies. They feel offended because the state is robbing them of their inner freedom and the sovereign command over their own body.

Beyond the core group, we find many individuals who work in technical professions or are self-employed and more strongly performance-oriented in their everyday lives, thus belonging rather more to the milieu of performers or the liberal-intellectual milieu. They practice yoga or believe in parapsychological phenomena, but

211

esotericism is not a central feature of their everyday lives. When trying to make sense of the world, they often draw on conspiracy theories. They are casual esoterics and vote for the AfD. Just like Ms Kleinschrod-Schüssler. She is 54 years old and cannot complain about a lack of work. She used to be a German and History teacher, but now she runs two hotels she inherited from her mother. She is Roman Catholic and describes her 'value framework' as Christian-humanist. She has left the AfD because of Björn Höcke but continues to vote for the party in elections. Although she rejects the notion of conspiracy theories, she considers the pandemic-related policies in general to be 'abysmal', indeed so utterly inadequate that there must be something else behind it all. Ms Kleinschrod-Schüssler believes that the measures are being implemented 'very much with intention, in order to control, or to better control the population. And [...] very different matters are being decided behind the scenes, which are not drawing any attention due to all the ostensible panic.' She names no specific actors, but we learn that she is currently reading a book by the aforementioned Klaus Schwab. Given the developments in Germany, Ms Kleinschrod-Schüssler plans to emigrate. She is no longer willing to pay taxes for this 'sick system' or to fund immigrant arrivals in the German social security system. This is a motive we will return to in the following chapter.

Libertarian-authoritarian counter-communities

Mr Zurbriggen describes himself as 'conspiracy practitioner'. He does not deny that there are dramatic cases of COVID-19 infections being treated in hospitals, but as soon as the pandemic began, he knew that the government would exploit the situation to push through a very different agenda. 'Bill Gates and Big Pharma' are determined to enforce vaccinations, he claims, but government apparatuses, too, always pursue ulterior agendas. Mr Zurbriggen considers himself a critic of capitalism, he is opposed to 'neoliberalism, Thatcher, Reagan'. He sums up his gripe about society's ills as follows: all 'that ever counts is money, money, money'.

As a trained civil engineering draughtsman, he has a keen interest in data and statistics. He, too, makes a point of always getting to the sources. Following his divorce, he lost his job because he increasingly immersed himself in shamanism and was getting on his co-workers'

212

nerves – though the fact that he was trying to conceal mistakes he had made in his work likely also played a part. Ever since, he has not managed to return to a stable path. He kept losing his jobs and currently is living in a shared apartment and training to become a 'healer'. Esoteric thinking is a key aspect of his biography. In the 1990s, he wore the orange robe of the disciples of the Rajneesh movement ('Oshoites') and became an advocate of anthroposophy. Today, he concerns himself with all kinds of conspiracy theories, and he even considers plausible the 'QAnon' theory – the narrative according to which senior members of the US Democrats are running an international child-trafficking cartel and committing ritual murder. After all, people have always performed sacrificial rituals, he says. Mr Zurbriggen has been an active member of civil society groups and organizations throughout his life, as community life matters a lot to him. As a child, he was in the gymnastics club, later he joined the Green Party, and today he has found a new home among the coronavirus critics. Even though the *Querdenker* articulate their protest with reference to individual freedom, they do not want to solipsistically stop there. They are not longing for organization (taken for an element of industrial modernity) but for community.

In contrast to the social movements in the past, the *Querdenker* neither have an agenda nor do they propagate any kind of positive political utopia. Slogans such as 'Peace, Freedom, Love' are merely the adhesive that loosely holds together this markedly fluid and amorphous movement in opposition to the pandemic-related restrictions and a new biopolitical governmentality. The latter manifests itself in recommendations and guidelines such as those pertaining to social distancing and mask-wearing. The movement's followers are united by shared frames of interpretation and, above all, a general distrust of political elites and scientific experts. They are eager to find like-minded people who have a similar worldview and who are just as 'excluded' as them. Precisely because they are highly individualist and oblivious to society at large, they seek close and emotional relationships. As a result, a 'community of distrust' emerges.[103] Zygmunt Bauman already anticipated this kind of transient networking as early as in 2000, noting that it provided a kind of temporary 'nail on which many solitary individuals hang their individual fears'.[104]

From a vantage point of utter distrust, social dependencies can be successfully negated and one can instead turn to developing counter-expertise and concern oneself with practical matters of everyday life in 'the resistance'. People adapt to the situation in counter-communities, such as health networks and dating platforms for the unvaccinated. They are driven by their yearning for a 'warm society' as opposed to a 'cold society'.[105] In these kinds of communities, an alternative reality can be constructed and sustained.[106] Love, as the antidote to functional reason, is referenced time and again – on placards, in slogans and, incidentally, in our interviews. But love can turn into its opposite at any time; say, when the atmosphere at a demonstration flips into aggressive disinhibition. Late modern 'neo-communities' as Andreas Reckwitz has termed them, are often charged with 'intense affectivity'.[107] As indicated above, the subject of children especially enraged many of our respondents. Over the course of the interviews, there was often a kind of gradual build-up of tension, until it was vented in some form of rhetorical escalation.

Of course, the *Querdenker* and Corona Rebels are only a minority in society, yet they find they have a relatively extensive echo chamber.[108] Around 38 per cent of the population display a general conspiratorial mentality, agreeing, for example, with the statement that secret organizations exert great influence on political decisions.[109] What is also revealed, in this context, is the strong link between esotericism, a conspiracy-theory mentality and authoritarianism.[110] The group of radical anti-statists, by contrast, remains relatively small, yet at the same time all the more determined to put up resistance. The vaccination rates have increased over more recent decades, though this is mainly because of the fact that the group of vaccination sceptics has shrunk. Members of this group, which often includes individuals who have completed intermediate or even higher education, are, however, less likely to have their children vaccinated than before.[111] More recently, the concern has been raised that society is becoming ever-more polarized. In our view, this is only true to a certain extent. The reality is rather more that the political attitudes at the margins are increasingly hardening.[112]

This hardening is noticeable particularly among those who previously tended to be left-leaning, before steadily drifting further towards libertarian-authoritarian positions in the course of the pandemic. Mockery and scorn are signs of an aggressive lust for destruction. There is no intention to achieve any corrections of a democracy that is allegedly developing in the wrong direction. Seeing as they believe they live in a 'dictatorship', they no longer feel bound by liberal norms. It is an *anomic* protest, which does reference values such as democracy and the rule of law, but which simultaneously vaunts its own contempt for the corresponding institutions.[113] Most of the protesters in fact oppose state interventions on libertarian grounds. Robert Nozick summarized this perspective quite succinctly: the state should neither coerce the population into practising solidarity nor 'prohibit activities to people for their *own* good or protection'.[114]

In the public debate, the *Querdenker* were labelled 'right-wing' from early on. This image was soon confounded by the fact that the demonstrations displayed no signs of pronounced nationalism and that many protesters were not remotely conservative, but quite obviously came from a very different political background. Their objective was not primarily closure – which constitutes a key register of right-wing forces – but opening: of borders, sports and cultural facilities, bars and restaurants.

This ostensible contradiction is resolved, however, when they are considered not as classic right-wingers but as *libertarian* authoritarians. They are *authoritarian* in the sense that they display several of the authoritarian personality traits as described by Adorno and his colleagues: authoritarian aggression, displays of 'toughness', destructiveness, cynicism, (conspiracy theory-based) projectivity and superstition can often be observed in severe and variously combined forms. Sexuality is only an issue in relation to the sovereignty over one's own body and that of children. Other characteristics of the traditional authoritarian syndrome, then, are either absent or coded differently: the *Querdenker* are not oriented towards the conventional values of the old middle classes but want to be unconventional. At the same time, they thereby adhere to the now conventionalized values of their milieu, among which self-realization takes centre stage. Subjectivity and imagination are not rejected – on the contrary. Above all, there is little indication of authoritarian submission.[115] They explicitly refuse to abide by government authorities. Their individualism, which they tie to a radical reified freedom vis-à-vis the state, ultimately makes them *libertarian* authoritarians, for they themselves are the only authorities they recognize.

This, as it were, anti-authoritarian element also manifests itself in two other respects: firstly, in the reorientation towards one's own experience-based knowledge, which implies the rejection of scientific expertise. Ms Weber puts this as follows: 'At this point, I really believe only what I've seen with my own eyes, or what those close to me have witnessed – like my partner, or my parents.' Secondly, in the rejection of experts. As we mentioned earlier, scientists such as Melanie Brinkmann and Christian Drosten gained considerable popularity and political influence during the pandemic. The *Querdenker*, however, blamed precisely these people for the broad restrictions on their freedom in their way of life. Consequently, they accused these figures, considered interpreters of a largely invisible threat, of serving sinister interests. This pattern was already anticipated by Ulrich Beck, when he wrote, in 1986, that risk societies are always *'scapegoat societ[ies]'*, too: 'suddenly it is not the hazards, but those who point them out, that provoke the general uneasiness.'[116] Scientific experts were repudiated; this was also, or primarily, due to the fact the detested 'mainstream' recognized these personalities as authorities. Dissident experts like the physician Sucharit Bhakdi, who claimed the virus was no more dangerous than a common flu, the doctors Bodo Schiffmann and Wolfgang Wodarg, as well as the financial scientist Stefan Homburg – and, apart from a few exceptions, they are all men – continue to be trusted, as their (former) reputation helps legitimize one's own doubts about the reality of reality through scientific arguments.[117]

In the universe of the *Querdenker*, Corona Rebels and critics of COVID-19 policies, there is a small number of more or less prominent leader figures who serve as 'alternative authorities'.[118] Authors such as Daniele Ganser play an important role in the practice of counter-epistemology. This slick Swiss historian, who is always keen to appear perfectly respectable, became more widely known for his anti-American conspiracy theories concerning NATO and 9/11 during the 2000s, and his books, YouTube videos and shows today reach an extensive audience. Beginning in summer 2020, he commented on the coronavirus, and in November 2021 he was among the initial signatories of a public appeal that warned against the dangers of lockdowns and vaccinations. Behind it all, this statement discerned the '"Great Reset" strategy of the forum of the super-rich, which calls itself the "World Economic Forum"'.[119] Ganser, who is a member of the advisory board of the above-mentioned portal *Rubicon*, was repeatedly referenced as a crucial factor in the respondents' *awakening*: 'The [...] person who changed my life, that was in fact Dr Daniele Ganser', emphasizes Mr Flückinger, for example. In contrast, Michael Ballweg, the founder of *Querdenker*, is anything

216

but a charismatic leader. Rather, he represents what researchers call a 'movement entrepreneur'.[120] A number of figures who purposefully styled themselves as tribunes of the people, such as Ken Jebsen or vegan cookbook author Attila Hildmann, also acquired a dubious fame.[121] Their usually raucous appearances and resentment-laden, frivolous political agitation are reminiscent of the 'false prophets' which Leo Löwenthal studied during the 1940s.[122] In the context of the Berkeley Group's studies, this long-standing colleague of Adorno and Horkheimer had analysed speeches, radio appearances and leaflets by proto-fascist agitators during the New Deal era. In his samples, he identified an alluring demagogy that activated pre-existing paranoia and prejudices and encouraged followers to embrace their destructive affects.

It seems appropriate, however, to add a qualification regarding the relationship between the *Querdenker* and these alternative authorities: although these prophets certainly have a vast fan base, we find no indication of authoritarian identification in our interviews. Respondents may well enthusiastically share their positions, but we detected no unbreakable faith in a leader figure. The *Querdenker*'s libertarian authoritarianism is subordinated to the abstract principle of individual freedom. It is the highest and – apart from themselves – the only authority they consider valid. Yet, in this rigid and ever-preconceived perspective, it turns into a reified freedom, which fails to reflect on its social conditionality.

During the 1980s, sociologist Niklas Luhmann referred to social movements as a part of society's 'immune system'.[123] Functional differentiation leads to risks which endanger the survival of the system as a whole, but which are unrecognizable to the individual sub-systems. Protest movements address these dangers and formulate certain 'no's'. These articulations, in turn, allow for successful adjustments: 'the system does not immunize itself *against the no* but *with the help of the no*'.[124]

The *Querdenker* certainly do address real problems, yet their critique is not aimed at correcting things in a democratic way but at the subversion of democracy and truth. That is to say, from this perspective, we are really looking at a kind of autoimmune disorder. The *Querdenker* issue a critique of domination, though, in our view, it is a *distorted* and a displaced critique of domination. At the same time, it seems appropriate to refrain from moral condemnation and instead to soberly point out the aforementioned function of social movements. It is true, by all means, that there was a void in this regard during the pandemic. Considering the extent of the restrictions on freedom, it was indeed surprising that there were hardly any established liberal or left-wing voices that might have – fundamentally, but in a reason-guided manner – challenged the measures. The function of systematic critique and, more importantly, of societal, scientific and political self-reflection was left vacant.[125]

American sociologist Barrington Moore has noted that social movements are primarily driven by a moral indignation that arises when people no longer believe the implicit social contract is being fulfilled.[126] In late modern societies, this contract states: whoever wants to indulge in individualism and is ready to perform will receive far-reaching (albeit reified) freedoms in return. Initially, during the lockdowns, these freedoms were curtailed for everyone, later only for those who refused to be vaccinated. Jürgen Habermas has argued that the restrictions of basic rights were justified because they served to protect the lives of citizens. The state, he asserts, 'was entitled to enforce' solidarity 'for functional reasons alone'.[127] As accurate as we believe Habermas's assessment is, he does not sufficiently take into account the reality that, ever since the onset of neoliberalism, solidarity has been included in the social contract as a kind of residual element at best. The obliviousness to the societal environment that characterizes reified freedom leaves little space for solidarity.[128] But this is not to say that the *Querdenker* are pure 'egomaniacs'. They are, by all means, socially minded, as our interviews reveal in many instances. And yet, this sociality does not encompass the state or society as a whole, but certain *communities* which in their view precede society and represent a self-directed counter-model to social relations somehow controlled by an external source, which many respondents were already wary of even before the pandemic.

What is more, the *Querdenker* operate within a distorted set of political coordinates, in which the critique of domination often appears unstructured in normative terms. The left has long ceased to be the leading force in these circles; indeed, during the pandemic, it largely supported the government's measures. In a way, the *Querdenker* thus constitute the continuation and radicalization of 'anti-politics', which has seen a rapid rise ever since the financial and Eurozone crisis at the end of the 2000s. The 'anti-politics' of movements like Occupy or Italy's Five Star Movement were an expression of moral rebellion.[129] Likewise, the yellow vests movement in France (*gilets jaunes*) indicated a profound alienation from liberal democracy. With a view to their direct democratic practices, we may regard these movements as constituents of a new counter-democracy. They articulated a profound critique of the modus operandi of liberal democracy and its institutions. What they lacked was an alternative social and political vision. The *Querdenker* are likewise an expression of political alienation, and they, too, have no political project. They appropriate the critique of domination, so to speak, *laterally*. The classic social movements' critique was usually directed against the (capitalist) state, whereas the *Querdenker* see a conspiracy at work.

When challenging the dominance of official experts, they follow, in a distorted way, the tradition of previous social movements: for example, the representatives of the anti-nuclear movement confronted the official expertise that implied the safety of nuclear power plants with a systematic and, importantly, scientific counter-expertise. The counter-experts of the social movements created a counter-public sphere which connected science with questions of power and everyday life.[130] The *Querdenker*, by contrast, rely on heretical experts, on renegades who draw their legitimacy exclusively from their antagonism towards the 'mainstream'.[131] The critique that is put forward is epistemic because it voices doubt about the reality of the virus, yet it has no theoretical basis of its own, as, for example, Marxism represented for the labour movement or feminism for the women's movement. In lieu of theory, there are only soundbites and snippets of argument that are erratically strung together; the *Querdenker* attach little value to a coherent line of argument. They imply that anyone can be an expert. Here, the democratization of knowledge turns into the individual presumption to knowledge. Just like in a distorting mirror, we find classic slogans of previous movements, too: while the slogan 'my body, my choice' refers to women's reproductive rights in the context of feminism, here it conveys the refusal to get vaccinated and practise solidarity with the rest of society. The *Querdenker* are emotional, ever-suspicious and, in a sense, always in opposition. In the name of democracy, they subvert democratic norms. Behind the slogans that celebrate freedom, justice and love, there is a more or less destructive nihilism – and this destructiveness in particular forms a key element of libertarian authoritarianism.

— Chapter 8 —

SUBVERSION AS A DESTRUCTIVE PRINCIPLE: REGRESSIVE REBELS

Ms Renz's world is no longer the one she once knew. In the past, the small county town in which she grew up and still lives was a bustling town with busy shopping streets. Today, she says, many shops have closed down, the streets are deserted, with one 'kebab shop' next to another. 'Life' as she used to know it has disappeared from her town. This masseuse, born in 1961, has witnessed the erosion of public infrastructure first-hand: her small parlour is in the same building that used to house the municipal hospital before it was closed down. 'Now they have taken away our hospital', she remarks with resignation, just like all the other 'big things' that were taken away. Along with the hospital's closure, Ms Renz, who has neither any friends nor a partner and relies on and trusts only her daughter, lost a significant number of her clients, too, and thus her contact with the social world. Although her massage parlour remained at the same address, the rest of the building was left vacant, and it was subsequently repurposed as accommodation for refugees. They brought life back into its empty rooms – but Ms Renz felt like her own life had been taken away. She felt surrounded by her new neighbours: 'They were above me, next to me, beneath me.' In her view, these asylum seekers had brought a different and alien 'mentality' and 'way of life' with them. They barbecued food on the balcony, made too much noise, listened to music until late at night, and approached her clients until they stopped coming altogether. Admittedly, the reason for this could also be related to the fact that she increasingly tried to set her clients against the refugees. While she places great emphasis on not submitting to conventions, she emphatically demands that the refugees do just that.

Ms Renz is far from acquiescing in her bleak existence, however. Even in her youth, she was always a 'revolutionary', never conforming and always 'taking a swipe' at differing opinions. During the conversation, she repeatedly bangs her hand on the table, talks herself into a rage and even verbalizes her violent fantasies. She refers to Cem Özdemir, the Green Party Minister of Agriculture who has a Turkish family background, as a 'w*g asshole' whom she would be happy to 'nail to the wall'. Whereas her mother was a dedicated volunteer election worker, she herself has always been a protest voter. Initially, she voted for the far-right Republikaner party, followed for several years by Die Linke. But when this left-wing party also advocated for 'open borders', Ms Renz turned away from it. Over the past years, she has pieced together her own world through alternative media. This may not be a coherent world, but it certainly channels her anger towards concrete images of the enemy. She rebels against the fees for a TV/radio licence, considers that Germany is not a 'sovereign state', possesses a '*Reichsbürger*' passport and believes that 'the Jews' want to 'wipe out' Germany. The only politician that gets her excited is Alice Weidel from the AfD, with her 'calm' and 'sarcastic' style. Renz is now an AfD member, as it is simply the 'strongest' party of the 'opposition'.

The biographical background of Ms Renz is typical of the ongoing regressive revolt. Although she already had an inclination towards authoritarianism in the past (her voting for a far-right party), it was democratically domesticated. Subsequently, she was able for many years to express her anti-establishment sentiment by voting for Die Linke – a party which promotes a decidedly anti-racist position. In 2015, however, she began drifting towards libertarian authoritarianism. Indeed, she still refuses to bow to any kind of conventions, and she is not submissive towards any external authority, but she is extremely aggressive and projective towards 'foreigners' and their strange customs. She vehemently rejects conforming to the 'mainstream'. Similar to the rebels, which the Berkeley Group around Adorno observed in their US exile during the 1940s, many of the people to whom we spoke have always had disregard for any kind of authority. They rebel against conventions and time and again come into conflict with their social environment. Their tendency towards the extreme, the excessive and the subversive has taken a rather destructive turn in more recent times. They rail against asylum seekers,

Muslim or Jewish people and, at times, bluster into violent fantasies. Most of them have experienced existential turning points or crises in their lives, for which they blame a corrupted system that supposedly restricts their freedoms and gives an advantage to 'strangers'. In this chapter, we shed light on the inner life of this out-of-control rebellion, the political views that structure the thought and action of the corresponding individuals, and the aversive emotional worlds that make their anti-capitalist-leaning social critique change over into resentment and anger. Alongside the type of the regressive rebel, we introduce the authoritarian innovator, essentially the former's more moderate comrade-in-arms. The latter also harbours xenophobic and authoritarian views but does not fundamentally question the democratic system.[1]

Engagement and alienation

Before the 'Alternative for Germany' (AfD) entered parliament as the third-strongest political force in 2017, a number of social movements and campaigns worked to prevent its looming electoral success. In 2016, the NGO Campact launched an online campaign in opposition to the right-wing populist party.[2] For this progressive organization, such a campaign was a novelty, as it had traditionally focused on ecological and social issues. After the campaign was rolled out, the activists at the organization's headquarters were rather startled by some of the reactions: a number of people on Campact's mailing list who had consistently supported the NGO's campaigns in the past now protested against this effort. They expressed their support for the AfD, and quite a few professed their intention to vote for this party. The puzzled NGO activists sought advice from researchers, and, eventually, we agreed to conduct a joint study to examine neo-authoritarian forms of political participation.[3] One question in particular was at the heart of this endeavour: how can it be that people who were dedicated supporters of campaigns for progressive causes, such as protesting and criticizing privatizations, have developed an affinity for the AfD? In order to find answers to our questions, we conducted sixteen biographical-narrative interviews in 2017.[4]

Whenever the success of right-wing populism is discussed, there are usually two dominant approaches to explaining its causes: a socio-economic one, and a socio-cultural one. While the former emphasizes economic problems, precarization and experiences of deprivation, the second argument focuses more on perceived threats to cultural values.[5] Over the course of our interviews, and once again in the subsequent analysis, it became clear that neither of the two approaches provides an adequate explanation. In our empirical sample, both people with and without severe experiences of deprivation were fighting the same *Kulturkampf*. Quite frequently, economic and cultural factors were closely interwoven.[6] Above all, the two existing explanatory approaches tell us very little about how the views of the followers of right-wing populist parties have changed over the course of their biographies. In this regard, our interviews managed to fill in a gap. These individuals – who had already been suspicious of official politics but translated this discontent into civil-society engagement for progressive causes before eventually turning towards the AfD – can thus help us better understand a counter-democracy that is ever more destructively turning against the social order. During our study, we encountered two distinct types associated with a drift towards the right. The first one constitutes a form that remains within the bounds of democratic conventions and probably most closely resembles the classic authoritarian. We refer to this group as the *authoritarian innovators*. The other type is that of the regressive rebels, a radical variant of libertarian authoritarianism. At the end of organized modernity – marked by socially regulated and relatively closed nation states – these people were cosmopolitans. But at the height of unbounded, deregulated and socially de-secured late modernity, their trajectory took a turn. They became reformed cosmopolitans, and now mutiny against liberal norms. Depending on the situation and group, they may rail against asylum seekers (in public), rebel against authorities, or declare that anyone with a differing opinion must be deluded. After fleshing out the common authoritarian characteristics of the two types, we introduce the type of the authoritarian innovator as a counterpoint that allows us to draw more clearly the analytical contours of the regressive rebel.

Ms Wimmer, born 1959, has all but stopped ever leaving her flat. She even has her groceries delivered to her door. Ever since 11 September 2001, her world has got continuously smaller, with only photographs and souvenirs telling of days gone by. At one point, they drove a Ford Mustang. She once travelled across the Middle East with her husband. Her voyages even took her to Thailand, where she converted to Buddhism. Today, she only barely ever musters up the courage to leave the house. She perceives the many migrants living in her neighbourhood as a threat. This spatial withdrawal, however, does not mean that she is politically apathetic: Ms Wimmer is an online animal rights activist. 'For me, animals come first', she says. Consequently, she signs all petitions she can find on the web, even when she does not understand the language they are written in. She considers the government to be a mere 'stage play', with 'the' economy and 'the' lobbyists acting as its directors.

Ms Wimmer's life situation and views could in various respects be regarded as prototypical of the entire interviewee population: they were or are active members of progressive organizations such as trade unions or, for example, Campact, and long adhered to solidarity-based and inclusive principles. But over recent years, they have retreated to the private sphere and their social circles have shrunken to a small cell to which they usually grant only very few people access – mostly family members. Their engagement, which used to be geared towards advancing a productive critique of society's defects, has transformed into a destructive distrust.[7] Almost all of our interview partners tell us that they have no or very little trust in parliaments, political parties and the EU. To reference Pierre Rosanvallon, they live in a 'society of estrangement'.[8] They trust neither politicians nor strangers in their own personal environment. When they get to speak at length, many of them point to neoliberalism and the austerity policy over the past thirty years as the reasons for this loss of trust. The social world became unstable, and welfare-state social security systems were gradually dismantled. Two disillusioned former SPD voters speak of 'predatory capitalism' and 'market-conforming democracy'. The decline of the SPD is in fact cited repeatedly. Should it not 'really be the party of the ordinary people, of the workers?', asks Mr Rupp, a retired bank clerk.[9] For many, the Schröder government's neoliberal reforms of the unemployment and welfare benefits system subsumed under the watchword 'Agenda 2010' marked the decisive turning point.

They feel increasingly powerless faced with the dominant political system. In their view, it has sealed itself off from any kind of contribution from civil society. They consider the parliaments to be controlled by professional politicians who are out of touch with reality. Oppositional forces have been shut down and degenerated into a 'pseudo-opposition', as Mr Rosowsky explains; he is a gym instructor who moved among far-right circles at one point. In his view, the state resembles a 'GDR 2.0' in which everyone is systematically monitored and all media have been brought into line. Our respondents criticize a 'consensus of the centre'[10] that morally de-legitimizes counter-democratic movements – an argument that we already came across while discussing the intellectuals associated with the now right-wing magazine *Tumult* (see chapter 6). Mr Kirchheimer, for instance, a lorry driver signed off sick who immerses himself in the books of the conspiracy-theorist publisher Kopp Verlag in his free time, shares this observation: 'It's all mishmash, all the same thing. There are no differences anymore. Because we're no longer being governed by politicians but by lobbyists, by the lobby.'

Among our interview partners, the crisis of representation has changed over into a fundamental scepticism that calls into question parliamentary democracy as such. They interpret political processes in that 'conspiracy-theory mode'[11] which we have come across more than once in this book. They speak of 'simulated democracy', 'manipulation' or intentional 'lies and misinformation'. In their view, the true powers-that-be pull the strings in gloomy back rooms, behind doors that remain closed to ordinary people. The more thoroughly the interviewees lose themselves in the thicket of conspiracy-theory thinking, the more likely they will claim that all *others*, the majority of the population, have lost touch with reality – quite similar to the *Querdenker*, who see themselves as the awakened as opposed to all the 'asleep sheep' (see chapter 7).

Our interview partners propose ideals of descriptive representation and direct democracy, as opposed to a politics that has abandoned the interests of ordinary people. Ms Renz sums up her demands to professional politicians as follows:

> Okay, I vote, but they are representatives of the people, I can't even stand to hear the word 'government' any more, but, so, they are representatives of the people, and they have to represent me, meaning, what I believe, my opinions, what benefits me, what is good for me. When I speak of myself, I mean everybody. Fine, everyone has a different opinion, but whatever they're doing, I want to be consulted. They live off my money, my taxes. I'm the one who pays them for what they do.

Mr Ludwig, a self-employed haulier, who has built a basin for drinking water in his garden and has stocked up food supplies for an emergency, demands more 'popular referendums'; others favour direct democracy along the lines of the Swiss model. The crisis of representative democracy is to be solved through direct representation. In this populist notion, a pathology of counter-democracy is discernible which can be described as *negative sovereignty*.[12] Key principles of parliamentary checks and balances, representation, delegation or intermediation by means of organization are treated with near-compulsive hostility. Decisions in which our respondents had no say or which they disagree with are regarded as the result of a conspiracy. In the name of the people, they advocate a reified freedom which rejects any kind of sociality. Here, counter-democracy has truly become *un*political, as it lacks the reference to a shared world.[13] The individual, personifying the populace at large, now rises to the role of sovereign.

Authoritarian political models are, however, welcome, whenever these serve their own interests. Mr Bollinger, for example, was a conservative all his life but has also voted for the Green Party. At the time of the interview, he was 72 years old and retired. In his view, Muslim men pose a threat to women, preventing them from moving about freely within the public space. In fact, these days his partner only leaves the house armed with her pepper spray. He thinks that drastic measures are needed to curb the unfettered and uninhibited chaos in the streets: 'We need doers in Germany, we don't need windbags, we've got enough windbags, doers are what we need.' Someone like Helmut Schmidt, he adds. It is probably no coincidence that six of our interview partners make the same positive reference to the late Social-Democratic German Chancellor who died in 2015, as he embodied precisely what they believe to have lost: the link between the political and the social order. After all, Schmidt was not only an SPD politician, he was also soldier-like and tough.

The idea of popular sovereignty, to which, according to Rosanvallon, counter-democracy lays claim, is reversed and turned into a destructive force (see chapter 3).[14] When asked about the AfD's appeal to her, Ms Wimmer replies: 'The fact that they are finally doing something, which Mummy "We-can-do-it" Merkel is incapable of.' Next, she explains the objectives of the AfD: 'And really, I want to hear German being spoken around me here in Germany and not feel as if I was in Africa.' In the imaginations of our interviewees, then, the 'people' are by no means identical with the population. Certain parts of the latter category are excluded from the former. They define 'the people' in dissociation from those who in their view do not belong to this group, regardless of whether they invoke political ('the people' vs. 'the elite'), moral ('corruption' vs. 'integrity') or ethnic ('natives' vs. 'immigrants') categories.[15] Mr Rosowsky, the gym instructor born in 1969, remarks in this context: 'Well, we have to live with our own, but not with the foreigners.' Here, similar to the nostalgic class struggle of certain intellectuals, the register of 'the majority' is used to exclude minorities (see chapter 6).

The remarks by Ms Wimmer and Mr Bollinger are representative of what is a major concern for all the study participants: anti-Muslim resentment and the scandalization of asylum policy. Immigration appears as a crucial driver of the erosion of the social order: 'You won't hear any German', Mr Rudolph says of his hometown in south-western Germany. To our interview partners, the urban social space in particular is replete with dystopian features. It appears as the hotbed of moral degeneration, lawlessness and violence, once again with a causal link to the Muslim population being constructed: 'Just go into the city, go to Essen or Cologne. Cologne is already a caliphate today', Mr Münziger believes. The town boundary sign, as the gateway to the urban space, marks the end of order; our study participants talk a lot about 'ghettoization', 'parallel societies' or 'no-go areas'.

As we have already mentioned: many of our interview partners cite biographical turning points and perceived losses of control. The have experienced the death of a family member, a painful end of a relationship or economic deprivation in the form of being made redundant or having to discontinue their own business. Quite a few have felt the 'silent compulsion of economic relations' in their lives, indeed, mostly long before the year 2015, which so frequently marks the crucial turning point in their accounts.[16] They remained silent for a long time. Only when the figure of the stranger entered the stage in 2015 did the rebellion against the dependence which they have experienced in moments (or, indeed, longer periods) of economic or social deprivation erupt in a destructive manner.

Moral condemnation and exclusionary critique

Mr Bollinger wants a well-ordered life:

> I'd put it this way: what I want is not a shift to the right. Currently, we have drifted so far to the left, in the media, on TV and also inside

227

the political parties. Just a small swing to the right. What I would like to see is just a bit more order, legal security, that our judges return to passing just verdicts, and for women to be able to walk the park at night or go shopping without being afraid.

The trained industrial business-management assistant, who was raised in the strict home of a 'staunch soldier' and repeatedly had to change career path, votes for the AfD. In his view, it is the only party that still represents the interests of ordinary people ('the centre'), which is why it is being censored by the establishment. He has been involved with Campact activities because he regards it as a citizens' movement that is not attached to any political parties. The then-acting chancellor Angela Merkel is no more than a 'stupid puppet' to him, acting at the command of George Soros, the 'Rothschilds and Bilderbergers'. He suspects that the European population is intentionally kept ignorant, and that the media have been brought into line so that the nation states can be secretly dissolved. As the moderator of various online conspiracy-theorist forums, however, he knows the truth: 'Sarrazin[17] is right, Germany really is abolishing itself.' To him, Germany has long been Islamicized, and the streets are no longer safe because of all the 'stabbers' and 'rapists'. And he emphatically stresses that he regards Islam to be the 'only real danger'. He loses himself in aversive emotional worlds which have taken on a menacing life of their own, and even demands 'labour camps' for Muslim asylum seekers and the determined use of armed force against criminal migrants. He is certain that civil war is just around the corner; then, finally, there will be some cleaning up. He knows of more and more people who are illegally arming themselves.

With his anger, his violent fantasies, and the imagination of a coming insurrection, Mr Bollinger represents an extreme position within the range of indignation which we encountered in our sixteen interviews. Even though most participants do not express themselves nearly as destructively as Mr Bollinger, they nevertheless share a notion of injustice that is advanced from a position of moral superiority. Mr Schmidt, for instance, a retired engineer, who leads an orderly structured life and has a secure socio-economic background, has a problem with asylum seekers' work ethic: 'But then they come here, and, well, lie down in our social safety net. Or, to put it more bluntly, hold their hand open and live off the rest of us.' Before voting for the AfD, he was a loyal SPD supporter and a union representative at his workplace. That is to say, he certainly seems to be somewhat sensitive to social injustices. And yet, he perceives the unemployment of asylum seekers not as a structural problem but as a question of ethics: surely, they could work, if only they wanted to. His outrage is sparked particularly by the image of the Muslim or Arab male. Almost obsessively, he assigns this figure disinhibited sexual characteristics. Mr Ludwig speaks of a group of Syrian men who 'sit around in the city all day long', pick up their groceries at the food bank, but drive a 'big Mercedes'. The self-employed lorry driver born in 1962, who is preparing for a state of emergency, makes a point of emphasizing how new and large this car is. It is but one example of the alleged illegitimate appropriation of assistance from the welfare state: 'Yes, someone has funded it [the car], probably me', he adds sarcastically. Almost all our interview partners favour an 'exclusionary solidarity'[18] which severely restricts welfare support measures and reserves them for the autochthonous population only. In other words, here we encounter an excluding concept of social justice that could be interpreted as a regressive side-effect of *negative performance thinking* that has proliferated along with the restructuring of the public solidarity-based welfare system. A large majority of our interviewees present themselves as willing to perform. Not only do they not abandon this principle, but, on the contrary, they virtually over-identify with it. However, despite their efforts, they are often unable to replicate their parents' professional success, have lost their job due to privatizations at the workplace, are struggling with poverty because of old age or sickness, etc. Performance now becomes a negative category of classification. Those whom they regard to be unwilling to perform are vilified. Considering their experiences of powerlessness and failure, they seek to assert their sovereignty by hating on strangers. The latter serve as surface on which to project the perceived injustice that causes their own diffuse anxiety in everyday life.

Interestingly, we were unable to detect a conflict between cosmopolitanism and communitarianism in our conversations, such as that claimed in some attempts to explain right-wing populism.[19] Unlike among parts of the intellectual milieu, the outrage here is rarely sparked by 'gender-asterisks', a third toilet door or veganism (see chapter 6). The critique is not so much culturalist in nature but rather motivated by certain notions of what social policies ought to be, and it is directed primarily against parliamentary democracy and its representatives as well as Muslim minorities.

The summary analysis of respondents' imagination with regard to libertarian authoritarian attitude patterns clearly reveals a tendency towards authoritarian aggression, a binary conception of power, and destructiveness. Another noticeable aspect is the tendency towards stereotyping, projectivity and sexuality, often conflated with the image of the Muslim male. In contrast, the attachment to conventional values is inconclusive: some were lifelong conservatives, but the majority espoused progressive positions before closing themselves off to the open society. What unites them is the diagnosis of a fundamental loss of order. And yet, the people we interviewed are not classic authoritarians. They are anything but submissive, *au contraire*: they are extremely suspicious of the state and any authority figure. And nor do they reject the sensitive, sensuous or the imaginative per se; they are committed to animal rights, or are themselves what might be regarded as the 'black sheep' of their families. In the discussion of the regressive rebels, the contrast with classic authoritarianism will become even clearer. These individuals found their parents' conformist lifestyle suffocating. They wanted to pursue self-realization, travelled to distant countries, turned to Far Eastern religious traditions or artistic activities. The regressive rebels in particular are highly individualist individuals, although they often lead a lonely, almost isolated existence. What unites all our interview partners is that they all at some point responded to experiences of powerlessness with social withdrawal. Yet, in each case this led them not to political passivity but to what can instead be understood as counter-democratic sovereignization.

Authoritarian innovators

The Schmitts are politically interested and reflected people who lead a neatly well-ordered life. That said, they have twice been struck by ill fate, as both of their sons have died. Unlike other respondents, they do not work themselves up into a rage when describing the problems in society; rather, they appear controlled and reasonable. Mr Schmitt is from a social-democratic working-class family that has been 'constantly advancing upwards'. Mr Schmitt, who has a degree in mechanical engineering, voted for the SPD and, as mentioned before, was an active union representative at his workplace. After a series of broken election promises, however, he entered into a 'reflection period', and he lost his faith in the SPD and the other parties. In the eyes of this couple – the two agree on just about all matters – politics has lost its credibility. As Mrs Schmitt states, the political parties 'in part' (and she emphasizes this qualification) see citizens merely as a 'stupid electorate' whom they even 'lie to at times'. This was their reason for turning towards the AfD. They resorted to this vote not so much for 'the faces' of this party, Mr Schmitt adds, but rather 'out of protest', because the AfD is supposedly 'pushing politics forward'. The couple has also voted for Die Linke in the past – specifically, because of Sahra Wagenknecht.

Reflecting on this change in their political attitude, the couple tell us: 'We moved, from being longstanding SPD voters, over a bit more to the right, because what Ms Merkel did two years ago is just not acceptable, in our view.' It was the government's asylum policy that motivated them to turn against the established party system – albeit without discarding it entirely. They get defensive when they are called 'racists' at their table tennis club, and regard their protest as a corrective to the unlimited admission of asylum seekers into Germany. They are not opposed to migrants per se, but to too many, seeing as 'people with a migrant background' have 'attracted negative attention' time and again. Mr Schmitt is anything but a typical racist: for a long time, he volunteered as a refugee aid worker, taught German classes, and the couple continues to provide tutoring for children from a school with a high proportion of migrants. After all, one should 'not only whine, you have to do something, too'. The Schmitts present themselves as reasonable and moderate; they are sceptical, but they want to reform parliamentary democracy from within. They thus constitute the type we identified as authoritarian innovators, as opposed to the regressive rebels. Here we are guided, among other things, by the considerations advanced by Robert K. Merton which we introduced in chapter 4. Just to recap: from the 1930s onwards, Merton concerned himself with the question of how social groups with limited resources react during periods of accelerated change and anomie, when they are no longer able to attain the goals regarded as legitimate through socially accepted means. In this context, Merton lists innovation and rebellion as two typical patterns: in the case of rebellion, resistance is dominant, and socially recognized aspirations are discarded. Things are different in the case of innovation: it is not that the goals as such are abandoned, but that the corresponding individuals somehow chose non-recognized paths to achieve them. The authoritarian innovators we encountered during our interviews continue to advocate what they understand by democracy and social cohesion. At the same time, they consider the established liberal democratic parties and the media to be unable to restore that democracy they feel they have lost – which is why they pin their hopes on the AfD in the sense of an innovation.[20]

Unlike the regressive rebels, authoritarian innovators are relatively well integrated socially: their occupational status is secure, or they look back on a successful professional career (three of them are already retired). They are moderately prosperous and live in well-ordered family structures. All of them place a high level of trust in their employers, and were, or are, employed full-time and with permanent contracts in mostly prestigious professions. Their jobs demand(ed) a high degree of social cooperation: in our sample, there is an engineer, a teacher, a plant manager, a worker from a high-tech company who runs an organic farm on the side, a bank clerk and a cultural worker who simultaneously works as a porter.

Of our 16 interview partners, we classified nine people as regressive rebels and six as authoritarian innovators, while one individual could not be assigned conclusively.[21] Given the striking genera-tional differences among the authoritarian innovators, we further divided this group into two age-based sub-groups. The older and retired individuals (cohorts 1944, 1946 and 1953) experienced social advance and professional success: from being the first or only one in the family with a degree on to becoming an engineer, from being a bank clerk to becoming a business manager, or from being an employed papermaker to becoming the plant manager. They looked back at standard biographies: school, professional training, first job, marriage, starting a family. They had traditional marriages, corresponding to the classic male breadwinner model with all its constraints, but also its securities. While the wife's tasks commonly included managing the household and rearing the children, the husband was free to advance professionally. They completed a 'family career',[22] whereby all of them rose up in the elevator together. The interview partners remember working extra hours and being overwhelmed, but their path ultimately paid off. Within the conven-tional tracks of a *secured* individualization, they were able to realize the dream of a middle-class life.

Three middle-aged interviewees (cohorts 1956, 1963 and 1964) still work, and they express overall satisfaction with their jobs and their salaries. Their social and occupational trajectories in life, however, are more heterogeneous and progressed in less linear patterns. They also started from largely unprivileged conditions (two have a basic school leaving degree, the third person was able to attend university in the GDR), but, compared to the older authoritarian innovators, their professional advancement was far more difficult. All of them report past or current financial problems, involuntary career changes, intermittent self-employment or juggling multiple jobs. And yet, they managed, through their own initiative, to master their difficulties. Even though they may not have a completely carefree future outlook, they have settled into fairly secure conditions. That said, their biographies do show how organized modernity's premises of social advancement and security gradually became more and more porous. They live in patchwork family contexts or indicate having had marriage problems. At the same time, what matters more to them is their desire for free self-determination and lifestyle choices: Mr Jung, born in 1964, works shifts in order to live his dream of running his own organic farm. Mr Lohmann, born in 1965, had to give up his job as sales agent when the print market collapsed and now produces inclusive films starring disabled actors. Their lives follow the winding, at times bumpy paths of *de-secured* individualization.

Furthermore, the two age groups also show differences with regard to their political socialization. The three older respondents indicate a family-based loyalty to the major parties. Besides Mr Schmitt, Mr Gruber is also from a working-class family closely connected to the SPD. His father was an industrial production worker: 'It's my father's influence: my dad was an SPD man, and the workers in our village were all SPD men, so that has an influence on you from early on.' The third, Mr Rupp, comes from a farmer's family. He grew up in a rural, conservative area: 'I'd simply say you were less political. In a way, you voted CDU and everything was fine.' People voted according to tradition, not based on specific identification. As a result, they state, their political consciousness did not form before they reached retirement, when their distrust started to grow. Although they need not fear ever losing their modest prosperity, the erosion of social security has left its mark on them nonetheless. They start brooding, and sense vague feelings of anxiety and fear, which, however, they articulate mainly via issues related to asylum or migration policies.

The three younger individuals, in contrast, have been politically active from an early age. Mr Jung became involved with local politics as young as his early twenties. He opposed the conservative-dominated politics in his hometown, but despite his profound ecological awareness he never joined the Green Party. Today, he votes for the AfD, as he regards immigration to pose a threat to 'German values'. Mr Lohmann, a conscientious objector, became a Greenpeace member during a trip to Canada as early as in the 1970s, left the Jusos (the SPD's youth organization) to join the Green Party and became involved in the anti-nuclear movement. Ms Krause grew up in the GDR, where she became a teacher as well as an activist with the reformist movement. Following German reunification, however, her options in the labour market were slim, and she retrained as an estate agent – a career that did not make her happy. She co-founded a private Catholic school and worked there as a teacher and board member. Today, she and her husband, with whom she has five grown-up children, produce their own food and live almost self-sufficiently, and concern themselves with ecological matters. Indeed, Mr Lohmann and Ms Krause do not vote for the AfD but describe themselves as sympathizers of the party.

The interviewees' political views and civil society engagement reflect the social trajectory we have just outlined. The authoritarian innovators, too, distrust the institutions of democracy, but they do not reject them per se. They are particularly suspicious of the political parties and the EU. Similarly, they are critical of the media, although they do not boycott them outright. They watch the *Tagesschau* news on the public national TV broadcaster, read national daily newspapers, or listen to public radio. They use alternative blogs or YouTube channels merely as a corrective. In short: they move on the terrain of a shared reality, yet they view it with suspicion. Unlike the regressive rebels, whom we shall turn to shortly, they make an effort not to violate the boundaries of acceptable discourse. Like the Schmitt couple, they attach great value to presenting a fact-based and nuanced argument. That is why they are so offended when being accused of racism by family members or friends, as they continue to position themselves within the publicly accepted range of opinions, albeit at its margin. They acknowledge other people's views, and they themselves speak of tolerance and freedom of opinion.

Their disappointment is precisely the result of their high expectations in democratic institutions. They see themselves as active, distrusting citizens who have established a great gulf between themselves and state authorities but want to hold these latter accountable and limit their power. They pay their taxes – and their dues – dutifully go and vote in elections, write protest letters to local and regional or state politicians, or attend political gatherings. They are active members of sports clubs and church congregations, attend parent-teacher associations or engage in volunteer work in local politics or trade unions. At the same time, they criticize the traditional channels of group representation as no longer responsive. In order to influence politics and society, they choose novel and, to them, unconventional avenues – such as openly promoting the AfD. Ultimately, they embody the contradictions which Rosanvallon has identified as counter-democracy's 'practical applications of distrust': 'Social distrust can encourage a salutary civic vigilance and thus oblige government to pay greater heed to social demands, yet it can also encourage destructive forms of denigration and negativity.'[23] While the destructive rejection of the shared political space surfaces openly among the regressive rebels, the authoritarian innovators exhibit the destructive element only in a mediated way or by means of stereotypes. Explicitly articulated aggression is very rare, yet their prejudices pushing to the surface certainly do come into conflict with their desire for conformity.[24] Mr Lohman, for instance, repeatedly points out his 'non-ideological' or 'neutral' stance while expressing his views on the government's asylum policy: 'Or that threat, which is in fact real, coming from all those people who have come into the country, and that's something you can say without being an AfD voter, 'cause it's a fact.' In order to justify his anxiety, he references supposed facts (although he presents them in a de-personalized manner by adding the indefinite pronoun 'one', as in, 'as one knows', 'one has heard', etc.). Even Adorno had already noticed in his analysis of prejudice that the corresponding individuals tended towards 'pseudorational discussions' in order to underpin their aversive emotions with legitimacy.[25]

It was also noticeable that the two age groups differed in the way they verbalized their xenophobic prejudices. Mr Rupp, who worked in a bank before retiring, was unable to keep his views on migration to himself at his men's choir group, where he expressed his outrage at the admission of refugees into the country: 'Why is it that young men are fleeing? And the women and children stay behind and are in danger?' Just like him, all our interview partners from the older cohorts tend towards moral scandalizing. In referencing the (in their view) moral misconduct of Muslim minorities or refugees, they draw a clear line of separation between the in-group and the out-group. This defence serves to protect their own values – for instance, in Mr Rupp's case, traditional ideals of family and masculinity. These age cohorts particularly regard language, work and starting a family as yardsticks of integration. To Mr Rupp, it is important that 'foreigners' participate in 'community life' and not just stay 'amongst themselves', that they go hiking with him, join the choir, etc. What frequently emerges during the conversations is a kind of hierarchy of debasement, allowing for prejudices to be verbalized without drawing negative attention as a xenophobe. Negative emotions are projected onto a partial group among migrants who are allegedly unwilling to integrate into society, while the other part, which is attributed this will, is mentioned to underscore one's own balanced and differentiated view.

The open resentment of outsiders, which appears only rarely among the older cohorts, who are more emotionally controlled, is clearly noticeable among the younger generation of authoritarian innovators: not only do they get more worked up about the issue of asylum seekers, but they also more often tend towards stereotyping generalizations that can take on the form of conspiracy theories. Mr Jung, for example, highlights that he has 'no problem with strangers', as long as they accept 'our, in quotation marks, Western values'. At the same time, however, he has noticed with great concern that his co-workers in the factory hardly speak German anymore. To him, this represents a dangerous development: 'It's really closing in, we have no offspring anymore, no German children.' Immigration represents a fundamental problem for the younger generation; to them it causes the delicate equilibrium of culture to fall out of balance, the reason being that the 'alien' value elements in society become too dominant, or because the high birth rate is detrimental to the ecological basis of social coexistence. The 'economic' function of stereotyping and prejudices for the psyche, which Adorno already diagnosed at the end of the 1940s, is more pronounced among younger cohorts.[26]

In the inner world of the authoritarian innovators, there is a simmering hostility – regardless of their outwardly controlled behaviour – that results from experiences of frustration and dependence. As a consequence, they feel deeply offended. And yet, the aggressive energies cannot be aimed directly at the root cause, the capitalist world that surrounds them: their inclination towards assimilating and their fear of being shamed are simply too great.

236

Hence, the rejection is projected onto another 'substitute object', in this case often asylum seekers who, in their view, are violating common conventions.

Regressive rebels

Mr Rudolph's kitchen table has hosted 'half the world'. Rudolph, a physiotherapist born in 1956, comes from a wealthy family whose business served customers around the globe. He used to be a cosmopolitan, who once travelled across the Middle East. Even as a young man, he felt an 'inner urge' to become politically active. He soon worked with the Green Party, became involved with the protests against 'Stuttgart 21'[27] from day one and is today an SPD member. However, he woke up and came to his senses following 'a few key experiences': 'When you see that your homeland is suddenly shrinking, that you can't communicate with others anymore'. This citizen of the world has transformed into a defender of the homeland and AfD voter. He feels betrayed by the established parties, sees the 'domination by foreigners' as the basic problem of German society. As a property manager, he explains, he has witnessed 'each wave of immigration' first-hand, which is why his assessment of the refugee crisis of 2015 is particularly accurate. Mr Rudolph is easily agitated, struggles to tolerate injustices, talks himself into a rage when relating to the letters he receives from migrant applicants for flats: 'Hundreds and hundreds! All from Arabs, all with an Arab background, and with an *unbelievable* sense of entitlement: "I want this, I want that, this is what I want to get, and this is what I want to get".' In contrast, the Germans in need that he knows get nothing. He knows many depressing stories of people whom the state has left to fend for themselves.

And neither is his own life short of a certain tragic nature. He had many opportunities, which, however, have all vanished into thin air. Of his parents' seven children, he is the downward-climber. Today, he is more or less penniless, physically unwell, and breaks into a bad cough repeatedly during our conversation. While he did not manage to complete his university degree because he was taking care of the father, his siblings were able to celebrate their middle-class educational successes (some of them became doctors). And yet, in his view, he was the one paying the price, as they hardly did their

237

part in caring for the parents. He is disillusioned, if not embittered about the generosity which he has shown in the past. As a result, he has now ended up all by himself, without a partner or children. He is 'so severely frustrated' with the political situation that he loses himself in fantasies of violence. If he had no personal obligations, he would catch up on 'military training', of which he was deprived due to his parents' pacifist stance: 'sniper training', in order to 'depart this life *in true mass-shooting style*'. While we are sitting together at his kitchen table, eating spritz cake, Mr Rudolph gives free rein to his imagination: 'A proper killing spree, and most certainly not just some harmless *tralala*-folks, but with a *real* bang. To *really kill*, to *murder*, two or three of those big wigs responsible for this Stuttgart 21 project.' Although he emphatically emphasizes that this is only a 'metaphor' that gives him comfort from time to time, not an actual plan, the image is nevertheless greatly disturbing.

Like Mr Rudolph, the other respondents whom we define as regressive rebels have also experienced personal disruption and dramatic turning points, crises or social decline. Their discontent with the political order and its representatives, which they almost compulsively refer to with hostility and contempt, runs deeper than in the authoritarian innovators. Among the regressive rebels, the distrust that has always accompanied the civil society counter-power that confronts established institutions morphs into destructiveness. They react to anomic experiences, one might say with reference to Merton, by discarding not only the legitimate means but also the socially recognized goals themselves.

Socially, the regressive rebels are caught in continuous descent. Instead of upward social mobility and stability later in life, they experienced deprivation and decline (here, the range of cohorts is broader: 1944, 1945, 1950, 1954, 1956, 1961 and three from 1962). Although they had comparatively favourable education opportunities (three had completed *Abitur*, one an advanced technical certificate, another three a secondary school leaving certificate (similar to O-levels) from a comprehensive state school, and two a qualification from a vocationally focused school similar to Britain's post-war secondary moderns), none of them managed to convert this into a successful professional career. Some of them lost the modest prosperity they had built up, others remained entirely deprived of advancement and success. They tell us about frequent and invol- untary career changes, working odd jobs, permanent disability due to accidents or health conditions, recurrent unemployment and looming old-age poverty. Like Mr Rudolph, two other respondents were also unable to complete their studies, almost all of them had to re-orientate their career paths at some point. Unlike the authoritarian innovators, the regressive rebels from our sample worked or work mainly in the service sector. Their social contacts were largely limited to their clients. They worked (or still work), for instance, as a lorry driver, masseuse or as gym coach and were (are) thus directly exposed to the domination of the customer and the anonymous authority of the market. They hardly experienced any cooperation or solidarity among co-workers, but instead reported conflicts with their employers or customers. Only three of nine interview partners trust(ed) their employer (including one disabled and one self-employed person).

At the time of the interviews, many were in a situation of anomie. Throughout their working life, they had to adjust their own expectations and claims, time and again, to a limited range of options. They look back at unsteady occupational biographies, as conventional paths led them nowhere. While the institutional framework conditions worked for the authoritarian innovators in the sense that they protected them from social decline, many of the regressive rebels have no one but themselves to rely on. For them, neither the education system nor the labour market or the market economy redeemed what they had promised. The regressive rebels also work hard to defend their social position, but often this is not enough. Many are threatened by social decline or had to settle with a position among the lower ranks in the social hierarchy. The retired Mr Briedenkamp, who, just like Mr Rudolph, comes from a wealthy family of industrialists, was a ballet dancer early in life, and his last occupation was as an alternative practitioner – but now he is looking at a retirement of poverty, loneliness and bitterness: 'Not enough to live, but too much to die.'

It is not just their occupational life that is marked by discontinuity. In their private existence, too, many suffer from separation and social isolation. Their partnership or family arrangements often deviate from conventional models. Many are permanently single ('Never a family, no partnership, nothing', says Mr Briedenkamp), two are in unmarried relationships, and only three are married. Many recount profound humiliations, difficult separations or divorces, and some of them have long since lost contact with their children. Ms Renz, for example, has two children, but she has never managed to stay with a partner for any long period of time. The regressive rebels were unable (and unwilling) to achieve a classic family life like that of the older generation of authoritarian innovators. But the improvised biography chosen by the younger generation of innovators is only rarely voluntarily self-selected, and is usually the result of years of disruptions. Only four out of nine respondents have children of their own, and two are (or were) single parents. Mr Kirchheimer, the lorry driver signed off sick, has been subject to a ban on contacting his children ever since his divorce. Only one of these respondents has raised a child together with her husband. The relationship with their own parents or siblings is often burdened with conflict: some have severed ties with their families, in other cases there were recurrent periods with no contact. As Adorno already observed with regard to authoritarian personalities, they, too, often have an ambivalent relationship with their father, vacillating between devoted idealization and aggressive rejection. In comparison with their parents, they are often deprived economically, which likely played a part in the fallings-out.

The regressive rebels, however, choose other means to reach their political goals. They have no intention of reforming the social order from within, but rebel against the system as a whole. Given that the social contract of meritocratic society has been breached, they no longer feel obligated by it. In terms of political socialization, they have already felt alienated from democratic institutions and procedures from early on. Politics was hardly or not at all discussed in the family context; often, they can only guess what their parents might have voted. Many of them have long been floating or protest voters. In the past, they voted mainly for smaller parties, such as the Green Party, the liberals (FDP) or Die Linke; three of them had already voted for far-right parties previously, albeit without developing a permanent attachment to them. They explain their changing party preferences in terms of their rebellious personalities. Masseuse Ms Renz, for example, describes herself as a 'revolutionary'; Mr Bollinger stresses that he has always taken an 'oppositional' stance. They easily get offended, and quickly get into arguments, whether in the family setting, with friends or at work. Their inner inclination towards rebellion seems to have become generalized. The political motives and positions may vary, what matters to them is staging a resistance. Mr Rosowsky, the gym instructor, voted for the SPD for some years, then the Green Party, but also was involved with the far-right NPD for a while – which was not easy for him as a gay man. He self-ironically remarks that he was primarily drawn by 'a bit of the masculinity cult, a bit of that martial attitude', and that he also enjoyed the paramilitary training. What seems to appeal to him in particular is the group's provocative appearance, especially at Nazi demonstrations. Although, he admits, he could have just as well joined the counter-demonstration, 'that would have been the emotionally easy way out, right?'. This is a negative, flamboyant rebellion, which may form situational alliances of convenience with new authorities but is ultimately characterized by a lust for the destructive. The fact that the regressive rebels we interviewed did not vote for right-wing parties for such a long time is, in this sense, part of the success story of the former West Germany, which managed for many years to integrate such individuals.

Moreover, interestingly, only some of them were already politically close to right-wing positions in previous periods in their lives. What we observed in strikingly many cases (five out of nine respondents), is a destructive deformation of an originally cosmopolitan attitude. These individuals are what we call *reformed cosmopolitans*; they used to represent a culturally open-minded lifestyle and a cosmo-politan attitude before abruptly abandoning this stance. They have travelled through the Middle East and beyond as backpackers, lived in India or Thailand, converted to Buddhism, devoted themselves to the search for meaning and practised meditative techniques of self-awareness – somewhat similar to the studied individuals from the *Querdenker* scene (see chapter 7). The regressive rebels, too, performed a fundamental U-turn which they frequently attribute to specific events that opened their eyes. Mr Rudolph, for instance, relates a situation he sees as his 'key experience': an encounter with 'four or five Turks' at a petrol station somewhere in the Black Forest, who 'did not bother to even look at' him, when he was thirsty and almost collapsing after a bicycle tour. After this experience he told himself: 'You *must* not become a stranger in your own country.' He thereby uses a phrase that sociologist Arlie Hochschild also came across several times when interviewing followers of the right-wing populist Tea Party movement in the United States and subsequently used for the title of her book *Strangers in Their Own Land*.[28] Just like Hochschild's interview partners, our respondents recount experiences of alienation and devaluation for which they blame foreigners, members of marginalized groups and the elites. That said, in our case it is precisely those people for whom a unique lifestyle and self-realization play a major role that are turning away from society in frustration. Their non-conformist individualist lifestyle entailed socio-economic failures; they were unable to attain their goals. Through their lives, their openness to the world has turned into introversion, yet they have not entirely shed their cosmopolitan convictions. They represent, more than communitarianism, a cosmopolitanism that has been turned in a regressive sense. They continue to see themselves as open-minded, enlightened individuals, but they regard multiculturalism and globalization as a fatally destructive threat to society.

The regressive rebels' opinions and civil society engagement are marked by a generalized distrust that extends to virtually all political and social institutions. The only form of democratic organization that at least earned the trust of five out of nine interviewees are citizens' initiatives. In their permanent hostility, the institutions of power (or 'oversight') are transformed into an authority so 'impenetrable' and 'so forbidding that [...] [c]itizens [feel] radically alienated'.[29] Absolute suspicion leads to a normative nihilism which discards all binding rules and is frequently accompanied by a lust for destruction. As we have pointed out, unlike the authoritarian innovators, the regressive rebels do not feel obligated by social conventions. On the contrary, they perceive rules and behavioural norms as an illegitimate restriction of their freedom of opinion and action. Essentially, they feel their freedom is being offended by a society shaped by immigration. In their view, they can no longer freely speak their mind or move around because of the many Muslims in the country. In contrast to the *Querdenker*, who advance the register of opening as opposed to closure (see chapter 7), the reverse is the case with the regressive rebels: as the reformed cosmopolitans that they are, they advocate a far-reaching closure. Their critique is not aimed at correcting but at abandoning the rules that restrict and patronize them. They are libertarian authoritarians whose prime motive is self-empowerment in the face of external barriers and inhibitions. Although they pay lip-service to democracy and the rule of law, their attempts at reasoning and rationalizing are frequently offset by their abusive language and defamatory speech. At times, their verbal assaults can morph into fantasies of violence against authorities, foreigners or those with different opinions. The efforts at self-adjustment, so typical of the authoritarian innovators, are

242

increasingly frustrated by destructive-subversive tendencies in the regressive rebels.

Established media, the daily national *Tagesschau* news programme on TV or national daily newspapers all draw their general suspicion. They bewail their biased reporting (particularly on the AfD or on migration policy issues). They refuse to participate in public discourse as critical voices, and instead turn to an alternative public: they are active on social media or watch YouTube videos. Similar to the *Querdenker*, reference to counter-knowledge and clandestine stocks of knowledge is essential for the regressive rebels. They list book titles and confidential sources, and refer to the relevant authors from the conspiracy theory scene. Among the regressive rebels, too, the crisis of political representation is linked to an epistemic crisis of 'better knowledge'. Conspiracy and mass delusion are frequently advanced social diagnoses. In contrast to the authoritarian innovators, they tend to regard their 'own opinion' as ostracized knowledge which they invoke against, to reference Bourdieu, the *doxa*. Mr Kirchheimer, who repeatedly refers to Thomas Wieczorek's book *Die verblödete Republik* (something along the lines of 'The gaga republic') (2009) and orders literature from the publisher Kopp Verlag on a regular basis, explains:

> I don't need *Heute Journal* nor *Tagesthemen* [the major national late-night news programmes on the public TV broadcasters ARD and ZDF], [...] seeing as these journalists are government-trained leftists. I don't need them to announce their opinion to me, I'd rather hear the news, I want to know what has happened, and then I can form my own opinion.

But, unlike in Merton's observation, here the rebellion against an anomic situation in life is not accompanied by visions of a better order but merely carries the desire for an overthrow of current conditions to extremes. The state of exception becomes a fundamental pattern of perceiving reality: the non-existence of the Federal Republic of Germany, the 'great replacement' ('*Umvolkung*'), civil war or world conspiracy. The emotional dramatization is a device for justifying extra-institutional means of resistance: they refuse to pay their TV/radio licence fees, hand in their ID cards, stock up with supplies (like Mr Ludwig) and document chemtrails. The changeover into the *Reichsbürger* (or 'sovereign citizens') scene is often a smooth

243

transition. In a twisted way, the regressive rebels are dissenters oriented towards autonomy. Narratives of blocked comments on the Internet, disputes and fallings-out in the family or with friends and when dealing with public authorities – or (less frequently) with customers and colleagues at work – all testify to this basic attitude. Going back on one's own position is regarded a weakness, and rebellion is declared a virtue. The rejection and exclusion they have experienced only harden their conviction, and even lead to a heroic self-elevation. On the whole, they lack an essential feature of the 'authoritarian syndrome' that Adorno and his colleagues described with a view to twentieth-century US society: subjugation. At the time, Adorno noted that the ambition for 'upward social mobility is expressed in terms of overt identification with those who are higher in the hierarchy of authority'.[30] Yet this no longer applies to the regressive rebels of our day: they rebel against the institutions and apparatuses that have prevented their social advancement. In their everyday way of leading their lives, they make an effort to preserve a middle-class façade while simultaneously engaging in (at times, secret) online exchanges with like-minded allies. Although it goes against their beliefs, they must conceal their positions to suit the context, which can lead to further frustrations. When they go online, they receive not only opposition but recognition, too.

Compared to the authoritarian innovators, their prejudices are more pronounced and emotionally charged, which helps flesh out the difference between the two types more clearly once again. For the authoritarian innovators, the prejudice about strangers or foreigners is primarily a 'means of social identification'[31] via the negative counterpoint of an outside group: the *others* are those who are lazy and unwilling to perform or who exhibit a morally questionable conduct. In the regressive rebels, this impulse is also present, but here it is even more important to an emotional economy that has spun out of control. Their contact with out-groups is very limited: they are neither active in the context of refugee assistance nor integration support and have no exchange with 'foreign' co-workers or neighbours to speak of. And yet, Muslim minorities in particular are more frequently identified as competition in the labour and housing markets or in welfare provision. Mr Ludwig vents his outrage: 'I had to work my ass off for my house, and they just get one for free.' That is to say, the prejudice is based not so much on negative experience with members of out-groups, but serves to channel feelings of declassification and frustration. For the Berkeley Group, the 'authoritarian syndrome' had a supporting function for the precarious psychodynamic: the strict demands of the super-ego which one is unable to fulfil are projected onto an 'object of special hatred'.[32] The rebels, too, ascribe all kinds of despised characteristics to an out-group: its members are freeloaders, greedy, lazy, sexually disinhibited or prone to violence. They elevate their own work ethic, more strongly so than the innovators, via the devaluation of minorities – a regressive outcome of the orientation towards performance and achievement that we have mentioned before. The self-loathing that emerges from having tried but failed turns into xenophobic hatred.

Ms Wimmer, who once travelled the Middle East with her husband and has left her flat only in emergencies ever since her retirement from public service, perceives Muslims as an abstract threat that poses a danger not only to her own life but to the social structure as a whole. 'They should adapt to us, not the other way around', she demands. She likewise constructs a minority that is allegedly seeking to impose its interests on the majority – a shift in the registers of critique which we have already seen in previous chapters (see chapter 6). When asked what she expects from politicians, she answers very clearly: 'Well, first of all, they should do more for Germans, for the pensioners who are not getting enough of a pension.' And she immediately adds: 'Out with the asylum seekers, all of them, out.' The authoritarian aggression is more direct in the regressive rebels, they openly articulate their hostility without inhibition. They are not ashamed of their anger, but *au contraire*, they frivolously put it on display. Mr Bollinger, for example, never tires of speaking of 'knife attacks' and 'rapes', while using a broad range of abusive terms. 'Does Islam belong to Germany?', he asks rhetorically. 'It belongs neither to Germany nor to Europe. Islam is simply shit [...]. We don't need child marriages, we don't need halal slaughter, we don't need stoning', he sums up, deeply enraged.

Unlike the authoritarian innovators, regressive rebels, furthermore, express antisemitic prejudice, sometimes covertly, at other moments quite blatantly. Particularly in the context of experiences of frustration or powerlessness, they draw on conspiracy theory-based explanatory models in which secretly operating power elites are coded in antisemitic terms: over and over, our interview partners refer to 'George Soros', 'Rockefeller', 'Rothschild', the 'Federal Reserve' or a 'world government'. They do not stop at a general suspicion but in fact trace

245

the sinister powers who control the world. Mr Jovanovic, who has developed an interest in political matters ever since he has been on sick leave, knows exactly who is taking advantage of the 'incitement against the AfD': 'Where exactly they are located, is also something I happen to be able to comment on; all with a Jewish background: Rockefeller [...] and the Rothschilds. All just nonsense? No! It's not nonsense. Most certainly not!'

Adorno assumed that in the case of antisemitism the 'imaginary foe' has become entirely detached from reality and the fantasies 'run wild'.[33] For the respondents' psychodynamic, however, such stereotyping has an important 'economic', i.e., compensating function:[34] Adorno suspected that antisemitic prejudice emerged from 'economic and professional envy' or the desire to 'get hold of the property of [one's] [minority] neighbour'.[35] Today's regressive rebels draw on antisemitic tropes in order to empower themselves (in an imaginary way). In this way, they can re-interpret their own powerlessness as a rebellion, without having to relate to actual social structures that make them aware of their dependence or deprivation. Mr Bollinger, for instance, who, after his training as an industrial management assistant, had to give up his business selling luxury goods (silverware, china dolls, premium quality glass vases and so forth) and 'struggle through' his last years until retirement working for a security service, emphasizes: 'Sure, I'm active, I'm not a windbag, I do something, but it's pointless.' His heroic, albeit futile struggle is directed against (the widespread conspiracy theory of) the 'great replacement' of the European population, for which he has supposedly gathered vast evidence. 'Those who call the shots, firstly, are the lobby, and above them is Soros, and above him is the new world order', he explains. 'these are not buzzwords; you can look all of this up. There are a few major, important forces that the people are totally unaware of. Due to my vast, extensive information, I know a little bit about the background.' Committing to the conspiracy-theorist techniques of examining and testing the aspects of reality that lie beyond one's own personal experience but nonetheless exert great influence over everyday life, the rebels can control reality and redirect their frustration towards a concrete target.

Not all of our interview partners express their antisemitic prejudice so openly. Rather, they tend to ask rhetorical questions which plant a fundamental doubt, and mobilize conspiratorial rumours that corroborate their existing assumptions. In this context, many of the regressive rebels apply forms of secondary antisemitism that question or trivialize the Holocaust (or its remembrance). As we observed, the respondents not only deny Germany's historical responsibility but simultaneously link this denial to a national reappreciation of the Germans. Correspondingly, Mr Kirchheimer clarifies: 'And the Germans, they ought to walk upright and show some backbone again and stop carrying all that past and what happened back then into the present so much.' The prejudices – and not only the antisemitic ones – are often presented as an existential matter: if one had to work hard and is still denied recognition, even experiencing humiliation and being offended, then others are being given an advantage – a 'deep story'[36] which Hochschild also encountered over and over during her research in the US. The conviction that the native population is being betrayed is particularly prevalent among the rebels, and it makes the prejudice towards elites and Muslim minorities more destructive than in the case of the authoritarian innovators. The interplay, with differing forms and intensities, of anti-Muslim and antisemitic prejudice and conspiracy theories allows the regressive rebels to process their own biographical predicaments and negative emotions and to rebel against modern Germany's social and political order. Their drifting caused them to turn off into a libertarian-authoritarian tunnel in which they can no longer be won over to social deliberation and – at least, so we fear – will not be won over anytime soon, either. Of all the libertarian authoritarians we analyse in this book, they are the most radical variant. They perceive the state and liberal norms as so repressive that they have developed an unashamed propensity to violence (even though it may appear only in symbolically verbalized form).

247

CONCLUSION

> Freedom implies the conscious realisation of those processes that lead to unfreedom, together with a power of resistance that neither seeks refuge from those processes in the romantic past nor submits to them blindly.
>
> Max Horkheimer and Theodor W. Adorno, 'Prejudice and Character' (1952)

The diagnosis advanced in this book holds that recent years have seen the rise of a libertarian authoritarianism. It is the product of a late modern society marked by paradoxical developments regarding individualization, democracy and equality. Moreover, it results from conflicts around knowledge, inclusion and exclusion, as well as from the transformation of the public sphere and the meaning of opposition.

In the Preface to *The Authoritarian Personality* published in 1950, Max Horkheimer spoke of 'the rise of an "anthropological" species we call the authoritarian type of man'.[1] The latter combines rationalism and anti-rationalism, and is 'at the same time enlightened and superstitious, proud to be an individualist and in constant fear of not being like all the others, jealous of his independence and inclined to submit blindly to power and authority'.[2] This authoritarian type of human being exhibits various similarities with libertarian authoritarians. If, to conclude, we again consider the traits identified by the Berkeley Group, we can ascertain a distinctive authoritarian aggression, projectivity, superstition and stereotypy, power thinking, destructiveness and cynicism. At the same time, the groups we studied differ in a number of key aspects: the *fallen intellectuals* tend

248

less towards superstition, but are instead driven by a sharp rejection of social sensitivity and non-binary gender identities. These latter categories apply less to the *Querdenker*, but superstition and projectivity are even more widespread among their ranks, whereas the dominant traits among the *regressive rebels* tend to be destructiveness and cynicism. However, there is one thing that distinguishes almost all libertarian authoritarians from the people Adorno and his colleagues described at the end of the 1940s: they do not rigidly advocate conventional values, if we understand 'conventional' to primarily denote classically conservative attitudes such as discipline, orderliness and diligence. They harbour the common conventions typical of late modern middle-class milieus as discussed throughout the chapters of this book. No noticeable authoritarian submissiveness is to be found. On the contrary: they often reject all and any social authorities, above all the state and 'mainstream' experts. They themselves are the only authority that they recognize. Freedom is an unconditional value to them, and they refuse to reconcile it with – let alone restrict it for the benefit of – the freedom of others. They conceive of this freedom as their sole right, which only they dispose of – what we earlier referred to as 'reified freedom'. In this sense, they are libertarians because they posit their own individual freedom as absolute. Yet this is simultaneously the proof of their *authoritarian* inclination. They devalue those who represent a concept of freedom that differs from their own. It is this form of aggressive disparagement that makes them libertarian authoritarians. In this, they resemble the 'crank' and the 'rebel' in the original studies on the authoritarian personality.

In our view, libertarian authoritarians have not replaced classic authoritarianism. The latter is still very much alive and present, albeit in a domesticated form.[3] The Berkeley Group was always aware that their theory had a 'temporal core'; it essentially condensed the 1930s and 1940s, the decades during which it was conceived.[4] Should society change, they noted, the psychodynamics of authoritarianism would differ as well. Hence, libertarian authoritarianism represents a kind of metamorphosis of the listed sub-types of classic authoritarianism that have today become more pronounced. Whether a new 'anthropological species' will emerge, as Horkheimer quite intentionally wrote in quotation marks at the time, remains to be seen – and studied. One indicator of changes in the form of authoritarianism is the fact that libertarian authoritarianism, in all of its variants, is linked to specific facets of social change in late modernity.

Although we are as free as never before, social constraints have not disappeared. Setting oneself apart, achieving self-realization and self-improvement – these are often no longer voluntarily chosen options, but requirements imposed on us: today, for example, in many professions, having your own social media profile is no longer optional to distinguish yourself from others and stand out from the crowd. It is necessary in order to compete in the labour market. All this takes place in an anxious world in which norms are constantly changing. Progress seems as if on stand-by and is at times paralleled by direct regressions. Moreover, late modern individuals are extremely prone to taking offence if they are unable to fulfil their aspirations for self-development. With their orientation towards self-realization and authenticity, they are entirely geared towards immanence, that is to say, they do not want to change the world, but instead improve themselves – and seek stability in alternative forms of transcendence precisely for this reason. It is a yearning that we came across over and over during our field research and in our interviews. Where does this longing for transcendence come from?

We have earlier discussed different aspects of social change that have facilitated the spread of libertarian authoritarianism. In this discussion, we have referred primarily to the concept of (late) modernity. Yet modernity is a *capitalist* modernity, which, as a permanent process of rationalization and secularization, constantly engenders what György Lukács called 'transcendental homelessness'.[5] Modern humans have lost their embedding in spiritual structures of meaning. For Lukács, reading novels was one way of dealing with this problem. One can immerse oneself in literature and imagine a different world. In our view, the growing esoteric communities and forms of practice and other kinds of spiritual sense-making are an indicator that there still is a considerable demand for a transcendental roof over our heads even today. Especially in a highly rationalized society, in which late modern market society 'as such becomes culture', there is a lack of meaning.[6]

Furthermore, in our view, this also indicates the emergence of a new 'anthropological species'. This species could also be described as hyper-individual. Empirically speaking, a general trend towards the hyper-empowerment of the individual has emerged in recent decades.[7] Due to the increased level of education, people have generally become more emancipated. However, this progress also has regressive consequences. Individual empowerment has generated a form of self-confidence, the underside of which is distrust in institutions. For them, institutions, with their necessary collective mediation services, represent an attack on their autonomy. People see themselves as experts in their own right, which is why they reject professional experts. Authoritarian liberalism is also responsible for this. It was not opposed to democracy as such, but it was intended to keep it away from the economy. It tried to seal itself off from the demos, from objections from below, by means of a 'thin model of democracy'. It focused on electoral democracy, institutional rules and restrictions as well as the comprehensive rule of law. Authoritarian liberalism promotes distrust of institutions and experts once again in its own specific way. Its ideology advocates economic, wealth-based elites that embody the market and performance – regardless of how they acquired their wealth. Democratic and state elites, however, are illegitimate; they are seen as representatives of left-wing liberal usurpation of a state that is not needed anyway.

The individuals whom we analysed were for the most part – though not exclusively – socialized in a post-authoritarian environment. Indeed, the post-war baby-boomer generation (in Germany roughly spanning the cohorts from 1955 to 1970) still largely had an authoritarian upbringing. However, for younger cohorts, this is no longer true to the same extent, either with regard to their socialization through family, school or political life. For the greater part of their lives, they harboured leftist, liberal or moderately conservative views and participated in a democratic system which they criticized in many regards but accepted overall. Now they see themselves as awakened or woken up, and perceive society as heading for dictatorship – or having long since become one. In our empirical material, we repeatedly encountered the theme of awakening. This was even more surprising as many of the respondents, implicitly or explicitly, distanced themselves from the *woke* (which equally refers to some sort of awakening) adherents of 'identity politics'.[8] The *awakened* libertarian authoritarians we studied constitute only a small proportion of the population, but they all exhibit diminishing social circles and interactions. The world of the *regressive rebels*, in particular, has become smaller, and they have lost many of their social contacts. Among the *Querdenker* or the *fallen intellectuals*, of course, things are rather different: during the COVID-19 pandemic, conflicts around freedom and solidarity extended deeply into people's private everyday lives. Friendships and families fell apart, and decades-old relationships were severed in a matter of a few weeks or months. Yet the *Querdenker* quickly found a new home in neo-communities of distrust – as did the one or other (fallen) intellectual.

Despite their intense critique of liberal democracy, libertarian authoritarians consider themselves democrats – although they move along the slippery slope of anti-political democracy, the denial of societal dependence and reified freedom. At the same time, they are usually not the fascistic personalities that Adorno considered all high-scorers on the F-scale to be. Today's libertarian authoritarians have been democratically socialized and profess participatory values. That said, they often have few reservations over standing side-by-side with fascists and are so disappointed with democracy that they become highly vulnerable to the authoritarian drift, meaning, not only taking a temporary right-wing turn but maintaining such a stance in the long run. It does not have to end this way. But more on that, later.

A critique of the state and the paradoxes of progress

Libertarian authoritarians' anger is directed against the modern state. Rather than the old class state with its origins in the Bismarck era, today it is a complex interventionist state, serving as an instrument for implementing social progress. At the same time, it produces inequalities, class positions and exclusions. The role of the state has once again changed considerably over the past two decades. Although it still has the strategic function of maintaining the capitalist order and stabilizing the concomitant class structures, it also encapsulates the conflicts around normative progress.[9] Particularly with a view to increasing global risks, the state is no longer only the ideal 'general capitalist' (as Friedrich Engels called it) but also the real 'general socializer' – as it accepts responsibility for the successful repro-duction of social relations. During the coronavirus pandemic, for example, inequalities did not decrease but rather became more aggra-vated in some respects. Yet the state also pursued a policy of universal health protection. In the past, the critique of the state (particularly that coming from the left) alleged, above all, that it ultimately did nothing to reduce or eliminate these inequalities, but perpetuated and even contributed to increasing them. In the eyes of classic neolib-erals, however, the state posed a threat to smoothly functioning markets and competitiveness. The more recently emerging libertarian authoritarians see it as no more than a machine restricting individual freedoms, be it through inclusionary policies, multiculturalism or the enforcement of solidarity with vulnerable groups during the pandemic. Some social groups, among them men of an advanced age, are losing their uncontested position of power, which they perceive as a loss of freedom. Society's normative democratization, inclusion and equalization restrict those subjective freedoms they previously enjoyed in their position within the class and status hierarchies.

The question of state power epitomizes most issues: in the eyes of libertarian authoritarians, the state restricts the exercise of their inalienable rights. Many of them consider themselves victims of supposed progressive usurpers ('left-liberal cosmopolitans'), who have seized power over the state, the universities and the media. To them, this entails a new divide: the antagonism between the illiberal rule of the left-liberal elites and the democratic majority, between a higher-educated centre and a hard-working periphery, alleging that cosmopolitans from urban milieus look down on the latter. We would not dispute that left-liberals have sometimes made irritating contributions there that may be perceived as condescending. At the same time, we have our doubts about an actual increase in such conflicts.[10] Mutual resentment between the cities and the countryside, between blue-collar and white-collar workers, etc., has always existed. What has actually changed, then, is the power balance inside the state structure. Exclusions and inequalities within the status systems were gradually reduced. In this sense, the reality is quite the opposite of what the sentimental freedom nostalgia ('In the past you could freely speak your mind') might suggest. In those retrospectively idealized times, women, for example, were not remotely permitted to say or do what they wanted, as they neither had the power to do so nor the required discursive position. In Switzerland, universal female suffrage was not introduced until 1971, as mentioned earlier. In Germany, the married housewife family model (*Hausfrauenehe*, lit.: 'housewife marriage') constituted applicable law until 1977, and it granted a husband the right to forbid his wife to work and terminate her employment contract.

The fact that many things could be said or done in the past that are considered unseemly today has little to do with the decline of the freedom of expression, but rather with the fact that those who were affected at the time lacked the (social) power to object to such statements or actions; and that people acquiesced in a kind of anticipatory obedience: many did not even think of protesting against sexist conventions or racist slurs. It took the civil rights movement for the N-word to disappear from the active vocabulary and for the legal discrimination of women to no longer be taken for granted. Today, freedom of expression is even greater, as more groups of people can express their opinions publicly. But discrimination continues even today, say, inside households, in the appointment of executive positions and, particularly, with regard to income. And yet, at least in normative terms, the realization of equality has never before been as advanced as it is today. The emotional charge of current conflicts is not the result of a new *(hyper)sensitivity* but of power struggles over questions of morality. Hard-won advancements have accumulated and engendered a new Tocqueville paradox. The reduction of exclusions has led to the social condemnation of gender- or ethnicity-related discrimination, non-representation and non-consideration. Social movements retrieve these phenomena from their social latency (because that was the key mechanism of their exclusion) and make them visible.

The expansion of democratic inclusion and equalization, however, comes at a price, which fuels today's battles over freedom. On the one hand, social rights were dismantled in parallel with – though not as a result of – moves towards democratic inclusion. For workers, unemployed and the poor, this signified a reduction of their individual liberties. For the established elites, the equalization and inclusion of previously excluded groups amounted to a loss of power. In this new power struggle, left-liberals often act exactly like those who have now partially lost their privileges: just like elites. They fight their rivals, and they certainly do so with the gloves off. By pursuing a 'progressive neoliberalism' while ignoring material social issues, left-liberalism has not only allowed libertarian authoritarians to present themselves as the representatives of 'ordinary people' – as right-wing populists, too, are eagerly seizing on this opportunity.

Libertarian authoritarians believe that they are fighting a *dictatorship*; they see themselves as heroic figures in the struggle for democracy, while they themselves subvert democratic norms. At times, this can get quite confusing. The disorder of our time entails a kind of babel: even those who are out to subvert and undermine democracy and freedom do so in the name of democracy and freedom. The widespread language of emancipation and the critique of domination, albeit with its substance inverted, also reflects the weakness of traditional progressive movements, whose followers have either deradicalized or moved into the state's institutions – often both. The old emancipation movements drew their force from the common struggle against ascriptions of social status, hierarchies and domination, against monarchs and the church. They fought for universal emancipation, for a democratic society of free citizens, for a democracy that constituted, governed and controlled itself, by itself. Since the last third of the twentieth century, many observers believe that freedom movements have lost this impetus because the great disruption – the constitution of civil rights and democracy – had already taken place. Henceforth, further progress was more about the incremental expansion of individual rights. Yet this changed the position of the critique, as it no longer referred to transforming capitalist totality but merely to its modification. The fundamental or comprehensive critique of capitalist modernity can barely be heard these days – and if it does make itself heard, it essentially lacks any prospect of ever being considered or implemented. The traditional critique of domination is weak and disoriented, revealing so many blind spots that its permanent opposition offers little perspective and has largely lost its purchase. Given that, following this metamorphosis, progressive forces no longer oppose the state, nor the media *doxa* (as they now occupy influential positions within this sector themselves), nor biopolitical government measures, and because they no longer convey socially critical thinking, i.e., 'the people's will', left-wing parties or social movements that embody a collective reality principle have lost their credibility as the mouthpieces of a critique of domination.

The coming truth conflicts

Is libertarian authoritarianism a temporary phenomenon? Or will it become a permanent attribute of late modern societies? The refugee crisis in 2015 was managed fairly successfully, and the coronavirus pandemic is over. It is also possible that the conflicts in the intellectual field will eventually be settled, either through clarification, convergence or simply because a new generation of intellectuals emerges that is less irreconcilable. Our concern, however, is that even in such a more optimistic scenario, libertarian authoritarianism would still not disappear ever so soon. Following the publication of our book in

Germany, the concept of libertarian authoritarianism was validated in two representative surveys. In the study by the University of Bielefeld, the proportion of libertarian authoritarians in the German population was estimated at 20 per cent.[11] In Austria, a study by the Austrian Academy of Sciences (ÖAW) came to the conclusion that almost a third of the population in the Alpine republic are libertarian authoritarians.[12] In other words, the social potential for conflicts over freedom is enormous.

Even before these surveys, Jürgen Habermas also spoke of a 'growing potential of an entirely new extremism of the centre that adopts libertarian forms', with regard to the COVID-19 protests.[13] One phenomenon we will likely continue to have to deal with even after the pandemic is the epidemic of half-truths and conspiracy narratives. This is due to the changed order of knowledge, expertise and scopes of action in late modern societies, to which we have referred repeatedly throughout this book. Alexander Bogner considers the different movements of 'consensus deniers' to epitomize an 'ideological campaign against the colonization of society by science'.[14]

On the one hand, access to information has become democratized; on the other hand, the result of scientific advancements, disciplinary specializations, and a lack of any sensory experience of risk (such as, in the past, smoke, dirt, etc.), is that individuals end up having a poorer understanding of the world that surrounds them. And yet, one nevertheless wants to remain an equally recognized discursive subject, albeit not so much through one's own knowledge, but rather through one's own opinion. In this context, then, it appears conducive to differentiate between fake news and post-truth. The former primarily refers simply to false statements that are declared facts, whereas post-truth as an attitude points to a deeper epistemic truth conflict. More specifically, post-truth implies the insistence that one's own opinion and one's own feelings should count just as much as scientific evidence in the assessment of a given question.[15] Here, we suspect a decisive pathology – constituting the basis of libertarian authoritarians' post-truth politics – in the simultaneity of the inability-to-know and a yearning for participation. They want *all* opinions (albeit primarily *their own ones*) to be taken seriously. In late modern conflicts over freedom, such as in the context of mask wearing in public, vaccinations and measures towards climate protection, libertarian authoritarians validate their views with proto-scientific evidence, rumours on Telegram or simply with fake news.

Of course, the classic critique of domination also refers to the individual's emotions and the subjective perception of a matter. Yet in the case of libertarian authoritarians, the registers of critique are frequently dislocated, distorted or inverted, so as to correspond to the pre-existing opinion. There are no channels through which feelings of powerlessness could be translated into a rational critique of domination. Faced with the impertinent complexities of the late modern world, libertarian authoritarians abandon the field. More than half a century ago, Adorno had already identified and summarized this mechanism:

> Paradoxically, a higher amount of insight might result in a reversion to attitudes that prevailed long before the rise of modern capitalism. For, while people recognize their dependence and often enough venture the opinion that they are mere pawns, it is extremely difficult for them to face this dependence unmitigated. Society is made of those whom it comprises. If the latter would fully admit their dependence on man-made conditions, they would somehow have to blame themselves, would have to recognize not only their impotence but also that they are the cause of this impotence and would have to take responsibilities which today are extremely hard to take. This may be one of the reasons why they like so much to project their dependence upon something else, be it a conspiracy of Wall Street bankers or the constellation of the stars.[16]

Accelerated social change provides a sounding board more conducive to conspiracy theories. Should conditions quieten down and a kind of 'normality' be restored, some people might manage to abandon their epistemic resistance against reality. That said, this would solve none of the problems, for it is precisely the supposed 'normality' that has so thoroughly prepared the ground for experiences of social humiliations.

What happens, though, if we do not return to normality? As terrifying as it sounds, this is not so unlikely a scenario at all. What if late modern societies enter into a series of crises – and, at times, multiple crises at once – which invariably entail the reduction and restriction of freedom? We already know of several problems that are inevitably going to arise. It is clear today, for example, that climate change will remain a permanent challenge for global society. Other major crises could have been anticipated far more prudently, such as the war in Ukraine, at least since Russia annexed Crimea in 2014. Other types of crises, such as the coronavirus pandemic, correspond to the 'black swan' principle: they are unlikely, but certainly contingent in this world, and then descend on reality with a bang, as a singular event.[17] Given the global character of late modern societies, the various crises become intertwined and mutually reinforcing: the coronavirus pandemic and the Ukraine war, for example, both threaten global supply chains and food supplies worldwide. The tightening supply in the corresponding sectors drives inflation, a scenario facilitated by the easy monetary policy of more recent years, which was itself a response to global economic problems. Although we cannot predict what risks may materialize, we would more or less rule out the possibility that late modern societies will return to a path of linear progress and attain a lasting, stable, everyday normality. Our fear is, therefore, that libertarian authoritarianism is here to stay, at least for the foreseeable future. There were plenty of indications of this in the summer of 2022. People who found the measures to counter the coronavirus pandemic exaggerated, for instance, also sensed an artificial dramatization – or even a welcome distraction from COVID-19 policies – in the reporting on the Ukraine war.[18] In many of the *Querdenker* scene's Telegram channels, the Russian invasion was downplayed or even justified.[19] From what we can tell at this point, however, this does not necessarily imply an authoritarian idealization of Putin, which would in any case contradict the libertarian authoritarians' mindset. For example, in our 2020 survey, only few *Querdenker* indicated a desire for a strong leader. In interviews we conducted after 24 February 2022, Putin himself was not referred to as an appealing figure, but the war was in part regarded as fabricated by the West. Ms Kleinschrod-Schüssler, a critic of the pandemic-related measures and AfD voter whom we met in the chapter on the *Querdenker*, or 'diagonalists', does not question the responsibility for the war. She does, however, express her suspicion that, once again, the situation is very dubious. In so doing, she draws on the register of social closure:

> To me, there was never a doubt that his [Putin's] invasion of Ukraine was a violation of international law. But how do we deal with this? I believe a debate about the matter should be possible. I'd say, those

people who were extreme supporters of the COVID-19 policies are about 90% identical with those who now want to supply heavy arms to Ukraine. And I think there must be a clear repatriation roadmap [for Ukrainian refugees]. Something along the lines of 'now you're here! But as soon as peace returns to your country, you should leave again'. Besides, the war isn't going on in every part of Ukraine. Because, if I see that the [coach operator] Flixbus runs from Germany to Kiev on a daily basis, I do have to say – my, what an interesting company this Flixbus operator is, driving into a war zone. And, I mean, that's when I ask myself, how can this be? And they're not leaving Ukraine, they're driving into Ukraine.

We consider it likely that the coming knowledge conflicts will see the formation of further awry fronts, linked via a distorted critique of domination. Although agreement with conspiracy-theorist statements on the topic of climate change was fairly low in our survey, it is already quite predictable today that coronavirus sceptics and conspiracy theorists will reject measures to mitigate climate change more vigorously in the future.[20] Driving bans, individual carbon budgets, price hikes for carbon-intensive consumer products ... such interventions can become 'trigger points'[21] for a reified understanding of freedom. The transformation of the world of work, digitalization and climate change are already having a considerable impact on the subjective experience of deprivation and are systematically linked to the development of right-wing attitudes.[22] The chances are that this link will not be weakened anytime soon.

If we expand our analytical gaze geographically, the phenomena of libertarian authoritarianism examined in this book can be understood as part of a wider international post-political rebellion. Naomi Klein's analysis of the American diagonalist movements in her 2023 book *Doppelganger* is very similar in many respects to the perspective on the *Querdenker* movement developed here.[23] Furthermore, the various forms of the sovereign citizen movement in the English-speaking world could be described as libertarian authoritarians. They claim to be independent, i.e., sovereign from the nation state, and refuse to obey any state authority. The sovereign citizens are mostly armed right-wing extremists, in Germany they are referred to as '*Reichsbürger*'. There is no certainty that said rebellion must necessarily develop towards the right, as it may just as well continue to take on a hybrid shape or shift more strongly to the left once again. For example, despite the structural contingency of authoritarianism in its midst, the *gilets jaunes* ('yellow vests') movement in France did not – thanks not least to a concerted intervention by the left – develop into a front organization of Marine Le Pen's right-wing *Rassemblement National*.[24]

Social freedom and democracy

We are a literary sociologist and a sociologist, and we have no magic solution to the problems we have analysed in the preceding pages. Rather, we regard this book as a contribution to a debate throughout society about the predicament that we find ourselves in. To conclude, we would therefore like to address only a few of the aspects that we consider most important – while keeping in mind that we obtained our findings in the context of an analysis of the paradoxical metamorphoses of late modern society.

In *The Dialectic of Enlightenment*, Horkheimer and Adorno concerned themselves with the question of how progress can turn into its opposite, and how 'instead of entering into a truly human state', humanity can sink into 'a new kind of barbarism'.[25] One answer that they gave to this question, which we have already mentioned, states that the Enlightenment destroys itself once it turns into a myth steeped in positivism. Horkheimer and Adorno were referring here to a kind of science that does not reflect its social function, a technology whose consequences remain hidden from view, and a market whose historical function of liberating people from feudal ties has been transformed into an autotelic apotheosis of capitalist relations. Indeed, their scepticism continues to be highly topical in our own time. In all three of these fields, there are factual restraints – ostensibly without any alternative – emerging today, which mark a regression that falls back behind one of the fundamental principles of the Enlightenment: thinking in alternatives. Horkheimer and Adorno were firmly convinced that 'freedom in society is inseparable from enlightenment thinking'.[26] From this perspective, the Enlightenment would have to be more self-reflective and think more in alternatives – and put them up for public debate, too. A late modern, renewed Enlightenment would be required to consider the conditions of the production of scientific evidence in its interpretation of the latter, so as to avoid lapsing into a positivism in which enlightenment becomes a 'myth of that which is the case'.[27] Was there really no alternative to the austerity policies of the past twenty-five years? After the repeated deployment of what German Chancellor Olaf Scholz once referred to as financial bazookas, we know today that there certainly must have been, but that they were prevented and overridden by political motives. Was the specific form of the pandemic policy without alternative? Not necessarily. It was also the result of a preceding short-sighted politics and the lack of systematic precautions. The risk of a pandemic was known long in advance. Is there no alternative to a neoliberal market economy? There probably is. But the neoliberal order is proclaimed as the only possible alternative to authoritarian regimes like the ones in China or Russia. The fact that further conceivable alternatives do exist, such as economic democracy, rarely features in public discourse.

We have shown in the chapters of this volume that many current disputes are the outcome of a conflict between democracy and state actions. Governments often have to react instantaneously to events for which no established management procedures yet exist. In the reality of democracy, there have been many cases of governments acting the wrong way or too slowly. Mistakes happen, they are part and parcel of politics. Yet, for the most part, their systematic examination, a self-reflective attitude, or a collective learning process, remained unfulfilled. As far as we are aware, neither politicians nor state representatives have self-critically enlightened the public as to what prompted the announcement during the early days of the pandemic that masks need not be worn, or that they could actually be unhealthy. While, after Russia's invasion of Ukraine, this kind of self-criticism is now occurring with regard to the formerly dominant conception of Germany's relationship with Russia, it is, in part, being inverted at the same time: while it is admitted that there was a grave misconception of the true fascistic character of the Putin regime, the reaction to cautiously expressed criticism – such as that by Jürgen Habermas which addresses the frequently bellicist tone of some of the demands raised – consists of mockery and malice. In our view, the range of alternatives would therefore have to include the following: needless to say, politicians must eventually make collectively binding decisions, but they could, firstly, present existing alternatives more openly and thus illuminate the consequences of each to the public, instead of simply citing factual restraints. Secondly, we would consider a distinctive form of self-reflection and, if need be, self-criticism to be appropriate.

261

Another aspect pertains to the expansion of the institutions and the normative foundations of freedom. If freedom is to mean more than just negative freedom, we must consider its thorough embeddedness in social relations.[28] Freedom rests on a whole mesh of interwoven subjective rights and institutional preconditions. Hence, economic, political and social *planning* becomes the very guarantor of individual freedom in outgoing late modernity: for instance, a welfare state that mitigates life's risks, a healthcare system that is prepared for any future pandemic, a disaster management mechanism capable of responding to extreme weather events, etc. Freedom can only truly be realized if mutual dependencies are acknowledged. Inevitably, then, this requires developing a new understanding of individualism. As independent, self-responsible or sovereign we may be as individuals, we are permanently bound to other human beings as living organisms, while, as subjects, we are bound to society. We can only ever be subjects in the simultaneous co-presence of other individuals, society and nature.[29] This does not contradict self-realization or singularization. Individuals must, however, achieve such self-realization with an awareness of its societal preconditions, rather than aiming for secession from the body politic. In this sense, Peter Wagner has criticized 'individualist liberalism'[30] as an insufficient (theoretical) foundation of social freedom. For him, its function in public debate is primarily to delegitimize other political values and responsibilities, as it neglects precisely the 'commitment to solidarity' that is so important for preserving freedom.[31] The freedom of the future requires solidarity. As Axel Honneth argues in *Freedom's Right*, a human subject 'is only "free" if it encounters another subject, within the framework of institutional practices, to whom it is joined in a relationship of mutual recognition; only then can it regard the aims of the other as the conditions for the realisation of its own aims'.[32] Here, Honneth imagines a society pervaded by democratic morality. Such a society, he believes, would not reduce individuality to lifeless conformity, but, on the contrary, enable it to finally develop freely and authentically.[33] It seems we still have a long way to go. One first step could be a return to thinking in alternatives, the retaining of options, and not affirming the status quo as the best of all worlds just because the alternatives existing in reality appear overly cruel. The democratization of democracy is certainly not ruled out in the world's horizon of possibility, and it would accommodate people's increased demands for participation as well as reducing their alienation from a political system which, in everyday life, they can often only experience in a mediated form or as an abstract principle.[34] However, alternatives only arise out of conflicts. French philosopher Miguel Abensour advocates an 'insurgent democracy' that challenges the state, thereby renewing democracy and turning it into a true democracy.[35] And yet, Abensour should not be mistaken for a *Querdenker* theoretician, as he is calling for the exact opposite: a vibrant grassroots critique of domination that does not seek to dispute reality, but to change it.

NOTES

Introduction

1 The following paragraph is in part taken from our essay in *New Statesman*: Carolin Amlinger and Oliver Nachtwey (2023), 'The new authoritarian personality: What is driving the resurgence of the libertarian far right?', *New Statesman*, 7 December, available at: https://www.newstatesman.com /ideas/2023/12/new-authoritarian-personality

2 See Matt Zwolinski and John Tomasi (2023), 'What is Libertarianism?', in: id., *The Individualists: Radicals, Reactionaries, and the Struggle for the Soul of Libertarianism*, Princeton, NJ: Princeton University Press, pp. 9–33; Quinn Slobodian (2023), *Crack-Up Capitalism: Market Radicals and the Dream of a World Without Democracy*, New York: Random House.

3 This term literally translates to 'diagonal thinker' and denotes something like 'contrarian' or 'maverick'. It emerged as a self-description by those who doubted the existence and/or severity of COVID-19 and staged protest marches against the pandemic-related restrictions. In the UK, for example, these groups were referred to simply as 'COVID deniers'. Here, we retain the term *Querdenker*, at times alternating with 'diagonalism' or 'diagonalist' in reference to Naomi Klein (2023), *Doppelganger: A Trip into the Mirror World*, New York: Farrar, Straus and Giroux; Will Callison and Quinn Slobodian (2021), 'Coronapolitics from the Reichstag to the Capitol: Defying conventional political labels and capitalizing on widespread distrust, a range of new movements share the conviction that all power is conspiracy', *Boston Review*, 12 January, available at: https://www.bostonreview.net/articles/quinn-slobodian-toxic-politics -coronakspeticism/

4 The term *Gleichschaltung* (which roughly translates to 'synchronization') refers to the systematic Nazification process in early 1930s Germany, during which all areas of society, from trade to culture and education, and particularly the media, were brought under the full control of the Nazi party, preparing the ground for its totalitarian rule.

5 Transl. note: the gender asterisk is used in German nouns to convey gender-neutral and non-binary language. Specifically, it is placed after the root word and before the female suffix '-*in*' (sg.) or '-*innen*' (pl.). For example,

the (male) *Lehrer* (teacher) thus becomes *Lehrer*in* (or *Lehrer*innen* in the plural).

6 Transl. note: This refers to the so-called *Reichsbürger* ('Reich citizens'), who do not recognize the post-war German state nor its democratic institutions. They constitute a contentious character comparable to the sovereign citizens movement.

7 See Oliver Decker and Elmar Brähler (eds.) (2020), *Autoritäre Dynamiken. Alte Ressentiments – neue Radikalität. Leipziger Autoritarismus-Studie 2020*, Gießen: Psychosozial-Verlag; Wilhelm Heitmeyer (2018), *Autoritäre Versuchungen. Signaturen der Bedrohung I*, Berlin: Suhrkamp; Wilhelm Heitmeyer et al. (2020), *Rechte Bedrohungsallianzen. Signaturen der Bedrohung II*, Berlin: Suhrkamp.

8 Theodor W. Adorno et al. (1950), *The Authoritarian Personality*, New York: Harper and Row, pp. 237–8.

9 Erich Fromm (2020 [1936]), *Studies on Authority and the Family. Sociopsychological Dimensions, Fromm Forum* 24, pp. 8–58, here: p. 54, available at: https://fromm-gesellschaft.eu/images/pdf-Dateien/1936a-eng .pdf

10 Erich Fromm (1984), *The Working Class in Weimar Germany: A Psychological and Sociological Study*, Oxford: Berg Publishers, p. 226.

11 Adorno, *Authoritarian Personality*, op. cit.

12 Ibid.

Chapter 1. Aporias of Enlightenment: the Critical Theory of freedom

1 See, for example, Peter Bieri (2001), *Das Handwerk der Freiheit. Über die Entdeckung des eigenen Willens*, Munich: Carl Hanser; Otfried Höffe (2021), *Kritik der Freiheit. Das Grundproblem der Moderne*, Munich: C.H. Beck; Axel Honneth (2014), *Freedom's Right: The Social Foundations of Democratic Life*, transl. by Joseph Ganahl, Cambridge: Polity; Carlo Strenger (2017), *Abenteuer Freiheit. Ein Wegweiser für unsichere Zeiten*, Berlin: Suhrkamp.

2 Cornelius Castoriadis (1987 [1975]), *The Imaginary Institution of Society*, transl. by Kathleen Blamey, Cambridge: Polity, pp. 146–7.

3 Montesquieu (1949 [1835/40]), *The Spirit of the Laws*, New York: Hafner, p. 149.

4 Werner Conze (1975), 'Freiheit', in: *Geschichtliche Grundbegriffe. Historisches Lexikon zur politisch-sozialen Sprache in Deutschland*, Vol. 2, ed. by Otto Brunner et al., Stuttgart: Klett-Cotta, pp. 425–542, here: p. 425.

5 For an overview, see Jonas Pfister (ed.) (2017), *Texte zur Freiheit*, Stuttgart: Reclam.

6 See the distinction made by Isaiah Berlin (1995 [1969]), 'Zwei Freiheitsbegriffe', in: id., *Freiheit. Vier Versuche*, Frankfurt am Main: Fischer, pp. 197–256.

7 Ernst Bloch (1986 [1959]), *The Principle of Hope*, Volume 2, Cambridge, MA: MIT Press, pp. 528–9.

8 Honneth, *Freedom's Right*, op. cit., p. 39.

9 Höffe, *Kritik der Freiheit*, op. cit., p. 32.

10 On the concept of progress, see Peter Wagner (2016), *Progress: A Reconstruction*, Cambridge: Polity.

11 Georg Wilhelm Friedrich Hegel (1975), *Lectures on the Philosophy of*

World History: Introduction, Reason in History (transl. from the German edition of Johannes Hoffmeister from Hegel papers assembled by H.B. Nisbet), New York: Cambridge University Press, pp. 89, 138.

12 On freedom consciousness in Hegel, see Andreas Arndt (2015), *Geschichte und Freiheitsbewusstsein. Zur Dialektik der Freiheit bei Hegel und Marx*, Berlin: Eule der Minerva.

13 See Höffe, *Kritik der Freiheit*, op. cit., pp. 29 f.

14 Honneth, *Freedom's Right*, op. cit., p. 15.

15 Ibid., p. 36.

16 Theodor W. Adorno (1973 [1966]), *Negative Dialectics*, London and New York: Routledge, p. 214.

17 Karl Marx (1975 [1844]), 'On the Jewish Question', in: *Marx Engels Collected Works* (MECW), Vol. 3, pp. 146–74, here: p. 163.

18 Theodor W. Adorno (2006 [1964–65]), 'Progress or Regression?', in: *History and Freedom: Lectures 1964–1965*, ed. by Rolf Tiedemann, transl. by Rodney Livingstone, Cambridge: Polity, pp. 3–9, here: p. 5.

19 See Alex Demirović (2019), 'Vernunft und Emanzipation', in: Uwe H. Bittlingmayer, Alex Demirović and Tatjana Freytag (eds.), *Handbuch Kritische Theorie*, Wiesbaden: Springer VS, pp. 187–210.

20 Max Horkheimer and Theodor W. Adorno (2002) *The Dialectic of Enlightenment: Philosophical Fragments*, Stanford, CA: Stanford University Press, p. xvi.

21 Ibid.

22 Gunnar Hindrichs (2020), *Zur kritischen Theorie*, Berlin: Suhrkamp, p. 92 (transl. added).

23 Jürgen Habermas (1983 [1969]), 'Theodor Adorno: The Primal History of Subjectivity – Self-Affirmation Gone Wild', in: id., *Philosophical-Political Profiles*, transl. by Frederick G. Lawrence, Cambridge, MA: MIT Press, pp. 99–111, here: p. 100.

24 Horkheimer and Adorno, *Dialectic of Enlightenment*, op. cit., p. 45.

25 Ibid., p. 43.

26 Max Horkheimer (1947), *Eclipse of Reason*, New York: Oxford University Press, p. 140.

27 For more on this subject, see also David Riesman, Reuel Denney, Nathan Glazer and Renate Rausch (1964), *Die einsame Masse. Eine Untersuchung der Wandlungen des amerikanischen Charakters*, Darmstadt: Rowohlt.

28 Andreas Reckwitz (2021), *The End of Illusions: Politics, Economy, and Culture in Late Modernity*, transl. by Valentine A. Pakis, Cambridge: Polity, p. 5.

29 Theodor W. Adorno (2000), 'Lecture Three, 30 April 1968', in: *Introduction to Sociology*, ed. by Christoph Gödde, transl. by Edmund Jephcott, Stanford, CA: Stanford University Press, p. 22.

30 On the discussion of Adorno's proclamation of the 'end of individuality', see Thorsten Bonacker (1998), 'Ohne Angst verschieden sein können. Individualität in der integralen Gesellschaft', in: Dirk Auer, Thorsten Bonacker and Stefan Müller-Doohm (eds.), *Die Gesellschaftstheorie Adornos. Themen und Grundbegriffe*, Darmstadt: Wissenschaftliche Buchgesellschaft (WBG), pp. 117–44, here: p. 142.

31 Theodor W. Adorno (2006 [1964–65]), 'Antinomies of Freedom', in: *History and Freedom: Lectures 1964–1965*, ed. by Rolf Tiedemann,

transl. by Rodney Livingstone, Cambridge: Polity, pp. 209–18, here: p. 213.

32 A discussion of Marcuse's theses in the context of the student movement, where they were both popular and controversial, can be found in Reimut Reiche (1969), *Sexualität und Klassenkampf. Zur Abwehr repressiver Entsublimierung*, Frankfurt am Main: Verlag Neue Kritik.

33 Herbert Marcuse (2011 [1963]), 'Obsolescence of Psychoanalysis', in: *Philosophy, Psychoanalysis and Emancipation: Collected Papers of Herbert Marcuse, Volume 5*, ed. by Douglas Kellner and Clayton Pierce, London and New York: Routledge, p. 115.

34 Herbert Marcuse (2002 [1964]), *One-Dimensional Man: Studies in the Ideology of Advanced Industrial Society*, London and New York: Routledge, pp. xlv–xlvi.

35 In his work *Eros and Civilization*, Marcuse posits his own interpretation of Freud against the so-called 'revisionist Neo-Freudian schools', by which he refers particularly to Erich Fromm: instead of discarding Freud's drive theory as biologistic like his colleagues did, Marcuse regards it as a 'social theory' that is 'sociological' in substance; Herbert Marcuse (2023 [1956]), *Eros and Civilization: A Philosophical Inquiry Into Freud*, London and New York: Routledge, p. 3.

36 Marcuse, 'Obsolescence of Psychoanalysis', op. cit., p. 120.

37 Ibid., pp. 120–1. In order to differentiate between 'true' and 'false' needs, Marcuse is ultimately forced to hold on to Freud's drive theory: to him, the instinctual energies inherent in all human beings entail an impulse for critique and thus for overcoming the social domination that oppresses them.

38 See Herbert Marcuse (2002 [1964]), 'The End of Utopia', in: *Five Lectures: Psychoanalysis, Politics, and Utopia*, transl. by Jeremy J. Shapiro and Shierry M. Weber, London: Penguin, pp. 62–82.

39 Marcuse, *One-Dimensional Man*, op. cit., p. 79.

40 Ibid.

41 Marcuse, 'Obsolescence of Psychoanalysis', op. cit., p. 118.

42 Although Erich Fromm played a leading role in developing the institute's 'programme of a Marxist social-psychology' during the early 1930s – a circumstance Jürgen Habermas reminded Herbert Marcuse of during a conversation shortly before the latter's death – Fromm was criticized for having undertaken a revisionist deviation from that very programme in his works from the 1940s onwards, as he had discarded Freud's drive theory; Jürgen Habermas (1977), 'Gespräch mit Herbert Marcuse', in: id., *Philosophisch-politische Profile*, Frankfurt am Main: Suhrkamp, pp. 265–318, here: p. 271 (transl. added).

43 On the break between the Institute for Social Research and Erich Fromm, see Rolf Wiggershaus (1986), *Die Frankfurter Schule. Geschichte. Theoretische Entwicklung. Politische Bedeutung*, Munich: Carl Hanser, pp. 298–307.

44 See Erich Fromm (1941), *Escape from Freedom*, New York: Holt, Rinehart and Winston.

45 Erich Fromm (1942), *Fear of Freedom*, London and New York: Routledge, p. 30.

46 Ibid., p. 29.

47 György (Georg) Lukács (1971 [1920]), *The Theory of the Novel: A historico-philosophical essay on the forms of great epic literature*, Cambridge, MA: MIT Press, pp. 46 ff.
48 Fromm, *Fear of Freedom*, op. cit., p. 101.
49 See ibid., pp. 106–7.
50 Ibid., p. 30.
51 Ibid., p. 121.
52 Ibid., p. 249.
53 In the current generation of Critical Theory, it is Hartmut Rosa who is following in Fromm's intellectual footsteps. He likewise regards the subject's inner urge for resonance as an inherent motivational force in humans; see Hartmut Rosa (2019), *Resonance: A Sociology of Our Relationship to the World*, Cambridge: Polity.
54 Adorno, 'Antinomies of Freedom', op. cit., p. 218.
55 Markus Schroer (2001), *Das Individuum der Gesellschaft. Synchrone und diachrone Theorieperspektiven*, Frankfurt am Main: Suhrkamp, p. 43 (transl. added).
56 Zygmunt Bauman (2000), *Liquid Modernity*, Cambridge: Polity, p. 22. The sentence continues: 'social institutions are only too willing to cede the worries of definitions and identities to the individual initiative, while universal principles to rebel against are hard to find.' Given the *Querdenker* movement's protests for freedom, this assessment would, of course, differ somewhat today.
57 See Peter Wagner (1994), *A Sociology of Modernity: Liberty and Discipline*, London and New York: Routledge.
58 Bauman, *Liquid Modernity*, op. cit., p. 25.
59 On this issue, see also, apart from Bauman: Hartmut Rosa (2013), *Social Acceleration: A New Theory of Modernity*, New York: Columbia University Press; Andreas Reckwitz (2020), *The Society of Singularities*, Cambridge: Polity.
60 Marcuse observed this rather clairvoyantly; see Marcuse, *One-Dimensional Man*, op. cit., pp. 254–5.
61 See Eric Hobsbawm (1994), *The Age of Extremes: The Short Twentieth Century: 1914–1991*, London: Michael Joseph; Hindrichs, *Zur Kritischen Theorie*, op. cit., pp. 46–90.
62 Herbert Marcuse (2009 [1968]), 'Foreword', in id., *Negations: Essays in Critical Theory*, London: MayFly Books, pp. xvii–xxiv, here: p. xvii.
63 Marcuse, Herbert (2009 [1968]), 'The Struggle against Liberalism in the Totalitarian View of the State', in id., *Negations: Essays in Critical Theory*, London: MayFlyBooks, pp. 1–30, here: p. 5.
64 Karl Marx (1976 [1867]), 'So-Called Primitive Accumulation of Capital', in *Capital, Volume One*, London: Penguin, pp. 873–942, here: p. 875.
65 Ibid., p. 899.
66 Ibid.
67 Marcuse, 'The Struggle against Liberalism', op. cit., p. 6.
68 Ludwig von Mises (1985 [1927]), *Liberalism in the Classical Tradition*, 3rd edn, New York and San Francisco: Cobden Press and Foundation for Economic Education, p. 51; quoted in: Marcuse, 'The Struggle against Liberalism', op. cit., p. 6.
69 Carl Schmitt (1998 [1932]), 'Strong State and Sound Economy: An

NOTES TO PP. 32–34

Address to Business Leaders', Address delivered to a conference of the Langnamverein in Düsseldorf, 23 November 1932, in: Renato Cristi, *Carl Schmitt and Authoritarian Liberalism: Strong State, Free Economy*, Cardiff: University of Wales Press, pp. 212–33. As Cristi notes: 'The *Langnamverein* was an association of Ruhr industrialists whose full name, *Verein zur Wahrung der gemeinsamen wirtschaftlichen Interessen in Rheinland und Westfalen* (Association for the Furtherance of the Joint Economic Interests of the Rhineland and Westphalia), forced its abbreviation to be "Long Name (Langnam) Association"'; see Cristi, p. 212, footnote 1.

70 Including, for example, for Alexander Rüstow; see Christoph Butterwegge, Bettina Lösch and Ralf Ptak (2016), *Kritik des Neoliberalismus*, Wiesbaden: VS Verlag für Sozialwissenschaften, pp. 31–8; on the relationship between liberalism and fascism, see the comprehensive study by Ishay Landa (2021), *Der Lehrling und sein Meister. Liberale Tradition und Faschismus*, Berlin: Dietz.

71 Schmitt, 'Strong State and Sound Economy', op. cit., pp. 217–18.

72 Ibid., p. 217.

73 Ibid.

74 Ibid., p. 225, brackets in the original.

75 Grégoire Chamayou (2021), *The Ungovernable Society: A Genealogy of Authoritarian Liberalism*, Cambridge: Polity, p. 207.

76 Hermann Heller (2015 [1933]), 'Authoritarian Liberalism', *European Law Journal*, 21(3), 295–301; on Heller's interpretation of Schmitt, see Wolfgang Streeck (2015), 'Heller, Schmitt and the Euro', *European Law Journal*, 1(3), 361–70.

77 Heller, 'Authoritarian Liberalism', op. cit., p. 300.

78 Hauke Brunkhorst (2019), 'Autoritärer Liberalismus', in: Karsten Fischer and Sebastian Huhnholz (eds.), *Liberalismus. Traditionsbestände und Gegenwartskontroversen*, Baden-Baden: Nomos, pp. 291–314, here: p. 291 (transl. added).

79 Chamayou, *The Ungovernable Society*, op. cit., p. 239.

80 Although Christoph Möllers emphasizes that the term 'authoritarian liberalism' serves mainly the 'polemics against liberalism', rather than an 'accurate classification of authoritarian systems', he thereby overlooks the economic functional logic of authoritarian liberalism that critics have proven; Christoph Möllers (2020), *Freiheitsgrade. Elemente einer liberalen politischen Mechanik*, Berlin: Suhrkamp, p. 32 (transl. added).

81 Friedrich Pollock (1933) 'Bemerkungen zur Wirtschaftskrise' [Remarks on the Economic Crisis], *Zeitschrift für Sozialforschung*, II(3), 321–54, here: p. 350; quoted in: Manfred Gangl (2016), 'The Controversy over Friedrich Pollock's State Capitalism', *History of the Human Sciences*, 29(2), 23–41, here: p. 26.

82 Adorno et al., *The Authoritarian Personality*, op. cit., p. 1.

83 Max Horkheimer and Theodor W. Adorno (1985), 'Vorurteil und Charakter' (1952), in: id., *Gesammelte Schriften*, Bd. 8: *Vorträge und Aufzeichnungen 1949–1973*, ed. by Gunzelin Schmid Noerr, Frankfurt am Main: Fischer, pp. 64–76, here: p. 69; available in English as typescript ('Prejudice and Personality', p. 6.) at: https://sammlungen.ub.uni-frankfurt .de/horkheimer/content/pageview/6593305

84 Theodor W. Adorno (1948), 'Remarks on 'The Authoritarian Personality' by Adorno, Frenkel-Brunswik, Levinson, Sanford', n.p. Available at: https://platypus1917.org/2016/11/08/remarks-authoritarian-personality -adorno-frenkel-brunswik-levinson-sanford/

85 See the table in Adorno et al., *The Authoritarian Personality*, op. cit., pp. 226–7.

86 Ibid., p. 228.

87 Ibid.

88 Ibid., pp. 262–9.

89 Ibid., p. 268.

90 See Fromm, *Sociopsychological Dimensions*, op. cit., p. 42.

91 Ibid., p. 16.

92 Ibid., p. 17.

93 Ibid., p. 43.

94 Ibid.

95 Ibid., p. 45.

96 Franz L. Neumann (2017 [1957]), 'Anxiety and Politics', *triple*, 15(2), 612–36, here: p. 615.

97 Ibid., p. 618.

Chapter 2. Freedom in dependence

1 For more on what follows in this section, see Andreas Reckwitz (2020), *Das hybride Subjekt. Eine Theorie der Subjektkulturen von der bürgerlichen Moderne zur Postmoderne*, Berlin: Suhrkamp. Reckwitz refers to subject cultures instead of social characters.

2 On this, see also the ground-breaking study by Wagner, *Sociology of Modernity*, op. cit., pp. 83–4.

3 Ibid., pp. 73 ff.; see also Marcuse, *One-Dimensional Man*, op. cit., pp. 3–20.

4 Although we are certainly aware of the diversity of forms of individuality, here and in the following we focus on the ideal-type reconstruction of individualization in order to flesh out its underlying overall social dynamic.

5 Karl Marx and Friedrich Engels (1976 [1848]), *Manifesto of the Communist Party*, MECW, Vol. 6, pp. 477–506, here: p. 506.

6 Ibid., pp. 486–7.

7 Ibid., p. 487. Zygmunt Bauman draws on this imagery in his interpretation of the historical process of modernization. In his view, this '"melting the solids" [leaves] the whole complex network of social relations unstuck – bare, unprotected, unarmed and exposed, impotent to resist the business-inspired rules of action and business-shaped criteria of rationality'; *Liquid Modernity*, op. cit., p. 4.

8 Karl Marx and Friedrich Engels (1986 [1857–58]), *Outlines of the Critique of Political Economy*, MECW, Vol. 28, pp. 49–561, here: p. 431; see also Marx, *Capital, Volume One*, op. cit., pp. 566 ff.

9 Marx and Engels, *Communist Manifesto*, op. cit., p. 487.

10 Max Horkheimer (1993), 'Egoism and Freedom Movements: On the Anthropology of the Bourgeois Era' (1936), in: id., *Between Philosophy and Social Science: Selected Early Writings*, Cambridge, MA: MIT Press, pp. 49–110, here: pp. 95–6.

11 For an overview, see Schroer, *Das Individuum der Gesellschaft*, op. cit.

12 See Hermann Korte (2011), *Einführung in die Geschichte der Soziologie*, Wiesbaden: Springer, pp. 161–3.
13 Norbert Elias (1994 [1939]), *The Civilizing Process*, Oxford: Blackwell, p. 369.
14 Ibid., p. 365.
15 See Norbert Elias (2001 [1987]), *The Society of Individuals*, ed. by Michael Schröter, London: Continuum, pp. 50 ff.
16 Sigmund Freud (2001 [1930]), *Civilization and Its Discontents*, in: *The Standard Edition of the Complete Psychological Works of Sigmund Freud, Volume XXI (1927–1931): The Future of an Illusion, Civilization and its Discontents, and Other Works*, New York: Vintage, p. 456.
17 Ibid., p. 454.
18 Especially during capitalism's period of primitive accumulation, women – and particularly their bodies – were made objects of subjugation and disciplining; see Silvia Federici (2004), *Caliban and the Witch: Women, the Body, and Primitive Accumulation*, New York: Autonomedia.
19 Bauman, *Liquid Modernity*, op. cit., p. 7.
20 Ibid., p. 32.
21 See Hans-Peter Müller (2005), 'Diagnostiker des Individualismus', *Merkur*, 59(675), 637–42, here: p. 638 (transl. added).
22 See Georg Simmel (1989), 'Über sociale Differenzierung' (1890), in: *Georg Simmel Gesamtausgabe* (GSG), Bd. 2: *Aufsätze 1887 bis 1890. Über sociale Differenzierung. Die Probleme der Geschichtsphilosophie (1892)*, ed. by Heinz-Jürgen Dahme, Frankfurt am Main: Suhrkamp, pp. 109–296; see also Georg Simmel (1977), 'Personal Identity', in: *The Problems of the Philosophy of History: An Epistemological Essay*, New York: Free Press, pp. 113–17.
23 Georg Simmel (2004), *The Philosophy of Money*, 3rd edn, London and New York: Routledge, p. 344.
24 Ibid., 284
25 Émile Durkheim (2010 [1951]), *Sociology and Philosophy*, New York: Routledge, p. 37.
26 Ibid., p. 37.
27 Nadia Urbinati (2015), *The Tyranny of the Moderns*, New Haven, CT: Yale University Press, p. 7.
28 Émile Durkheim (1969), 'Individualism and the Intellectuals', transl. by Steven Lukes, *Political Studies*, XVII(1), 14–30, here: p. 25.
29 Peter Wagner (2008), *Modernity as Experience and Interpretation: A New Sociology of Modernity*, Cambridge: Polity, p. 36.
30 Thomas Hobbes (1651), *Leviathan. or: The Matter, Forme, and Power of a Common-wealth Ecclesiasticall and Civill*, London: Andrew Crooke, p. 129.
31 Honneth, *Freedom's Right*, op. cit., p. 23.
32 John Stuart Mill (1978 [1859]), *On Liberty*, Indianapolis, IN: Hackett Publishing Co., p. 12.
33 Ibid., p. 9.
34 Isaiah Berlin (2002), 'Two Concepts of Liberty' (1958), in: *Liberty: Incorporating Four Essays on Liberty*, ed. by Henry Hardy, Oxford: Oxford University Press.
35 See Ulrich Beck (1992), *Risk Society: Towards a New Modernity*, Newbury Park, CA: Sage, pp. 127–38.

36 Theodor W. Adorno, et al. (1989), 'Die verwaltete Welt oder: Die Krise des Individuums. Aufzeichnung eines Gesprächs im Hessischen Rundfunk am 4. September 1950', in: Max Horkheimer, *Gesammelte Schriften*, Vol. 13: *Nachgelassene Schriften 1949–1972*, ed. by Gunzelin Schmid Noerr, Frankfurt am Main: Fischer, pp. 121–42.
37 Elias, *The Society of Individuals*, op. cit., pp. 135–6.
38 See the Preface in *The Civilizing Process*, op. cit., pp. ix–xv; see also Norbert Elias (1978), *What is Sociology?*, London: Hutchinson, pp. 118–22.
39 See Elias, *The Society of Individuals*, op. cit., pp. 153–238.
40 Beck, *Risk Society*, op. cit., p. 131.
41 Ibid., p. 130.
42 On this, see the remarks on Alain Ehrenberg in chapter 4.
43 Adorno, *History and Freedom* (Lecture 23), op. cit., p. 212.
44 See Bauman, *Liquid Modernity*, p. 39; Beck, *Risk Society*, op. cit., p. 131.
45 On the shrunken middle class, see Bertelsmann Stiftung/OECD (eds.) (2021), *Bröckelt die Mittelschicht? Risiken und Chancen für mittlere Einkommensgruppen auf dem deutschen Arbeitsmarkt*, Gütersloh: Bertelsmann Stiftung; on the underclass, see Nicole Mayer-Ahuja and Oliver Nachtwey (2021), 'Verkannte Leistungsträger:innen. Berichte aus der Klassengesellschaft', in: Nicole Mayer-Ahuja and Oliver Nachtwey (eds.), *Verkannte Leistungsträger:innen. Berichte aus der Klassengesellschaft*, Berlin: Suhrkamp, pp. 11–46.
46 See Pierre Rosanvallon (2013), *The Society of Equals*, Cambridge, MA: Harvard University Press, p. 14; Robert Castel (2003), *From Manual Workers to Wage Laborers: Transformation of the Social Question*, New Brunswick, NJ: Transaction Publishers.
47 See Oliver Nachtwey (2018) *Germany's Hidden Crisis: Social Decline in the Heart of Europe*, London: Verso, pp. 10 f.; Hartmut Rosa (2012), 'Wettbewerb als Interaktionsmodus. Kulturelle und sozialstrukturelle Konsequenzen der Konkurrenzgesellschaft', in: id., *Weltbeziehungen im Zeitalter der Beschleunigung*, Frankfurt am Main: Suhrkamp, pp. 324–56, here: p. 201; Rosa, *Social Acceleration*, op. cit., pp. 117–19.
48 See, e.g., Richard Sennett (1998), The *Corrosion of Character: The Personal Consequences of Work in the New Capitalism*, New York: W.W. Norton; Sighard Neckel (2000), 'Identität als Ware. Die Marktwirtschaft im Sozialen' (1996), in: id., *Die Macht der Unterscheidung. Essays zur Kultursoziologie der modernen Gesellschaft*, Frankfurt am Main: Campus, pp. 37–47.
49 See Oliver Nachtwey (2017), *Decivilization: on regressive tendencies in Western societies*, in Heinrich Geiselberger (ed.), *The Great Regression*, Cambridge: Polity, pp. 130–42.
50 See Thomas Meyer (2004), 'Die Agenda 2010 und die soziale Gerechtigkeit', *Politische Vierteljahresschrift*, 45(2), 181–90.
51 See Nachtwey, *Germany's Hidden Crisis*, op. cit., pp. 99–101.
52 Oliver Nachtwey (2009), *Marktsozialdemokratie. Die Transformation der SPD und Labour Party*, Wiesbaden: VS Verlag, pp. 225–6.
53 Honneth, *Freedom's Right*, op. cit., p. 78.
54 See Nachtwey, *Germany's Hidden Crisis*, op. cit., pp. 93–4, 152–61.
55 See Theodor W. Adorno (2006), 'Freedom and Bourgeois Society', in:

id., *History and Freedom: Lectures 1964–1965* (Lecture 21), Cambridge: Polity, pp. 190–9, here: p. 197.

56 For more on the meritocratic principle's function for domination, see the still-ground-breaking study by Claus Offe (1975), *Berufsbildungsreform. Eine Fallstudie über Reformpolitik*, Frankfurt am Main: Suhrkamp.

57 See Sighard Neckel (2008), *Flucht nach vorn. Die Erfolgskultur der Marktgesellschaft*, Frankfurt am Main: Campus, pp. 62–3.

58 Ibid., p. 12.

59 As early as 1949, Robert K. Merton spoke of a virtual 'cult of success' in the context of American capitalism's unbridled orientation towards social advancement; Robert K. Merton (1968), *Sociological Theory and Social Structure*, New York: The Free Press, p. 189.

60 See Mayer-Ahuja and Nachtwey, 'Verkannte Leistungsträger:innen', op. cit., pp. 14–20.

61 See Mark Lutter (2013), 'Strukturen ungleichen Erfolgs. Winner-take-all-Konzentrationen und ihre sozialen Entstehungskontexte auf flexiblen Arbeitsmärkten', *Kölner Zeitschrift für Soziologie und Sozialpsychologie*, 65(4), 597–622; Sighard Neckel (2014), 'Oligarchische Ungleichheit. Winner-take-all-Positionen in der (obersten)Oberschicht', *Westend. Neue Zeitschrift für Sozialforschung*, 11(2), 51–63.

62 See Carolin Amlinger (2021), *Schreiben. Eine Soziologie literarischer Arbeit*, Berlin: Suhrkamp.

63 See Oliver Nachtwey and Philipp Staab (2016), 'Market and Labour Control in Digital Capitalism', *tripleC*, 14(2), 457–74.

64 Michael Hartmann (2002), *Der Mythos von den Leistungseliten. Spitzenkarrieren und soziale Herkunft in Wirtschaft, Politik, Justiz und Wissenschaft*, Frankfurt am Main: Campus.

65 Sam Friedman, Dave O'Brien and Ian McDonald (2021), 'Deflecting Privilege. Class Identity and the Intergenerational Self', *Sociology*, 55(4), 716–33.

66 Neckel, *Flucht nach vorn*, op. cit., p. 12.

67 Ibid., p. 16 (transl. added).

68 Ibid., p. 64 (transl. added).

69 See Adrian Daub (2020), *What Tech Calls Thinking: An Inquiry into the Intellectual Bedrock of Silicon Valley*, New York: Farrar, Straus & Giroux, pp. 133–50.

70 See Bauman, *Liquid Modernity*, op. cit., p. 34.

71 In his classic work *The Sociological Imagination* (2000, Oxford: Oxford University Press), which was originally published at the end of industrial modernity in 1959, American sociologist C. Wright Mills showed that private problems always simultaneously indicate existing public problems, too (pp. 10 f.). This awareness of society has today been lost.

72 See Neckel, *Flucht nach vorn*, op. cit., p. 188.

73 See Bundesregierung (German Federal Government) (2021), *Lebenslagen in Deutschland. Der Sechste Armuts- und Reichtumsbericht der Bundesregierung*, Berlin; Bertelsmann Stiftung/OECD (eds.), *Bröckelt die Mittelschicht?*, op. cit.; Nachtwey, *Germany's Hidden Crisis*, op. cit.

74 In the 1970s, British cultural sociologist Paul Willis studied the resistance staged by working-class adolescents in the educational context. He was able to show how these youths seek to assert themselves by displaying their

contempt for school, by consuming alcohol, and representing 'manliness', yet at the same time thereby fully intentionally exclude themselves, because they essentially already know that they will end up on the factory line and will not manage to advance upward in society. In reference to Willis, the processes described here may be regarded as a modernized form of self-exclusion; see Paul Willis (1978), *Learning to Labour: How Working Class Kids Get Working Class Jobs*, Westmead, UK: Saxon House.

75 On the issue of upward social advancement in gangster rap music, see Martin Seeliger (2022), *Soziologie des Gangsta-Rap. Popkultur als Ausdruck sozialer Konflikte*, Weinheim: Beltz Juventa.

76 Rosa, 'Wettbewerb als Interaktionsmodus', op. cit., p. 326 (transl. added). As early as at the beginning of the 1980s, Jürgen Habermas had famously warned against the 'colonisation of the lifeworld'; Jürgen Habermas (1987), *Theory of Communicative Action*, Vol. 2, Boston, MA: Beacon Press, pp. 322, 391.

77 Neckel, *Flucht nach vorn*, op. cit., p. 15 (transl. added).

78 See Marion Fourcade (2014), 'Ordinalization. Lewis A. Coser Memorial Award for Theoretical Agenda Setting 2014', *Sociological Theory*, 34(3), 175–95.

79 Marion Fourcade and Alex V. Barnard (2021), 'Das Unbehagen an der Ordinalisierung', *Kölner Zeitschrift für Soziologie und Sozialpsychologie*, 73(1), 113–35, here: p. 131 (transl. added).

80 Ibid.

81 See William Davies (2018), *Nervous States: How Feeling Took Over the World*, London: Vintage. Although Davies's reflections mainly concerned the United Kingdom and the US, similar developments can also be confirmed in the German case: even though overall prosperity has grown, the life expectancy of pensioners with high earnings has risen far more strongly than that of their peers who receive only a small pension; see Georg Wenau, Pavel Grigoriev and Vladimir Shkolnikov (2019), 'Socioeconomic Disparities in Life Expectancy Gains among Retired German Men, 1997–2016', *Journal of Epidemiology and Community Health*, 73(7), 605–11.

82 See Thomas H. Marshall (2020 [1951]), 'Staatsbürgerrechte und soziale Klassen', in: Jürgen Mackert and Hans-Peter Müller (eds.), *Citizenship – Soziologie der Staatsbürgerschaft*, Wiesbaden: VS Verlag, pp. 45–102; Rosanvallon, *Society of Equals*, op. cit.

83 See Martin Kohli (1988), 'Normalbiographie und Individualität. Zur institutionellen Dynamik des gegenwärtigen Lebenslaufregimes', in: Hanns-Georg Brose and Bruno Hildebrand (eds.), *Vom Ende des Individuums zur Individualität ohne Ende*, Opladen: Leske & Budrich, pp. 33–53.

84 Reckwitz, *Das hybride Subjekt*, op. cit., p. 29 (transl. added).

85 Initially, in his book *Das hybride Subjekt* ('The Hybrid Subject'), Reckwitz still referred to this era as 'postmodernity'; only in his later writings did he change his terminology – with reference to the works of Anthony Giddens – to 'late modernity'; see Reckwitz, *Society of Singularities*, op. cit.; Anthony Giddens (1991), *Modernity and Self-Identity: Self and Society in the Late Modern Age*, Stanford, CA: Blackwell. Here, we follow Reckwitz's concise systematization, which is indeed very useful for further developing our argument. However, it would perhaps be appropriate – in another context

– to address a blind spot in Reckwitz's analysis, namely the complete absence of working-class subcultures.

86 Undine Eberlein refers to this metamorphosis of individuality as 'romantic individualism'; see Undine Eberlein (2000), *Einzigartigkeit. Das romantische Individualitätskonzept der Moderne*, Frankfurt am Main: Campus.

87 Regarding the historical roots of this, see Colin Campbell (1987), *The Romantic Ethic and the Spirit of Modern Consumerism*, Oxford: Basil Blackwell.

88 See Axel Honneth (2004), 'Organized Self-Realization: Some Paradoxes of Individualization', *European Journal of Social Theory*, 7(4), 463–78, here: p. 469.

89 See Luc Boltanski and Ève Chiapello (2005 [1999]), *The New Spirit of Capitalism*, London: Verso.

90 Claus Offe (1989), *Arbeitsgesellschaft. Strukturprobleme und Zukunftsperspektiven*, Frankfurt am Main: Campus.

91 See Frithjof Bergmann (2019), *New Work, New Culture: Work We Want and a Culture that Strengthens Us*, Alresford: John Hunt/Zero Books.

92 See Jan Guldner (2021), 'Moderner und billiger, da kann man nicht nein sagen', Interview with Nick Kratzer, in: *Wirtschaftswoche*, 12 September, available at: https://www.wiwo.de/erfolg/homeoffice/desksharing-moderner-und-billiger-da-kannman-nicht-nein-sagen/27469168.html

93 See Nachtwey, *Germany's Hidden Crisis*, op. cit.

94 See Andreas Reckwitz (2023), 'The Theory of Society as a Tool', in Andreas Reckwitz and Hartmut Rosa, *Late Modernity in Crisis: Why We Need a Theory of Society*, Cambridge: Polity, pp. 9–94, here: p. 61; Reckwitz, *The End of Illusions*, op. cit., p. 116f; Reckwitz, *The Society of Singularities*, op. cit., pp. 199–213.

95 Nils C. Kumkar, Uwe Schimank, Karin Gottschall, Betina Hollstein and Stefan Holubek-Schaum (2022), *Die beharrliche Mitte. Wenn investive Statusarbeit funktioniert*, Wiesbaden: Springer VS (transl. added).

96 Reckwitz, *Society of Singularities*, op. cit., p. 12.

97 Ibid., pp. 242–51.

98 Reckwitz, *The Society of Singularities*, op. cit., p. 8; Reckwitz, 'The Theory of Society as a Tool', op. cit., p. 43.

99 See Undine Eberlein (2006), 'Serielle Einzigartigkeit und Eigensinn', in: Günter Burkart (ed.), *Die Ausweitung der Bekenntniskultur – neue Formen der Selbstthematisierung?*, Wiesbaden: VS Verlag, pp. 127–43.

100 Simmel, *Philosophy of Money*, p. 216.

101 See Edgar Cabanas and Eva Illouz (2019), *Manufacturing Happy Citizens: How the Science and Industry of Happiness Control our Lives*, Cambridge: Polity, p. 9.

102 Anja Röcke (2021), *Soziologie der Selbstoptimierung*, Berlin: Suhrkamp, p. 10 (transl. added); see also: Daniel Nehring and Anjy Röcke (2023), 'Self-optimisation: Conceptual, Discursive and Historical Perspectives', *Current Sociology*, https://doi.org/10.1177/00113921221146575

103 Reckwitz, 'The Theory of Society as a Tool', op. cit., p. 67.

104 See Greta Wagner (2017), *Selbstoptimierung. Praxis und Kritik von Neuroenhancement*, Frankfurt am Main: Campus.

105 Max Weber (1992 [1930]), *The Protestant Ethic and The Spirit of Capitalism*, London: Routledge, p. 77.

106 On self-tracking, see Steffen Mau (2017), *Das metrische Wir. Über die Quantifizierung des Sozialen*, Berlin: Suhrkamp, pp. 167–84; Simon Schaupp (2016), *Digitale Selbstüberwachung. Self-Tracking im kybernetischen Kapitalismus*, Münster: Verlag Graswurzelrevolution; Stefanie Duttweiler, Robert Gugutzer, Jan-Hendrik Passoth and Jörg Strübing (eds.) (2016), *Leben nach Zahlen. Self-Tracking als Optimierungsprojekt?*, Bielefeld: transcript.

107 See Ulrich Bröckling (2016), *The Entrepreneurial Self: Fabricating a New Type of Subject*, Los Angeles, CA: Sage.

108 Bauman, *Liquid Modernity*, op. cit., p. 34.

109 And yet, an incipient reversal of this trend can be observed, too: younger people born around the turn of the millennium attach greater value to spending time with their friends and family. They yearn for more collegiality, but, more importantly, for a meaningful job that is more than just a source of income. However, this is still no more than a counter-movement to the dominant mode of competitive subjectivity; on this, see the regularly published Deloitte Millennial Surveys.

110 See, with regard to the regulation of emotions, Arlie Russell Hochschild (1983), *The Managed Heart: Commercialization of Human Feeling*, Berkeley, CA: University of California Press.

111 See Cabanas and Illouz, *Manufacturing Happy Citizens*, op. cit.; Bröckling, *The Entrepreneurial Self*, op. cit.; Ulrich Bröckling (2017), *Gute Hirten führen sanft. Über Menschenregierungskünste*, Berlin: Suhrkamp, pp. 113–39.

112 See Sighard Neckel, Greta Wagner and Anna Katharina Schaffner (eds.) (2017), *Burnout, Fatigue, Exhaustion: An Interdisciplinary Perspective on Affliction*, Cham: Palgrave Macmillan.

113 Honneth, 'Organized Self-Realization', op. cit., p. 474.

114 Bauman, *Liquid Modernity*, op. cit., pp. 16–17.

115 Max Horkheimer (1966), 'On the Concept of Freedom', *Diogenes*, 14(53), 73–81, here: p. 75.

116 Robert Nozick (1974), *Anarchy, State, and Utopia*, Oxford: Blackwell.

117 John Rawls (1971), *A Theory of Justice*, Cambridge, MA: Harvard University Press.

118 See Peter Niesen (2002), 'Die politische Theorie des Libertarianismus. Robert Nozick und Friedrich A. von Hayek', in: André Brodocz and Gary S. Schaal (eds.), *Politische Theorien der Gegenwart*, Vol. 1, Opladen: UTB, pp. 69–110.

119 Nozick, *Anarchy, State, and Utopia*, op. cit., p. 52.

120 Wagner, *Modernity as Experience and Interpretation*, op. cit., p. viii.

121 Alexis de Tocqueville (2000 [1840]), *Democracy in America*, Chicago, IL: University of Chicago Press, pp. 719, 714.

122 György (Georg) Lukács (2000 [1923]), *History and Class Consciousness*, Cambridge, MA: MIT Press, p. 83.

123 Ibid., p. 86.

124 Marx, *Capital, Volume One*, op. cit., p. 165. This whole passage by Marx on the commodity relation reads as follows: 'It is a physical relation between physical things. As against this, the commodity form, and the value-relation of the products of labour within which it appears, have absolutely no connection with the physical nature of the commodity and

the material [*dinglich*] relations arising out of this. It is nothing but the definite social relation between men themselves which assumes here, for them, the fantastic form of a relation between things.'

125 Timo Jütten (2011), 'Verdinglichung und Freiheit', *Deutsche Zeitschrift für Philosophie*, 59(5), 717–30, here: p. 719 (transl. added).

126 For more on this, see C.B. Macpherson (2011 [1962]), *The Political Theory of Possessive Individualism. Hobbes to Locke*, Oxford: Oxford University Press; Habermas also refers to possessive individualism; see Habermas, *Theory of Communicative Action*, op. cit., p. 325.

127 Habermas, *Theory of Communicative Action*, Vol. 2, op. cit., p. 355. In this instance, Habermas presents a 'theory of late-capitalist reification, reformulated in terms of system and lifeworld' that seeks to explain the 'cultural impoverishment and fragmentation of everyday consciousness'.

128 See Ole Nymoen and Wolfgang M. Schmitt (2021), *Influencer. Die Ideologie der Werbekörper*, Berlin: Suhrkamp.

129 The 'wheels of the juggernaut' is the metaphor Marx uses to depict an unstoppable process of accumulation (Marx, *Capital, Volume One*, op. cit., p. 799). The term juggernaut (derived from the Sanskrit 'Jagganath') refers to the temple chariots used in Hindu processions, which can hardly be stopped once they have picked up pace.

130 Robert Castel (2011), *Die Krise der Arbeit. Neue Unsicherheiten und die Zukunft des Individuums*, Hamburg: Hamburger Edition, p. 21 (transl. added); see also Robert Castel (2016), 'The Rise of Uncertainties', *Critical Horizons*, 17(2), 160–7.

131 Marcuse, *One-Dimensional Man*, op. cit., p. 12.

132 Adorno, too, had anticipated this scenario. His concern was that individuals who identify with the course of world capitalism 'do so in an unhappy, neurotically damaged way, which effectively leads them to reinforce the world as it is. And that, I would say, is the truth about the situation of human beings in history.' Adorno, *On History and Freedom* (Lecture 8), op. cit., p. 76.

133 Marx, 'On the Jewish Question', op. cit., p. 167.

134 Adorno, *On History and Freedom* (Lecture 24), op. cit., p. 217.

Chapter 3. The order of disorder: social change and regressive modernization

1 Reckwitz, *Das hybride Subjekt*, op. cit., p. 28 (transl. added).

2 Reckwitz, 'The Theory of Society as a Tool', op. cit., p. 72.

3 Ulrich Beck (1996), 'The Age of Side-Effects: On the Politicization of Modernity', in: id., *The Reinvention of Politics: Rethinking Modernity in the Global Social Order*, Cambridge: Polity, pp. 11–60, here: p. 35.

4 See Martin Hartmann and Axel Honneth (2010), 'Paradoxien kapitalistischer Modernisierung', in: id., *Das Ich im Wir*, Berlin: Suhrkamp, pp. 222–48; Axel Honneth and Ferdinand Sutterlüty (2011), 'Normative Paradoxien der Gegenwart – eine Forschungsperspektive', *Westend. Neue Zeitschrift für Sozialforschung*, 8(1), 67–85.

5 Oliver Nachtwey and Martin Seeliger, (2020), 'Transformation of Industrial Citizenship in the Course of European Integration', *The British Journal of Sociology*, 71(5), 852–66.

6 See Simon Schaupp (2022), 'Algorithmic Integration and Precarious (Dis)obedience: On the Co-constitution of Migration Regime and

Workplace Regime in Digitalised Manufacturing and Logistics', *Work, Employment and Society*, 36(2), 310–27; Steven Vallas and Juliet B. Schor, (2020), 'What Do Platforms Do? Understanding the Gig Economy', *Annual Review of Sociology*, 46, 273–94.

7 See Nachtwey, *Germany's Hidden Crisis*, op. cit.; id., *Decivilization*, op. cit., pp. 130–42.

8 See Horkheimer and Adorno, *The Dialectic of Enlightenment*, op. cit., p. 28.

9 Claus Offe (2010), 'Was (falls überhaupt) können wir uns heute unter politischem Fortschritt vorstellen?', *Westend. Neue Zeitschrift für Sozialforschung*, 7(2), 3–14, here: p. 13 (transl. added).

10 Wagner, *Progress*, op. cit.; see also Ingolfur Blühdorn, Felix Butzlaff and Margaret Haderer, (2021), 'Emancipatory Politics at its Limits? An Introduction', *European Journal of Social Theory*, 25(1), 3–25.

11 See Reinhart Koselleck (2006 [1980]), '"Fortschritt" und "Niedergang" – Nachtrag zur Geschichte zweier Begriffe', in: id., *Begriffsgeschichten. Studien zur Semantik und Pragmatik der politischen und sozialen Sprache*, Frankfurt am Main: Suhrkamp, pp. 159–81, here: p. 159.

12 See Pippa Norris and Ronald Inglehart (2019), *Cultural Backlash: Trump, Brexit, and Authoritarian Populism*, Cambridge: Cambridge University Press, pp. 25–35, 77–101. Another frequently made observation is that of increased social polarization; for a critical treatment, see Steffen Mau (2022), 'Kamel oder Dromedar? Zur Diagnose der gesellschaftlichen Polarisierung', *Merkur*, 76(874), 5–18.

13 Critics object to this form of diversity and the corresponding recruitment of staff, alleging that considerations of skill and qualifications thus go overlooked. And yet, research has proved extensively that diversity engenders a higher overall competence level. Furthermore, the critique is somewhat trite, as it suggests that the criterion of competence had actually played a significant role previously. But if that had been the case, then why did Andreas Scheuer remain Federal Minister of Transport right till the end of the grand coalition's term in office (even after his failed project of a toll system for the German Autobahn cost taxpayers an estimated €243 million)?

14 See Beck, *Risk Society*, op. cit.; id., 'The Age of Side-Effects', op. cit.; Claus Offe (1987), 'The Utopia of the Zero-Option: Modernity and Modernization as Normative Political Criteria', *PRAXIS International*, (1), 1–24.

15 See Jürgen Habermas (1986), 'The New Obscurity: The Crisis of the Welfare State and the Exhaustion of Utopian Energies', *Philosophy and Social Criticism*, 11(2), 1–18.

16 For a more elaborate treatment of this aspect, see Zygmunt Bauman (2017), *Retrotopia*, Cambridge: Polity.

17 See Fredric Jameson (2005), *Archaeologies of the Future: The Desire Called Utopia and Other Science Fictions*, London: Verso, p. 199.

18 Henry Ford, Samuel Crowther, and William A. Levinson (2013 [1922]), *The Expanded and Annotated 'My Life and Work'*, Boca Raton, FL: CRC Press, p. 54.

19 See Eli J. Finkel, Paul W. Eastwick, Benjamin R. Karney, Harry T. Reis and Susan Sprecher (2012), 'Online Dating: A Critical Analysis from the

Perspective of Psychological Science', *Psychological Science in the Public Interest*, 13(1), 3–66.

20 Corresponding data are available at: https://www.destatis.de/DE/Themen /Gesellschaft-Umwelt/Bevoelkerung/Haushalte-Familien/Tabellen/4-3-lr -alleinstehende.html

21 Bauman, *Liquid Modernity*, op. cit., p. 62; see also Rosa, *Social Acceleration*, op. cit.

22 Bauman, *Liquid Modernity*, op. cit., p. 61.

23 Slavoj Žižek (1999), *The Ticklish Subject: The Absent Centre of Political Ontology*, London: Verso, p. 408.

24 Slavoj Žižek (2000), 'Why We All Love to Hate Haider', *New Left Review*, 2, 37–46.

25 Žižek, *The Ticklish Subject*, op. cit., p. 408.

26 This also applies, albeit to a lesser extent, to ethnicity.

27 See Nachtwey, *Germany's Hidden Crisis*, op. cit., pp. 63–4.

28 Reckwitz, *The End of Illusions*, op. cit., pp. 41–50.

29 Mayer-Ahuja and Nachtwey, 'Verkannte Leistungsträger:innen', op. cit.

30 See Nachtwey, *Germany's Hidden Crisis*, op. cit., pp. 81–93.

31 See Cas Wouters (1999), *Informalisierung. Norbert Elias' Zivilisationstheorie und Zivilisationsprozesse im 20. Jahrhundert*, Opladen/Wiesbaden: Westdeutscher Verlag.

32 This term was coined by Norbert Elias; See Norbert Elias (1986), 'Wandlungen der Machtbalance zwischen den Geschlechtern. Eine prozess-soziologische Untersuchung am Beispiel des antiken Römerstaats', *Kölner Zeitschrift für Soziologie und Sozialpsychologie*, 38, 425–49.

33 See Aladin El-Mafalani (2018), *Das Integrationsparadox. Warum gelungene Integration zu mehr Konflikten führt*, Cologne: Kiepenheuer & Witsch.

34 Sabine Hark and Paula-Irene Villa (2017), *Unterscheiden und herrschen. Ein Essay zu den ambivalenten Verflechtungen von Rassismus, Sexismus und Feminismus in der Gegenwart*, Bielefeld: transcript, p. 26 (transl. added).

35 Armin Nassehi (2021), *Unbehagen. Theorie der überforderten Gesellschaft*, Munich: C.H. Beck, p. 194 (transl. added).

36 On this subject, see Norris and Inglehart, *Cultural Backlash*, op. cit.

37 This was not only true for American trade unions; see Sigrid Koch-Baumgarten (1999), 'Vom "Arbeitnehmerpatriarchat" zur Quotengewerkschaft? Ein Rückblick auf 50 Jahre Geschlechterverhältnisse in den Gewerkschaften der Bundesrepublik', *Femina Politica. Zeitschrift für feministische Politikwissenschaft*, 8(1), 36–48.

38 See Arlie Hochschild (2016), *Strangers in Their Own Land: Anger and Mourning on the American Right*, New York: The New Press.

39 See Nancy Fraser (2017), 'Progressive Neoliberalism versus Reactionary Populism: A Hobson's Choice', in: Heinrich Geiselberger (ed.), *The Great Regression*, Cambridge: Polity, pp. 40–8.

40 Beck, *Risk Society*, op. cit., p. 19.

41 Ibid., p. 161.

42 Ibid., p. 28.

43 Adorno, *History and Freedom*, op. cit., p. 195.

44 Alexander Bogner (2021), *Die Epistemisierung des Politischen. Wie die Macht des Wissens die Demokratie gefährdet*, Ditzingen: Reclam.

45 William Davies (2018), *Nervous States: How Feelings Took Over the World*, London: Vintage, p. 75.
46 Beck, *Risk Society*, op. cit., p. 47.
47 Ibid., p. 49.
48 See Ulrich Beck (2009), 'Knowledge or Non-Knowing? Two Perspectives of "Reflexive Modernization"', in: id., *World at Risk*, Cambridge: Polity, pp. 115–28, here: p. 123.
49 Ibid.
50 Pierre Rosanvallon (2008), *Counter-Democracy: Politics in an Age of Distrust*, transl. by Arthur Goldhammer, Cambridge: Cambridge University Press, pp. 3f.
51 Ulrich Beck (2009) *World at Risk*, Cambridge: Polity, pp. 24–46.
52 Beck, *Risk Society*, op. cit., p. 53.
53 Ulrich Beck (2006), 'Living in the World Risk Society. A Hobhouse Memorial Public Lecture given on Wednesday 15 February 2006 at the London School of Economics', *Economy and Society*, 35(3), 329–45, here: p. 336.
54 Beck, *Risk Society*, op. cit., p. 75.
55 See Reckwitz, *The Society of Singularities*, op. cit., p. 9.
56 Hartmut Rosa (2023), 'Best Account: Outlining a Systematic Theory of Modern Society', in: Hartmut Rosa and Andreas Reckwitz, *Late Modernity in Crisis: Why We Need a Theory of Society*, Cambridge: Polity, pp. 95–158, here: 128; see also Rosa, *Resonance*, op. cit., pp. 414–20.
57 Most famously, these include Colin Crouch (2004), *Post-Democracy*, Cambridge: Polity; see also Jacques Rancière (1999 [1995]), *Disagreement: Politics and Philosophy*, Minneapolis, MN: University of Minnesota Press; id. (1996), 'Demokratie und Postdemokratie', in Alain Badiou and Jacques Rancière, *Politik der Wahrheit*, Vienna: Turia & Kant, pp. 119–56.
58 See Peter Mair (2013), *Ruling the Void: The Hollowing of Western Democracy*, London: Verso.
59 See Žižek, *The Ticklish Subject*, op. cit., pp. 198–205, 334–47.
60 See, e.g., Göran Therborn (2020), *Inequality and the Labyrinths of Democracy*, London: Durnell Marston.
61 See Lea Elsässer (2018), *Wessen Stimme zählt? Soziale und politische Ungleichheit in Deutschland. Vol. 91*, Frankfurt am Main: Campus.
62 See Armin Schäfer and Michael Zürn (2021), *Die demokratische Regression*, Berlin: Suhrkamp; Philip Manow (2020), *(Ent-)Demokratisierung der Demokratie*, Berlin: Suhrkamp.
63 Peter Wagner (2012), *Modernity: Understanding the Present*, Cambridge: Polity, p. 101.
64 See Manow, *(Ent-)Demokratisierung der Demokratie*, op. cit.
65 See Ingolfur Blühdorn (2013), *Simulative Demokratie. Neue Politik nach der postdemokratischen Wende*, Berlin: Suhrkamp; John Keane (2009), *The Life and Death of Democracy*, London: Simon & Schuster.
66 Rosa, 'Best Account', op. cit., p. 127.
67 Technically, this would also apply to the climate crisis, but here the slowing of decision-making is often intentional.
68 See Rosanvallon, *Counter-Democracy*, op. cit.
69 Ibid., p. 8.
70 Ibid., p. 23.

71 See Dieter Rucht (1999), 'Gesellschaft als Projekt – Projekte in der Gesellschaft', in: Ansgar Klein, Hans-Josef Legrand and Thomas Leif (eds.), *Neue soziale Bewegungen. Impulse, Bilanzen und Perspektiven*, Opladen: VS Verlag für Sozialwissenschaften, pp. 15–27 (transl. added).
72 Rosanvallon, *Counter-Democracy*, op. cit., p. 23.
73 See ibid., pp. 173–90.
74 Ibid., p. 185.
75 Otto Kirchheimer (1966), 'The Transformation of the Western European Party Systems', in: Joseph La Palombara and Myron Weiner, *Political Parties and Political Development (SPD-6)*, Princeton, NJ: Princeton University Press, pp. 177–200, here: p. 200.
76 See Mair, *Ruling the Void*, op. cit.
77 A closer inspection of this development would certainly merit a study in its own right.
78 See Anthony Downs (1957), *An Economic Theory of Democracy*, New York: Pearson.
79 See Tariq Ali (2015), *The Extreme Centre: A Warning*, London: Verso.
80 Chantal Mouffe (2018), *For a Left Populism*, London: Verso, p. 17.
81 See Chantal Mouffe (2005), *On the Political*, London and New York: Routledge, pp. 8–34.
82 Manow, *(Ent-)Demokratisierung der Demokratie*, op. cit., p. 21 (transl. added).
83 Kirchheimer, 'Transformation', op. cit., pp. 177–200, here: p. 200.
84 Davies, *Nervous States*, op. cit., p. 61.
85 Luc Boltanski, for example, has objected that the various critical theories merely argue 'metacritically' these days and no longer correspond to the verdicts individuals articulate in everyday life; see Luc Boltanski (2008), *Soziologie und Sozialkritik. Frankfurter Adorno-Vorlesungen 2008*, Berlin: Suhrkamp, pp. 15–28.
86 In his critique of Hegel, Marx emphasizes that an idea can only become 'a material force as soon as it has gripped the masses'. (Karl Marx (1975 [1844]), Contribution to the Critique of Hegel's Philosophy of Law. Introduction, *MECW*, Vol. 3, New York: Intl. Publishers, pp. 175–87, here: p. 182.)
87 See Oliver Nachtwey and Fabienne Décieux (2014), 'Occupy. Proteste in der Postdemokratie', *Forschungsjournal Soziale Bewegungen*, 27(1), 75–89.
88 See Oliver Nachtwey (2017), 'Citizenship-Proteste? Zum Wandel des sozialen Konflikts', in: Priska Daphi, Nicole Deitelhoff, Dieter Rucht and Simon Teune (eds.), *Protest in Bewegung. Zum Wandel von Bedingungen, Formen und Effekten politischen Protests*, Leviathan special vol. 33, Baden-Baden: Nomos, pp. 147–70.
89 See Nachtwey and Décieux, 'Occupy', op. cit.
90 See Priska Daphi, Dieter Rucht, Wolfgang Stuppert, Simon Teune and Peter Ullrich (2014), 'Occupy Frieden. Eine Befragung von Teilnehmer/innen der "Montagsmahnwachen für den Frieden"', in: *IPB Working Papers*, Berlin.
91 Jürgen Habermas (1987), 'Technology and Science as "Ideology"', in: *Towards a Rational Society. Student Protest, Science, and Politics*, Cambridge: Polity, pp. 81–122, here: p. 85.
92 Here, we are not referring to the postcolonial critique of the Enlightenment,

which addresses the un-enlightened and in part racist preconditions of the Enlightenment.

93 See the – still very worthwhile – critiques and social-theoretical reconstructions by Fredric Jameson (1991), *Postmodernism, or, the Cultural Logic of Late Capitalism*, Durham, NC: Duke University Press, and Alex Callinicos (1989), *Against Postmodernism: A Marxist Critique*, Cambridge: Blackwell.

94 See Albrecht Koschorke (2018), 'Linksruck der Fakten', *Zeitschrift für Medien- und Kulturforschung*, 9(2), 107–18, here: p. 117 (transl. added).

95 See Wolfgang Welsch (2008), *Unsere postmoderne Moderne*, Berlin: Akademie Verlag, p. 40.

96 Philipp Sarasin (2021), *1977. Eine kurze Geschichte der Gegenwart*, Berlin: Suhrkamp, p. 21 (transl. added).

97 See Scott Lash (1994), 'Expert-Systems or Situated Interpretation? Culture and Institutions in Disorganized Capitalism', in: Ulrich Beck, Anthony Giddens and Scott Lash, *Reflexive Modernization: Politics, Tradition and Aesthetics in the Modern Social Order*, Stanford, CA: Stanford University Press, pp. 198–215, here: p. 202.

98 See Jean-François Lyotard (1984 [1979]), *The Postmodern Condition: A Report on Knowledge*, Manchester: Manchester University Press.

99 See Michel Foucault (1995 [1975]), *Discipline and Punish: The Birth of the Prison*, 2nd edn, New York: Vintage.

100 See Jean Baudrillard (2010 [1978]), *The Agony of Power*, Cambridge, MA: Semiotext(e).

101 Carolin Amlinger (2020), 'Rechts dekonstruieren. Die neue Rechte und ihr widersprüchliches Verhältnis zu Postmoderne', *Leviathan*, 48(2), 318–37, here: p. 334 (transl. added).

102 See Paul Feyerabend (2010), *Against Method: Outline of an Anarchistic Theory of Knowledge*, 4th edn, London: Verso.

103 Alexander Bogner (2021), *Die Epistemisierung des Politischen. Wie die Macht des Wissens die Demokratie gefährdet*, Ditzingen: Reclam, p. 61.

104 Ibid., p. 64 (transl. added).

105 See Bruno Latour (2009 [1999]), *Das Parlament der Dinge. Für eine politische Ökologie*, Frankfurt am Main: Suhrkamp.

106 For a more elaborate treatment, see Carolin Amlinger (2022), 'Men Make Their Own History. Conspiracy as Counter-narrative in the German Political Field', in: Ben Carver, Dana Craciun and Todor Hristov (eds.), *Plots: Literary Form and Cultures of Conspiracy*, London and New York: Routledge, pp. 179–200.

107 Bogner, *Die Epistemisierung des Politischen*, op. cit., p. 79 (transl. added).

108 Ingolfur Blühdorn (2021), 'Liberation and Limitation: Emancipatory Politics, Socio-ecological Transformation and the Grammar of the Autocratic-authoritarian Turn', *European Journal of Social Theory*, 25(1), 26–52.

109 Ibid., pp. 33–40.

110 Although we reference Blühdorn with approval here, the intensity of his critique leads in the wrong direction. Although he does decipher the emergence of democratic regressions, his argument ultimately turns conservative because he implicitly gives preference to a coherent subject in the Kantian sense.

111 Nicos Poulantzas (1978), *State, Power, Socialism*, London: NLB.

112 On non-governability, see Claus Offe (1979), '"Unregierbarkeit". Zur Renaissance konservativer Krisentheorien', in: *Stichworte zur 'Geistigen Situation der Zeit'*, ed. by Jürgen Habermas, Vol. 1: *Nation und Republik*, Frankfurt am Main: Suhrkamp, pp. 294–318.

113 See David Harvey (2005), *A Brief History of Neoliberalism*, Oxford: Oxford University Press.

114 See Nachtwey, *Germany's Hidden Crisis*, op. cit., pp. 38–56.

115 See Quinn Slobodian (2018), *Globalists: The End of Empire and the Birth of Neoliberalism*, Cambridge, MA: Harvard University Press; Thomas Biebricher (2018), *The Political Theory of Neoliberalism*, Stanford, CA: Stanford University Press.

116 See Jamie Peck (2001), *Workfare States*, New York: The Guilford Press; Loïc Wacquant (2009), *Punishing the Poor: The Neoliberal Government of Social Insecurity*, Durham, NC: Duke University Press.

117 In this regard, see Michel Foucault (1991), 'Governmentality', in: Graham Burchell, Colin Gordon and Peter Miller (eds.), *The Foucault Effect: Studies in Governmentality*, Chicago, IL: University of Chicago Press, pp. 87–104; Michel Foucault (2007), *Security, Territory, Population, Lectures at the Collège de France, 1977–78*, Basingstoke: Palgrave Macmillan; Michel Foucault (2008), *The Birth of Biopolitics. Lectures at the Collège de France, 1978–79*, Basingstoke: Palgrave Macmillan.

118 For a ground-breaking analysis, see Ulrich Bröckling, Susanne Krasmann and Thomas Lemke (eds.) (2011), *Governmentality: Current Issues and Future Challenges*, Abingdon and New York: Routledge. Governmentality studies, however, do tend to play down the state's role as an independent actor; see also the critique by Loïc Wacquant and Ulf Kadritzke (2012), 'Der neoliberale Leviathan. Eine historische Anthropologie des gegenwärtigen Gesellschaftsregimes', *Prokla. Zeitschrift für Kritische Sozialwissenschaft*, 42(169), 677–98.

119 See Richard H. Thaler and Cass R. Sunstein (2003), 'Libertarian Paternalism', *American Economic Review*, 93(2), 175–9.

120 On this subject, see David Graeber (2015), *The Utopia of Rules: On Technology, Stupidity and the Secret Joys of Bureaucracy*, London: Melville House, pp. 3–44; Giandomenico Majone (1994), 'Paradoxes of Privatization and Deregulation', *Journal of European Public Policy*, 1(1), 53–69.

Chapter 4. Social aggrievement: on the social character of aversive emotions

1 See Svenja Flaßpöhler (2021), *Sensibel. Über moderne Empfindlichkeit und die Grenzen des Zumutbaren*, Stuttgart: Klett-Cotta.

2 See, for example, Ursula Orlowsky and Rebekka Orlowsky (eds.) (1992), *Narziss und Narzissmus im Spiegel von Literatur, Bildender Kunst und Psychoanalyse. Vom Mythos zur leeren Selbstinszenierung*, Munich: Fink.

3 Ovid (2000), *Metamorphoses*, III, Houston, TX: Boarders Classics, pp. 437–73, here: p. 463.

4 On the conflation of Narcissus and narcissism, see Ursula Orlowsky and Rebekka Orlowsky (2002), 'Einleitung: Intention und Aufbau des Buches', in: id. (eds.), *Narziss und Narzissmus im Spiegel von Literatur, Bildender Kunst und Psychoanalyse. Vom Mythos zur leeren Selbstinszenierung*, Stuttgart: Brill/Fink, pp. 19–28, here: p. 19.

5 Almut-Barbara Renger (2002), 'Vorwort: Narcissus – "Selbsterkenntnis"

und "Liebe als Passion". Gedankengänge zu einem Mythos', in: id. (ed.), *Narcissus. Ein Mythos von der Antike bis zum Cyberspace*, Stuttgart/ Weimar: J.B. Metzler, pp. 1–12.

6 The aspect of recognition is pointed out by Martin Altmeyer; see Altmeyer (2000), 'Narzißmus, Intersubjektivität und Anerkennung', *Psyche*, 54(2), 143–71, here: p. 143 (transl. added).
7 Ovid, *Metamorphoses*, op. cit., pp. 339–510, here: p. 474.
8 Almut-Barbara Renger (1999), 'Vorwort', in: id. (ed.), *Mythos Narziss. Texte von Ovid bis Jacques Lacan*, Leipzig: Reclam, pp. 14–21, here: p. 16 (transl. added).
9 Particularly during the 1970s, narcissism became a somewhat excessively used reference point for many a diagnosis of decay, which we shall return to at a later point.
10 Adorno, *History and Freedom* (Lecture 12), op. cit., p. 210.
11 Peter Sloterdijk (2021), 'Warum treten zunehmend Leute aus der Wirklichkeit aus?', in: id., *Der Staat streift seine Samthandschuhe ab. Ausgewählte Gespräche und Beiträge 2020–2021*, Berlin: Suhrkamp, pp. 149–71, here: p. 169 (transl. added).
12 Christopher Lasch (1979), *The Culture of Narcissism: American Life in An Age of Diminishing Expectations*, New York: W.W. Norton, p. 22.
13 On New Age, spirituality and the sense of time, see Sarasin, *1977*, op. cit., pp. 190–200.
14 Beck, *Risk Society*, op. cit., p. 100, original emphasis.
15 Alain Ehrenberg (2010), *La Société du Malaise: Le Mental et le Social*, Paris: Odile Jacob, p. 23 (transl. from the German, *Das Unbehagen in der Gesellschaft* (2011), Berlin: Suhrkamp, added).
16 Axel Honneth defines social pathologies as developments in which 'some or all members of society systematically misunderstand the rational meaning of a form of institutionalised praxis' (Honneth, *Freedom's Right*, op. cit., p. 113). Our own endeavour, however, focuses on the subjective consequences of this socially induced restriction.
17 See Reinhard Haller (2015), *Die Macht der Kränkung*, Salzburg: Ecowin, p. 36.
18 See Georg Simmel (1984), *On Women, Sexuality, and Love*, ed. by Guy Oakes, New Haven, CT: Yale University Press, p. 183.
19 See John Steiner (2006), *Seeing and Being Seen: Emerging from a Psychic Retreat*, London and New York: Routledge.
20 Georg Simmel (1992 [1901]), 'Zur Psychologie der Scham', in: *Schriften zur Soziologie. Eine Auswahl*, ed. by Heinz-Jürgen Dahme and Otthein Rammstedt, Frankfurt am Main: Suhrkamp, pp. 140–50, here: p. 145 (transl. added).
21 Sighard Neckel (1991), *Status und Scham. Zur symbolischen Reproduktion sozialer Ungleichheit*, Frankfurt am Main: Campus, p. 99 (transl. added); see also: Sighard Neckel (2020), 'Sociology of Shame: Basic Theoretical Considerations', in: Liz Frost, Veronika Magyar-Haas, Holger Schoneville and Alessandro Sicora (eds.), *Shame and Social Work: Theory, Reflexivity and Practice*, Bristol: Policy Press.
22 Sighard Neckel (1993), 'Achtungsverlust und Scham. Die soziale Gestalt eines existentiellen Gefühls', in: id., *Die Macht der Unterscheidung*, op. cit., pp. 92–109, here: p. 106 (transl. added).

23 For a more extensive treatment of this issue, see Léon Wurmser (1990), *Die Maske der Scham. Die Psychoanalyse von Schamaffekten und Schamkonflikten*, Berlin and Heidelberg: Westarp.

24 Heinz Weiß (2008), 'Groll, Scham und Zorn. Überlegungen zur Differenzierung narzißtischer Zustände', *Psyche*, 62(7), 866–86, here: p. 874 (transl. added). Weiß links the three narcissistic emotional states grudge, shame and anger to distinct perspectives, which allows for a more accurate delineation of the specific relationship being denied. Our analysis is strongly influenced by his approach.

25 Transl. note: Sighard Neckel provides a helpful introduction of this term to English language readers: 'Turning to the etymology of grudge, in German the word for this is *Grollen*. According to the standard Duden dictionary, *Groll* stands for secret, entrenched animosity or concealed hatred, and a suppressed displeasure that is prevented from turning outward by internal or external resistance. It corresponds to the English "grudge" or "rancour". This rancour takes on a specific tonality: muttering and murmuring, the dark tonal colours or timbres are also evident in the English "grumbling" and "grunting". Old German also used the words *Grimm* (ire) and *Ingrimm* (wrath) to express its tense, cramping nature, which is also related to the English "grim" or "grimace".' (Sighard Neckel [2023], 'Grudge: The emotional side of resentment', *Emotions and Society*, 5(2), pp. 139–46, here: p. 139.)

26 Weiß, 'Groll, Scham und Zorn', op. cit., pp. 867 f. (transl. added).

27 Ibid., p. 868.

28 Rainer Paris (2004), 'Ohnmacht als Pression. Über Opferrhetorik', *Merkur*, 58(665–666), 914–23, here: pp. 917–18. However, the scholar of the sociology of power and organizational sociology Rainer Paris frequently uses this insight to trivialize disadvantaged groups' experiences of discrimination. Given his criticism of queer/feminist positions, he became an author for the right-wing magazine *Tumult*, which we discuss in Chapter 6.

29 Haller, *Die Macht der Kränkung*, op. cit., p. 84 (transl. added).

30 See Weiß, 'Groll, Scham und Zorn', op. cit., p. 868.

31 Neckel, 'Grudge', op. cit., here: p. 141.

32 Haller, *Die Macht der Kränkung*, op. cit., p. 85 (transl. added); see Michael Feldman (1997), 'Groll, die zugrundeliegende ödipale Konfiguration', in: Ronald Britton, Michael Feldman and John Steiner (eds.), *Groll und Rache in der ödipalen Situation*, Tübingen: Brandes & Apsel, pp. 51–96.

33 The representatives of Affect Studies go even further, claiming that affects create (political) events: see, for example, Kathleen Stewart (2007), *Ordinary Affects*, Durham, NC: Duke University Press; Janet Staiger, Ann Cvetkovich and Ann Reynolds (eds.) (2010), *Political Emotions*, New York: Routledge. As Simon Strick emphasizes, they conceive of '"feelings" and "identities" as provisional states, seeking to process a confusing concourse of intensities, desires, fleeting impressions, blockades, inhibitions, and atmospheres into something that becomes intelligible as a meaningful everyday life and can thus (but need not necessarily) be "experienced".' (Simon Strick [2021], *Rechte Gefühle. Affekte und Strategien des digitalen Faschismus*, Bielefeld: transcript, p. 72, transl. added.)

34 See Pankaj Mishra (2017), *Age of Anger: A History of the Present*, New York: Farrar, Straus and Giroux; Uffa Jensen (2017), *Zornpolitik*,

Berlin: Suhrkamp; Cornelia Koppetsch (2019), *Die Gesellschaft des Zorns. Rechtspopulismus im globalen Zeitalter*, Bielefeld: transcript.

35 With his 2010 essay 'Der Wutbürger' ('The angry citizen'), journalist Dirk Kurbjuweit created a name for the new political figure: Dirk, Kurbjuweit (2010), 'Der Wutbürger. Stuttgart 21 und die Sarrazin-Debatte. Warum die Deutschen so viel protestieren', *Der Spiegel*, 11 October (transl. added), available at: https://www.spiegel.de/spiegel/a-724587.html

36 See Jan-Werner Müller (2016), *Was ist Populismus? Ein Essay*, Berlin: Suhrkamp, p. 42.

37 Weiß, 'Groll, Scham und Zorn', op. cit., p. 878.

38 See Jensen, *Zornpolitik*, op. cit., p. 79.

39 Heinrich Popitz (2017), *Phenomena of Power: Authority, Domination, and Violence*, New York: Columbia University Press, pp. 10–12, 48.

40 Heinz Kohut (1975 [1971]), 'Überlegungen zum Narzißmus und zur narzißtischen Wut', in: id., *Die Zukunft der Psychoanalyse. Aufsätze zu allgemeinen Themen und zur Psychologie des Selbst*, Frankfurt am Main: Suhrkamp, pp. 205–51.

41 Peter Sloterdijk (2010), *Rage and Time: A Psychopolitical Investigation*, New York: Columbia University Press, p. 21.

42 Ibid., p. 221; see Jensen, *Zornpolitik*, op. cit., pp. 119–23.

43 Friedrich Nietzsche (2006 [1887]), *On the Genealogy of Morality*, transl. by Carol Diethe, ed. by Keith Ansell-Pearson, Cambridge: Cambridge University Press, p. 20.

44 Ibid.

45 Regarding Weber's analysis of Nietzsche's conception of slave morality, see Hermann Kocyba (2019), 'Max Weber. Ressentiment und Rationalität – Zur Genealogie des modernen Menschen', in: Eicke Brock and Jutta Georg (eds.), '– ein Leser, wie ich ihn verdiene'. Nietzsche-Lektüren in der deutschen Philosophie und Soziologie, Stuttgart: J.B. Metzler, pp. 293–317.

46 Max Scheler (1998 [1915]), *Ressentiment*, 5th edn, Milwaukee, WI: Marquette University Press, p. 7. Nietzsche also describes the independent dynamic which the suffering develops: 'The sufferers [...] rummage through the bowels of their past and present for obscure, questionable stories that will allow them to wallow in tortured suspicion, and intoxicate themselves with their own poisonous wickedness' (Nietzsche, *Genealogy of Morality*, op. cit., p. 94).

47 Horkheimer and Adorno, *Dialectic of Enlightenment*, op. cit., p. 158.

48 Thomas Bedorf regards personalization as a feature of populism; see Thomas Bedorf (2019), 'Zur Rhetorik des politischen Ressentiments', *Zeitschrift für Praktische Philosophie*, 6(1), 239–56, here: p. 252 (transl. added).

49 Scheler, *Ressentiment*, op. cit., p. 7.

50 Ibid., p. 8.

51 Although our focus here is on the social causes of people taking offence, this is not to imply that aversive emotions are the typical or only mode of reaction to the tensions we are about to investigate. They are simply more likely in those individuals who are particularly exposed to such tensions.

52 Tocqueville, *Democracy in America*, op. cit., p. 744.

53 Hans-Peter Müller (2004), 'Soziale Ungleichheit und Ressentiment', *Merkur*, 58(665–666), 885–94, here: p. 888 (transl. added).

54 Ibid., p. 889 (transl. added).
55 Tocqueville, *Democracy in America*, op. cit., p. 72.
56 On envy as a democratic emotion, see Johannes Voelz (2017), 'Wendungen des Neids. Tocqueville und Emerson zum Paradox einer demokratischen Leidenschaft', *Westend. Neue Zeitschrift für Sozialforschung*, 26(1), 141–54.
57 Tocqueville, *Democracy in America*, op. cit., p. 749.
58 Müller, 'Soziale Ungleichheit und Ressentiment', op. cit., p. 890 (transl. added).
59 Elias, *Society of Individuals*, op. cit., p. 52.
60 See Nachtwey, 'Decivilization', op. cit., p. 227.
61 Norbert Elias (1996 [1989]), *The Germans: Power Struggles and the Development of Habitus in the Nineteenth and Twentieth Centuries*, Cambridge: Polity, p. 184.
62 Scheler, *Ressentiment*, op. cit., p. 14.
63 Ibid., pp. 7–8.
64 Ibid., p.11.
65 Ibid., p. 12.
66 Émile Durkheim (2002 [1897]), *Suicide: A Study in Sociology*, London and New York: Routledge, p. 216.
67 Helmut Thome concisely addresses this aspect: Helmut Thome (2016), 'Zur Normalität von Anomie in funktional differenzierten Gesellschaften', *Zeitschrift für Soziologie*, 45(4), 261–80, here: p. 263 (transl. added).
68 Durkheim, *Suicide*, op. cit., p. 209.
69 Ibid., p. 215.
70 Ibid., p. 268.
71 The theory of institutional anomie attributes deviant modes of behaviour in economic institutions to a market-oriented mentality; see Steven F. Messner, Richard Rosenfeld and Andreas Hövermann (2019), 'Institutional Anomy Theory: An Evolving Research Program', in: Marvin D. Krohn, M., Nicole Hendrix, Gina Penly Hall and Alan J. Lizotte (eds.), *Handbook on Crime and Deviance*, New York: Springer, pp. 161–77.
72 Neckel, 'Identität als Ware', op. cit., p. 45 (transl. added).
73 Scheler, *Ressentiment*, op. cit., p. 13.
74 Ibid., pp. 14–15.
75 Joseph Vogl (2021), *Kapital und Ressentiment. Eine kurze Theorie der Gegenwart*, Munich: C.H. Beck, pp. 162 f. (transl. added).
76 See Jan Slaby and Christian von Scheve (eds.) (2019), *Affective Societies: Key Concepts*, London and New York: Routledge.
77 Mishra, *Age of Anger*, op. cit., p. 14.
78 Ibid., pp. 9, 89.
79 Sighard Neckel (1999), 'Blanker Neid, blinde Wut? Sozialstruktur und kollektive Gefühle', in: id., *Die Macht der Unterscheidung*, op. cit., pp. 110–32, here: p. 119 (transl. added).
80 Michael J. Sandel (2020), *The Tyranny of Merit: What's Become of the Common Good?*, New York: Farrar, Straus and Giroux, p. 22.
81 Ibid., pp. 24 ff.
82 Ibid., p. 25.
83 See also Neckel, 'Blanker Neid, blinde Wut?', op. cit., p. 129.
84 Merton, *Sociological Theory and Social Structure*, op. cit., p. 221.

85 Ibid., p. 217.
86 Reckwitz, *Society of Singularities*, op. cit. Although narcissism is often associated with the cult of 'stars', it is just as much a generator of envy and feelings of inferiority.
87 Heinrich Popitz (1980), *Die normative Konstruktion der Gesellschaft*, Tübingen: Mohr Siebeck, p. 10 (transl. added).
88 Heinrich Popitz (2017), 'Social Norms', *Genocide Studies and Prevention: An International Journal*, 11(2), 3–12. This article is a translation of an excerpt from: Heinrich Popitz (2006), *Soziale Normen*, ed. by Friedrich Pohlmann and Wolfgang Eßbach, Frankfurt am Main: Suhrkamp.
89 Merton, *Sociological Theory and Social Structure*, op. cit., p. 246.
90 Christian Baron depicts this rather impressively in his novel *Ein Mann seiner Klasse* (Berlin: Ullstein, 2020).
91 Fromm, *Fear of Freedom*, op. cit., p. 103.
92 Popitz, 'Social Norms', op. cit., p. 8.
93 Ibid.
94 See Sahra Wagenknecht (2021), *Die Selbstgerechten. Mein Gegenprogramm – für Gemeinsinn und Zusammenhalt*, Frankfurt am Main: Campus, p. 102 (transl. added). Around the time this translation is being completed, this former left-wing politician has just formed her new party (*Bündnis Sahra Wagenknecht*), which, according to Wagenknecht, is supposed to be 'neither right-wing nor left-wing'.
95 Merton, *Sociological Theory and Social Structure*, op. cit., p. 238.
96 See Heinz Weiß and Heinrich Merkt (2021), 'Eine pathologische Organisation auf der Grundlage des Strebens nach Perfektion', in: Vera King, Benigna Gerisch und Hartmut Rosa (eds.), *Lost in Perfection. Zur Optimierung von Gesellschaft und Psyche*, Berlin: Suhrkamp, pp. 225–38, here: p. 225.
97 See King et al. (eds.), *Lost in Perfection*, op. cit.
98 Hartmut Rosa (2010), *Alienation and Acceleration: Towards a Critical Theory of Late-Modern Temporality*, Aarhus: NSU Press, p. 32.
99 See Edgar Cabanas and Eva Illouz (2019), *Manufacturing Happy Citizens: How the Science and Industry of Happiness Control our Lives*, Cambridge: Polity, pp. 139–44.
100 Merton, *Sociological Theory and Social Structure*, op. cit., p. 237. The efforts towards assimilation, however, may well be non-conformist, as Greta Wagner has impressively illustrated in her study on the use of performance-enhancing drugs; see Wagner, *Selbstoptimierung*, op. cit.
101 Merton, *Sociological Theory and Social Structure*, op. cit., p. 241.
102 Berlin, 'Two Concepts of Liberty', op. cit., pp. 166–217, here: p. 181.
103 Merton, *Sociological Theory and Social Structure*, op. cit., p. 243.
104 Alain Ehrenberg (2010 [1998]), *The Weariness of the Self: Diagnosing the History of Depression in the Contemporary Age*, Montreal: McGill-Queen's University Press, pp. 222–3.
105 Merton, *Sociological Theory and Social Structure*, op. cit., p. 196.
106 Sennett, *Corrosion of Character*, op. cit., pp. 62–3.
107 Lutz Eichler (2014), *System und Selbst. Arbeit und Subjektivität im Zeitalter ihrer strategischen Anerkennung*, Bielefeld: transcript, p. 301 (transl. added).
108 See Nicola Gess (2021), *Halbwahrheiten. Zur Manipulation von*

Wirklichkeit, Berlin: Matthes & Seitz, pp. 49–63; Sighard Neckel (2000 [1897]), 'Bluffen, Täuschen und Verstellen. Bemerkungen zu einer Variante des Leistungsprinzips', in: id., *Die Macht der Unterscheidung*, op. cit., Frankfurt am Main: Campus, pp. 60–6.

109 See Nymoen and Schmitt, *Influencer*, op. cit.
110 Merton, *Sociological Theory and Social Structure*, op. cit., pp. 209–10.
111 Ibid., p. 210.
112 Ibid., p. 211.
113 See also Maurits Heumann and Oliver Nachtwey (2021), 'Autoritarismus und Zivilgesellschaft', *IfS Working Paper No. 16*, Frankfurt am Main, pp. 29–60.
114 Lasch, *Culture of Narcissism*, op. cit., p. 15.
115 Ibid., p. 16.
116 Ibid., p. 63.
117 See ibid., pp. 231–2.
118 Ehrenberg, *Das Unbehagen in der Gesellschaft*, op. cit., p. 163.
119 On this, see Philip Cushman (1990), 'Why the Self is Empty. Toward a Historically Situated Psychology', *American Psychologist*, 45(5), 599–611.
120 Richard Sennett (1977), *The Fall of Public Man*, London/New York: Penguin.
121 Ibid., p. 325.
122 Ibid., p. 338.
123 Ibid., p. 326.
124 See Koschorke, 'Linksruck der Fakten', op. cit., pp. 107–18.
125 The prevalence (i.e., the commonness of occurrence) of narcissistic personality disorders is usually estimated at below 1 per cent; see Kathrin Ritter and Claas-Hinrich Lammers (2007), 'Narzissmus – Persönlichkeitsvariable und Persönlichkeitsstörung', *Psychotherapie, Psychosomatik, Medizinische Psychologie*, 57(2), 53–60, here: p. 56; Aline Vater, Stefan Roepke, Kathrin Ritter and Claas-Hinrich Lammers (2013), 'Narzisstische Persönlichkeitsstörung. Forschung, Diagnose und Psychotherapie', *Psychotherapeut*, 58, 599–615, here: p. 607; on the inflationary use of the diagnosis of narcissism in negative depictions of cultural developments, see Kristin Dombek (2016), *Die Selbstsucht der anderen. Ein Essay über Narzissmus*, Berlin: Suhrkamp; on the revaluation of narcissism as an anthropological constant, see Katharina Ohana (2022), *Narzissten wie wir. Vom Streben nach Aufwertung – ein ehrlicher Blick auf uns Menschen*, Weinheim: Beltz.
126 Jean M. Twenge and W. Keith Campbell (2009), *The Narcissism Epidemic: Living in the Age of Entitlement*, New York: Atria.
127 Jean M. Twenge, Sara Konrath, Joshua D. Foster, W. Keith Campbell and Brad J. Bushman (2008), 'Egos Inflating Over Time. A Cross-Temporal Meta-Analysis of the Narcissistic Personality Inventory', *Journal of Personality*, 76(4), 875–902.
128 Twenge and Campbell, *The Narcissism Epidemic*, op. cit., pp. 73–88.
129 Ibid., pp. 89–106.
130 Yaida T. Uhls and Patricia M. Greenfield (2011), 'The Rise of Fame: An Historical Content Analysis', *Cyberpsychology. Journal of Psychosocial Research on Cyberspace*, 5, n.p.
131 C. Nathan DeWall, Richard S. Pond Jr., W. Keith Campbell and Jean M.

Twenge (2011), 'Tuning in to Psychological Change. Linguistic Markers of Psychological Traits and Emotions over Time in Popular US Song Lyrics', *Psychology of Aesthetics, Creativity, and the Arts*, 5(3), 200–7.

132 Twenge and Campbell, *The Narcissism Epidemic*, op. cit., pp. 107–22.

133 Timo Gnambs and Markus Appel (2017), 'Narcissism and Social Networking Behavior: A Meta-analysis', *Journal of Personality*, 86(2), 200–12.

134 Twenge and Campbell, *The Narcissism Epidemic*, op. cit., pp. 123–40.

135 In contrast to the findings of Twenge und Campbell, a research team led by Eunike Wenzel was able to detect a continuous decline in narcissism among US university students since the 1990s. In particular, the sense of entitlement, i.e., the feeling of one's own superiority, had become less pronounced; see Eunike Wetzel, Anna Brown, Patrick L. Hill, Joanne M. Chung, Richard W. Robins and Brent W. Roberts (2017), 'The Narcissism Epidemic Is Dead; Long Live the Narcissism Epidemic', *Psychological Science*, 28(12), 1833–47.

136 See Aline Vater, Steffen Moritz and Stefan Roepke (2018), 'Does a Narcissism Epidemic Exist in Modern Western Societies? Comparing Narcissism and Self-esteem in East and West Germany', *PLoS ONE*, 13(5), 1–16; Paul K. Piff (2013), 'Wealth and the Inflated Self: Class, Entitlement, and Narcissism', *Personality and Social Psychology Bulletin*, 40(1), 34–43; Peter K. Hatemi and Zoltán Fazekas (2018), 'Narcissism and Political Orientations', *American Journal of Political Science*, 62(4), 873–88; Virgil Zeigler-Hill, Destaney Sauls and Paige Malay (2021), 'Through the Eyes of Narcissus: Competitive Social Worldviews Mediate the Associations with Ideological Attitudes', *Self and Identity*, 20(6), 811–40.

137 On the concept of the social figure, see Tobias Schlechtriemen and Sebastian J. Moser (2018), 'Sozialfiguren. Zwischen gesellschaftlicher Erfahrung und soziologischer Diagnose', *Zeitschrift für Soziologie*, 47(3), 164–80.

Chapter 5. Libertarian authoritarianism: a movement for a reified freedom

1 See Wendy Brown (2015), *Undoing the Demos: Neoliberalism's Stealth Revolution*, New York: Zone Books.

2 Wendy Brown (2018), 'Neoliberalism's Frankenstein: Authoritarian Freedom in Twenty-First Century "Democracies"', *Critical Times*, 1(1), pp. 60–79, here: p. 65.

3 Ibid., p. 70.

4 Ibid., p. 71.

5 Heitmeyer, *Autoritäre Versuchungen*, op. cit., p. 86.

6 Marcuse, 'Obsolescence of Psychoanalysis', op. cit., p. 120.

7 Blühdorn, 'Liberation and Limitation', op. cit., p. 14.

8 Lütjen identifies this as the origin of the populist quest for 'self-empowerment': although populism accepts modern rationality and its methods, it attacks all established authorities of knowledge production and dissemination: populism's appeal implies 'that "the people" are capable of speaking for themselves and to deal with the complexities of politics and society on their own. [...] At the core of right-wing populism, we find, as counterintuitive as it might sound, a narrative of individual self-empowerment'; see Torben Lütjen (2021), 'The Anti-authoritarian Revolt: Right-wing Populism as Self-empowerment?', *European Journal of Social Theory*, 25(1), 75–93, here: pp. 77, 84, 89.

9   See Eichler, *System und Selbst*, op. cit., p. 459. In his commendable study, Lutz Eichler attempts to trace the metamorphoses of social subjectivity and relate them to sociological theory development.

10 Adorno et al., 'Die verwaltete Welt', op. cit.

11 Theodor W. Adorno (1982), 'Freudian Theory and the Pattern of Fascist Propaganda', in: Andrew Arato and Eike Gebhardt (eds.), *The Essential Frankfurt School Reader*, New York: Continuum International Publishing Group, pp. 118–37, here: p. 134.

12 Freud, *Civilization and Its Discontents*, op. cit., p. 96.

13 Adorno, 'Freudian Theory and the Pattern of Fascist Propaganda', op. cit., p. 122.

14 See Sigmund Freud (1949 [1921]), *Group Psychology and the Analysis of the Ego*, New York: Liveright Publishing, pp. 90 ff.

15 Oliver Decker (2019), 'Prothetische Ergänzungen und narzisstische Plomben. Zur Psychoanalyse der autoritären Dynamik', *Swiss Archives of Neurology, Psychiatry and Psychotherapy*, 170, 1–9, here: p. 1 (transl. added).

16 Freud, *Group Psychology and the Analysis of the Ego*, op. cit., p. 74.

17 Fromm, *Fear of Freedom*, op. cit., p. 141.

18 Adorno et al., *The Authoritarian Personality*, p. 613.

19 Marcuse, 'Obsolescence of Psychoanalysis', op. cit., pp. 109–22.

20 Oliver Decker (2022), 'Flight into Authoritarianism: The Dynamics of Right-Wing Extremism at the Centre of Society', in: Oliver Decker, Johannes Kiess and Elmar Brähler (eds.), *The Dynamics of Right-Wing Extremism within German Society: Escape into Authoritarianism*, transl. by David West, London/New York: Routledge, pp. 1–37, here: pp. 20 ff.

21 On this, see the *Leipziger Autoritarismus-Studien zu rechtsextremen und politischen Einstellungen in Deutschland* (LAS, 'Leipzig Authoritarianism Studies on Extreme Right-Wing and Political Attitudes in Germany'), which have modernized the authoritarianism theory of Critical Theory and translated it into a quantitative survey; Decker et al. (eds.), *The Dynamics of Right-Wing Extremism*, op. cit.

22 Marx, *Capital, Volume I*, op. cit., p. 280.

23 Angelika Ebrecht-Laermann has studied the social figure of the 'lone fighter' as a revenant of authoritarianism and reached similar conclusions. In both rap songs and the self-representation of ISIS militants, she observes a 'negative narcissism' that conveys the desire for 'total de-differentiation' and 'self-empowerment'; see Angelika Ebrecht-Laermann (2019), 'Einzelkämpfer – Wiedergänger des Autoritarismus?', in: Oliver Decker and Christoph Türcke (eds.), *Autoritarismus. Kritische Theorie und Psychoanalytische Praxis*, Gießen: Psychosozial Verlag, pp. 29–48, here: p. 44.

24 See Herbert Marcuse et al. (2009 [1968]), 'Aggressiveness in Advanced Industrial Societies' (and further contributions), in: id., *Negations: Essays in Critical Theory*, London: MayFlyBooks, pp. 187–202.

25 See Fromm, *Fear of Freedom*, op. cit. Fromm had regarded the 'rebel' as a para-type.

26 Adorno et al., *Authoritarian Personality*, op. cit., p. 234.

27 See Alexander Mitscherlich (1969), *Society without the Father: A Contribution to Social Psychology*, London: Tavistock Publications.

28 Marcuse, 'Obsolescence of Psychoanalysis', op. cit., p. 112.
29 Marcuse, *Eros and Civilization*, op. cit., p. 28.
30 Gunnar Hindrichs (2022), 'Autoritär-kulturindustrieller Charakter', *Psyche*, 76(4), 1–29, here: p. 24 (transl. added). Unlike in the authoritarian personality, according to Hindrichs, the ego weakness today is a symptom of a 'cultural-industrial character', which rests on the self-restriction of the id. Proceeding from the diagnosis of Critical Theory that the cultural industry merely provides unsublimated pre-pleasure because it is both 'prudish and pornographic' at once, the adjustment effort of the psychodynamic also changes, turning into a 'self-restriction of the id' (ibid., p. 19).
31 *Abitur* (or *Matura* in Austria and Switzerland) is the secondary school leaving certificate that qualifies for university entrance (comparable to the UK's A-levels).
32 Ibid., p. 27 (transl. added).
33 Adorno et al., *The Authoritarian Personality*, pp. 751 f.
34 Ibid., p. 753.
35 Ibid.
36 Horkheimer, *Eclipse of Reason*, op. cit., p. 111.
37 Ibid., p. 113. The fact that this same gesture is turned on its head in conspiracy theory thinking is addressed in more detail in Chapter 7.
38 Fromm, *Fear of Freedom*, op. cit., p. 145.
39 Adorno et al., *The Authoritarian Personality*, p. 763.
40 Ibid.
41 Ibid.
42 Ibid., p. 764.
43 Marcuse, 'Obsolescence of Psychoanalysis', op. cit., pp. 115–16.
44 See Adorno et al., *The Authoritarian Personality*, op. cit., p. 763; Fromm, *Fear of Freedom*, op. cit., p. 145.
45 Adorno et al., *The Authoritarian Personality*, op. cit., p. 765.
46 Ibid., pp. 766–7.
47 Ibid., p. 765.
48 Ibid. Here, Adorno also introduces the trait of 'semi-erudition'.
49 See Gess, *Halbwahrheiten*, op. cit.
50 Ibid.
51 See Fromm, *Fear of Freedom*, op. cit., p. 122.
52 Freud, 'Group Psychology and the Analysis of the Ego', op. cit., p. 53.
53 Oliver Decker, Katharina Rothe, Marliese Weißmann, Johannes Kiess and Elmar Brähler (2013), 'Economic Prosperity as "Narcissistic Filling": A Missing Link Between Political Attitudes and Right-wing Authoritarianism', *International Journal of Conflict and Violence*, 7(1), 135–49.
54 Eva von Redecker (2020), 'Ownership's Shadow: Neoauthoritarianism as Defense of Phantom Possession', *Critical Times*, 3(1), 33–67, here: p. 35. In their depiction of neo-authoritarianism, both Redecker and Decker draw on the semantics of artificial surrogates which help conceal a deficiency. While Redecker introduces the term 'Phantom Possession' – 'Like phantom pain, phantom possession is felt after amputation' (ibid.) – Decker, in reference to Fromm, speaks of the 'prosthetic security' of authoritarianism; Decker, 'Prothetische Ergänzungen und narzisstische Plomben', op. cit., pp. 4–6.
55 See Birgit Sauer (2017), 'Gesellschaftstheoretische Überlegungen zum

europäischen Rechtspopulismus. Zum Erklärungspotenzial der Kategorie Geschlecht', *Politische Vierteljahresschrift*, 58(1), 3–22. For an overview of the research on right-wing populism and gender, see Vincent Streichhahn (2021), 'Das Geschlecht des Rechtspopulismus. Ein Forschungsüberblick', in: Seongcheol Kim and Veith Selk, *Wie weiter mit der Populismusforschung?*, Baden-Baden: Nomos, pp. 293–318.

56 On the concept of the milieu, see Michael Vester, Peter von Oertzen, Heiko Geiling, Thomas Hermann and Dagmar Müller (2001), *Soziale Milieus im gesellschaftlichen Strukturwandel. Zwischen Integration und Ausgrenzung*, Frankfurt am Main: Suhrkamp; Ronald Hitzler and Anne Honer (1984), 'Lebenswelt – Milieu – Situation. Terminologische Vorschläge zur theoretischen Verständigung', *Kölner Zeitschrift für Soziologie und Sozialpsychologie*, 36(1), 56–74; Stefan Hradil (1987), *Sozialstrukturanalyse in fortgeschrittenen Industriegesellschaften. Von Klassen und Schichten zu Lagen und Milieus*, Opladen: VS Verlag für Sozialwissenschaften.

57 Sven Reichardt (2014), *Authentizität und Gemeinschaft. Linksalternatives Leben in den siebziger und frühen achtziger Jahren*, Berlin: Suhrkamp, p. 40 (transl. added).

58 Vester et al., *Soziale Milieus im gesellschaftlichen Strukturwandel*, op. cit., p. 311 (transl. added here and in the following).

59 Ibid.

60 On the explanatory power of the Sinus Milieus for a tendency towards right-wing populism independently of milieus, see Bertram Barth and Berthold Bodo Flaig (2018), 'Aktuell und zukunftssicher', in: Bertram Barth, Berthold Bodo Flaig, Norbert Schäuble and Manfred Tautscher (eds.), *Praxis der Sinus-Milieus. Gegenwart und Zukunft eines modernen Gesellschaftsund Zielgruppenmodells*, Wiesbaden: Springer VS, pp. 30–3. The Leipzig Authoritarianism Study also compiles clusters for grouping political syndromes present among the population according to common features. These clusters, however, do not represent social milieus, but rather pertain to aspects of personality, values and political orientations; see Oliver Decker et al., 'Das autoritäre Syndrom heute', in: Decker et al. (eds.), *The Dynamics of Right-Wing Extremism*, op. cit., pp. 117–56, here: pp. 132–4.

61 Since sociology has thus far failed to develop a comparable long-term milieu research agenda, the Sinus Milieus are frequently used as an interpretive heuristic for social diagnoses; see the discussion between Nils C. Kumkar, Uwe Schimank and Andreas Reckwitz: Nils C. Kumkar and Uwe Schimank (2021), 'Drei-Klassen-Gesellschaft? Bruch? Konfrontation? Eine Auseinandersetzung mit Andreas Reckwitz' Diagnose der "Spätmoderne"', *Leviathan*, 49(1), 7–31; Andreas Reckwitz (2021), 'Auf der Suche nach der neuen Mittelklasse – Replik auf Nils Kumkar und Uwe Schimank', *Leviathan*, 49(1), 33–61. This exchange prompted a debate about the use of a milieu model that was originally designed for market research. For example, Patrick Sachweh criticized the method for being untransparent and neither intersubjectively comprehensible nor replicable; see Patrick Sachweh (2021), 'Klassen und Klassenkonflikte in der postindustriellen Gesellschaft', *Leviathan*, 49(2), 181–8, here: p. 184. We are aware of these shortcomings, and in the following draw on the Sinus Milieus only as a

template in order to zero in on the social spaces of libertarian authoritarianism. Surely there is a need for further in-depth studies in this regard, which could corroborate our analysis advanced here.

62 See Vester et al., *Soziale Milieus im gesellschaftlichen Strukturwandel*, op. cit., pp. 311–27; see also Helmut Bremer and Andrea Lange-Vester (2014), 'Zur Entwicklung des Konzeptes sozialer Milieus und Mentalitäten', in: Helmut Bremer and Andrea Lange-Vester (eds.), *Soziale Milieus und Wandel der Sozialstruktur. Die gesellschaftlichen Herausforderungen und die Strategien der sozialen Gruppen*, Wiesbaden: Springer, pp. 13–41.

63 Vester et al., *Soziale Milieus im gesellschaftlichen Strukturwandel*, op. cit., p. 315; on the methodology of the Sinus Milieus, see also the self-presentation by Barth et al. (eds.), *Praxis der Sinus-Milieus*, op. cit.

64 Vester et al., *Soziale Milieus im gesellschaftlichen Strukturwandel*, op. cit., p. 509; for a more detailed analysis of the alternative milieu, see Reinhardt, *Authentizität und Gemeinschaft*, op. cit.

65 Franz Walter (2010), *Gelb oder Grün? Kleine Parteiengeschichte der besserverdienenden Mitte in Deutschland*, Bielefeld: transcript, p. 73.

66 Vester et al., *Soziale Milieus im gesellschaftlichen Strukturwandel*, op. cit., p. 510.

67 Ibid.

68 See Blühdorn, 'Liberation and Limitation', op. cit.

69 Reckwitz, 'Auf der Suche nach der neuen Mittelklasse', op. cit., p. 38.

70 See Sinus Markt- und Sozialforschung (2021), *Die Sinus-Milieus in Deutschland. Infopaket für Lehrzwecke*, Heidelberg, pp. 25–31 (transl. added here and in the following). An English-language overview of the Sinus Milieus is available at: https://www.sinus-institut.de/en/sinus-milieus/sinus-milieus-germany

71 Ibid., p. 26.

72 Vester et al., *Soziale Milieus im gesellschaftlichen Strukturwandel*, op. cit., p. 507.

73 Sinus, *Die Sinus-Milieus*, op. cit., pp. 33–9.

74 Ibid., pp. 34, 65–71, 67, 66, 89–95, 91.

75 Vester et al., *Soziale Milieus im gesellschaftlichen Strukturwandel*, op. cit., p. 521.

76 Sinus, *Die Sinus-Milieus*, op. cit., p. 90.

77 On the sociological debate, see the contributions in Martin Endreß and Andrea Maurer (eds.) (2015), *Resilienz im Sozialen. Theoretische und empirische Analysen*, Wiesbaden: Springer VS.

78 See Bauman, *Liquid Modernity*, op. cit., pp. 51–2.

79 Vester et al., *Soziale Milieus im gesellschaftlichen Strukturwandel*, op. cit., pp. 509 f.

80 Bröckling, *The Entrepreneurial Self*, op. cit.

81 See Blühdorn, 'Liberation and Limitation', op. cit., pp. 14–15.

82 See Inglehart and Norris, *Cultural Backlash*, op. cit.

83 See Philipp Lepenies (2022), *Verbot und Verzicht. Politik aus dem Geiste des Unterlassens*, Berlin: Suhrkamp.

Chapter 6. The demise of the truth seekers: fallen intellectuals

1 Hans Ulrich Gumbrecht (2020), 'Die Debatte läuft sich tot', *Neue Zürcher Zeitung*, 8 August, p. 29 (transl. added).

2 Émile Zola (1996), *The Dreyfus Affair: 'J'accuse' and Other Writings*, New Haven, CT: Yale University Press, pp. 43–52.

3 Andreas Franzmann (2004), *Der Intellektuelle als Protagonist der Öffentlichkeit. Krise und Räsonnement in der Affäre Dreyfus*, Frankfurt am Main: Humanities Online, p. 536; see also Ulrich Oevermann (2003), 'Der Intellektuelle. Soziologische Strukturbestimmungen des Komplementär von Öffentlichkeit', in: Andreas Franzmann, Sascha Liebermann and Jörg Tykwer (eds.), *Die Macht des Geistes. Soziologische Fallanalysen zum Strukturtyp des Intellektuellen*, Frankfurt am Main: Humanities Online, pp. 13–75 (transl. added).

4 See Hauke Brunkhorst (2010), 'Die Macht der Intellektuellen', *Aus Politik und Zeitgeschichte*, 40(10), 32–7.

5 The popular formula of the 'unattached intelligentsia' was coined by Karl Mannheim, who himself adopted it from Alfred Weber. It refers to the social independence from any specific stratum that allows intellectuals to develop a normatively independent judgement; see Karl Mannheim (1997 [1929]), *Ideology and Utopia*, London and New York: Routledge, p. 137; for Alfred Weber's original concept, see Wolfgang Eßbach (2013), 'Intellektuellensoziologie zwischen Ideengeschichte, Klassenanalyse und Selbstbefragung', in: Thomas Kroll and Tilman Reitz (eds.), *Intellektuelle in der Bundesrepublik Deutschland. Verschiebungen im politischen Feld der 1960er und 1970er Jahre*, Göttingen: Vandenhoeck & Ruprecht, pp. 21–40. A 'recurring tableau of lines of argument attributed' to intellectuals is compiled in: Thomas Jung and Stefan Müller-Doohm (2008), 'Vorwort: Fliegende Fische. Zeitgenössische Intellektuelle zwischen Distanz und Engagement', in: Thomas Jung and Stefan Müller-Doohm (eds.), *Fliegende Fische. Zeitgenössische Intellektuelle zwischen Distanz und Engagement*, Frankfurt am Main: Fischer, pp. 9–18, here: pp. 14 ff.

6 Hans-Peter Müller (2021), 'Wozu (noch) Intellektuelle? Versuch einer Standortbestimmung', *Merkur*, 66(760–761), 878–85, here: p. 878 (transl. added).

7 Among intellectuals' efforts to situate their own position – frequently conceived as the generalization of their own commitments – the one advanced by Jean-Paul Sartre has proven particularly efficacious. His model of the 'total' or 'universal' intellectual refers to a universal truth concept, which, in turn, legitimizes public intervention in just about all public matters. His definition reads as follows: 'The intellectual is someone who meddles in what is not [their] business.' (Jean-Paul Sartre (1976), 'A Plea for Intellectuals', in: *Between Existentialism and Marxism*, New York: William Morrow, pp. 228–85, here: p. 230.)

8 Dietz Bering has historically reconstructed the varying use of the term 'intellectual' in a comprehensive study: Dietz Bering (2010), *Die Epoche der Intellektuellen. 1898–2001. Geburt Begriff Grabmal*, Berlin: Berlin University Press. More recent research on intellectuals is summarized by Hans Manfred Bock (2011) in: 'Der Intellektuelle als Sozialfigur. Neuere vergleichende Forschungen zu ihren Formen, Funktionen und Wandlungen', *Archiv für Sozialgeschichte*, 51, 591–643.

9 On the difficulty of defining conservatism, see Martin Greiffenhagen (1986), *Das Dilemma des Konservatismus in Deutschland*, Frankfurt am Main: Suhrkamp, pp. 27–36.

10 Hauke Brunkhorst (1987), 'The Intellectual in Mandarin Country: The

West German Case', in: Alain G. Gagnon (ed.), *Intellectuals in Liberal Democracies*, New York: Praeger, pp. 121–43, here: p. 139; on conservative thinking in Germany, see Sebastian Liebold and Frank Schale (eds.) (2017), *Neugründung auf alten Werten? Konservative Intellektuelle und Politik in der Bundesrepublik*, Baden-Baden: Nomos.

11 M. Rainer Lepsius (1964), 'Kritik als Beruf. Zur Soziologie der Intellektuellen', *Kölner Zeitschrift für Soziologie und Sozialpsychologie*, 16(1), 75–91, here: p. 88 (transl. added).

12 For example, the accomplished scholar of research on intellectuals, Hans Manfred Bock, noted in 2012: 'Even if the intellectuals succeed in preserving their position of critique and independence, in future they will likely legitimize themselves less through a reference to universal values, but rather through specialist expertise and thus by engaging with real-life political action instead of long-term political goals.' Hans Manfred Bock (2012), 'Nekrologe auf Widerruf. Legenden vom Tod des Intellektuellen', *Merkur*, 66(760–761), 866–77, here: p. 877. Another publication that same year was: Philipp Korom (2012), 'Der Aufstieg der Expertenintellektuellen. Eine kritische Auseinandersetzung mit Bourdieus Soziologie der Intellektuellen', *SWS-Rundschau*, 52(1), 69–91. We shall return to the hypothesis of the expert intellectual below.

13 See Diedrich Diederichsen (2015), 'Postideologische Querfronten', *Jahrbuch der Zeitschrift 'Theater heute'*, pp. 14–20 (transl. added).

14 Jürgen Habermas (2008 [2006]), 'Ein avantgardistischer Spürsinn für Relevanzen. Die Rolle des Intellektuellen und die Sache Europas', in: id., *Ach, Europa. Kleine Politische Schriften XI*, Frankfurt am Main: Suhrkamp, pp. 77–87, here: p. 81 (transl. added).

15 See Bock, 'Nekrologe auf Widerruf', op. cit., p. 866 (transl. added).

16 See Müller, 'Wozu (noch) Intellektuelle?', op. cit., p. 878 (transl. added).

17 See Frank Schirrmacher (2008), 'Der Solschenizyn-Schock', *Frankfurter Allgemeine Zeitung*, 4 August, available at: https://www.faz.net/aktuell /feuilleton/buecher/sieg-ueber-die-geschichteder-solschenizyn-schock -1677319.html

18 Jean-Francois Lyotard (1983), 'Tomb of the Intellectual', in: id., *Political Writings*, London: ECL Press, pp. 3–8.

19 Ingrid Gilcher-Holtey (2013), 'Konkurrenz um den "wahren" Intellektuellen. Intellektuelle Rollenverständnisse aus zeithistorischer Sicht', in: Thomas Kroll and Tilman Reitz (eds.), *Intellektuelle in der Bundesrepublik Deutschland*, Göttingen: Vandenhoeck & Ruprecht, pp. 41–54, here: p. 45 (transl. added); on the different social figures of intellectuals, see Stephan Moebius (2010), 'Intellektuellensoziologie – Skizze zu einer Methodologie', *Sozial.Geschichte Online*, 2, pp. 37–63, 47–50.

20 Mark Fisher (2009), *Capitalist Realism: Is there no Alternative?*, Alresford: Zero Books, p. 2.

21 Axel Honneth (2017), *The Idea of Socialism: Towards a Renewal*, Cambridge: Polity, p. 41 (transl. added).

22 Müller, 'Wozu (noch) Intellektuelle?', op. cit., p. 881.

23 Amlinger, 'Rechts dekonstruieren', op. cit., p. 320.

24 Müller, 'Wozu (noch) Intellektuelle?', op. cit., p. 881.

25 Zygmunt Bauman (1987), *Legislators and Interpreters: On Modernity, Post-Modernity and Intellectuals*, Cambridge: Polity, p. 5.

NOTES TO PP. 157–159

26 See Georg Vobruba (2019), *Die Kritik der Leute. Einfachdenken gegen besseres Wissen*, Weinheim: Beltz Juventa, pp. 107–16 (transl. added).

27 See Martin Carrier (2007), 'Engagement und Expertise. Die Intellektuellen im Umbruch', in: Martin Carrier and Johannes Roggenhofer (eds.), *Wandel oder Niedergang? Die Rolle der Intellektuellen in der Wissensgesellschaft*, Bielefeld: transcript, pp. 13–32.

28 Michel Foucault (1980), 'Truth and Power', in: *Power/Knowledge: Selected Interviews and Other Writings, 1972–1977*, ed. by Colin Gordon, New York: Pantheon Books, p. 126; see Ingrid Gilcher-Holtey, *Eingreifendes Denken*, Metternich: Velbrück Wissenschaft, pp. 359–91.

29 Foucault, 'Truth and Power', op. cit., p. 133.

30 Philipp Korom proposes the term 'expert intellectuals' in this regard; see Korom, 'Der Aufstieg des Expertenintellektuellen', op. cit.

31 Foucault, 'Truth and Power', op. cit., pp. 82, 128.

32 See Gangolf Hübinger (2006), *Gelehrte, Politik und Öffentlichkeit. Eine Intellektuellengeschichte*, Göttingen: Vandenhoeck & Ruprecht, p. 14.

33 See Frank Furedi (2004), *Where Have All the Intellectuals Gone?*, New York: Continuum.

34 Bock, 'Der Intellektuelle als Sozialfigur', op. cit., p. 613.

35 Richard Münch (2011), *Akademischer Kapitalismus. Über die politische Ökonomie der Hochschulreform*, Berlin: Suhrkamp, p. 14 (transl. added).

36 Carlos Spoerhase, for instance, emphasizes that 'wherever, whenever, and in what form something is published [...] has a significant impact on whose research is noticed, who receives a position at a renowned university, whom the major funding institutions are willing to support, the way in which claims to knowledge can be articulated and challenged, and what kind of follow-up communication these articulations entail.' (Carlos Spoerhase (2022), 'Filetierte Vernunft. Veröffentlichen in den Geistes- und Sozialwissenschaften', *Mittelweg 36*, 31(2), 4–13, here: p. 5, transl. added).

37 Thomas H. Macho (1992), 'Geistesgegenwart. Notizen zur Lage der Intellektuellen', in: Martin Meyer (ed.), *Intellektuellendämmerung? Beiträge zur neuesten Zeit des Geistes*, Munich: Carl Hanser, pp. 38–56, here: p. 45 (transl. added).

38 See Axel Schildt (2020), *Medien-Intellektuelle in der Bundesrepublik*, ed. by Gabriele Kandzora and Detlef Siegfried, Göttingen: Wallstein, pp. 611–22.

39 See Stephan Moebius (2010), 'Der Medienintellektuelle', in: Stephan Moebius and Markus Schroer (eds.), *Diven, Hacker, Spekulanten. Sozialfiguren der Gegenwart*, Frankfurt am Main: Suhrkamp, pp. 277–90.

40 Habermas, 'Ein avantgardistischer Spürsinn für Relevanzen', op. cit., p. 83 (transl. added).

41 See Amlinger, *Schreiben*, op. cit., pp. 636–8.

42 Ekkehard Knörer (2012), 'Demokratisierung der Kritik? Von Experten und Metaexperten', *Merkur*, 66(760–761), 945–56, here: p. 952 (transl. added).

43 See Martin Seeliger and Sebastian Sevignani (eds.) (2021), *Ein neuer Strukturwandel der Öffentlichkeit?*, *Leviathan Sonderband 37*, Baden-Baden: Nomos.

44 Vogl, *Kapital und Ressentiment*, op. cit., p. 178 (transl. added).

45 Jürgen Habermas (2022), 'Reflections and Hypotheses on a Further

Structural Transformation of the Political Public Sphere', *Theory, Culture & Society*, 39(4), 145–71, here: p. 159.

46 See Pablo Barberá (2020), 'Social Media, Echo Chambers, and Political Polarization', in: Nathaniel Persily and Joshua A. Tucker (eds.), *Social Media and Democracy: The State of the Field, Prospects for Reform*, Cambridge: Cambridge University Press, pp. 34–55.

47 Thomas Petersen (2021), 'Die Mehrheit fühlt sich gegängelt', *Frankfurter Allgemeine Zeitung*, 16 June, p. 8.

48 In an empirical cross-country study, Pippa Norris examined how far the perception of a 'cancel culture' depends on the congruity of individual values and the dominant culture. Making reference to the concept of the 'Spiral of Silence' developed by Elisabeth Noelle-Neumann, she assumes that the norms and values of social 'mainstream' eventually assert themselves and become the prevalent culture, whereas deviating minority voices fall silent due to the pressure towards conformism. Norris thus concludes that in post-industrial, liberal societies, it is especially right-wing scientists that feel excluded, while in so-called developing countries with a traditional moral culture, this tendency applies mainly to left-wing scientists; see Pippa Norris (2023), 'Cancel Culture: Myth or Reality?', *Political Studies*, 71(1), 145–74. What Norris overlooks, however, are the internal contradictions and fragmentations of what is understood to be a homogeneous majority or minority.

49 On the history of the political use of the term, see Meredith D. Clark (2020), 'Drag Them. A Brief Etymology of So-called "Cancel Culture"', *Communication and the Public*, 5(3–4), 88–92; on the American origins of this term and the concomitant debate in the United States, see Adrian Daub (2022), *Cancel Culture Transfer. Wie eine moralische Panik die Welt erfasst*, Berlin: Suhrkamp.

50 See Sighard Neckel (2005), 'Political Scandals: An Analytical Framework', *Comparative Sociology*, 4(1–2), 101–11.

51 Ingrid Gilcher-Holtey (2014), 'Skandalisierung des Skandals. Intellektuelle und Öffentlichkeit', in: Andreas Gelz, Dietmar Hüser and Sabine Ruß-Sattar (eds.), *Skandale zwischen Moderne und Postmoderne. Interdisziplinäre Perspektiven auf Formen gesellschaftlicher Transgression*, Berlin: De Gruyter, pp. 217–34, here: pp. 219 f. (transl. added).

52 Ibid., pp. 221–8.

53 Norbert Elias and John L. Scotson (1994), *The Established and the Outsiders: A Sociological Enquiry into Community Problems*, Collected Works of Norbert Elias, Volume 4, 2nd edn, Thousand Oaks, CA: SAGE, p. xxxii.

54 Robin Celikates (2019), 'Moralischer Fortschritt, soziale Kämpfe und Emanzipationsblockaden. Elemente einer Kritischen Theorie der Politik', in: Ulf Bohmann and Paul Sörensen (eds.), *Kritische Theorie der Politik*, Berlin: Suhrkamp, pp. 397–425, here: p. 409 (transl. added).

55 Petersen, 'Die Mehrheit fühlt sich gegängelt', op. cit., p. 8.

56 See Karsten Schubert (2020), 'Umkämpfte Kunstfreiheit. Ein Differenzierungsvorschlag', *Zeitschrift für Menschenrechte*, 14(2), 195–204.

57 Albrecht Koschorke (2021), 'Identität, Vulnerabilität und Ressentiment. Positionskämpfe in den Mittelschichten', *FGZ Working Paper 1*, Leipzig: FGZ, p. 5.

58 Harald Martenstein (2021), 'Über Sternchenpausen, Bösewichtinnen und neue Erwerbsquellen für den Duden', *Zeit-Magazin*, 28 April, available at: https://www.zeit.de/zeit-magazin/2021/18/harald-martenstein-gendern-kritik-sprachesprachentwicklung-duden. To some observers, Martenstein is himself a victim of cancel culture, after he left the Berlin-based national daily newspaper *Der Tagesspiegel* in February 2022 following the deletion of a controversial column of his titled 'Nazi-Vergleiche' ('Nazi Comparisons'). In this column, he had stated that it was 'certainly not antisemitic' for COVID-19 protesters to wear 'Jewish badges' displaying the word 'unvaccinated' at their marches, as those who wore them allegedly identified with Jewish victims; see Claudia Tieschky (2022), 'Harald Martenstein verlässt "Tagesspiegel"', *Süddeutsche Zeitung*, 20 February, available at: https://www.sueddeutsche.de/medien/martensteintagesspiegel -1.5532655

59 Anna Schneider (2021), 'Weit weg von der Lebensrealität', *Die Welt*, 21 June, available at: https://www.welt.de/debatte/kommentare/plus231996405 /Diskriminierungssensible-Medien-Weit-weg-von-der-Lebensrealitaet.html. Schneider also takes a radically libertarian position with regard to the government's COVID-19 measures; see, e.g., Anne Schneider (2021), 'Die Freiheit beginnt beim Ich', *Die Welt*, 20 November, available at: https:// www.welt.de/debatte/kommentare/plus235159368/Anna-Schneider-zu -Individualismus-und-Covid-Freiheit-beginnt-beim-Ich.html

60 For an in-depth treatment of the politics of 'anti-genderism', see Sabine Hark and Paula-Irene Villa (eds.) (2015), *Anti-Genderismus. Sexualität und Geschlecht als Schauplätze aktueller politischer Auseinandersetzungen*, Bielefeld: transcript.

61 Koschorke, 'Identität, Vulnerabilität und Ressentiment', op. cit., p. 2.

62 See Paula-Irene Villa, Richard Traunmüller and Matthias Revers (2021), 'Lässt sich "cancel culture" empirisch belegen?', *Aus Politik und Zeitgeschichte*, 71(46), 26–33, here: p. 27.

63 Diedrich Diederichsen (2021), 'Am Stammtisch der Sachlichkeit. Markiertes Sprechen in Deutschland', *Merkur*, 75(868), 5–18, here: p. 6 (transl. added).

64 Which is reflected in the fact that the research literature on Sloterdijk remains negligible despite his extensive works. Exceptions include, for example, Sjoerd van Tuinen, (2006), *Peter Sloterdijk. Ein Profil*, Paderborn: UTB; Sjoerd van Tuinen, (ed.) (2007), *Peter Sloterdijk, Cultural Politics*, 3(3) (Special Issue); Jean-Pierre Couture (2016), *Sloterdijk*, Cambridge: Polity; Christian Hein (2021), *Peter Sloterdijk. Der Briefkurier der POST-Moderne*, Würzburg: Königshausen & Neumann.

65 *Bild* is the most influential German tabloid.

66 Willem A. Tell (2015), 'Was fasziniert die Deutschen an Helene Fischer? 8 Fragen an Deutschlands wichtigsten Philosophen', Interview with Peter Sloterdijk, *Bild*, 26 June, available at: https://www.bild.de/unterhaltung /kultur/helene-fischer/warumlieben-die-deutschen-den-schlagerstar -41518092.bild.html

67 Peter Sloterdijk (2013), 'Reflexionen eines nicht mehr Unpolitischen' ('Reflections of a no-longer apolitical man'), acceptance speech for the Ludwig Börne Prize 2013, Berlin: Suhrkamp, p. 32 (transl. added).

68 Ibid., p. 35.

69 Peter Sloterdijk (2013), *You Must Change Your Life: On Anthropotechnics*, Cambridge: Polity, p. 443.

70 Peter Sloterdijk (1987), *Critique of Cynical Reason*, Minneapolis, MN: University of Minnesota Press, p. 103.

71 See van Tuinen, *Peter Sloterdijk*, op. cit., p. 19.

72 See Peter Sloterdijk (2009), 'Die Revolution der gebenden Hand', *Frankfurter Allgemeine Zeitung*, 13 June), available at: https://www.faz.net/aktuell/feuilleton/debatten/kapitalismus/diezukunft-des-kapitalismus-8-die-revolution-der-gebenden-hand-1812362.html; see also the volume *Die nehmende Hand und die gebende Seite. Beiträge zu einer Debatte über die demokratische Neubegründung von Steuern* (Berlin: Suhrkamp, 2010), which assembles various of Sloterdijk's contributions on this matter; see also Jan Rehmann and Thomas Wagner (eds.) (2010), *Angriff der Leistungsträger? Das Buch zur Sloterdijk-Debatte*, Hamburg: Argument/Ariadne.

73 The German version *Zorn und Zeit* was published in 2006, the English version in 2010: Peter Sloterdijk (2010), *Rage and Time*, New York: Columbia University Press, pp. 41, 31.

74 Ibid., p. 40.

75 Christoph Schwennicke (2016), 'Es gibt keine moralische Pflicht zur Selbstzerstörung. Peter Sloterdijk über die Flüchtlingskrise', Interview with Peter Sloterdijk, in: *Cicero*, 28 January (transl. added), available at: https://www.cicero.de/innenpolitik/peter-sloterdijk-luegenaether-fluechtlinge-koelnsilvester/plus

76 Unlike a number of other intellectuals, Sloterdijk had little understanding/sympathy for the COVID-19 demonstrations: 'I cannot understand these people. [...] [T]his rapid spread of an invisible, treacherous X called SARS-CoV-2 from one person to another is not simply a matter of opinion' (Sloterdijk, 'Der Staat zeigt seine eiserne Faust', in: id., *Der Staat streift seine Samthandschuhe ab*, op. cit., p. 62, transl. added).

77 See Diederichsen, 'Postideologische Querfronten', op. cit., p. 20 (transl. added).

78 Volker Weiß (2020), 'Querfront. Die Allianz der Populisten', in: *Stichworte zur Zeit. Ein Glossar*, ed. by Heinrich-Böll-Stiftung, Bielefeld: transcript, pp. 227–40, here: p. 227 (transl. added).

79 See Stefan Breuer (1993), *Anatomie der konservativen Revolution*, Darmstadt: Wissenschaftliche Buchgesellschaft.

80 See Axel Schildt (1981), *Militärdiktatur mit Massenbasis? Die Querfrontkonzeption der Reichswehrführung um General von Schleicher am Ende der Weimarer Republik*, Frankfurt: Campus.

81 For a critique of extremism theory, which assumes structural similarities between left-wing and right-wing positions, see Eva Berendsen, Katharina Rhein and Tom Uhlig (eds.) (2019), *Extrem unbrauchbar. Über Gleichsetzungen von links und rechts*, Berlin: Verbrecher.

82 Yuri M. Lotman (1991), *Universe of the Mind. A Semiotic Theory of Culture*, transl. by Ann Shukman, Bloomington, IN: Indiana University Press, p. 142; on this, see also Uwe Wirth (2012), 'Zwischenräumliche Bewegungspraktiken', in: id. (ed.), *Bewegen im Zwischenraum*, Berlin: Kulturverlag Kadmos, pp. 7–34.

83 See Albrecht Koschorke (2023), 'Lechts und rinks. Seitenwechsel in Zeiten der Polarisierung', *Mittelweg 36*, 32(1), 66–78.

84 See Diederichsen, 'Postideologische Querfronten', op. cit., p. 16 (transl. added).
85 See Julian Müller (2023), 'Der politische Konvertit als Fürsprecher seiner selbst', *Mittelweg 36*, 32(1), pp. 17–27.
86 Thea Dorn, Juli Zeh and Daniel Kehlmann (2021), 'Der Einspruch der Künstler. Es geht nicht darum, wer recht hat', *Die Zeit*, 29 April, pp. 47f. (transl. added).
87 See 'Jan Josef Liefers', 22 April 2021, available at: https://www.youtube.com/watch?v=Ux_j8ALQiQY (transl. added).
88 See 'Volker Bruch', 22 April 2021, available at: https://www.youtube.com/watch?v=sOCi3B9wJ5U (transl. added). Volker Bruch and director Jeana Paraschiva continued the campaign with the title #allesaufdentisch (roughly: '#allfactsonthetable'); now, artists and experts were supposed to start a critical dialogue.
89 See Peter Kümmel (2021), 'Büschn schämen', *Die Zeit*, 29 April, p. 49 (transl. added).
90 Transl. note: In January 2024, Maaßen, who was a member of the centre-right Christian Democrats (CDU) for many years, officially withdrew from the party. He announced that the organization he had simultaneously belonged to all along, the *Werte Union* – an ultraconservative circle, founded in 2017, operating both in and outside the CDU, claiming to represent this party's conservative core – was going to form a political party in its own right, aiming to stand candidates for the first time in the 2024 state elections in Thuringia, Saxony and Brandenburg. Ironically, as also became known in January 2024, the domestic intelligence service that Maaßen headed from 2012 to 2018 (*Verfassungsschutz*) keeps a record on him in its 'right-wing extremism' database.
91 Ibid. (transl. added).
92 Giorgio Agamben (2021), 'The Invention of an Epidemic', in: id., *Where Are We Now?: The Epidemic as Politics*, London: Eris, pp. 11–13.
93 Giorgio Agamben (1998), *Homo Sacer: Sovereign Power and Bare Life*, Stanford, CA: Stanford University Press, pp. 166–80.
94 Agamben, 'The Invention of an Epidemic', op. cit., p. 12.
95 Benjamin Bratton (2021), 'Agamben WTF, or How Philosophy Failed the Pandemic', *Verso Blog*, 28 July, available at: https://www.versobooks.com/en-gb/blogs/news/5125-agamben-wtf-or-how-philosophy-failed-the-pandemic; on the continuities in Agamben's thought, see Thomas Assheuer (2022), 'Haben wir das Sterben verlernt? Kritik an Corona-Maßnahmen', *Zeit online*, 15 January, available at: https://www.zeit.de/kultur/2022-01/kritik-corona-massnahmen-intellektuelle-philosophie
96 Giorgio Agamben (2021), 'Foreword', in: id., *Where Are We Now?: The Epidemic as Politics*, London: Eris, pp. 7–10, here: p. 7.
97 See Carolin Amlinger and Nicola Gess (2020), 'Reality Check. Wie die Corona-Krise kritische und weniger kritische Theorien auf den Prüfstand stellt', *Geschichte der Gegenwart*, 1 July, available at: https://geschichtedergegenwart.ch/reality-check-wie-diecorona-krise-kritische-und-weniger-kritische-theorien-auf-denpruefstand-stellt/
98 Agamben, 'Foreword', op. cit., p. 9.
99 Ibid., p. 8.
100 Ibid., p. 10.

101 The following passage is based on the Wolf quotations, descriptions and analyses presented in Naomi Klein's 2023 book *Doppelganger: A Trip into the Mirror World*, New York: Farrar, Straus and Giroux.

102 Klein, *Doppelganger*, op. cit., p. 77.

103 Ulrike Guérot (2022), *Wer schweigt, stimmt zu. Über den Zustand unserer Zeit. Und darüber, wie wir leben wollen*, Frankfurt am Main: Westend, p. 134 (transl. added).

104 Diagonalist Ulrike Guérot, for example, envisaged the following post-pandemic scenario: 'First, we'll all have to make a clean sweep, all of us in their own country. We will transfer those responsible to the International Court of Justice, should it turn out that it was not a bat but a laboratory that brought us the virus [...]. We'll ask the US to take care of Fauci and Bill Gates. We'll shut down the WHO and comb through its financial ties to the pharmaceutical industry. We will not let the shady figures at Pfizer and friends get away' (ibid., p. 116, transl. added).

105 Marx and Engels, *Manifesto of the Communist Party*, MECW, Vol. 6, op. cit., pp. 477–519, here: p. 495.

106 In this regard, see the critique presented by Richart Rorty (1998) *Achieving Our Country: Leftist Thought in Twentieth-Century America*, Cambridge, MA: Harvard University Press, pp. 73 ff.

107 See, for example Mark Lilla (2017), 'Das Scheitern der Identitätspolitik. Trumps Amerika. Lehren für die Linke', *Blätter für deutsche und internationale Politik*, 62, 41–55 (transl. added).

108 See the reconstruction in Emma Dowling, Silke van Dyk and Stefanie Graefe (2017), 'Rückkehr des Hauptwiderspruchs? Anmerkungen zur aktuellen Debatte um den Erfolg der Neuen Rechten und das Versagen der "Identitätspolitik"', *Prokla*, 47(3), 411–20, here: p. 413 (transl. added).

109 Ibid.

110 Bernd Stegemann (2017), 'Der liberale Populismus und seine Feinde', *Blätter für deutsche und internationale Politik*, 4, 81–94, here: p. 89 (transl. added).

111 Ibid., p. 92 (transl. added).

112 Ibid. Silke van Dyk in fact concludes from this quote a readiness to enter into a strategic *Querfront* with right-wing populism; see Silke van Dyk (2017), 'Krise der Faktizität? Über Wahrheit und Lüge in der Politik und die Aufgabe der Kritik', *Prokla*, 47(3), 347–67, here: p. 361.

113 Bernd Stegemann (2021), *Die Öffentlichkeit und ihre Feinde*, Stuttgart: Klett-Cotta, p. 62 (transl. added).

114 Robert Pfaller (2017), *Erwachsenensprache. Über ihr Verschwinden aus Politik und Kultur*, Frankfurt am Main: Fischer, p. 21 (transl. added).

115 Ibid., p. 23 (transl. added).

116 Ibid., p. 24; regarding Stegemann's reconstruction of the deliberative public sphere according to Habermas, see *Die Öffentlichkeit und ihre Feinde*, op. cit., pp. 39–50 (transl. added).

117 Bauman, *Retrotopia*, op. cit.

118 For the most part, Fraser is directly referenced; see, e.g., Pfaller, *Erwachsenensprache*, op. cit., p. 19 (transl. added).

119 See Jürgen Link (2009), *Versuch über den Normalismus. Wie Normalität produziert wird*, Göttingen: Vandenhoeck & Ruprecht.

120 Wagenknecht, *Die Selbstgerechten*, op. cit., p. 25 (transl. added).

121 Pfaller, *Erwachsenensprache*, op. cit., pp. 19–20 (transl. added).
122 Ibid., p. 204. Svenja Flaßpöhler also advances a similar critique in her book *Sensibel. Über moderne Empfindlichkeit und die Grenzen des Zumutbaren* (Stuttgart, 2021). Flaßpöhler, however, does take into account the progressive dynamic of sensitization throughout the history of civilization, too.
123 Pfaller, *Erwachsenensprache*, op. cit., pp. 14–15 (transl. added).
124 Bernd Stegemann (2020), 'Keine Macht den Denunzianten und Reinheitsfanatikern der Kulturszene!', in: *Schweizer Monat 1077*, available at: https://schweizermonat.ch/keine-macht-dendenunzianten-und -reinheitsfanatikern-der-kulturszene (transl. added).
125 See Koschorke, 'Linksruck der Fakten', op. cit.
126 Jürgen Habermas (1981), 'Modernity – An Incomplete Project', *New German Critique*, 22, pp. 3–15, here: p. 14.
127 See Amlinger, 'Rechts dekonstruieren', op. cit.
128 Quoted in Philipp Felsch (2015), *Der lange Sommer der Theorie. Geschichte einer Revolte 1960–1990*, Munich: Fischer, p. 163 (transl. added).
129 Frank Böckelmann, et al. (1978), *Das Schillern der Revolte*, Berlin: Merve.
130 Quoted in Felsch, *Der lange Sommer der Theorie*, op. cit., p. 163 (transl. added).
131 See Karin Priester (1995), 'Philosophie der Apokalypse. Geistige Pfadfinder der Neuen Rechten', *Blätter für deutsche und internationale Politik*, 10, 1241–51.
132 Felsch, *Der lange Sommer der Theorie*, op. cit., pp. 198–206.
133 Transl. note: During the mid-1960s, this – fairly small – group, mainly active in southern West Germany and West Berlin, which had emerged from the Munich-based artists' group SPUR and was explicitly oriented towards Critical Theory, staged provocative public actions and happenings to convey a critique of society and consumerism. The group's publication *Anschlag* provided an outlet for a wide range of emancipatory leftist theory.
134 Tumult, 'Über Tumult', available at: https://www.tumult-magazine.net /ueber-tumult (transl. added).
135 Frank Böckelmann (1979), 'Die urbane Katastrophe', in: *Tumult. Zeitschrift für Verkehrswissenschaften*, 1, 3–24, here: p. 3 (transl. added).
136 Jean Baudrillard (1978), *Kool Killer. Oder Der Aufstand der Zeichen*, Berlin: Merve (transl. added).
137 Frank Böckelmann and Horst Ebner (2014), 'Tumult. Vierteljahresschrift für Konsensstörung', *Tumult. Vierteljahresschrift für Konsensstörung* (summer), p. 1 (transl. added).
138 Frank Böckelmann and Horst Ebner (2015), 'Gibt es wenigstens eine einzige Lebensform?', *Tumult. Vierteljahresschrift für Konsensstörung* (autumn), pp. 4–6, here: p. 5 (transl. added).
139 Frank Böckelmann (2015/16), 'Völkerfußwanderung 2015?', *Tumult. Vierteljahresschrift für Konsensstörung* (winter), pp. 4–7, here: p. 5 (transl. added).
140 Böckelmann and Ebner, 'Gibt es wenigstens eine einzige Lebensform?', op. cit., p. 6 (transl. added).
141 Ernst Jünger (2012 [1938]), *The Adventurous Heart (Second Edition): Figures and Capriccios*, Candor: Telos, p. 69.

142 See Luc Boltanski (2011), *On Critique: A Sociology of Emancipation*, Cambridge: Polity; Ulrich Bröckling (2013), 'Der Kopf der Leidenschaft. Soziologie und Kritik', *Leviathan*, 41(2), 309–23, pp. 314–16.

143 Koschorke, 'Identität, Vulnerabilität und Ressentiment', op. cit., p. 6.

144 See Diederichsen, 'Postideologische Querfronten', op. cit., p. 20.

Chapter 7. The re-enchantment of the world: 'diagonalist' protests

1 Malte Thießen (2021), *Auf Abstand. Eine Gesellschaftsgeschichte der Coronapandemie*, Frankfurt am Main: Campus, p. 42.

2 Ibid.

3 Ibid., pp. 80–8; see also Frank M. Snowden (2019), *Epidemics and Society: From the Black Death to the Present*, New Haven, CT: Yale University Press.

4 See Thießen, *Auf Abstand*, op. cit., pp. 45–54.

5 See Ulrich Beck (1999), *World Risk Society*, Cambridge: Polity, pp. 52–71.

6 Thießen, *Auf Abstand*, op. cit., pp. 80–104.

7 Ibid., p. 76.

8 Bogner, *Die Epistemisierung des Politischen*, op. cit., p. 21.

9 See Richard Münch (2021), 'Benevolenter Paternalismus. Regieren nach SARS-CoV-2', in: Sebastian Büttner and Thomas Laux (eds.), *Umstrittene Expertise. Zur Wissensproblematik der Politik*, *Leviathan (Special Ed.)*, 38, Baden-Baden: Nomos, pp. 409–32.

10 Alexander Gauland, quoted in Thießen, *Auf Abstand*, op. cit., p. 72.

11 The following paragraphs are partly based on Carolin Amlinger and Oliver Nachtwey (2021), 'Sozialer Wandel, Sozialcharakter und Verschwörungsdenken in der Spätmoderne', *Aus Politik und Zeitgeschichte*, 71(35–36), 13-19, here: pp. 14 f.

12 See Klaus Schwab and Thierry Malleret (2020), *COVID-19: The Great Reset*, Geneva: World Economic Forum.

13 Bogner, *Die Epistemisierung des Politischen*, op. cit., p. 26.

14 Alexander Bogner and Wolfgang Menz (2021), 'Wissen und Werte im Widerstreit. Zum Verhältnis von Expertise und Politik in der Corona-Krise', *Leviathan*, 49(1), 111–32. Caspar Hirschi criticizes the rise of an 'expertocracy' during the pandemic and laments that virologists such as Berlin-based Christian Drosten in particular acquired too much power; see Hirschi (2021), 'Expertise in der Krise. Zur Totalisierung der Expertenrolle in der Euro-, Klima- und Coronakrise', in: Büttner and Laux (eds.), *Umstrittene Expertise*, op. cit., pp. 159–86, here p. 161. Judging by our observations, his legitimate critique in part flashes to hostility towards Drosten in particular and experts in general; see the critique by Nils C. Kumkar of Hirschi's diagnosis: Kumkar (2021), 'Politisierung von Expertise? In der Pandemie auf jeden Fall!', *Frankfurter Allgemeine Zeitung*, 15 December, available at: https://www.faz.net/aktuell/wissen/geist-soziales/wie-caspar-hirschi-vor-politisierung-virologischerexpertise-warnt-17683142.html

15 See also the depictions and analyses in: Heike Kleffner and Matthias Meisner (eds.) (2021), *Fehlender Mindestabstand. Die Coronakrise und die Netzwerke der Demokratiefeinde*, Freiburg: Herder; Wolfgang Benz (ed.), *Querdenken. Protestbewegung zwischen Demokratieverachtung, Hass und Aufruhr*, Berlin: Metropol-Verlag.

16 See, e.g., Will Callison and Quinn Slobodian (2021), 'Coronapolitics from the Reichstag to the Capitol', *Boston Review*, 12 January, available at: https://bostonreview.net/articles/quinn-slobodiantoxic-politics -coronakspeticism/

17 For the sociological debate on the role of frames for collective action, see: Robert D. Benford and David A. Snow (2000), 'Framing Processes and Social Movements: an Overview and Assessment', *Annual Review of Sociology*, 26, 611–39.

18 Our analyses also indicate that the involvement of far-right forces in the *Querdenker* movement was greater, from early on, in eastern Germany compared to western Germany, marking a particular contrast with the movement in the southwestern state of Baden-Württemberg; see Nadine Frei and Oliver Nachtwey, 'Quellen des "Querdenkertums". Eine politische Soziologie der Corona-Proteste in Baden-Württemberg', *SocArXiv Preprint*, available at: https://osf.io/preprints/socarxiv/8f4pb

19 The demonstration in Konstanz and the atmosphere during the event reminded the attending observers from the local research group of a hybrid between an alternative subculture and a church convention; see Johannes Pantenburg, Sven Reichardt and Benedikt Sepp (2021), 'Wissensparallelwelten der "Querdenker"', in: Sven Reichardt (ed.), *Die Misstrauensgemeinschaft der 'Querdenker'. Die Corona-Proteste aus kultur- und sozialwissenschaftlicher Perspektive*, Frankfurt am Main: Campus, pp. 29–66, here: p. 30.

20 See, e.g., the demonstration report by Basel-based sociologists: Nadine Frei et al. (2021), '"Liebe, Freiheit, Frieden". Ethnographische Beobachtung des Corona-Protests in Konstanz', *SocArXiv Preprint*, available at: https://osf .io/vzf6a

21 See Christine Hentschel (2021), 'Das große Erwachen. Affekt und Narrativ in der Bewegung gegen die Corona-Maßnahmen', *Leviathan*, 49(1), 62–85, here: p. 63.

22 Thießen, *Auf Abstand*, op. cit., p. 140.

23 Italian social movement researcher Alberto Melucci considers dissociation from other groups as key for building a collective identity – and, in order to refer to the corresponding mechanisms and strategies that are applied to create such an identity, he uses a term that has today become rather contro-versial: 'identity politics'; see Alberto Melucci (1995), 'The Process of Collective Identity', in: Hank Johnston and Bert Klandermans (eds.), *Social Movements and Culture*, Minneapolis, MN: University of Minnesota Press, pp. 41–63.

24 Hentschel, '"Das große Erwachen"', op. cit., p. 64.

25 With regard to the following section, see Oliver Nachtwey, Robert Schäfer and Nadien Frei (2020), 'Politische Soziologie der Corona-Proteste', *SocArXiv Preprint*, available at: https://osf.io/preprints/socarxiv/zyp3f. Given the epidemiological situation, we decided not to conduct our quantitative survey – as we had originally intended – with paper-and-pencil questionnaires at demonstrations, but to recruit participants for an online survey from an open Telegram group. The online survey was completed from 18 to 24 November 2020. The pool of respondents comprised individuals who, at the time of our research, were members of an open Telegram group with more than 200 subscribers that was

directly associated with the political scene of the corona critics. This approach helped us contact a large number of potential participants (3,700 individuals clicked on the survey's start page). A total of 1,152 completed questionnaires were generated, which represents a decent basis for an analysis of the group who did respond. That said, it nevertheless remains a sample of convenience, not a representative survey. The open Telegram groups that allowed for effectively posting ads comprised around 75,000 members in total, many of whom were likely active members of several groups, however. Incidentally, we were blocked in some groups – from the larger and more professionally run ones in particular – by moderators or bots. As a result, we were unable to ascertain the number of people who followed the link to the survey in each Telegram group and can therefore gauge the response rate only insufficiently. We may assume an overrepresentation of individuals seeking to present the movement of corona critics in a better light. Seeing as participation occurred via self-selection, it was impossible for us to weight or correct this imbalance.

26 Our survey also included a small number of participants from Austria, though we have not subjected them to any separate analysis given the slim sample.

27 Mario Luis Small (2011), 'How to Conduct a Mixed Methods Study: Recent Trends in a Rapidly Growing Literature', *Annual Review of Sociology*, 37, 57–86. This multi-perspectivity allows for what is called a 'triangulation' of data in order to validate the results by cross-comparison; see Uwe Flick (2017), *Doing Triangulation and Mixed Methods*, London: SAGE.

28 On this, see Frei and Nachtwey, 'Quellen des "Querdenkertums"', op. cit. Subsequent representative surveys found that the followers of the Green Party mostly, and indeed increasingly, rejected the protests against policies to deal with the pandemic; see, e.g., Edgar Grande, Swen Hutter, Sophia Hunger and Eylem Kanol (2021), 'Alles Covidioten? Politische Potenziale des Corona-Protests in Deutschland', *WZB Discussion Paper* ZZ 2021–601, available at: https://bibliothek.wzb.eu/pdf/2021/zz21-601 .pdf. However, this does not contradict our findings, seeing as our sample includes only *former* followers of the Green Party.

29 See also the findings presented by Sebastian Koos, 'Konturen einer heterogenen "Misstrauensgemeinschaft"', in: Reichardt (ed.), *Die Misstrauensgemeinschaft der 'Querdenker'*, op. cit., pp. 67–90.

30 Today, there is extensive research on the individual psychological factors that lead people to believe in conspiracy theories; for an overview, see: Karen M. Douglas et al. (2019), 'Understanding Conspiracy Theories', *Political Psychology*, 40, 3–35.

31 We refer to a *latent* tendency towards antisemitism because almost 30 per cent of study participants effectively evaded judgement on the statement 'Even today, Jews continue to have great influence on politics' by selecting 'prefer not to say'. This might be a sign of socially demanded response behaviour, but only further investigations can tell us conclusively. Compared to the representative Leipzig authoritarianism study, moreover, the disapproval rate concerning this item was lower. The studies can be compared only to a limited extent, however, as the investigation from Leipzig did not provide the option 'prefer not to say' in the questionnaire, as it followed a forced-choice procedure.

32 Opposition to vaccination, however, is not only motivated by anthropo-sophical and esoteric thinking alone, but can also often be found among men in whom it originates in an 'overestimation of their own physical resil-ience' rather than in actual scepticism; see Yasemin El-Menouar (2021), *Zwischen individueller Freiheit und Gemeinwohl. Sieben Wertemilieus und ihre Sicht auf Corona*, Gütersloh: Bertelsmann Stiftung, p. 28.

33 The conversational interviews were largely conducted via Zoom. Unless indicated otherwise, the following quotes from individual *Querdenkers* are taken from the interviews, which were anonymized for analysis.

34 We are grateful to all members of the working group 'Corona protests and conspiracy thinking' at the Department of Sociology, in the autumn term of 2021, for their support in generating empirical data for this study.

35 See also the analysis by Pantenburg et al., 'Wissensparallelwelten der "Querdenker"', op. cit., p. 3.

36 For more on the initial analyses which we draw on in the following section, see Nadine Frei, Robert Schäfer and Oliver Nachtwey (2021), 'Die Proteste gegen die Corona-Maßnahmen. Eine soziologische Annäherung', *Forschungsjournal Soziale Bewegungen*, 34(2), 249–58; Oliver Nachtwey et al., 'Generalverdacht und Kritik als Selbstzweck. Empirische Befunde zu den Corona-Protesten', in: Benz (ed.), *Querdenken*, op. cit., pp. 194–213.

37 See Niklas Luhmann (1968), *Vertrauen. Ein Mechanismus der Reduktion sozialer Komplexität*, Stuttgart: Enke, pp. 92–101.

38 See Michael Butter (2018), *'Nichts ist, wie es scheint'. Über Verschwörungstheorien*, Berlin: Suhrkamp; Michael Butter and Peter Night (eds.) (2020), *Routledge Handbook of Conspiracy Theories*, London: Routledge.

39 Imke Schmincke (2015), 'Das Kind als Chiffre politischer Auseinandersetzung am Beispiel neuer konservativer Protestbewegungen in Frankreich und Deutschland', in: Hark and Villa (eds.), *Anti-Genderismus*, op. cit., pp. 93–108.

40 The alleged increase in the suicide rate could not be verified, however; see Daniel Radeloff, Jon Genuneit and Christian J. Bachmann (2022), 'Suizide in Deutschland während der COVID-19-Pandemie. Eine Analyse auf der Grundlage von Daten zu elf Millionen Einwohnern 2017–2021', *Deutsches Ärzteblatt*, 119, available at: https://www.aerzteblatt.de/archiv/225003/Suizide-in-Deutschland-waehrend-der-COVID-19-Pandemie

41 See Beck, *Risk Society*, pp. 80 ff.

42 See also Frei and Nachtwey, 'Quellen des "Querdenkertums"', op. cit.

43 We base ourselves here on an unpublished evaluation of our survey data.

44 Fabian Beckmann and Anna-Lena Schönauer, 'Spaltet Corona die Gesellschaft? Eine Milieuanalyse pandemiebezogener Einstellungen', in: Birgit Blättel-Mink (ed.), *Gesellschaft unter Spannung. Der Verhandlungsband des 40. Kongresses der Deutschen Gesellschaft für Soziologie (DGS) vom 14.–24. September 2020*, p. 8.

45 See El-Menouar, *Zwischen individueller Freiheit und Gemeinwohl*, op. cit.; see also Helene Thaa (2020), 'Corona-Skepsis als Rebellion der Individualist*innen', *Soziologieblog*, 9 September, available at: https://soziologieblog.hypotheses.org/13718

46 On this, see Carolin Amlinger and Oliver Nachtwey (2021), 'Die Risikogesellschaft und die Gegenwelt. Theorien von Ulrich Beck und Luc

Boltanski eröffnen soziologische Perspektiven auf das Corona-Rebellentum', *Frankfurter Allgemeine Zeitung*, 17 February, p. N3.

47 Beck, *Risk Society*, op. cit., p. 72.
48 Ibid., p. 73.
49 See Jaron Harambam and Stef Aupers (2015), 'Contesting Epistemic Authority: Conspiracy Theories on the Boundaries of Science', *Public Understanding of Science*, 24(4), 466–80.
50 Bogner, *Die Epistemisierung des Politischen*, op. cit., p. 104.
51 See also Carolin Amlinger (2020), 'Über das Querdenken. Der epistemische Widerstand der Corona-Proteste', *Zeitschrift für Fantastikforschung*, 8(1), 20–6.
52 For more on this, see Pantenburg et al., 'Wissensparallelwelten der "Querdenker"', op. cit.
53 See Amlinger and Nachtwey, 'Die Risikogesellschaft und die Gegenwelt', op. cit.
54 Nils C. Kumkar notes a similar observation regarding the use of alternative facts; see Nils C. Kumkar, *Alternative Fakten*, op. cit., pp. 54, 154.
55 See also Florian Buchmayr (2019), 'Im Feld der Verschwörungstheorien. Interaktionsregeln und kollektive Identitäten einer verschwörungstheoretischen Bewegung', *Österreichische Zeitschrift für Soziologie*, 44(4), 369–86.
56 See Pierre Bourdieu (2014) *On the State: Lectures at the Collège de France 1989–1992*, Cambridge: Polity, p. 163.
57 Ibid., pp. 164, 168, 184.
58 Pierre Bourdieu (1991 [1981]), 'Political Representation: Elements for a Theory of the Political Field', in: id., *Language and Symbolic Power*, ed. by John B. Thompson, transl. by G. Raymon and M. Adamson, Cambridge: Polity, pp. 171–202, here: p. 172.
59 Concerning the following section, see Buchmayr, 'Im Feld der Verschwörungstheorien', op. cit.; Oliver Kuhn (2010), 'Spekulative Kommunikation und ihre Stigmatisierung – am Beispiel der Verschwörungstheorien', *Zeitschrift für Soziologie*, 39(2), 106–23; Andreas Anton, Michael Schetsche and Michael Walter (2014), 'Einleitung: Wirklichkeitskonstruktion zwischen Orthodoxie und Heterodoxie – zur Wissenssoziologie von Verschwörungstheorien', in: Andreas Anton, Michael Schetsche and Michael Walter (eds.), *Konspiration*, Wiesbaden: Springer VS, pp. 9–25.
60 Luc Boltanski (2011), *On Critique. A Sociology of Emancipation*, Cambridge: Polity, p. xi.
61 Ibid., pp. 9, 57. Apart from this, however, Boltanski strongly distances himself from Bourdieu's critical sociology, as he considers it to take subjects insufficiently seriously.
62 See Amlinger and Nachtwey, 'Sozialer Wandel', op. cit., p. 13.
63 Boltanski, *On Critique*, p. 113.
64 Ibid., p. 114.
65 Ibid.
66 See Michel Foucault (2011), *The Courage of the Truth. The Government of Self and Others II*, Lectures at the Collège de France 1983–1984, Basingstoke: Palgrave Macmillan, pp. 1–32.
67 See Eva Barlösius (1997), *Naturgemäße Lebensführung. Zur Geschichte*

der Lebensreform um die Jahrhundertwende, Frankfurt am Main: Campus; Bernd Wedemeyer-Kolwe (2017), *Aufbruch. Die Lebensreform in Deutschland*, Darmstadt: Philipp von Zabern/WBG.

68 See Johannes Weiß (1986), 'Wiederverzauberung der Welt? Bemerkungen zur Wiederkehr der Romantik in der gegenwärtigen Kulturkritik', in: Friedhelm Neidhardt et al. (eds.), *Kultur und Gesellschaft (Sonderheft 27 der Kölner Zeitschrift für Soziologie und Sozialpsychologie)*, by Opladen: VS Verlag für Sozialwissenschaften.

69 Karl Mannheim (1986), *Conservatism: A Contribution to the Sociology of Knowledge*, ed. by David Kettler, Volker Meja and Nico Stehr, New York: Routledge, p. 64.

70 See Andreas Speit (2021), *Verqueres Denken. Gefährliche Weltbilder in alternativen Milieus*, Berlin: Ch.Links; Detlef Siegfried and David Templin (eds.) (2019), *Lebensreform um 1900 und Alternativmilieu um 1980. Kontinuitäten und Brüche in Milieus der gesellschaftlichen Selbstreflexion im frühen und späten 20. Jahrhundert*, Göttingen: V&R Unipress.

71 See Eberhard Wolff (2019), 'Über das Impfen', *Schweizerische Ärztezeitung*, 100(25), 868; Eberhard Wolff (1998), 'Einschneidende Maßnahmen. Pockenschutzimpfung und traditionale Gesellschaft im Württemberg des frühen 19. Jahrhunderts', *Medizin, Gesellschaft und Geschichte*, Supplement 10; Jonathan M. Berman (2020), *Anti-Vaxxers. How to Challenge a Misinformed Movement*, Cambridge, MA: MIT Press.

72 See Malte Thießen (2017), *Immunisierte Gesellschaft. Impfen in Deutschland im 19. und 20. Jahrhundert*, Göttingen: Vandenhoeck & Ruprecht, pp. 31–7.

73 For the UK case, see Nadja Durbach (2005), *Bodily Matters. The Anti-Vaccination Movement in England, 1853–1907*, Durham, NC: Duke University Press; Wolff, 'Einschneidende Maßnahmen', op. cit.

74 Ibid.

75 See Thießen, *Immunisierte Gesellschaft*, op. cit., pp. 132 f.

76 Barlösius, *Naturgemäße Lebensführung*, op. cit., p. 7.

77 See Cornelia Klinger (1993), 'Romantik und Neue Soziale Bewegungen', in: *Athenäum. Jahrbuch für Romantik*, Vol. 3, ed. by Ernst Behler et al., Paderborn: Brill/Schöningh, pp. 223–44.

78 See also Luc Boltanski and Ève Chiapello (2005 [1999]), *The New Spirit of Capitalism*, London: Verso, p. 37.

79 See Reichardt, *Authentizität und Gemeinschaft*, op. cit., pp. 784–90.

80 See Barbara Ehrenreich (2018), *Natural Causes: An Epidemic of Wellness, the Certainty of Dying, and Killing Ourselves to Live Longer*. New York: Twelve.

81 Speit, *Verqueres Denken*, op. cit., p. 90.

82 Ibid., pp. 90–3; Sarasin, *1977*, op. cit., pp. 169–221.

83 The following section is based on Frei and Nachtwey, 'Quellen des "Querdenkertums"', op. cit.

84 See Helmut Zander (2019), *Die Anthroposophie. Rudolf Steiners Ideen zwischen Esoterik, Weleda, Demeter und Waldorfpädagogik*, Paderborn: Brill/Schöningh.

85 Mateo Kries (2011), 'Ein Stecker für die höheren Energien', Interview with Peter Sloterdijk, *Die Welt*, 25 October, available at: https://www.welt.de/print/die_welt/kultur/article13679318/Ein-Stecker-fuer-die-hoeheren-Energien.html

86 Zander, *Die Anthroposophie*, op. cit., p. 252.
87 Ibid., p. 247.
88 For a more detailed depiction, see Frei and Nachtwey, 'Quellen des "Querdenkertums"', op. cit.
89 In the extensive research literature, see, e.g., N. Fournet et al. (2018), 'Under-vaccinated Groups in Europe and their Beliefs, Attitudes and Reasons for Non-vaccination; Two Systematic Reviews', *BMC Public Health*, 18(1), 1–17; Edzard Ernst (2011), 'Anthroposophy: A Risk Factor for Noncompliance with Measles Immunization', *The Pediatric Infectious Disease Journal*, 30(3), 187–9.
90 See Jennifer Reich (2016), *Calling the Shots: Why Parents Reject Vaccines*, New York: New York University Press.
91 Zander, *Die Anthroposophie*, op. cit., pp. 252, 35.
92 See Speit, *Verqueres Denken*, op. cit., p. 91.
93 See ibid., pp. 111–12.
94 Karl Mannheim also regarded romanticism and rationalism as mutually referential in a complementary manner; see Mannheim, *Conservatism*, op. cit., p. 65.
95 See Paul Heelas (2008), *Spiritualities of Life. New Age Romanticism and Consumptive Capitalism*, Hoboken: Wiley-Blackwell.
96 This was Adorno's comment on astrology; Theodor W. Adorno (1962), 'Aberglaube aus zweiter Hand', in: *Gesammelte Schriften*, Vol. 8: *Soziologische Schriften I*, Frankfurt am Main: Suhrkamp, pp. 147–76, here: p. 173.
97 In this instance, the term 'milieu' refers not to lifestyles within the social space, as it has been applied thus far, but exclusively to the shared quasi-religious practices.
98 See Franz Höllinger and Thomas Tripold (2014), *Ganzheitliches Leben. Das holistische Milieu zwischen neuer Spiritualität und postmoderner Wellness-Kultur*, Bielefeld: transcript, pp. 12, 26–35; Wouter J. Hanegraaff (1977), *New Age Religion and Western Culture, Esotericism in the Mirror of Secular Thought*, New York: Brill, op. cit., pp. 125–57.
99 See Charlotte Ward and David Voas (2011), 'The Emergence of Conspirituality', *Journal of Contemporary Religion*, 26(1), 103–21. However, claims as to this phenomenon's novel character are also subject to criticism; for more on this subject, see: Egil Asprem and Asbjørn Dyrendal (2015), 'Conspirituality Reconsidered. How Surprising and How New Is the Confluence of Spirituality and Conspiracy Theory?', *Journal of Contemporary Religion*, 30(3), 367–82; Robert Schäfer and Nadine Frei (2021), 'Rationalismus und Mystifikation. Zur formalen Pathetik des Dagegenseins', *Zeitschrift für Religion, Gesellschaft und Politik*, 5, 391–410.
100 See Nachtwey et al., 'Politische Soziologie der Corona-Proteste', op. cit., pp. 44–9; on the aspect of gender, see Nadine Frei and Ulrike Nack, 'Frauen und Corona-Proteste', *SocArXiv Preprint*, available at: https://osf .io/preprints/socarxiv/bn8vk/
101 Höllinger and Tripold, *Ganzheitliches Leben*, op. cit., pp. 208–18.
102 See also Nils B. Weidmann (2022), 'Esoteric Beliefs and Opposition to Corona Restrictions', *Working Paper Series/Cluster of Excellence 'The Politics of Inequality'*, No. 10, University of Konstanz.

103 See Reichardt (ed.), *Die Misstrauensgemeinschaft der 'Querdenker'*, op. cit.

104 Zygmunt Bauman (2000), *Liquid Modernity*, Cambridge: Polity, p. 37.

105 On this figure of thought, see Winfried Gebhardt (1999), '"Warme Gemeinschaft" und "kalte Gesellschaft". Zur Kontinuität einer deutschen Denkfigur', in: Günter Meuter and Henrique R. Otten (eds.), *Der Aufstand gegen den Bürger. Antibürgerliches Denken im 20. Jahrhundert*, Würzburg: Königshausen & Neumann, pp. 165–84.

106 See Heinrich Popitz (1994), 'Realitätsverlust in Gruppen', in: id., *Soziale Normen*, op. cit., pp. 175–86, 177.

107 Andreas Reckwitz (2019), *Die Gesellschaft der Singularitäten. Zum Strukturwandel der Moderne*, Berlin: Suhrkamp, p. 63.

108 A representative study by the Berlin Social Science Center (WZB) highlights the considerable and relatively stable mobilization potential of the corona protests. One in five respondents approves of the protests to a great or even very great degree. One in ten people indicates a general readiness to attend a protest rally. The majority of those in support of the protests position themselves in the political centre ground. Furthermore, the study highlights that the protests are primarily motivated not by economic concerns but by 'feared restrictions of freedom'; see Grande et al., 'Alles Covidioten?', op. cit.; for similar results, see Sebastian Koos and Nicolas Binder, 'Wer unterstützt die "Querdenker"?', in: Reichardt (ed.), *Die Misstrauensgemeinschaft der 'Querdenker'*, op. cit., pp. 295–320.

109 Oliver Decker et al., 'Das autoritäre Syndrom', op. cit., p. 201. Conspiracy theories related to the coronavirus proliferated in both Germany and Switzerland during the pandemic; see, for example, Sarah Anne Kezia Kuhn et al. (2022), 'Coronavirus Conspiracy Beliefs in the German-speaking General Population. Endorsement Rates and Links to Reasoning Biases and Paranoia', *Psychological Medicine*, 52(16), pp. 4162–76.

110 See Clara Schließler et al. (2020), 'Aberglaube, Esoterik und Verschwörungsmentalität in Zeiten der Pandemie', in: Oliver Decker and Elmar Brähler (eds.), *Autoritäre Dynamiken. Alte Ressentiments – neue Radikalität. Leipziger Autoritarismus-Studie 2020*, Gießen: Psychosozial-Verlag, pp. 283–308.

111 Claudia Diehl and Christian Hunkler (2022), 'Vaccination-related Attitudes and Behavior across Birth Cohorts: Evidence from Germany', *PLoS ONE*, 17(2), e0263871.

112 See Thomas Lux, Steffen Mau and Aljoscha Jacobi (2022), 'Neue Ungleichheitsfragen, neue Cleavages? Ein internationaler Vergleich der Einstellungen in vier Ungleichheitsfeldern', *Berliner Journal für Soziologie*, 32, 173–212; Mau, 'Kamel oder Dromedar?', op. cit.

113 See Hentschel, '"Das große Erwachen"', op. cit.

114 Nozick, *Anarchy, State, and Utopia*, op. cit., p. ix.

115 However, Decker et al. consider superstition to be part of authoritarian submission as well – though this deviates from the classic F-scale (or fascist scale), where it represents a separate dimension in its own right; see Decker et al., 'Das autoritäre Syndrom', op. cit., p. 193.

116 Beck, *Risk Society*, op. cit., p. 75.

117 In the case of the QAnon conspiracy theory, too, we find a counter-epistemology issued by a counter-expert – namely Q – who knows about the government's secrets and exposes them; see Jeremiah Morelock and Felipe

NOTES TO PP. 216-222

Ziotti Narita (2022), 'The Nexus of QAnon and COVID-19. Legitimation Crisis and Epistemic Crisis', *Critical Sociology*, 48(6), 1005–24.

118 Boris Holzer et al., 'Einleitung: Protest in der Pandemie', in: Reichardt (ed.), *Die Misstrauensgemeinschaft der 'Querdenker'*, op. cit., pp. 7–28, here: p. 18.

119 This 'Neuer Krefelder Appell' is available at: https://peaceappeal21.de/

120 Jochen Roose (2013), 'Soziale Bewegungen als Basismobilisierung. Zum Verhältnis von Basis und Führungspersonal in den Ansätzen der Bewegungsforschung', in: Rudolf Speth (ed.), *Grassroots-Campaigning*, Wiesbaden: Springer VS, pp. 141–57.

121 Even in the 1920s, there was a host of such 'prophets' surrounding the *Lebensreform* movement. Some of them were rather left-leaning, others drifted towards fascism; see Ulrich Linse (1983), *Barfüßige Propheten. Erlöser der zwanziger Jahre*, Berlin: Siedler.

122 See Leo Löwenthal (2015 [1987]), *False Prophets: Studies on Authoritarianism*, London: Routledge.

123 See Niklas Luhmann (1995), *Social Systems*, Stanford, CA: Stanford University Press, pp. 402–4.

124 Ibid., p. 371; for more on this, see also Kai-Uwe Hellmann, 'Einleitung', in: Niklas Luhmann, *Protest. Systemtheorie und soziale Bewegungen*, ed. by Kai-Uwe Hellmann, pp. 7–45, here: p. 26.

125 Regarding such an approach, see Alex Demirović (2022), 'Kapitalistischer Staat und Pandemie (Teil 1)', *Prokla. Zeitschrift für Kritische Sozialwissenschaft*, 52(206), 11–32; see also Thomas Ebermann (2021), *Störung im Betriebsablauf. Systemrelevante Betrachtungen zur Pandemie*, Hamburg: KVV 'konkret'.

126 See Barrington Moore and Detlev Puls (1978), *Injustice: The Social Bases of Obedience and Revolt*, London: Palgrave Macmillan.

127 Jürgen Habermas (2021), 'Corona und der Schutz des Lebens. Zur Grundrechtsdebatte in der pandemischen Ausnahmesituation', *Blätter für deutsche und internationale Politik*, 9, 65–78, 66.

128 For a perspective on a 'neoliberal' concept of freedom, see: Samia Mohammed (2020), 'Verletzliche Freiheit? Zur Kritik neoliberaler Freiheitsverständnisse in der Corona-Krise', in: Clara Arnold, Oliver Flügel-Martinsen, Samia Mohammed and Andreas Vasilache (eds.), *Kritik in der Krise. Perspektiven politischer Theorie auf die Corona-Pandemie*, Baden-Baden: Nomos, pp. 33–48.

129 Jacques de Saint Victor (2015), *Die Antipolitischen*, Hamburg: Hamburger Edition, p. 10.

130 See Dieter Rucht (1988), 'Gegenöffentlichkeit und Gegenexperten', *Zeitschrift für Rechtssoziologie*, 9(2), 290–305.

131 Johannes Pantenburg and Benedikt Sepp (2021), 'Wissen, hausgemacht. Selbstverständnis, Expertisen und Hausverstand der "Querdenker"', in: Büttner and Laux (eds.), *Umstrittene Expertise*, op. cit., pp. 468–82.

Chapter 8. Subversion as a destructive principle: regressive rebels

1 This chapter is largely based on the research collaboration between Maurits Heumann and Oliver Nachtwey. The analysis presented here is taken from: Heumann and Nachtwey, 'Autoritarismus und Zivilgesellschaft', op. cit.

2 Campact specializes mainly in online campaigns and has a mailing list with

more than two million subscribers; further information on the organization is available at: https://www.campact.de/campact/; For more on Campact's anti-AfD campaign, see: https://blog.campact.de/2016/03/steuern-bildung-hartz-iv-was-die-afd-wirklich-will/

3 The study received financial support from the Demokratie-Stiftung Campact and the Rosa Luxemburg Foundation. We would like to thank Flurin Dummermuth, Farah Grütter and Moritz Dolinga for their cooperation in both the survey and the data analysis.

4 In one case we interviewed a married couple. In another two of our interviews, partners/family members of our respondents were temporarily present.

5 For an overview of the varying explanatory approaches, see Bettina Kohlrausch and Linus M. Höcker (2020), 'Ursachen für rechtspopulistische Einstellungen. Ein Überblick über den Forschungsstand', *Working Paper Forschungsförderung 178*, Düsseldorf: Hans-Böckler-Stiftung.

6 The exploratory study was based on self-selective sampling of people from the Campact mailing list who had criticized the NGO's campaign. In total, we retrieved more than thirty hours of interview material, which we complemented with ethnographic field notes and a standardized questionnaire on the social structure and electoral preferences. Aided by the analytical software MAXQDA, we coded the interview material with reference to deductive criteria, in keeping with the method of qualitative content analysis and following the open procedure developed in Grounded Theory; on methodical aspects, see Philipp A.E. Mayring (2015), *Qualitative Inhaltsanalyse. Grundlagen und Techniken*, Weinheim: Beltz; Anselm L. Strauss and Juliet Corbin (1990), *Basics of Qualitative Research: Grounded Theory Procedures and Techniques*, London: SAGE; Jörg Strübing (2014), *Grounded Theory. Zur sozialtheoretischen und epistemologischen Fundierung eines pragmatistischen Forschungsstils*, Wiesbaden: Springer VS. On this basis, we were then able to reconstruct two 'empirically founded types' of the new authoritarianism which exhibit a condensation of shared ideas, biographical developments and socio-structural features; on this method, see Uwe Kelle and Susanne Kluge (2010), *Vom Einzelfall zum Typus. Fallvergleich und Fallkontrastierung in der qualitativen Sozialforschung*, Wiesbaden: VS Verlag für Sozialwissenschaften, p. 90. Our typology allows us to reconstruct shared beliefs and modes of reaction in correlation to participants' social trajectory and political socialization and, moreover, conclusively to interpret these data with a view to anomie-induced experiences of alienation and the political processing thereof. It is important to note that the interviews took place in the context of a public media debate around Germany's asylum policy and the rise of the AfD and are therefore strongly influenced by what Adorno et al. referred to as the 'cultural climate' and the 'ideological influence upon the people of most media for moulding public opinion'; Adorno, *Authoritarian Personality*, op. cit., p. 655.

7 Rosanvallon, *Counter-Democracy*, op. cit., pp. 8, 23.

8 Ibid., p. 10.

9 On the transformation of social-democratic parties, see Oliver Nachtwey (2009), *Marktsozialdemokratie. Die Transformation von SPD und Labour Party*, Wiesbaden: VS Verlag für Sozialwissenschaften.

10   Mouffe, *For a Left Populism*, op. cit., p. 4.
11   Nils C. Kumkar (2017), 'Realitätsverlust und Autoritarismus. Das Krisenerleben des klassischen Kleinbürgertums und die Attraktivität Donald Trumps', *Psychologie und Gesellschaftskritik*, 41(3–4), 87–107, here: p. 94 (transl. added).
12   Rosanvallon, *Counter-Democracy*, op. cit., p. 14.
13   Ibid., p. 22.
14   Ibid., p. 12.
15   Ibid., p. 266.
16   Karl Marx (1976 [1867]), 'So-Called Primitive Accumulation of Capital', in *Capital, Volume One*, London: Penguin, pp. 873–942, here: p. 899; see also Søren Mau (2023), *Mute Compulsion: A Marxist Theory of the Economic Power of Capital*, London: Verso.
17   Transl. note: Thilo Sarrazin, a politician and erstwhile longstanding SPD member (until 2020). He made his name with his 2010 *Deutschland schafft sich ab* ('Germany Is Abolishing Itself'), a highly controversial book on immigrants and immigration policy in Germany, in which he rails against multiculturalism and insinuates that Muslim immigrants are civilizationally inferior.
18   See Klaus Dörre (2018), 'In der Warteschlange. Rassismus, völkischer Populismus und die Arbeiterfrage', in: Karina Becker, Klaus Dörre and Peter Reif-Spirek (eds.), *Arbeiterbewegung von rechts? Ungleichheit – Verteilungskämpfe – populistische Revolte*, Frankfurt am Main: Campus, pp. 49–81; see also Klaus Dörre (2018), 'A Right-Wing-Workers' Movement? Impressions from Germany', *Global Labour Journal*, 9(3), 339–47.
19   See, among others, Cornelia Koppetsch (2017), 'Rechtspopulismus, Etablierte und Außenseiter. Emotionale Dynamiken sozialer Deklassierung', in: Dirk Jörke and Oliver Nachtwey (eds.), *Das Volk gegen die (liberale) Demokratie, Leviathan Sonderheft 32*, Baden-Baden: Nomos, pp. 208–32; Reckwitz, *The End of Illusions*, op. cit.; Wolfgang Merkel (2017), 'Kosmopolitismus versus Kommunitarismus. Ein neuer Konflikt in der Demokratie', in: Philipp Harfst, Ina Kubbe and Thomas Poguntke (eds.), *Parties, Governments and Elites: The Comparative Study of Democracy*, Wiesbaden: Springer VS, pp. 9–23.
20   Apart from participants' differing vulnerability to anomie, further differences in political attitudes and prejudices as well as in their professional and private biographical trajectories were cause to subdivide the group into two sub-groups.
21   Partners or family members who were only temporarily present during the interviews, such as Ms Schmitt, were not considered in the analysis.
22   See Rüdiger Peukert (1997), 'Die Destabilisierung der Familie', in: Wilhelm Heitmeyer (ed.), *Was treibt die Gesellschaft auseinander?*, Frankfurt am Main: Suhrkamp, pp. 187–328.
23   Rosanvallon, *Counter-Democracy*, op. cit., p. 24.
24   Adorno, *Authoritarian Personality*, op. cit., p. 756.
25   Ibid., p. 607.
26   Ibid., p. 759.
27   Transl. note: Stuttgart 21 is a railway and urban development project in Stuttgart, primarily involving the reconstruction of the central train station

as a subterranean rail hub, with dozens of kilometres of new regular and high-speed tracks and 30 new tunnels being built. Due to the skyrocketing costs (the originally estimated budget, the bulk of which was to be funded with taxpayer money, more than doubled from about €4.5bn in 2009 to over €9bn by 2022) and widespread doubt about the overall direction of the project, there was a broad protest movement which staged regular large-scale demonstrations, at the height of which there were various episodes of violent confrontations with police. Ultimately, the project was resumed, with operations supposed to begin by December 2025.

28 See Hochschild, *Strangers in Their Own Land*, op. cit.
29 Rosanvallon, *Counter-Democracy*, op. cit., p. 269.
30 Adorno, *Authoritarian Personality*, op. cit., p. 760.
31 Ibid., p. 759.
32 Ibid., pp. 611, 619.
33 Ibid., pp. 612, 613.
34 Ibid., p. 759.
35 Ibid., p. 618 (transl. mod.).
36 See Hochschild, *Strangers in Their Own Land*, op. cit., pp. 135–52.

Conclusion

1 Adorno, *Authoritarian Personality*, p. ix.
2 Ibid.
3 See Decker et al. (eds.), *Dynamics of Right-Wing Extermism*, op. cit.; Wilhelm Heitmeyer (2024, forthcoming), *Authoritarian Temptations and Right-Wing Threat Alliance: The Crisis of Capitalist Societies in an Uncertain Future*, Berlin: Springer.
4 Horkheimer and Adorno, 'Preface to the New Edition' (1969), in: *Dialectic of Enlightenment*, op. cit., pp. xi–xii, here: p. xi.
5 Lukács, *The Theory of the Novel*, op. cit., p. 41.
6 Neckel, 'Identität als Ware', op. cit., p. 38.
7 Wade M. Cole, Evan Schofer and Kristopher Velasco (2023), 'Individual Empowerment, Institutional Confidence, and Vaccination Rates in Cross-National Perspective, 1995 to 2018', *American Sociological Review*, 88(3), 379–417.
8 At the same time, one's own being-revived (or 'awakened') might help explain the strong projectivity towards left-liberal identity politics, particularly among intellectuals.
9 See Bob Jessop (2016), *The State: Past, Present and the Future*, Cambridge: Polity.
10 See Lux, et al., 'Neue Ungleichheitsfragen, neue Cleavages?', op. cit.; Steffen Mau, Thomas Lux and Fabian Gülzau (2020), 'Die drei Arenen der neuen Ungleichheitskonflikte. Eine sozialstrukturelle Positionsbestimmung der Einstellungen zu Umverteilung, Migration und sexueller Diversität', *Berliner Journal für Soziologie*, 30(3), 317–46.
11 Eva M. Groß, Andreas Hövermann and Amelie Nickel (2023), 'Entsicherte Marktförmigkeit als Treiber eines libertären Autoritarismus', in: Andreas Zick, Beate Küpper and Nico Mokros (eds.), *Die distanzierte Mitte. Rechtsextreme und demokratiegefährdende Einstellungen in Deutschland 2022/23*, Bonn: Dietz, pp. 243–56.
12 Alexander Bogner (ed.) (2023), *Nach Corona. Reflexionen für zukünftige*

Krisen. Ergebnisse aus dem Corona-Aufarbeitungsprozess, Vienna: Austrian Academy of Sciences.

13 Jürgen Habermas (2021), 'Corona und der Schutz des Lebens. Zur Grundrechtsdebatte in der pandemischen Ausnahmesituation', *Blätter für deutsche und internationale Politik*, 9, 65–78, here: p. 68 (transl. added).

14 Alexander Bogner (2021), *Die Epistemisierung des Politischen. Wie die Macht des Wissens die Demokratie gefährdet*, Ditzingen: Reclam, pp. 95, 93 (transl. added).

15 See Frank Fischer (2021), *Truth and Post-Truth in Public Policy*, Cambridge: Cambridge University Press, pp. 6f.; Rose McDermott (2019), 'Psychological Underpinnings of Posttruth in Political Beliefs', *Political Science & Politics*, 52(2), 218–22, here: p. 219.

16 Theodor W. Adorno (1994), 'The Stars Down to Earth: The Los Angeles Times Astrology Column', in: id., *The Stars Down to Earth and Other Essays on the Irrational in Culture*, New York: Routledge, pp. 46–171, here: p. 154.

17 See Nassim Nicholas Taleb (2007), *The Black Swan: The Impact of the Highly Improbable*, New York: Random House.

18 See, for example, the survey data of the COSMO project, available at: https://projekte.uni-erfurt.de/cosmo2020/web/topic/vertrauen-ablehnung -demos/30-verschwoerung/

19 See Carla Reveland and Volker Siefert (2022), '"Querdenker" für Putin', *Tagesschau.de*, 4 March, available at: https://www.tagesschau.de/investigativ /reaktionen-auf-putin-von-querdenkernund-verschwoerungsideologen-101 .html

20 On this aspect, see also the data of the COSMO project, available at: https://projekte.uni-erfurt.de/cosmo2020/web/topic/politik/20-akzeptanz/ #von-corona-krise-und-klima-krise-stand-15.06.21

21 Regarding this term, see Steffen Mau (2021), 'Wut kann Impulse setzen, aber keine Probleme bearbeiten', Interview by Nils Markwardt, in: *Philomag.de*, 15 April, available at: https://www.philomag.de/artikel/steffen-mau-wut -kann-impulse-setzen-aber-keineprobleme-bearbeiten

22 See Andreas Hövermann, Bettina Kohlrausch and Dorothea Voss-Dahm (2022), 'Wie Arbeit, Transformation und soziale Lebenslagen mit anti-demok-ratischen Einstellungen zusammenhängen. Befunde einer repräsentativen Bevölkerungsumfrage', *Working Paper Forschungsförderung 241*, Düsseldorf: Hans-Böckler-Stiftung.

23 See Klein, *Doppelganger*, op. cit.

24 Pascal Wagner-Egger, et al. (2022), 'The Yellow Vests in France. Psychosocial Determinants and Consequences of the Adherence to a Social Movement in a Representative Sample of the Population', *International Review of Social Psychology*, 35(1), pp. 1–14, here: p. 2.

25 Max Horkheimer and Theodor W. Adorno (2002 [1944/1947]), 'Preface' (1944 and 1947), in: id., *Dialectic of Enlightenment: Philosophical Fragments*, Stanford, CA: Stanford University Press, p. xiv.

26 Ibid., p. xvi.

27 Horkheimer and Adorno, 'Preface to the New Edition' (1969), op. cit., p. xii.

28 Elisabeth Anker goes further and criticizes the term 'negative freedom' as 'ugly freedom', as it also implies the freedom to exploit and subjugate

others and degrade and destroy the climate. See Elisabeth R. Anker (2022), *Ugly Freedoms*, Durham, NC: Duke University Press.

29 See Benjamin Bratton (2021), *The Revenge of the Real: Politics for a Post-Pandemic World*, London: Verso.
30 Wagner, *Modernity as Experience and Interpretation*, op. cit., p. 39.
31 Ibid.
32 Honneth, *Freedom's Right*, op. cit., p. 45.
33 See also Marx and Engels, 'The German Ideology' (1845/46), *MECW*, Vol. 5, pp. 19–581, here: p. 74.
34 Adorno, *Freedom and History* (Lecture 10), op. cit., p. 97.
35 See Miguel Abensour (2011), *Democracy Against the State: Marx and the Machiavellian Moment*, Cambridge: Polity.

INDEX